STUDIES IN THE
NEW TESTAMENT
II

STUDIES IN THE NEW TESTAMENT

BY

J. DUNCAN M. DERRETT

D.C.L. (Oxon.), LL.D., Ph.D. (Lond.), of Gray's Inn, Barrister;
Professor of Oriental Laws in the University of London

VOLUME TWO
MIDRASH IN ACTION
AND AS A LITERARY DEVICE

LEIDEN
E.J. BRILL
1978

By the Same Author

Law in the New Testament (Darton, Longman & Todd, London)
Jesus's Audience (Darton, Longman & Todd)

also

Religion, Law and the State in India (Faber & Faber, London)
Introduction to Legal Systems (edited) (Sweet & Maxwell, London)
Dharmaśāstra and Juridical Literature (Harrassowitz, Wiesbaden)
Bhāruci's Commentary on the Manusmṛti (Steiner, Wiesbaden)
Essays in Classical and Modern Hindu Law (Brill, Leiden)
and (translation)
R. Lingat, Classical Law of India (University of California Press)

ISBN 90 04 05634 3

Copyright 1978 by E.J. Brill, Leiden, The Netherlands

PRINTED IN BELGIUM

TABLE OF CONTENTS
(with particulars of original locations)

PREFACE

Apart from acknowledgements I have only minor points to add to my Preface to Volume I.

As for acknowledgements, it is proper I should thank editors and publishers for permission to reprint photographically matter reproduced here. The sources are indicated in the Table of Contents. But it is time I thanked editors of all the journals with which I have been associated for seventeen years for their interest and care. In at least three cases minute solicitude has been used with the presentation of the texts, and I admire the editorial patience and sympathy of which I, and of course my readers, have been beneficiaries. I have taken the opportunity of cleaning out some slips which even vigilant editors and printers have been unable to obviate. It is the spirit that counts, and my *de facto* collaborators deserve recognition.

This was particularly so in the earlier days. 'Midrashic' research was regarded not so much as *avant garde* as, rather, highly speculative. Only certain consecrated names were thought fit to 'indulge' in it. The situation is very different now. J. M. Ford comes out with a suggested new explanation of the very obscure Mark xi.16, finding that σκεῦος could very well mean 'money bags' if one searched out uses of *kelîm* in the Mishnah.[1] B. McNeil uses the Targum of Is.ix.5 to explain John xii.34.[2] J. Bernard relies extensively on rabbinic material to illuminate the healing at Bethesda.[3] Adventures into rabbinics are made without self-consciousness or apology. That is a revolution indeed. M. Wilcox's use of Qumran material to explain 'upon a tree' is not the less startling for the fact that Qumran novelties are now acceptable information.[4]

But there has been an even more interesting discovery, which has been a particular joy to me. The Sermon on the Mount has been the object of intense scrutiny by the learned for at least sixteen centuries. The ethical information in it has formed the basis of innumerable disquisitions and many huge tomes. The man in the

---

[1] *Bibl.* 57 (1976), 249-53. My own treatment differs: *Downside Rev.* 95, no. 319, April 1977, 79-94.

[2] *NT* 19 (1977), 22-33.

[3] *Mél.sc.rel.* 33 (1976), 3-34, 34 (1977), 12-44.

[4] *JBL* 96/1 (1977), 85-99.

street would not think it possible that a sentence could be plausibly retranslated so as to change entirely its meaning and potential. Like so many I had thought something was wrong with Matt. v.28. The Greek was awkward, but where others had not shown doubts I too was lulled into a false security. But blessed is he who does not take the assumptions of the masters for truth! K. Haacker modestly, and to my mind convincingly, shows that the words βλέπων γυναῖκα πρὸς τὸ ἐπιθυμῆσαι αὐτὴν ἤδη ἐμοίχευσεν αὐτὴν ἐν τῇ καρδίᾳ mean 'looking at a married woman with the object of arousing her (sexual) desire has already, so far as his intention goes, made her into an adulteress'.[5] This has the merit of creating a proper antithesis with the standard Jewish piety of Jesus's time and later, and has other far-reaching consequences for our understanding of Jesus's teaching which the magnificent article duly points out. If such discoveries can be made without altering a letter of the text, and even without more than a glance at the Jewish background, my contention that the specialists evince an unjustifiable complacency is amply substantiated.

This decided me to reprint here my study of Jesus as a law-teacher which, on the surface, is somewhat out of keeping with the rest. This brief systematic view of his activity neither depends from midrash as such nor requires a reexamination of literary devices and conventions. It is therefore presented in a tone different from the other contents of the volume. But it can be linked in this sense, that the critics' misunderstandings of the nature of law in the environment of Jesus lead them imperceptibly into an unfortunate estimate of the function of scripture and the role of its self-appointed exegete who is, by the same token, a spiritual and ethical leader. To teach law automatically means to project halakhic midrashim, and I have attempted to suggest what he was about. His particular brand of utopianism and millenarianism is anchored in the Bible, and he intended it to be put into practice.

J.D.M.D.

---

[5] *BZ* 21/1 (1977), 113-16.

LIST OF ABBREVIATIONS

The references to tractates of the *Mishnāh* or the Talmuds are simple abbreviations (*e.g.* Berakot is shown as Ber.) and the tractates can readily be located by reference to a table of contents or the spines of the volumes. Complete consistency was not possible in this present work since its parts were published separately.

b.	Babylonian Talmud
Bauer-Arndt-Gingrich	W.F. Arndt and F.W. Gingrich, *A Greek-English Lexicon of the New Testament* (1957)
Bibl.	Biblica
Billerbeck	H.L. Strack and P. Billerbeck, *Kommentar zum Neuen Testament aus Talmud und Midrasch* (1924/1961)
Blackman	P. Blackman, *Mishnayoth* (1951-5)
Blass-Debrunner	F. Blass and A. Debrunner, *A Greek Grammar of the New Testament and other Early Christian Literature* (1961)
BSOAS	Bulletin of the School of Oriental and African Studies, London
BZ	Biblische Zeitschrift
CBQ	Catholic Biblical Quarterly
CD	Zadokite Document, otherwise Damascus Document, or Damascus Rule
Chavel	*The Commandments. Sefer Ha-Mitzvoth of Maimonides*, trans. C.B. Chavel (1967)
C.I.J.	*Corpus Inscriptionum Judaicarum*
Cod.	Justinian's *Codex* in the *Corpus Iuris*
C.P.J.	*Corpus Papyrorum Judaicorum*
CR	Community Rule, or Manual of Discipline
Danby	H. Danby, *The Mishnah* (1933)
Dig.	Justinian's *Digesta* (or Pandects) in the *Corpus Iuris*
DSW	The War Rule, or War Scroll
Dupont-Sommer	A. Dupont-Sommer, *Les Ecrits Esséniens découverts près de la Mer Morte*, 3rd edn (1968)
ET or *Exp.T.*	Expository Times
F.Gr.Hist.	J. Jacoby, *Die Fragmente der Griechischen Historiker* (1958)
H.T.R. or H.Th.R	Harvard Theological Review
Horowitz	G. Horowitz, *The Spirit of the Jewish Law* (1953)
HUCA	Hebrew Union College Annual
ICLQ	International and Comparative Law Quarterly
IEJ	Israel Exploration Journal
j.	Jerusalem Talmud
JBL	Journal of Biblical Literature
JE	Jewish Encyclopedia
JJP or *J.Jur.Pap.*	Journal of Juristic Papyrology
JJS	Journal of Jewish Studies
J.N.E.S.	Journal of Near Eastern Studies
Jos.	Flavius Josephus
JRL	B. Cohen, *Jewish and Roman Law* (1966)
JQR	Jewish Quarterly Review
JThS or *J.T.S.*	Journal of Theological Studies
LNT	Derrett, *Law in the New Testament* (1970)

Lohse   E. Lohse, *Die Texte aus Qumran* (1954)
LXX   The Septuagint
m   Mishnah
M.T.   The Masoretic Text or Maim., *Mishneh Torah* (= 'Code')
Maim.   Maimonides
Midr. R.   Midrash Rabbah
Moulton-Milligan   J. H. Moulton and G. Milligan, *The Vocabulary of the Greek New Testament* (1914-30)
NEB   New English Bible
NKZ   Neue kirchliche Zeitschrift
NT   Novum Testamentum
NTS   New Testament Studies
PG   Migne, *Patrologia*, Series Graeca
PL   Migne, *Patrologia*, Series Latina
Q   Scroll from Qumran, the preceding numeral referring to the Cave: 1 *QS* = *CR*
RB   Revue Biblique
RE   Pauly's *Real-Encyclopädie der classischen Altertumswissenschaft*
R.H.P.R.   Revue d'Histoire et Philosophie Religieuses
RIDA   Revue Internationale des Droits de l'Antiquité
SBE   Sacred Books of the East
Sonc.   I. Epstein, ed., *The Babylonian Talmud*, English translation (London, The Soncino Press) or the English translation of the *Midrash Rabbah* (various editors) published by the same Press
STh   Studia Theologica
T.L.Z.   Theologische Literaturzeitung
ThWzNT   *Theologisches Wörterbuch zum Neuen Testament* (1933/1957-) originally edited by G. Kittel. An English version is appearing in America.
TuU   Texte und Untersuchungen zur Geschichte der altchristlichen Literatur
TQ   Theologische Quartalschrift
VT   Vetus Testamentum
y   *see* j
ZDMG   Zeitschrift der Deutsche Morgenländische Gesellschaft
ZKT   Zeitschrift für katholische Theologie
ZNW or *Z.N.T.W.*   Zeitschrift für die neutestamentliche Wissenschaft
ZRGG   Zeitschrift für Religions- und Geistesgeschichte
ZSS   **Zeitschrift der Savigny-Stifung für Rechtsgeschichte**
ZTK   Zeitschrift für Theologie und Kirche
ZVR   Zeitschrift für vergleichende Rechtswissenschaft

Leek-beds and Methodology

As research into the Targumim and Midrashim continues, resistance grows to use of discoveries therefrom in the exegesis of the New Testament. It is surmised that neither Jesus nor the evangelists can have used multiple biblical allusion in their respective works [1]. There is resentment at the suggestion that some of the accretions to or interpretations of scripture, which we now know existed in early times, were so well known to the man in the street that parables, for example, could be built up on the supposition that allusions to them would not be wasted. But men then knew their bibles by heart, and synagogue sermons will have utilised the Targumim that had just been recited. Yet the proposition that St. Mark expected his hearers to grasp what are to us recondite allusions, and left practically no clues to help them, is still unacceptable to many. In this miniature note I show the usefulness of midrashic technique, as can be done well when one takes up a notoriously difficult passage in Mark.

At Mk. vi. 40 we learn that (according to the N. E. B.) 'they sat down in rows, a hundred rows of fifty each'. The R. S. V., more faithful to the original, has 'they sat down in groups, by hundreds and by fifties'. The last phrase is interesting as it suggests a semi-military array [2], but parallel expressions in the Damascus Document and the Messianic Rule prove that this is not to be accepted [3]. The concept of eating by companies (Mk. vi. 39: συμπόσια = ḥavûrôt) [4] can recall the style of eating the Passover, which is eaten by companies, and which St. John thought immediately relevant to our present story [5]. The words translated 'in rows', 'in groups', πρασιαὶ πρασιαί, mean literally 'garden-beds, garden-beds' [6], i. e. in semitic idiom (and indeed that of other Asian languages) 'by garden-beds distributively'. The phrase πρασιαὶ πρασιαί is unexampled elsewhere; and while some semitic parallels are linguistic and only vaguely relevant [7], the phrase ganûnyôt ganûnyôt ('by companies' with a pun on 'garden[s]') in a late text from a most interesting context [8], puts us directly in touch with a notion Mark uses.

The explanation is simple. πρασιά is etymologically a bed for leeks (Germ. Lauch) [9]. Leeks need much water, and in the Middle East must be irrigated. In order to be irrigated effectively they must be planted in

---

[1] *Helmut Merkel*, «Recht im Neuen Testament», ZRGG 1973, 266–269. But Mark writes symbolically: *I. Drury*, J. T. S. 24/2 (1973), 367–379.

[2] The idea appealed to *Lohmeyer*, ad loc. Cf. ἑκατόνταρχος, πεντηκόνταρχος * (Exod. xviii. 21, 25; 4 Ki. i. 9).

[3] CD XIII. 1: *C. Rabin, Zadokite Documents* (Oxford, 1958), 64; *Manual of Discipline* II. 21; *M. Burrows, Dead Sea Scrolls* II/2 (New Haven, 1951).

[4] See below. Also *Abrahams*, cited below.

[5] Jn. vi. 4.

[6] *Billerbeck, Kommentar zum Neuen Testament* II, 13, followed by *Klostermann*, ad loc, copied by *Grundmann* ad loc.

[7] *J. Moffatt* at Exp., 8th ser., 7 (1914), 89–90. He rightly but too shortly referred to the Midrash on S. S. viii. 13.

[8] Billerbeck's reference to Kohut's *Aruch Completum* (Vienna, 1878-), ad verb. *Gan*, no. 6 (vol. 1, p. 315, col. ii), seems confused.

[9] *Liddell–Scott–Jones, Lexicon* ad voc. For πράσον in papyri see *Preisigke, Wört.* ii, 354; *Kießling, Wört.* 231.

quite straight rows, which is the way (in the East) diners must sit if they are to be served from bowls or similar containers. I have often sat in such a row to be served, and one describes (in Sanskrit) a ritually observant person as 'one who purifies his row'. I will not go so far as to say that leeks require more water than water-melons, but they need much, hence Num. xi. 5. That verse seems to run inconsequentially after the reference to 'flesh' before, perhaps contrasting (which may be the point) with the gift of the quails (*šlw*, cf. *slw*, the mysterious name for him who is to come at Gen. xlix. 10, 4QPB). 'In Egypt we had *fish* for the asking, cucumbers, and water-melons, leeks and onions and garlic.' All these need much water. Haggadah tells us that when the Children of Israel went through the Red Sea they were provided with fresh water, and every delicious fruit one can think of. Perhaps vegetables figured too? The word for 'leek' (Heb. *ḥaṣir*, Aram. *karatey* or *qaḥloṯ*) appears in the LXX as πράσα (only here).

Neither Matthew nor Luke found the phrase in Mark suitable. Perhaps its implications were lost on them? The Feeding of the Five Thousand is a demonstration of what the Messianic Age is like [10], and the bread is like the manna of the desert, sufficing (irrespective of quantity) for all the souls who depended on each individual gatherer (Exod. xvi. 16–18 Targ. Pal.). The 'beds' are intelligible. The recipients were arranged in rows like the leeks, etc., in Egypt to show that in the World to Come the righteous will be sated like the well-irrigated vegetables which the stupid and unbelieving Israelites 'lusted for' in the desert.

This far-fetched idea is strengthened by two images from the Old Testament in which garden-beds occur plainly. Sir. xxiv. 31 (no Heb. available) speaks of irrigating the leek-bed; the context is plainly Wisdom's sating with the Word (ibid., 33, cf. Matt. iv. 4). The Song of Songs contains two important passages. S. S. vi. 2 should have been translated, according to Aquila, not with φιάλαι (as the LXX: 'beds', [round] 'basins', for the Heb. 'gardens') but with πρασιαί. The traditional rabbinical interpretation is that the 'beloved' is God, the garden houses of study, and the gathering of lilies is taking (to Paradise) the righteous of Israel. Hence it relates also to the Garden of Eden, and, by a short step, to the Messianic Kingdom [11]. That S. S. vi. 2 applied to the death of the righteous and to the Messianic Age is proved by its structural function in Jn. xix. 39–40 (hitherto unexplained!). Further, S. S. viii. 13, which is connected with vi. 2 by 'gardens' and 'companies' (i. e. scholars) refers to the Messianic banquet for the righteous [12].

Thus when the Messiah, as God's agent, came [13] (Mark seems to hint) he went down to, and delighted in, his garden-beds, which are to be

---

[10] A view shared by many older exegetes, e. g. *Pfleiderer, Primitive Christianity*, II, 25f, with the accent on the eucharistic aspect; the manna theme is properly stressed by O. Betz, *What do we know about Jesus?* (London, 1968), 67.

[11] Midrash Rabbah, S. S. VI. 2, 1 (Soncino translation, 206) also §§ 2–4; so Midrash Rabbah Gen. LXII. 2 (Soncino trans., 551–552). Yalqûṭ Šimʿoni § 991.

[12] Babylonian Talmud, B. B. 75a (Soncino trans. 299) (alleging Job xl. 30). It is from S. S. viii. 13 that the idea seems to have come, much noticed since Billerbeck, that scholars sit in rows compared to a garden.

[13] That the Targum on S. S. and Yalqûṭ thereon apply the text in many places to the Messiah has been known since A. Edersheim, *Life and Times of Jesus the*

visualised as leek-beds. The Children of Israel in the desert were pining (as they say: Num. xi. 6) with thirst (cf. συμπόσια). What was sent them was *flesh* every day until it came out of their nostrils (so Num. xi. 20) (all this is summarised in Ps. cv. 40). St. Mark's account of the Feeding of the Five Thousand at many points improves on the wilderness story (e. g. the presence of *grass*). With the loaves and fish a large number are satisfied (cf. Jn. vi. 12), without the need for the quails, or the Rock, or indeed of the wells that, according to haggadah (Num. xx. 1–2 Targ.) existed until the death of Miriam. The satisfying of plants that need a lot of water by opening the dike, or otherwise operating the system of irrigation, must have been then, as it is still, a most agreeable, signifi-cant, and well-known operation. The true explanation of Mk. vi. 39–40 is not that they are prettily [14] arranged as if in a vineyard, which has been suggested, but they, like the righteous, and like students, themselves played the role of the leeks which waited patiently for the essential irrigation which would enable them to grow. This literally satisfies the requirement of Ps. cv. 40b, 'he sent (not 'gave') them bread from heaven *to satiety'*.

FURTHER ANNOTATION

p. [101], n. 2. The πεντηκόνταρχος at Is. iii.3 is the Messiah: Midr. Rab. Num. XVIII.21.

Messiah (1883) (London, 1906), ii, 722–723. The wildly far-fetched Targum on Cant. vi. 1 shows that the actor is the Lord, giving rest to the people, assembling them from captivity, ordaining the temple service, and feeding delicately, like a son, the congregation gathered from Babylon. Thus the idea of gardenbeds is successively glossed in terms of peace and order, arrangement, worship, and *feeding*. These are the ideas that a Hebrew reader of the Masoretic text could then legitimately entertain. It has a bearing on Mk. vi. 39.

[14] So interestingly, if sentimentally, *I. Abrahams, Studies in Pharisaism and the Gospels* iii (Cambridge, 1924), 210–211 (Mishnah, Yoma I. 7 is irrelevant), and more imaginatively, *P. Carrington, According to Mark* (Cambridge, 1960), 136 (taking many useful hints from Billerbeck).

FURTHER LIGHT ON THE NARRATIVES
OF THE NATIVITY

The large literature on the infancy narratives [1]) justified by the intrinsic interest of the subject-matter, has promoted substantial advances in the last few years [2]). The extraneous material utilised has been slight and unconvincing, but, that notwithstanding, critical techniques have gone far to revealing something which had not been suspected until recently, namely the functions of both narratives as a preparation for the hearing of the gospels as a whole, and, in Luke's case, for the gist of Acts as well. Here little will be offered by way of recapitulation of what has been published already, and it is assumed that previous publications are available to the reader. Important extraneous material has been neglected

---

[1]) Items mentioned below contain bibliographies of their own. I would mention also W. SOLTAU, *The Birth of Jesus Christ* (London, 1903) (apart from the correspondence with Is. lx 6 amongst other passages, there can be no doubt that none of the other details about the Magi grew up on Jewish soil, but they are all based upon heathen mythology (!)); E. NESTLE, 'Die Hirten von Bethlehem', *Z.N.W.* 7 (1906), 257-9 (usefully links the shepherds with Mi. iv 8 and birth in the field with Mi. ix 10); E. J. HOUDOUS, 'The Gospel of the Epiphany,' *C.B.Q.* 6/1 (1944), 69-84 (a pre-midrashic study); H. J. RICHARDS, 'The three kings...' *Scripture* 8 (1956), 23-8 (the star represents metaphorically the leading of astrologers); D. DAUBE, 'The earliest structure of the gospels,' *N.T.S.* 5 (1958-9), 184-5 (theme of persecution of Jacob by Laban; Rachel is Jacob's wife and Herod is Laban) (cf. NELLESSEN, inf. p. 96, n. 60, pp. 69-71); S. MUÑOZ IGLESIAS, *Estud. Bibl.* 16 (1957), 5-36 (heroic, including Indian tales, and the infancy narratives); K. STENDAHL, 'Quis et unde? An analysis of Mt. i-2', *Judentum, Urchristentum, Kirche (Festschrift J. Jeremias)* (Berlin, 1960), 94-105; S. BEN-CHORIN, *Bruder Jesus* (Munich, 1970), 30-38; M. D. GOULDER, *Midrash and Lection in Matthew* (London, 1974), 236-42 (good on Joseph and dreams; development of themes taken up by DAUBE, above). I have not seen J. DUCHESNE-GUILLEMIN, 'Jesus' trimorphism and the differentiation of the Magi', in SHARPE and HINNELLS, ed., *Man and his Salvation. Essays... S.G.F. Brandon* (Manchester, forthcoming), cf. 8. For Mr. BARNETT's recent notion see below, p. 83 n. 10.

[2]) J. DANIÉLOU, *The Infancy Narratives* (London, 1968). LEGRAND, inf. p. 106, n. 97. BENOIT, inf, p. 94, n. 48. NELLESSEN, inf. p. 96, n. 60.

in both cases, viz. regarding the Census and the Magi, and some relevant biblical references have been overlooked. It is astonishing that this can be so, but so it is.

I. *The Census of Augustus*

1. Luke starts his story of the birth of Jesus with a reference to the decree of Caesar Augustus. It has been argued from SCHÜRER onwards interminably, fortified by the editors of the second edition of that classic [3]), and by a historian (to whom they do not refer) working on the colonies of the empire [4]), that there could have been no census under Augustus in Judaea before A.D. 6, and that Quirinius was not, indeed could not have been, available to conduct any such operation prior to that date [5]). Sadly, historians say, Luke was confused or himself confused the sequence of events, even in a matter which could easily have been checked, and has

---

[3]) E. SCHÜRER, *The History of the Jewish People in the Age of Jesus Christ, New English Version*, ed. G. VERMES and F. MILLAR, I (Edinburgh, 1973), 399-427. (1) History does not otherwise record a general imperial census in the time of Augustus; (2) under a Roman census, Joseph would not have been obliged to travel to Bethlehem, and Mary would not have been required to accompany him there [misunderstanding]; (3) a Roman census could not have been carried out in Palestine during the time of king Herod [unnecessary presupposition]; (4) Josephus knows nothing of a Roman census in Palestine during the reign of Herod [ditto]; he refers rather to the census of A.D. 6/7 as something new and unprecedented; (5) the census held under Quirinius could not have taken place in the time of Herod, for Quirinius was never governor of Syria during Herod's lifetime. G. OGG, 'The Quirinius question today', *Ex. T.* 79 (1968) 231-6, well argued, is otiose if I am right in my present contentions.

[4]) B. LEVICK, *Roman Colonies in Southern Asia Minor* (Oxford, 1967), 206-14: in spite of obscurities, there is no room (p. 210) for Quirinius on the list of governors of Syria between 13 and 4 B.C., but even if there were, it is highly unlikely that he conducted a census of Judaea before it was reduced to provincial status in A.D. 6. A study of Sentius Saturninus (Consul 19 B.C.) in our context was done by EVANS, inf. n. 5.

[5]) See also OGG, cited n. 3 above. See also C. F. EVANS, 'Tertullian's references to Sentius Saturninus and the Lukan Census', *J. T. S.* 24/1 (1973), 24-39. Sir Ronald SYME, strongly urging L. Calpurnius Piso (*cos.* 15 B.C.) as the *ignotus* subject of the eulogium of the Titulus Tiburtinus (in *Vestigia* 17, 1973, 585-601), denied that there was any previous census in Judaea, admitted Luke's 'discrepancy', censured those that attempted to explain it away, offered as a genuine explanation the fact that Judaea knew two major crises (4 B.C. and A.D. 6), in both of which Judas the Galilaean figured, so that conflation and amalgamation were encouraged by inadvertence—but he assumed (wrongly) that 'Herod' was Herod the Great. His conclusion, however, 'When the year (of the Nativity) came to excite curiosity and interest, it lay beyond human ascertainment...', seems correct.

been as poor a historian in this rather important context as he is
known to have been in some minor ones [6]). So much for Luke
the historian! However, a very sensible suggestion, based upon
known retrospective biography in China at a period not so very
remote from ours [7]), would remove the discussion from the realm
of mere chronology and introduce an *as-if* chronology [8]), in order
to attribute to the child features which may have existed, or may
not, but which in some sense proleptically corroborate what was
known and thought about him after he had become famous. This
approach is a valid one, and is particularly appropriate to the study
of Matthew's nativity stories. Dreams, after all, were solemnly
related as history by Josephus (*B.J.* ii.112-16; *Ant.* xvii.345-53)
whom everyone acknowledges to be a historian [9]). However, the
entire hypothesis is otiose in this context since the 'Herod the
King' in whose reign the angel appeared to Zechariah could clearly
be Herod Archelaus. Since we must presume Luke could have
checked his chronology, the 'Herod' must not be presumed to be
Herod the Great until evidence is forthcoming that it was he. And
there is no such evidence. Scholars have been confused by Matthew,
and have fallen into a pre-critical harmonisation of the two gospels.

It has been argued [10]) that Luke has an internal chronology of
his own, that Jesus was about 30 years of age in A.D. 29/30 (Lk. iii
1, 21, 23) and that if the census was not a Roman census at all but
an administrative arrangement whereby the whole Jewish popula-
tion was organised by Herod the Great to swear allegiance to
Caesar's government and to himself, this could well have been
about 7 B.C.: thus Jesus would have been about 36 or so. However,

---

[6]) Acts v 36 f. (anachronistic). SCHÜRER [2], 425. See also comments on
Lk. xxiii 45 at DERRETT, *Jesus's Audience* (London, 1973), 126.

[7]) Samuel N. C. LIEU has drawn my attention to the work of Ssu-ma
Ch'ien (died *c.* 90 B.C.): Burton WATSON, *Records of the Grand Historian of
China* (New York, 1961), 77-81 (*biography* of Kao-Tsu). The sign of the dragon
hovering over his mother while she was sleeping in the field (like the story
of the conception of Samson this may go back to an extremely ancient
mythical form, in which the Alexander-legend merely shares); the reigning
emperor, warned by astrologers, attempted to suppress the expected threat
(near-historical, as with Herod's behaviour) (this *might* go back to the
Alexander-legend, which certainly penetrated as far East as Mongolia).

[8]) For the meaning of *as-if*, DERRETT, *Jesus's Audience*, 101-6, 126.

[9]) It is notorious, too, how carefully Josephus relates portents, dreams
apart: DERRETT, *op. cit.*, 117-18.

[10]) P. W. BARNETT, '*Apographe* and *apographesthai* in Luke 2', *Exp. T.*
85/12 (1974), 377-80.

there is no evidence that *apographé* could apply to such a proceeding, nor that very humble families would need to travel distances for the purpose, nor that ordinary people in general were tendered the oath to which Josephus refers at *Ant.* xv.369, xvii.42. It seems more likely that the oath was tendered to groups notorious for their hostility to his government or to any non-theocratic government. Further, if Jesus was born (as I suppose) *in St. Luke's view* in A.D. 6, this would make him about 24 years of age. Neither figure is really near '30', but that, in any case, has nothing to do with chronology, the figure being taken from 2 Sam. v 4, for it was right that the Son of David should inaugurate his activities at David's age (32 and 35 were ages connected with less satisfactory characters).

Archelaus was called Herod [11]) just as Antipas was called Herod, and the coins of Archelaus call him simply 'Herod the Ethnarch' [12]), which is a significant and appropriate title. Hence Luke's chronology is consistent, and he places the birth of Jesus in A.D. 6 or later. I have detected [13]) in the name Quirinius [14]) the root letters QRN, which can suggest (as a glance at Jastrow's dictionary will confirm) (a) a hard instrument, (b) capital [as opposed to income] (it was under his orders that the taxgathering machine was effectively put into operation, and a valuation of land was a part of the process as Stauffer has shown clearly), and (c) horn, namely the horn of the Messiah (Ps. lxxxix 24-27, xcii 10; Lk. i 69; b. Ber. 29a) (!).

---

[11]) *Der Kleine Pauly* II (1967) 1092, ll. 15-16, no. 3. Dio Cassius, *Hist. Rom.* lv. 27, 6. Josephus did not call Archelaus 'Herod' because he gave this name to Herod the Great, to whom he refers in the same breath with Archelaus a vast number of times, and also to Herod Antipas, whom he occasionally calls 'Herod' when confusion with the father was unlikely.

[12]) M. A. LEVY, *Gesch. der Jüd. Münzen* (Leipzig, 1855), 73 f. F. W. MADDEN, *Coins of the Jews* (London, 1881). 114-18. J. MESHORER, *Maṭbe'ot ha-Yehudim bime Bayit Sheni* (Tel Aviv, 1966), 92-3. SCHÜRER [2], 416. Jos., *B.J.* ii. 93.

[13]) Notes circulated at a lecture given in December 1970. See JASTROW's *Dictionary* for the scope of *qeren*.

[14]) The census of Quirinius (Jos., *Ant.* xvii. 355, xviii. 1 ff.: see W. LODDER, *Die Schätzung des Quirinius bei Fl. Josephus*, Leipzig, 1930); to the valuable bibliography of L. H. FELDMAN, ed., *Josephus* (Loeb edn.), ix (1969), App. B, add the important E. STAUFFER, 'Die Dauer des Census Augusti' in *Fest. E. Klostermann* (Berlin, 1961), 9-34 (a work insufficiently studied because its conclusions gave too much room to Luke!). ἀπογραφή also in Acts v 37; Jos., *B.J.* vii. 253. It is likely that ἀπογραφὴ πρώτη means 'earlier census', as if Luke knew of subsequent and more characteristic arrangements in Palestine: G. M. LEE, *Bibl.* 51 (1970), 238.

Jews liked to play with letters, and puns on Greek names are not at all uncommon. Small wonder that the name was remembered.

The coincidence of a census and the birth of the Messiah is based upon two midrashim of Old Testament texts. It is odd that scholars have noticed neither. NESTLE, indeed, noted the psalm as far back as 1910, but his comment was ignored [15]). The prophet Micah tells how God will give over the Jews to the gentiles until one that is to bear a child shall give birth. From this it was deduced that the Messiah would come (i.e. be born) nine months after the rule of Rome was effectively extended over the whole (including the Judaean) world [16]). One could say that Rome was effectively ruler as early as Herod the Great's time (Matthew took that view, seemingly); or one could say that Rome effectively ruled Judaea only on the removal of Archelaus in A.D.6 [17]). That was the view for which Luke seems to have opted. The godless king was 'dead' (according to prophecy?), the fight was over, and Israel was awaiting the true shepherd: ἕκαστος εἰς τὴν ἑαυτοῦ πόλιν (1 K. xxii 36; cf. 17 and add Jdg. xxi 24-25). It implies that actual information about the birth of Jesus was meagre. That is likely. Several emperor's birth-dates were unknown shortly after their times. I myself have known Asian lads who were unaware of the date of their births and invariably referred me to their parents as being 'likely to remember'. Luke's extreme interest in the pregnancy of Mary, and the apparently fortuitous occurrence of the birth in Bethlehem are explained when we have placed the text   * of Micah in its perspective:

Mi. v 1 καὶ σύ, Βηθλεεμ οἶκος τοῦ Εφραθα, ὀλιγοστὸς εἶ τοῦ εἶναι ἐν χιλιάσιν Ιουδα· ἐκ σοῦ μοι ἐξελεύσεται τοῦ εἶναι εἰς ἄρχοντα ἐν τῷ Ισραηλ, καὶ αἱ ἔξοδοι αὐτοῦ ἀπ'ἀρχῆς ἐξ ἡμερῶν αἰῶνος. 2 διὰ τοῦτο

---

[15]) See inf. p. 87, n. 24.

[16]) b. Yoma 10a = Soncino translation 44. Also Yalquṭ on Mic. v 3 (Rab   * so reported) ('until the time' = nine months). Mi. v 1-5 itself is most thoroughly studied with the fullest references by J. COPPENS, 'Le cadre littéraire de Michée V:1-5', in H. GOEDICKE, ed. Albright Fest. (Baltimore, 1971), 58-62. In his view the MT of v. 2 should be translated, '. . . c'est pourquoi (dans l'entretemps) il les abandonnera jusqu'à l'époque où celle qui doit engendrer aura engendré, et (alors) le reste de ses frères reviendra vers les fils d'Israël. . .'. On the text of the LXX and Lucian see the important material in G. HOWARD's study at J.Q.R. 62 (1971), 51 ff., 59. The Dead Sea Scroll reading supports LXX Ms. W.

[17]) For Archelaus's banishment see Jos., B.J. ii. 111, 167; Ant., xvii. 342-4.

δώσει αὐτοὺς ἕως καιροῦ τικτούσης τέξεται, καὶ οἱ ἐπίλοιποι τῶν ἀδελ-
φῶν αὐτῶν ἐπιστρέψουσιν ἐπι τοὺς υἱοὺς Ισραηλ. 3 καὶ ὄψεται καὶ
ποιμανεῖ τὸ ποίμνιον αὐτοῦ ἐν ἰσχύι κυρίου, καὶ ἐν τῇ δόξῃ τοῦ ὀνόματος
κυρίου τοῦ θεοῦ αὐτῶν ὑπάρξουσιν·διότι νῦν μεγαλυνθήσεται ἕως ἄκρων
τῆς γῆς. 4 καὶ ἔσται αὕτη εἰρήνη· ὅταν Ἀσσύριος ἐπέλθη ἐπὶ τὴν
γῆν ὑμῶν καὶ ὅταν ἐπιβῇ ἐπὶ τὴν χώραν ὑμῶν. . .

The second biblical text upon which the chronology in Luke is
founded is Ps. lxxxvii. There we are told that all the peoples of the
world, including those that had treated the Jews ill, shall come
and seek to be inscribed along with the Jews as children of Jerusalem. The whole psalm is of interest, especially when one thinks of
the Magi. The reader's attention must also be called to the phrase
'I have called to mind (as if calling a roll) Rahab. . .' Now Rahab,
referring no doubt to Egypt [18]), is of course also the ex-harlot who
became a proselyte, a Jewish heroine, and mother of priests who
were also prophets [19]), and eventually, according to Matt. i 5, an-
cestress of the Messiah Jesus. The text, with midrashim to be found
in the Targum, the LXX, *Midrash on Psalms* [20]), and elsewhere,
has its major fascinations, but the important idea for us is that
when God writes down the peoples, i.e. makes a census of the world,
this man, or Man [21]), will be born there, i.e. in Jerusalem, the ritual
limits of which (as Passover practice showed) included Bethlehem.
Jerusalem was to be a world-metropolis in a spiritual sense. Midrash makes it plain that the Messiah will be born at the time when
God counts up all the peoples [22]). God's opposition to census is well
known [23]), but there would come a time when that would be waived.

---

[18]) Rahab is a kingdom according to *Midr. Ps.* Ps. 8 § 3, Ps. 90 § 15 (see
also Is. xxx 7). *J. E.* x (1905), 308-9.
[19]) Rahab in midrash: *J.E.* x (1905), 309.
[20]) See especially *Midr. Ps.*, Ps. 87 § 6 (trans. W. BRAUDE, II, 77).
[21]) The Heb. ʾiš ʾiš is capable of any imaginative rendering, 'everyman'
being perhaps the most faithful to the original. Yet midrashic technique
starts from there, it does not stop there. *Midr. Ps.*, also Yalqûṭ (§ 838):
'this man and that man' refers to the Messiah's of the Lord, the Messiah the
son of David and the Messiah the son of Ephraim. "'This man that he was
born there' means that it will be as if such men were *newly born*". [At the
time of God's census all converts will be as if newly born.]
[22]) See MT, Targ., and *Midr. Ps.* ad loc.
[23]) Ex. xxx 12 f.; 2 Sam. xxiv 1; 1 Chr. xxi 1; cf. Jos., *Ant.* vii. 318-22; b.
Pes. 64b = Soncino trans. 326 (Agrippa I [or II, A.D. 66 ?] wanting to
know the number of the people while avoiding the prohibition, asked the
High Priest to count the paschal sacrifices; cf. Jos. *B.J.* vi. 422-5). Cf. Ezk.
xiii 9 (connected by Hugh BROUGHTON with Ps. lxxxvii 6); Heb. xii 22-3.

Thus Jewish learning, or what passed for learning, confirmed that the Messiah would come at the time of a census. No very exact coincidence is required for this, but, as everyone who has looked for coincidences knows, a fairly near concurrence is readily grasped as an exact coincidence. Rabbis, commenting on our psalm, said that *at that time* the nations of the earth would bring gifts to the King Messiah, for Ps. lxxxvii is to be read with Ps. lxviii 32 (*Midr. Ps.*, Ps. lxxxvii § 6; Yalquṭ § 838; Targ. Is. 16.1; b. Pes. 118b): the gifts would be very peculiar, as we shall see, and whether that midrash was available or not in Matthew's time is an open question, but very little ingenuity is needed to see how it could very well consist with his picture of the Magi (see below).

ψ lxxxvi οἱ θεμέλιοι αὐτοῦ ἐν τοῖς ὄρεσι τοῖς ἁγίοις· Ἀγαπᾷ κύριος τὰς πύλας Σιὼν, ὑπὲρ πάντα τὰ σκηνώματα Ἰακωβ. Δεδοξασμένα ἐλαλήθη περὶ σου, ἡ πόλις τοῦ Θεοῦ. Μνησθήσομαι Ρααβ καὶ Βαβυλῶνος τοῖς γινώσκουσί με·καὶ ἰδοῦ ἀλλόφυλοι, καὶ Τύρος, καὶ λαὸς τῶν Αἰθιό- πων, οὗτοι ἐγεννήθησαν ἐκεῖ. Μήτηρ Σιὼν, ἐρεῖ ἄνθρωπος· καὶ ἄνθρωπος ἐγεννήθη ἐν αὐτῇ, καὶ αὐτὸς ἐθεμελίωσεν αὐτὴν ὁ Ὕψιστος. Κύριος διηγήσεται ἐν γραφῇ λαῶν καὶ ἀρχόντων, τούτων τῶν γεγεννημένων ἐν αὐτῇ. Ὡς εὐφραινομένων πάντων ἡ κατοικία ἐν σοί. . .

That the early church knew this as relating to the birth of the Saviour is proved by the Byzantine liturgy [24]: on Christmas Eve, the third hour, the first psalm is this very psalm. That a census, and exacting of tribute, would coincide with the messianic era and the glory of Jerusalem can easily be read in Is. lx 17 (*wᵉ nogśayich ṣᵉdāqâ*), if one has this psalm in mind, and indeed the Magi and their gifts are not far off (Is. lx. 16-17)!

2. We now come to the journey of Joseph and Mary to Bethle- hem. It is generally regarded as a very implausible tale, the very stuff of myth. Why, in a mythically self-conscious age, did Luke commit himself, a historian to such a story? As a matter of fact it is not only plausible, but just a little too lifelike. Luke takes a plausible story in order to make a quasi-political, biblical-exegetical point out of it. These people were Jews, and everyone would be-

GINZBERG, *Leg. J.* iii, 146. J. G. FRAZER, *Folk-lore in the Old Testament* (London, 1923), 307-13.

[24] Μηναῖα τοῦ ὅλου ἐνιαυτοῦ, II (Rome, 1892), 635 (Service of the great or imperial hours). The relevance is noted in scholia to ψ 88 (87) (ed. 1587) as explained by E. NESTLE, 'Die Schatzung in Lukas 2 and Psalm 87 (86). 67', *Z.N.W.* 11 (1910), 87!

lieve that Joseph would hesitate to turn down an opportunity of saving money. Luke has told us exactly why, and we have been ignorant enough to miss the point. Most hearers of Luke will have been Christians, or would-be Christians who knew of the Jews' predicament in Egypt, which was still in exactly the same position as it was in the time of Christ: the dreadful upheavals in Judaea were not reflected in Egypt, and it was very easy to suppose that the outlines, at least, of the Egyptian situation had had their counterparts in Judaea when the census began. The reason why Christians would be sensitive to the predicament of the Jews was simply this, that many of them were claiming to be Israel, and to participate in its privileges, as I have explained in a coming study on the Jews as religious persecutors in the time of St. Paul (apropos of I Cor. xii 1-3). Jews wanted more privileges than they had, and they were alarmed lest Christians caused them to lose those they did possess. Consequently a great many Christians were concerned at the negative side of their new status: unless they could claim to be Greeks (and not part of the Israelite *ethnos*) they would suffer from the Jews' disabilities!

The better opinion is that the census in Egypt was an affair of long standing, with roots at least in the Ptolemaic age [25]. It was a pattern for bureaucracy. There never was a bureaucracy like that in Egypt, and all parts of the empire in the time of Augustus and Tiberius would have been glad to emulate its standards and achievements. We have some of the contents of a few of its archives (or waste-paper baskets?), and so are in a good position to know what went on. When Quirinius and his assistants took up the mammoth task of making a census of the inhabitants of Judaea, by no means the passive natives that were subject to the λαογραφία in Egypt, they will have had the Egyptian system as their blueprint (for there was no other) and they will have added some optimism to

---

[25] M. HOMBERT and C. PRÉAUX, *Recherches sur le Recensement dans l'Égypte romaine* (Leiden, 1952) (magnificent for our purposes). κατ' οἰκίαν ἀπογραφαί certainly existed before A.D. 33/34 (p. 50) and the fourteen-year cycle may well have preexisted that date. Males were subject to λαογραφία (= census) in 94 or 61 B.C.: P. Tebt. 103, 121, 189. V. A. TCHERIKOVER and A. FUKS, *Corpus Papyrorum Judaicarum* I (Cambridge, Mass., 1957), 60: λαογραφία (LXX 3 Macc. ii 28, 30) was introduced into Egypt by Augustus in 24/23 B.C. TCHERIKOVER minimises the influence of pre-Roman poll-tax arrangements. S. L. WALLACE (below) would have placed the first Roman census in 24/23 B.C. if the Ptolemaic system really provided a model, or the first census was in 10/9 B.C.

determination in attempting to put the scheme into effect [26]). S. L. WALLACE is obviously right in pointing out that the census in Judaea *need* not have proceeded along the Egyptian lines—but what other model was in existence, and if any was how (if we know nothing of it) would Luke's hearers be informed about it?

By Luke's time, if he wrote after A.D. 70, everyone will have known how successful Quirinius was, leaving aside the rebellion his task provoked. One factor will have been very well known, namely the Jews' indignation at having been treated as second-class subjects of the empire, being classed with the Egyptian natives [27]). Having done all they could to infiltrate into the gymnasium and so qualify for citizenship of Alexandria and other Greek cities (this involved an element of plastic surgery in the majority of cases, so idiotic was the search for prestige!) [28]), they remained furious when, unsuccessful in an attempt to achieve a mass 'passing' to free status, they were officially declared (Josephus, *Ant.* xix. 280-5) to be non-citizens of the Greek cities, barred from entry to the rolls of citizens, and thus confined to the other status' available to non-citizens of the cities [29]). All over the empire the second-class status of Jews will have been known, a very sore point to them! In the homeland of the *ethnos* the same jealousy will have existed. The cities founded by the Seleucids and by Herod the Great, inhabited by mixed colonists, most of whom claimed to be Greeks, could claim total immunity from the λαογραφία, that is to say if the

---

[26]) H. BRAUNERT, 'Der römische Provinzialzensus', *Historia* 6 (1957), 192-214 (an excellent reference I owe to Mr. Sam LIEU) throws no new light on our problem such as would contradict the other authorities cited in this study, whilst carefully distinguishing census of citizens of Rome from that of other inhabitants of the empire (see pp. 199-200). His reference to Cassius Dio LVI 28, 6 is particularly valuable. He attributes Luke's dating to Jewish nationalistic tendencies prior to the crucifixion and taken over by the early church (see *J.B.L.* 65 [1946], 123 ff.).

[27]) See note 25. Also V. A. TCHERIKOVER, *Hellenistic Civilisation and the Jews* (Jerusalem, 1959), 311-12, 317-18, 326.

[28]) See works on the edict of Claudius in the bibliography (next note), commencing with U. WILCKEN, *Zum Alexandrinischen Antisemitismus* (Abh. d. k. Sach. Gesellsch. d. Wiss., Phil. -Hist. Kl. 27) (Leipzig, 1909). TCHERIKOVER and FUKS, above: 'Just as the gymnasium education was a mark of distinction proper to Greeks, so the payment of poll-tax was a sign of degradation marking the Egyptians'. Greeks were exempt from poll-tax: R. TAUBENSCHLAG, *Law of Greco-Roman Egypt* (1944), 108.

[29]) An excellent bibliography on the citizenship of Alexandrian Jews and on the edict of Claudius is at L. H. FELDMAN, *op. cit.*, App. Q (pay special attention to the works of TCHERIKOVER).

Egyptian pattern was followed. As for 'mother' cities in the remaining territory the citizens could claim a reduction in the poll-tax amounting to 50% [30]). We do not know if that was actually the case in any city other than Jerusalem, mother-city or no mother-city: but the Egyptian pattern is quite clear. A citizen of a *metropolis* paid only a half of the tax *even if he lived in one of the villages* [31]). It was a question of being on the rolls. The tax was levied on all adults *as members of a household*, and was assessed not merely on the basis that they owned property in a particular place. That indeed along with other considerations determined where they had to file their assessment declarations—especially if they had ἰδία to which they might return for the purpose of filing them [32]). Their place of residence at the time of the census (γραφὴ ἐνοικίων) was also significant. The paper, addressed to the relevant official, commenced, after the formal address, with the word ἀπογράφομαι [33]) and just above the names or signatures of the witnesses, a statement that the deponent took an oath as to the correctness of his declaration [34]). That oath must have annoyed the Jews, and must have been one of the reasons for the furious opposition to the procedure, but we do not know how Quirinius' officials got around it. I say the tax was levied on all adults. Boys under 14 and men over 60 or 61 were exempt [35]). It was therefore absolutely necessary to know the date of birth. The registers kept in the registry offices were used to prove

---

[30]) λαογραφούμενοι ἀπὸ τῆς μητροπόλεως: a privileged class. HOMBERT-PRÉAUX, 104, 120 § 2. Sherman LEROY WALLACE, *Taxation in Egypt* (Princeton, 1938), 96 ff., 120. SCHÜRER [2], 402 n. 10.

[31]) WALLACE, 121: if they made proper census returns.

[32]) After HOMBERT-PRÉAUX (above) the next chief study is V. A. TCHERIKOVER, 'Syntaxis and Laographia', *J. Jur. Pap.* 4 (1950), 179-207. The place of birth was not significant generally (HOMBERT-PRÉAUX, 65). But the ἐφέστια (? ancestral or permanent domicile) was also a basis for registration. H.-P. are judicious (pp. 67-8) in refusing to confirm that registrants must return to their ἰδία for the purpose of registration, seeing that uncertainty over the obligatory location seems to have been common (P. Oxy. 1157, 3d cent.). Luke's τὴν ἑαυτοῦ πόλιν takes, to my mind, advantage of a popular notion that returning to one's ἰδία was a normal, if not compulsory proceeding. In Egypt it was especially rural, not urban.

[33]) Many examples are given verbatim by HOMBERT-PRÉAUX.

[34]) HOMBERT-PRÉAUX, 124-7. P. Oxy. 255 (Oct. A.D. 48): ὀμνύω Τιβέριον . . . Αὐτοκράτορα εἰ μὴν . . . ἐπ' ἀληθείας ἐπιδεδωκέναι τὴν προκειμένην γραφὴν τῶν παρ' ἐμοὶ οἰκούντων . . . P. Milanesi 3 (A.D. 1-14): ὀμνύω Καίσαρα.

[35]) A point made as early as U. WILCKEN, *Grundzüge* I (Leipzig/Berlin, 1912), 189. SCHÜRER [2], 403 n. 12. In *Syria* the age-range for liability to the poll-tax was 14-65. Thus concern about age (and therefore date of birth) is known for the relevant region.

dates of birth and death and relationship for purposes of marriage and inheritance; they were legal testimony [36]). Hence, as soon as we know that a census was being held we know that registers, and pedigrees furnished by the deponents themselves, were available. Quite apart from the fact that Jewish sources refer openly to ascertainable pedigrees [37]), the *sarcasm* against such pedigrees as we have, suggesting that no one knew his ancestry (apart from being implausible in an underdeveloped territory, where pedigrees are of great social and financial value), is well wide of the mark [38]).

Boys over 14 had to pay, and all newly born boys had to be registered at the census, which had a recurrence every 14 years for that very reason [39]). *Privileged* families were naturally most concerned to get their boys registered. If registered in the κατ' οἰκίαν ἀπογραφή their citizenship by *birth* could not be disputed! [40]) If the *pater familias* was not available to make the declarations personally, he stood the risk that his deputy would bungle the ἀπογραφή [41]). The ἀκρόασις was an official scrutiny, or semi-judicial

---

[36]) κατ' οἰκίαν ἀπογραφαί were used to prove membership of the sacerdotal order on the mother's side, rights to land, rights to heirship (see H.-P.). P. Lond. 324 illustrates proof of relationship by birth to living persons. The authenticity of the copy in the archives (βιβλιοθήκη ἐγκτήσεων) is shown: ἐπιδείξω τὰ ἴσα ἐν καταχωρισμῷ.

[37]) Jos., *Vita* 6; Ezra ii 63; Mishnah, Ta'an. IV.5, Qidd. IV.5; Targ. Zech. iii 3-4; b. Pes. 62b. Z. W. FALK, *Introduction to Jewish Law of the Second Commonwealth* (Leiden, 1972), 136. j. Ta'an. IV.2, 68a. J. Z. LAUTERBACH, *J.Q.R.*, NS, 8, 401 ff. b. Yev. 49b = Soncino trans. 324. Cf. EUSEB., *Hist. Eccl.* I.7, 13.

[38]) SCHÜRER [2], 411, 412 n. 1. The reference to J. JEREMIAS, *Jerusalem in the Time of Jesus* (1969), 275-302, is unfortunate. Mishnah, Ta'an. IV.5 does not imply that everyone was of unknown descent in recent generations. The arena of thought is the coming of Elijah to sort out genealogies back to Aaron and Moses!

[39]) See also p. 88, n. 25. HOMBERT-PRÉAUX, 75: children born after the last census had to appear personally and not otherwise (or we cannot prove personal appearance thereafter). Non-registration of children was a penal offence: children ἀναπόγραφοι ἐκ πολλῶν ἤδη ἐτῶν (B.G.U. 983) (ibid. p. 98). Children are declared as ἀναγεγραμμένος or more often as μὴ ἀναγεγραμμένος ἐν ἐπιγεγενημένοις. Daughters were *not* mentioned—metropolites acquired their status through *males*! (ibid. p. 116-17). Minor sons are registered: Stud. Pal. IV, p. 62, l.29 and p. 70 (Jews) (also B.G.U. 971, l. 18): ἀπολογισμός ἀφηλίκων υἱῶν λαογραφουμένων.

[40]) P. Oxy. 1157. HOMBERT-PRÉAUX, 76. The very important edict of C. Vibius Maximus (A.D. 103/4) asking people to return to their normal places of residence to work there has been underevaluated at SCHÜRER [2], 412, correctly and cautiously evaluated by HOMBERT-PRÉAUX, 67-8.

[41]) P. Oxy. 1157.

hearing [42]) at which the deponents could be questioned on discrepancies, and the truth of allegations regarding births and deaths
could be checked [43]). A census system which relied entirely on the
declarations of the assessees themselves would be moonshine. The
great detail of surviving depositions shows that their makers were
afraid of discrepancies coming to light [44]). All residents and their
relationships to each other had to be declared. There were penalties
for false declaration [45]). To make sure that the child's birth was
correctly recorded a personal appearance with the child, if born by
the time of the census (which was obviously not a matter of a
couple of days), was highly desirable [46]).

But there was a more arcane reason tending to the same end. It
must be remembered that according to Luke Joseph's *domicile* was
in Nazareth, which was in the territory of Antipas, and he was
not therefore personally liable to the poll-tax unless ownership
of property in Judaea could conceivably be construed as requiring
assessment. By treaty between Rome and Antipas it was possible
for the residents in the territory of the latter to be extradited to
meet charges arising out of revenue demands made on behalf of the
former. The delicacy of such relationships is evidenced by Luke
himself (xxiii 6-12). We know nothing of any such treaty, yet it is
inconceivable that such arrangements were not *contemplated*,
whether or not they were effectuated! Moreover, if Antipas's rule
was precarious, and all hearers of Luke knew that it was, Roman
rule was impending even for residents at Nazareth (as was the
case), and in that case assessment to poll-tax (at the preferential
rate) once for all would take care of the family wherever they were
domiciled, and wherever they held property indefinitely. Luke's

---

[42]) See ἀκροατής, judge: Jos., *Ant.* ii.275, xvii.91; arbitrator, PREISIGKE,
Wört., I. 49; id., LAMPE, *Patr. Greek Lex.*, ad v., I.c; ἀκρόασις, hearing (judicial): Jos., *Ant.* xvii.94, xviii.170, 178, 179; ἀκροατήριον, courtroom:
Justinian, Nov. 21. This was what the Jews objected to (Jos., *Ant.* xviii.2-3):
ἐν δεινῷ φέροντες τὴν ἐπὶ ταῖς ἀπογραφαῖς ἀκρόασιν ὑποκατέβησαν . . .
ἀπετίμων τὰ χρήματα μηδὲν ἐνδοιάσαντες. The study of this passage by
STAUFFER, *ubi cit.*, p. 84, n. 14 above, at 25-6 is excellent, with citations
regarding oppressive methods of interrogation (ibid. 26 n. 1). SCHÜRER [2]
mentions only ἐπικρίσις (p. 404, n. 19): an examination to determine status
and consequent liability to poll-tax.
[43]) Last note. The account of HOMBERT-PRÉAUX agrees.
[44]) HOMBERT-PRÉAUX, 127
[45]) Ibid.
[46]) See p. 91, n. 39 above! Men and women were registered. Husbands
could make returns on behalf of their wives (HOMBERT-PRÉAUX, 53, 63).

picture of Joseph's behaviour was thus factually plausible; and it had the special quality (possibly the decisive one in the eyes of its author) of portraying Joseph as voluntarily, even eagerly, submitting himself to Roman jurisdiction, utterly unlike the turbulent Zealots and their fellow-travellers as depicted by Josephus (*B.J.* vii.253 ff.). Joseph's family, whatever their conscious motives (!), actually voluntarily submitted Jesus to be born under direct Roman rule, though he was conceived under a semitic princeling. It is well known that according to rabbinical law every Jew owns a fraction of the land of Israel: the principle is that the right by descent cannot be alienated indefinitely under biblical principles, whatever the actual possession, since land cannot be acquired (in this view) by possession alone. All Jews must have acquired some right by intestate succession, even though the fraction might be quite illusory, and the location forgotten. Purely ornamental inheritances must have been a commonplace in the first century, when the Hellenistic *de facto* legal system upon which the governments based their fiscal arrangements recognised sales, including revenue-sales, and other transfers, especially by testament, which were unknown to the holy scripture and to principles based upon it. Joseph claimed to be of the 'house of David'—with the jargon of the Egyptian ἀπογραφή in mind we find a new significance in ἐξ οἴκου καὶ πατριᾶς (Lk. ii. 4b)—and his *city*, therefore, was Bethlehem. Whether or not he ever lived there, which he may have done, he could probably prove his descent, and a tiny fraction of landed property there (say 1/500 of an acre), a token citizenship of what is depicted quite obviously as a metropolis. Bethlehem, though insignificant in those days, was the mother city of Jerusalem itself. If Jerusalem was 'mother' in the words of the psalmist, how much more was Bethlehem, the city of the man who bought the threshing-floor ! In order to establish his own pedigree and his own citizenship rights in the paternal line (cf. Lk. iii 23-31) Joseph could well have needed to be there. He could claim to be assessed to poll-tax at the privileged rate whether he had visible assets there or not. And not he only, but his wife also. But Mary's presence there, as scholars seem to have failed to notice, was not in order to be enrolled (ἀπογράψασθαι is of course the correct technical term) for that could easily have been done on her behalf by the head of the household where they lodged, but because the child, if born there, and legitimately descended from a citizen (for mere birth in a *polis* did not admit one to the rolls though it provided a claim to admission), would qualify as a citizen by birth, and, if a male child, liable to poll-tax at the age of fourteen, would be able to claim after due admission to the register the reduction of the tax to 50%. To get the child born there his mother must necessarily travel with her husband. The ancestral dwelling (if, as seems likely, that is indeed the correct implication of the word κατάλυμα, which literally links the story with the grotesque experience of Moses and his uncircumcised child)[47]), was then so choked with people doing exactly what Joseph was doing that he was obliged to shack up in a cave, possibly underneath the dwelling or in its very close vicinity [48]).

3. Something more should be said about the manger. That it was a niche cut from the living rock I am unable to doubt. The grotesque and farfetched meanings and allusions in the story are beginning to come to hand. They must not be rejected on purely *a priori* grounds. The word φάτνη, otherwise πάθνη, implies a socket [49]). I have already explained that a rock receptacle carries the implications of ritual purity [50]), and that birth in a cave had then overtones of special fitness for ensuring ritual purity for others [51]). 'Manger' was also used to mean, almost in slang terms, a place for feeding, for stuffing oneself [52]); it was also, as a translation of the Hebrew *'ebûs*, a 'picnic basket' [53]), and thus very appropriate for the shepherds who were just coming off watch [54]). The notion that

[47]) Ex. iv 24-26 and Targ. Ginzberg, *Leg. J.* ii, 295; v, 423 n.149. Jub. xlviii 2. b. Ned. 32a = Soncino trans. 94. B. S. CHILDS, *Myth and Reality in the Old Testament* (London, 1960), 58 ff.

[48]) A substantial advance was made by P. BENOIT, ' "Non erat eis locus in diversorio" (Lc.2, 7)', *Mélanges. . . Rigaux* (Gembloux, 1970), 173-86. κατάλυμα can be a lodging one owns, or a shepherds' encampment (out in the open!): LXX Jer. 40 (33), 12. A temporary lodging, also a festive chamber (whether or not hired) (see Lk. xxii 11; Mk. xiv 14). It does not follow that the manger was in a different locale.

[49]) As manger: Test. Iobi xl. For other meanings see LIDDELL-SCOTT-JONES, *Lexicon*, ad verba.

[50]) 'The Manger, ritual law and soteriology', *Theol.* 74 (1971), 566-71. Use is made of Mishnah, Parah III.2-3, etc.

[51]) See last note.

[52]) Plato, *Tim.* 70E; Philo, *Spec. Leg.* I.148 (Loeb edn., viii.182-4).

[53]) Mishnah, Ned. IV.4, as explained by me at *Conoscenza Religiosa* 4 (1973), 439-44. See also *'ebûs* as a common meal for workers at j. Dem. III.1 (trans. Schwab II, 1878, 156).

[54]) See references at DERRETT, 'The Manger at Bethlehem: light on St. Luke's technique from contemporary Jewish religious law', *Studia Evangelica* VI (T. & U. 112) (Berlin, 1973), 86-94, esp. p. 89.

the child there was the second Adam is conveyed by the midrash which explains Adam's fear and Adam's reprieve. Farfetched as these ideas are, they are connected, because *bread* connects the pair of them. Adam was afraid of being tied to the manger, eating bent double like an ass [55]). Jesus is associated with the manger, as the second Adam and as the food of the righteous [56]). I have already expounded the parallel between the story of the manger, the story of Moses, and the entombment of Christ. This is corroborated by a strange discovery. The death-feasts dear to pagans, and annual commemorations of the dead, which it seems some non-observant Jews had more than a taste for, took place in tombs, which were provided with tables and with niches (for seats) cut out of the living rock around the tables: these niches were naturally called φάτναι [57]). Thus the notion is corroborated on several footings, that the shepherds were going down to Bethlehem in order to visualise partaking of the baby in an environment prefiguring the tomb (place of rebirth). As soon as born he was declared to be their saviour and their food. This cannot be viewed historically as meaningful for any actual shepherds, but it fits the true purpose of the passage, to which we come at sect. III below.

II. *The Magi*

4. The question of Matthew's chronology can well wait until the main problem is tackled. We must be grateful for the unfashionable study by P. GAECHTER, which, basically, takes the Magi story as plausible [58]). Many have felt that their dealings with

---

[55]) Explained from Targ. ps. Jon., Gen. iii 18 at Theol. 74 (1971) 569-70 (references at 569 n. 3), repeated at *Jesus's Audience*, 108, and *Con. Rel.* 4 (1973), 440, with variations.

[56]) Prof. E. ZOLLA informs me that in the Greek liturgy the *discos* for the wafers is the crib, on which the *prosphora* are placed at the *proskomidia* in a pattern, the Lamb being in the middle, the Holy Virgin on the right side of the Lamb.

[57]) A. A. BARB, 'Krippe, Tisch und Grab. . .', *Mullus. Fest. Theodor Klauser. Jahrb. Ant. Christ. Ergänzungsband* 1 (Münster/W., 1964), 17-27. T. KLAUSER, 'Das altchristliche Totenmahl nach dem heutigen Stande der Forschung', in *Ges. Arb.*, ed. E. DASSMANN, *Jahr. Ant. Christ., Ergänzungsband* 3 (ibid., 1974), 114-20.

[58]) P. GAECHTER, 'Die Magierperikope', *Z. kath. Theol.* 90 (1968), 257-95 (a comprehensive study) (nowhere else have I seen the idea that when the Magi and Joseph compared notes *they* said to *him* 'You had better get moving' and *he* said to *them* 'You will be doing me a good turn if you disappear sharpish'). H. NELLESSEN (inf.) rejects this approach to the story (p. 119).

Herod, and especially the sentence 'Herod was troubled and all Jerusalem with him' had a very plausible ring. Herod's behaviour fits his record [59]. We must be grateful, too, for a totally different study, the elaborate, well-balanced, highly scholarly, and progressive work of NELLESSEN [60]. Neither scholar knew what was going on, yet both contributed to an understanding of Matthew's tale.

It is fairly generally agreed that Matthew makes extensive use of Jewish midrashim on Old Testament texts, yet uses them in an inside-out way: the facts of the Christ story are a commentary upon the Old Testament [61]. The discrepancies in analysis and diagnosis of the curious Matthaean use of Old Testament midrash and haggada melt before NELLESSEN's excellent summary [62]. But, as we see in the first gospel so often, the artist's commentary is a projection of his understanding of his material; he does not create it. The Magi cannot be dismissed as a fabrication, still less a fabrication based upon some embassy of a Parthian king to Nero, years after the event about to be described [63]. However, are they primarily a symbol, as everyone has suspected, a coming-to-life of biblical texts such as have been identified long since (the texts are Is. xviii 1-3, 7 [see b. Sanh. 98a]; xlv 14-15; lx 6; Zeph. iii 10; Ps. lxviii 28 ff.; lxxii 10-11; cf. 1 En. liii 1), or were they representatives of, or even a portrayal of real people ? Who were they, and what were they doing there ? The answer is complex.

---

[59] GAECHTER, amongst others, points (p. 286) to Josephus's accounts of Herod's fears of insurrections and cruelty of repression. Matthew's hearers would believe anything of that ogre: but what of the unimpeached Roman examples of the same sort of behaviour ?

[60] E. NELLESSEN, *Das Kind und seine Mutter. Struktur und Verkündigung des 2. Kapitels im Matthäusevangelium* (Stuttgart, 1969). At p. 79 he opines that *prior to Matthew* two palestinian, probably Galilaean traditions of a legendary character has been fused into a whole, and Matthew preserved and improved on both (judicious!). At p. 120 he links the Magi with missions. There is no need to talk of a pseudo-Matthew, as R. E. WITT at *Stud. Patr.* XI, 92-8 and *J.R.A.S.* 1974/1, 51.

[61] NELLESSEN, 61-3. GAECHTER, 280. At p. 281 G. denies that there is true haggada or midrash here. Haggada certainly, and midrash of a peculiar type! An early admission that we have a Christian midrash here appeared at W. K. LOWTHER CLARKE, *Divine Humanity* (London, 1936), 41-51.

[62] At pp. 61-69.

[63] Dio Cassius, *Hist. Rom.* LXIII.7.1 (Loeb edn., viii.146). A. DIETERICH, 'Die Weisen aus dem Morganlande', *Z.N.W.* 3 (1902), 1-14; F. CUMONT, 'L'Adoration des Mages et l'art triomphal de Rome', *Atti della Pontificia Accademia Romana di Archaeologia*, ser. III, 3 (1932), 82-105.

5. The story can be briefly recapitulated.

After Jesus had been born in Bethlehem in Judaea in the time of Herod the Great, some μάγοι coming from the East arrived at Jerusalem asking where was the man who had been born king of the Jews, for they had seen his star in its rising [64]) and come to worship him. When king Herod heard this he was disturbed and all Jerusalem with him. He summoned all the chief priests and scribes of the nation and enquired where the Messiah was born (he identified 'king of the Jews' with the Messiah!), and they said in Bethlehem in Judaea, as the prophet Micah had indicated. Then Herod quietly summoned the mages and discovered when the star appeared. He sent them to Bethlehem to enquire for the child, to tell him, and thus enable him to worship him also. They went and the star they had seen in its rising led them on till it stood over the place where the child was ... they worshipped him, opened their treasure-chests and gave him gifts, gold and frankincense and myrrh ... they returned to their country by another way. Later on Herod realised that he had been deceived by the mages...

The beautiful story tells us many definite things. Its literary cadre, and chronological cadre deserve to be looked into separately. The presupposition behind the tale is that even about the time of Jesus's birth the hostility of the upstart semite kings, not less Archelaus [65]) than Herod his father, was combined with an ironical desire to welcome the Messiah. The distinction between 'king of the Jews', a title analogous to Ethnarch (hardly a *pagan* notion, as GAECHTER would have it), and ruler of Judaea was plain enough. In a special sense the Messiah was king, Lord Messiah, for pious Jews everywhere. And the horrid Idumaean was likely to be aware of this, and unconsciously admit it. Yet the kingdoms of the world were in the gift of Satan. One cannot but suspect their pretended worship of him who was to come. As for the historicity of this notion, I shall have something to say presently. Irrespective of the biblical prophecy that the nations would come to the Messiah bringing him gifts [66]), and enabling the dispersed to be reunited, Messianic expectations existed in many eastern lands [67]). And in such expectations the messianic movements in Israel will have

---

[64]) So HOUDOUS convincingly. That ἐστάθη ἐπάνω means 'it stood at its zenith' (p. 82) is not so clear.

[65]) Matt. ii 22 (an imputation, the source and objective justification for which remains unknown).

[66]) See above, p. 96. Note the Assyrians at Mic. v 4 (above) who can well appear in the guise of suppliants. See also *Midr. Rabba Esther* I.4 (Ps. lxviii 30, lxxii 11).

[67]) GUILLEMIN, inf. p. 103, n. 86 (referring to Vergil's fourth eclogue and the Sibylline books). NELLESSEN, 120. Citing J. HASENFUSS, 'Drei Könige', *L. Th.K.²* III (1959), 566 f., he opines that the Magi may well be associated with a genuine Zoroastrian desire to link with a Jewish saviour.

found leadership. Apart from this religiously-awakened folk, Jewish and pagan, in the Middle East looked, and had long been looking to the East for wisdom. It is not sufficiently appreciated that at the period and for at least two centuries previously the East was considered the abode of wisdom and spiritual insight [68]), often with bizarre results. The same phenomenon has been at work ever since India was rediscovered by European travellers, reaching what could be its climax in the last half-century. The 'Light from the East' syndrome is by no means without genuine causes, and I should be the last to pretend that such fancies were baseless. But for our purpose it is sufficient to recognise that Matthew's hearers will have shared what was then a common sentimental attitude to eastern religions, taking it for granted that spiritual men in the East, by which they meant Babylon, Iran, and India, knew a great deal more about life than mere westerners [69]). Stories of men going to eastern climes on tours of wisdom-collection proliferated, and no one doubted but that, for example, the Brahmins (amongst whom the gymnosophists stood out prominently) [70]) had much to teach the Mediterranean world.

This outlook was heavily reinforced by the Alexander-romance [71]),

[68]) Dio Chrysostom, XXXVI 41, XLIX 7. The point about fashionable interests in eastern religions is made forcibly by A. D. NOCK in his *Essays* (Oxford, 1972), ch. 15 of which deals extensively with *magos* and *magia*. For good and true Magi see e.g. Philo, *Spec. Leg.* III.100 (Loeb edn., vii.538, also ibid. 635-6, remarks by F. H. COLSON).

[69]) Dio Chrysostom, XXXV 22 (one of the sources of Palladius, inf.). The behaviour of Apollonius of Tyana is most expressive: Philostratus, *Vita Ap.* v. 30. A. DIHLE, 'Indische Philosophen bei Clemens Alexandrinus', *Mullus* (sup. p. 95, n. 57), 60-70 (apropos of Clem. Al., *strom.* 1, 71, 3/6). Excellent for our purpose is Philo, *Quod Omnis* 74 (Loeb edn., ix, 52) (see Strabo xv. 1, 59 [Megasthenes]): mages and gymnosophists equally lauded.

[70]) Basic references at *Der Kleine Pauly*, II, 892-3. H. GREGOR, *Das Indienbild des Abendlandes* (Wien, 1964). The gymnosophists were historical, but transmodified into mirrors for the greedy West by first cynic and later Christian apologetic. For *maga* Brahmins see McCRINDLE's *Ancient India as Described by Ptolemy* [2], ed. Surendranath MAJUMDAR, Sastri, Calcutta, 1927, Notes, pp. 381-2, also remarks by H. W. BAILEY at *J.R.A.S.* 1972/2, 107-8. *Bhaviṣya-purāṇa* I.2, 139-47.

[71]) This enormous subject can be introduced with a short bibliography which carries the reader to further bibliographies: the *texts* of Pseudo-Callisthenes have appeared as follows: the A version edited by Karl MÜLLER in 1846 (ARRIAN, *Anabasis et Indica*, ed. Fr. DUBNER, Paris), superseded by W. KROLL *Historia Alexandri Magni, Pseudo-Callisthenes*, I *Recensio Vetusta* (Berlin, 1926) except as to the Brahmin episode; the λ version was edited by H. VAN THIEL (Bonn. 1959); the γ version in part by H. ENGELMANN, *Der griechische Alexanderroman* ... (Meisenheim am Glan, 1963), and in part by

which, with the Jesus story, was soon to conquer the civilised world, and be its prime source of story-telling. Tales of Solomon and Alexander moved in all quarters, and the Jews were, as merchants, great purveyors of such tales. The Alexander-romance, having its toes (if not a whole foot) in true history, was based on

F. PARTHE, *Der griech. Alexanderroman...Buch III* (Meisenheim am Glan, 1969), while we have the β version by L. BERGSON (Stockholm-Göteborg-Uppsala, 1965) (see Ross, *Gnomon*, 38, 1966, 447-9). The history of the text and its transmission: R. MERKELBACH, *Die Quellen des Griechischen Alexanderromans* (Munich, 1954) (major source for all episodes); D. J. A. Ross, *Alexander Historiatus* (London, 1963) (with an important supplement at *J. Warburg & Courtauld Inst.* 30 (1967), 383 ff.); O. MAZAL, 'Der griechische und byzantinische Roman in der Forschung von 1945 bis 1960', *Jahrb. der oesterr. byzantinischen Gesellsch.* 11-12 (162/3), 30-50. Of all the episodes in Ps. Callisthenes which testify to the wisdom-from-the-east fantasy of the Greeks the Brahmin episode is the most extensive and fascinating, supported as it is in many respects by true history and available at all points in the development of the Alexander-romance: DERRETT, 'The history of 'Palladius on the races of India and the Brahmans', *Class. Med.* 21 (1960), 64-135; G. C. HANSEN, 'Alexander und die Brahmanen', *Klio* 43-5 (1965), 351-80; W. BERGHOFF, *Palladius de Gentibus Indiae et Bragmanibus* (Meisenheim am Glan, 1967) (see HANSEN, *Gnomon*, 41, 1969, 344-7). If our Magi represent Asians historically-bibliographically identifiable as Brahmins (or pseudo-Brahmins), the conception of Jesus links with the conception of Alexander. On Olympias's experience see D. J. A. Ross, 'Olympias and the serpent', *J. Warburg & Courtauld Inst.* 26 (1963), 1-21 (widely illustrated this myth was well-known in the first century A.D.). On the Jewish origin of much of the Alexander-romance see Fr. PFISTER, *Alexander der grosse in den Offenbarungen der Griechen, Juden, Mohammedaner und Christen* (Berlin, 1956) (also MERKELBACH, ROSS), and there is also D. J. A. Ross at *Z. Deut. Altertum u. Deut. Literatur* 98/4 (1969), 292-307. The link between Olympias and Alcmene is obvious and verifiable. The Olympias-Nectanebus [king-*magos*]-Philip story figures in many derivative versions, e.g. E. A. WALLIS BUDGE, *The History of Alexander the Great, being the Syriac Version of the Pseudo-Callisthenes* (Cambridge, 1889), I, chh. iv, xi. See also R. RAABE, *Historia Alexandrou. Die Armenische Übersetzung...* (Leipzig, 1896). *Ancient* fragments of the debate between Alexander and the Brahmins occur, e.g. Pap. Soc. It. 743; b. Tamid 31b-32a. A mediaeval Hebrew version draws on the Yosippon and earlier sources: I. J. KAZIS, *The Book of the Gests of Alexander of Macedon. Sefer Toledot...* (Cambridge, Mass., 1962). Jewish material from this romance percolated into Christian sources of the 2d cent.: J. RENDEL HARRIS, *The Rest of the Words of Baruch: a Christian Apocalypse of the year 136 A.D.* (Lond. 1889). M. GASTER, *Studies and Texts* ii (London, 1925-8), 816. Alexander-romance material was known to, and was circulated and developed by Jewish literateurs before and during the time of Matthew. It was an art-form which, like the gospels (*mutatis mutandis*), they shared with their Greek neighbours and rivals. PLINY (A.D. 50-77) tells how a freedman got to Ceylon, whose king sent to the West for red coral and an embassy to Rome in A.D. 41-54 (on *N.H.* VI. 81-91 see SCHWARZ, *J. As. Hist.* 8, 1974, 21-48; *Rhein. Mus.* 117, 1974, 166-76). One Lysas left graffiti in the Eastern Desert (*J.R.S.* 43, 1953, 38-40). The Levant liked Asian comings-and-goings, in which myth came alive.

much older material, which the historical narratives of Alexander's adventures had fused into a lump. It infected in turn the Jewish tales of the birth of Moses [72]), and that of Abraham[73]). Moving westward it produced similar tales regarding the births of Roman heroes [74]). The infiltration of themes from the legendary birth-stories of Alexander, themselves the work of Jewish imagination (most probably in Alexandria itself), into the biographies of Romans [75]) is a close parallel with the Matthaean nativity story. The movement *eastwards* of messianic and Alexander material at various, including very early stages of history is of much more interest chronologically than it is thematically [76]).

---

[72]) B. BEER, *Leben Moses* (Leipzig, 1863) (a magnificent repertory). S. DE BENEDETTI, *Vita e morte di Mosè. Leggende ebraiche tradotte* ... (Pisa, 1879). B. S. CHILDS, 'The birth of Moses', *J.B.L.* 84 (1965), 108-122. I. LEVI, 'Le lait de la mère et le coffre flottant', *R.É.J.* 59 (1910), 1-13 (esp. p. 8). R. BLOCH, 'Moïse dans la tradition rabbinique', *Cah. Sion.* 1954; also 'Quelques aspects de la figure de Moïse dans la tradition rabbinique', *Moïse, l'homme de l'Alliance* (Paris, 1955); C. PERROT, 'Les récits de l'enfance dans la haggada antérieure au IIe siècle de notre ère', *Recherches de Sc. Relig.* 55 (1957). The antiquity of much of this haggada is certified by Jos., *Ant.* ii.205-6, 210-17 (Amram's [cf. Nectanebus's] dreams) (cf. MEKILTA ad loc.); Midr. R. Exod. on i 22. DAUBE, *N.T.S.* 5(1958-9), 184. Amram was a sinless person: b. B.B. 17b = Soncino translation 86-7. On mythological thinking see E. BRUNNER-TRAUT, 'Pharao und Jesus als Söhne Gottes', *Antaios* 2/3 (1960), 266-84.

[73]) B. BEER, *Leben Abrahams* (Leipzig, 1859). M. DOCTOR, *Abram. Jugend-geschichte des Erzvaters Abraham nach der talmud. Sage* (Frankfurt a.M., 1905). LEVI, last note (p. 9). *Midr. Ps.*, Ps. cxviii § 11 (BRAUDE, II, 238). E. NESTLE, 'Zu Mt. 2', *Z.N.W.* 8 (1907), 73-4, refers to *J.E.* i.86: the star of Abraham's birth swallowed four other stars; councillors said to Nimrod, buy the child and kill it! On the relevance of all this to the Jesus story see M. M. BOURKE at *C.B.Q.* 22 (1960), 174 commented upon by NELLESSEN, 72.

[74]) Contemporaries of the apostles were aware of the ubiquity of the myth of the escaping child/future king (Sargon, Moses, Perseus, Oedipus, Cyrus, Romulus: see Dio Chrysostom vi. 53!). See Suetonius, *Aug.* 94.3 (Loeb edn., i. 264) (includes Julius Marathus's account of an attempt to prevent male children being reared!). Scipio Africanus: Gellius, *Noct. Att.* 6. SOLTAU, *op.cit.*, 38, 46. Inscriptions in honour of Augustus (provision to celebrate his birthday), ibid., 67 ff. Nero: Suetonius, *Nero* 36 (N. orders death of eminent men and children of conspirators are killed horribly). Suet. *Aug.* 94.4 tells the tale of the serpent (cf. Alexander: Ross, *JWCI*, sup., 21) and Augustus's mother, and of astrologers' predictions (94.5).

[75]) Actually recognised by Suetonius at *Aug.* 94.5! So Livy XXVI. 19.7. Egypt was the origin of these ideas. R. REITZENSTEIN, *Poimandres* (Leipzig, 1904), 308-10; A. ELTER, *Donarem pateras* (Bonn, 1907), apropos of Hor., *Carm.* IV.8, 22-3, 29, 30. See also Plut., *Alex.* ii.4.

[76]) For the myths regarding the conception and birth of the (Śākyamuni) Buddha, available in the *verse* Jātakas (probably B.C. in date: placed very early by D. SCHLINGLOFF, 'The unicorn', *German Scholars on India*, I [Va-

6. Two major complex themes arise in this connection: first the theme of the supernatural impregnation of the mother by a deity, the birth of a world-leader foretold by mage stargazers or at least by soothsayers, whose prognostications lead to hostility on the part of a wicked king (a theme obviously much older than Exodus, but strongly exemplified and fortified by it); and secondly the theme of the search for wisdom and immortality in the remotest East. Present massively in the Alexander-romance, which long antedated the gospels and is known to have circulated in sophisticated forms contemporaneously with them [77]), these two themes are ingeniously woven together in Matthew's nativity story in order to produce an impression that Jesus is greater than Moses, Abraham, and Alexander all together. That this is indeed the matrix of the Magi is indicated by Plutarch's account (*Alex.* III. 3-4)of the behaviour of the Magi at Ephesus, when Alexander was born: they declared that a great calamity for Asia had been born, judging from a spontaneous fire in Artemis's temple. It has already been urged that the Exodus haggada hardly fitted the Magi, in the sense that the evil Egyptians, so well known to Paul and his contemporaries [78]), were no model for the pious Magi [79]). But this would miss the point. It is the partial coincidence and partial discrepancy which provide the beauty and the significance of Matthew's composition, as with his uses of the scriptural material themselves.

---

ranasi, 1973], 299) see E. WINDISCH, *Buddha's Geburt* (Abh. d. k. Sächs. Gesellsch. d. Wissensch., Philol-Hist. Kl. 26/2) (Leipzig, 1908) (discussing the literature at 212-13), also J. B. AUFHAUSER, *Buddha und Jesus in ihrer Paralleltexten* (LIETZMANN's *Kleine Texte*, 157) (Bonn. 1926). Sculpture confirms the B.C. age of such myths: A. CUNNINGHAM, *The Stūpa of Bharhut* (London, 1879); A FOUCHER, 'Les représentations de Jātaka dans l'art Bouddhique', *Mémoires concernant l'Asie orientale* III (Paris, 1919). DERRETT, 'Greece and India: the Milindapañha, the Alexander-romance and the gospels', *Z.R.G.G.* 19 (1967), 33-64; 'Greece and India again: the Jaimini-Aśvamedha, the Alexander-romance and the gospels', *Z.R.G.G.* 22 (1970), 19-44; ' "Every valley shall be exalted": borrowings from Isaiah in ancient India', *Z.R.G.G.* 24 (1972), 153-5.

[77]) V. MARTIN, 'Un recueil de diatribes cyniques, Pap. Genev. inv. 271', *Mus. Helveticum* 16/2 (1959) 77-95, discussed critically by DERRETT (1960) and HANSEN (1965) (p. 99, n. 71 sup.).

[78]) JANNES and JAMBRES (CD V 18-19 [Lohse, 76; Vermes, 102]; 2 Tim. iii 8). J. DANIÉLOU, *History of Early Christian Doctrine* II, *Gospel Message and Hellenistic Culture* (London/Philadelphia, 1973), 490.

[79]) GOULDER, *Midrash and Lection*, 238 n.

The star may not have been Jupiter [80]), and there is hardly any reason to believe it was a conjunction such as was suggested years ago [81]). That the Messiah, being a king, would have a star no contemporary would care to doubt, even if there were no propensity to cite in support Num. xxiv 15-20 [82]). But what is of real interest in the story is that no chief priest, scribe, or other 'of the nation' was looking for it. For such expectation and knowledge one must look to the simple and to eastern nations, some of which could be relied on to recognise leadership (as indeed Tiridates had done in his theatrical way) [83]), much as the Egyptian seers had foretold the birth of Moses and the Chaldean seers had foretold the birth of Abraham. That contemporaries of Matthew believed in portentous stars which stood over a city is certain, for a warning star was seen to hang over Jerusalem before its destruction, according to Josephus [84]). And the Queen of Sheba, so it was said long afterwards, found a star or some such bright heavenly light to greet her when she came to visit Solomon [85]). Stars have guided travellers in the desert and across the continents and oceans, and it is not surprising that readers of Matt. ii have imagined that the star led the Magi. In fact the text tells us merely that the Magi saw a star at its rising,

[80]) Jupiter is preferred by GAECHTER, 283.

[81]) Kepler's idea of a conjunction (7/6 B.C.): HOUDOUS, *ubi cit.* NELLESSEN, 117-18, ibid., 119 (not a natural phenomenon at all: I agree; N. should have cited the Josephus parallel). W. GRUNDMANN, *Das Evangelium nach Matthäus* (Berlin, 1968), 80-1 refers to H. G. VOIGT, *Die Geschichte Jesu und die Astrologie* (Leipzig, 1911)) and H. H. KRITZINGER, *Der Stern der Weisen* (Gütersloh, 1911) (elaborate works possibly based upon inadequate literary-critical hypotheses).

[82]) Some say every righteous man has his star (*Midr. Ps.*, Ps. 148 § 1, BRAUDE, ii, 375; cf. ibid., 90 § 2, BRAUDE, II, 87). E. LOHMEYER, 'Der Stern der Weisen', *Theol. Blätter* 17 (1938), coll. 288-99 deals with Balaam, etc. (Num. xxiii 8; xxii 5; xxiv 8, 17, 18, at p. 298). NELLESSEN, 74. J. DANIÉLOU, 83, refers to uses of Num. xxiv 17 at CD VII 19-21 (LOHSE, 80; VERMES, 104), also 1 QM XI 6 (LOHSE, 204; VERMES, 138), IV Q Test. 12-13 (LOHSE, 250; VERMES, 248) showing the importance of the star for messianic-apocalyptic visionaries. So Test. Levi xviii 3; Test. Jud. xxiv 1. G. VERMES, *Jesus the Jew* (London, 1973), 133-4, 136.

[83]) See above, p. 96, n. 63. SOLTAU, 39. NELLESSEN, 75-6 (parallels are poor).

[84]) *B.J.* vi. 289: ὑπὲρ τὴν πόλιν ἄστρον ἔστη. GAECHTER's naturalistic interpretation (p. 290) may be insufficient without being unrealistic.

[85]) J. E. BRUNS, 'The Magi episode in Matt. 2', *C.B.Q.* 23 (1961), 51-4, refers to the Queen of Sheba and legends figuring in M. GRÜNBAUM, *Neue Beiträge* (Leiden, 1893), 220, and N. AUSUBEL, *Jewish Folklore* (Leiden, 1972), 482. BRUNS points to the gifts of the Queen of Sheba at 1 K. x 1-13 (LXX) and identifies Jesus as Wisdom and Herod as the antithesis of Wisdom.

and this (we are to imagine) led them to enquire for the new king amongst the Jews—the paradox was especially gratifying to Jewish hearers, to whom the low condition of Judaea had failed to match with their fantasy of world hegemony. The nations would come one day to Jerusalem and claim to be enrolled as worshippers of the Jewish deity. Abraham was born in a star-gazing culture, and was a stargazer himself; it was from contemplating stars that he came, spontaneously, to know the unity of God. So these would-be proselytes from pagan religions are led by reading a star to find the Messiah.

7. The gifts of the Magi are very significant, and once again what was well enough known has not been understood. The midrashic connection with the Joseph of antiquity and his pagan buyers (see Gen. xxxvii 25) has been ignored. All three gifts mean worship. The suggestion that gold implies tribute, and that the Magi were really kings (a notion easily explained from Is. xix 11; lx 3, 11, 16; Ps. lxviii 28 ff.; lxxii 10-11; cf. Test. Iobi 28) and that myrrh implies medical, healing skill [86]), are both otiose. The Alexander story tells how Alexander, once well into the midst of Asia, sent quantities of frankincense and myrrh to Leonides, his old preceptor, to *facilitate his ritual* [87]). A Seleucid monarch sent gold (in the form of vessels), frankincense and myrrh to a temple in order to *facilitate worship there* [88]). The Magi bowed down before

---

[86]) Elaborately contended for by L. OLSCHKI, 'The Wise Men of the East in oriental tradition', in W. J. FISCHEL, ed., *Semitic and Oriental Studies...W. Popper* (Berkeley, 1951), 375-95 citing Plut., *Alex.* 25; Pliny, *N.H.* XII. 62, XXIV.17, 160. OLSCHKI is elaborated on by U. MONNERET DE VILLARD, *Le Leggende Orientali sui Magi Evangelici* (*Studi e testi* 163) (Vatican, 1952). Lowther CLARKE (sup. p. 96 n. 61) thought the gifts were for magical incantations (by whom ?). DUCHESNE-GUILLEMIN, 'Die drei Weisen aus dem Morgenlande und die Anbetung der Zeit', *Antaios* 7/3 (1965/6), 234-52 (a reference I owe to Prof. M. BOYCE), thought that the incense brought by the kings to fumigate Job on his dunghill (Test. Iobi 28, ed. BROCK, 1967, 41) was a parallel to the Magi!

[87]) The circumstances are clearly set out at Plut., *Alex.* 25.4 (p. 679C): ἀπεστάλκαμέν σοι λιβανωτὸν ἄφθονον καὶ σμύρναν, ὅπως παύσῃ πρὸς τοὺς θεοὺς μικρολογούμενος. WETSTENIUS (*ad loc.*) saw this—as also Josephus's grasp of the haggada on Pharao, *Ant.* ii.205-6, 210-17—but he has been ignored.

[88]) C.I.G. 2852, PAULY-WISSOWA, *R.E.* XVI.1 (1933), *myrrha*, col. 1134 f.; 1145. Seleucus II, king of Antioch (243 B.C.) to the temple of Apollo in Miletus. Gold is for the sanctuary: *Midr. Ps.*, Ps. 104 § 13 (BRAUDE, II, 173); Gen. ii 12, Deut. iii 25. Frankincense represents the priesthood: *Midr. Ps.*, Ps. 45 § 6 (BRAUDE, I, 453): Lev. ii 2, 16; Is. lxvi 3. Myrrh: see Exod. xxx 23; Ps. xlv 8 (Messiah). See also Is. lx 6; Jer. vi 20. Not that kings could not be

him (as the family of the ancient Joseph had bowed down before
him): the paradox was that he was a living deity, and in bowing
before him they acknowledged the deity, Yahweh, whose worship
they were facilitating. The rabbinical tradition that the gifts of
the nations to the Lord Messiah (Is. lxvi 20 and Cant. iv 8 as
interpreted at *Midr. Ps.* 87 § 6; Yalqût § 839; Ps. Sal. 17.31b:
the idea is based on Is lx 4, 9) were the children of Israel themselves
fits well enough here: the sumptuous gifts of the Magi are the tribes
of Israel gathered from the dispersion as the Jews of the diaspora
return to Yahweh through Jesus when the heathen worship him
as a deity. True Justin, who was tolerably well informed, believed
(*Dial.* 7, 7—8, 88) that the Magi came from Arabia; but that was
merely because incense, etc., was exported from that quarter,
wheresoever it originated from.

The whole is to be seen from the situation post A.D. 70. The
destiny of the Jews lies not in recovering fantasies of world-do-
minion, but in bringing salvation to all nations. The way to God
lies through the baby of Bethlehem. The hostility of the Idumaean
kings, long since consigned to oblivion except as ogres, represents
the ignorance and prejudice of the old Israel, paradoxically
shamed by the eagerness and endurance of the pagans [89]), when
these are enlightened by divine providence. The Magi went back
by a different way, i.e. they did not return by the way they came,
which is symbolic of frustration. They went on, and, Matthew
indicates, they are still going on (like Melchizedek, who came from
no one knows where, and went no one knows whither), to their
country or countries, taking their submission to the Messiah with
them [90]). Until the time of Christ all nations had looked to the
East, and even the Jews claimed, or were thought to claim some
affinity even with the remote Brahmins[91]). Alexander, though a

---

honoured in a similar way: Polybius, *Hist.* XIII.9, 5 (the Gerraeans and
Antiochus, early 3d cent. B.C.) (silver, frankincense and *stacte*); cf. Herod.
III.109. For what did the kings use such tribute?

[89]) So Matt. viii 11-12.

[90]) See below, p. 107, n. 98.

[91]) Clearchus on Education traced the descent of the Indian gymnosophists
from the Magi, and Diogenes Laertius, proem. 9, adds, 'some assert that the
Jews also are descended from the Magi'. Jews and Brahmins are associated by
Megasthenes (Clem. Al., *strom.* 1.72, 5 = JACOBY, *F.Gr.H.* 737.8). Josephus
reports that Clearchus said that Aristotle said Jews were descended from
Indian philosophers called Kalanoi (cf. Plut., *Alex.* 65!) (Jos., *c. Ap.* I.176-9,
Loeb edn., i, 235 n. *b*). The nonsense in F. NORK, (pseud. Fr. KORN), *Bra-*

deity by birth, went and was stupified by them and gave them,
so we are told, the means of worship [92]), which was all they would
accept from him. Now the east comes to a new Alexander, and
makes its own gifts in the region of Jerusalem, an Asian city on the
edge of the western world. No reader or hearer of Matthew could
suppose that Mary did not make some gift to the Magi, for in the
East each gift requires a reciprocation, if only a token one. Matthew does not say what she gave them; our artists show the child
bestowing a blessing. Syrian tradition says he gave them a wonderful stone [93]). The point of the story is that in return for their
sumptuous gifts they must have obtained supersubstantial benefits
in return. This summarises the mission to the gentiles, who should
give what is appropriate for worship.

III. *The Chronology and the Message*

8. Luke's chronology would place the birth of Jesus in or after
A.D. 6. Matthew's places it prior to 4 B.C., a discrepancy of not
less than ten years. Matthew carefully dates the birth before the
division of Herod the Great's kingdom into tetrarchies. In his
view, it would seem, Micah (whom he quotes) told that the Messiah
would come, and be greeted by the nations, after the dominion
of Rome had superseded Jewish rule [94]), and that supersession he
saw as having coincided with Herod the Great's rule. It was certainly arguable that Herod's special relationship with Augustus   *
was an effective replacement of true Jewish leadership with a
non-Jewish, foreign-backed, empire. Neither Luke nor Matthew
need have known the date of Jesus birth. Each scheme was devised
to tell its own story. Luke speaks of the coming of Rome as the
arrival of the Messiah from Edom [95]). Roman rule enables the

---

minen und Rabbinen oder: *Indien Stammland der Hebräer und ihrer Fabeln*
(Meissen, 1836) includes some kernels of sense. That the Alexander-romance
was known to first-century haggadists is proved by Jos., *Ant.* ii.348 (what is
known of the former will authenticate the latter!).

[92]) Palladius, *de vita Bragmanorum* II.36, 38-9; that the material goes
back into the first century is shown by Pap. Genev. inv. 271, which is dat-
able A.D.-150, and the particulars appear in V. MARTIN, *op. cit.*, 88-9, with
some material at p. 95 (frag. B, l. 3).

[93]) On this see DE VILLARD, *cit.sup.*, p. 103, n. 86, also B. M. METZGER,
'Names for the nameless in the New Testament', in P. GRANFIELD and J. A.
JUNGMANN, ed., *Kyriakon. Fest.Quasten* I (Münster/W, 1970), 79-85.

[94]) Above, p. 85.

[95]) WELLHAUSEN already saw the Idumaean rulers as representing Edom/
Rome. W. VISCHER, 'Das Evangelium von der Weisen aus dem Morgenlande',

messianic movement to achieve the widest publicity and an entrée to the imperial capital itself. Matthew sees the same story as something internal to the Jewish people: their Messiah, unrecognised by the bastard princes, indeed hated by them, and worshipped only in the unconscious, in an ironical hypocrisy, was the fulfilment of so many dreams and tales, and brought the pagans indeed to worship the true God. The births of all the great cannot but have been attended by portents, and this was the portent which was most significant and characteristic. The true Israel was capable of being made up by all mankind. Thus from neither Luke nor Matthew can we find out the date of Jesus's birth. Both stories are a kind of history, retrospective biography, a genre dear to the ancient world. We cannot take bits of either and combine them to form a history of Jesus in the modern sense. Points where the stories agree can be said to give rise to a presumption (and no more) that prior to both evangelists it was generally believed amongst the faithful that Jesus was born of a virgin (an unpenetrated female) called Mary, betrothed to a man called Joseph of the Davidic stock, in or near Bethlehem in Judaea about the time when a change from native to imperial government was becoming finalised. Can we go beyond that?

We have gone far enough. Both evangelists are really explaining in their own ways what the further spread of Christianity would be. Luke, in his story of the angel and the shepherds, depicts the task of the episcopate [96] and the preachers who will spread their knowledge of the Saviour and of his eternal presence with the faithful throughout the Jews and through them to the world. The language of the pericope has been compared with the technical vocabulary associated with the preaching of the gospel, and the coincidences are compelling [97]. The hearers of Luke identified

---

Fest. E. Vischer (Basel, 1935), 7 ff., at 8-10. Is. lxiii 1 and midrashim thereon. *Midr. Ps.* Ps. 22 § 9.

[96]) *Stud. Evangel.* VI (1973), 89 n. 3.

[97]) L. LEGRAND, 'L'Évangile aux bergers: essai sur le genre littéraire de Luc. ii 8-20', *R.B.* 75 (1968), 161-87. The ironical contrast between the good news of the Saviour and the good news of the birth of an imperial cult-object is striking (the inscription at Priene, Dittenb. *O.G.I.* II.458: see L. CERFAUX, J. TONDRIAN, *Le Culte des Souverains dans la civilization Gréco-romaine*, Paris-Tournai, 1957, 321, 332, 380, 450: here at pp. 162-3). On the eschatological triumph of Yahweh, LEGRAND cites Is. lii 7, lxi 1; Ps. xcvi 2 ff. On σήμερον see Ps. ii 7 and Acts xiii 33. *Signs* dominate the apostolic mission (169-73). An apocalyptic and christological scene. Cf. M. DE JONGE and A. S. VAN DER WOUDE, *N.T.S.* 12 (1965-6), 307.

themselves with the shepherds and went out to tell the good news to others. Matthew likewise tells how the gospel will be spread amongst the heathen [98]), the death and resurrection of Jesus eventually means the worship of God through him in all parts of the known world after the pattern of the worship of the baby by the representatives of all the soothsayers and stargazers in creation. The massacre of the innocents, not so absurd a story as Roman counterparts show, depicts the human wastage which must be a by-product of the hostility of the evil kingdoms, to many of which any Christian polity is intolerable. Divine providence has foreseen this loss, and in the children up to the age of two we are shown the simple people due for martyrdom [99]).

9. It remains to raise a conjecture. While the Jewish state flourished, while cash flowed in the kingdom of that great builder, Herod the Great, is it inconceivable that mages of eastern countries could have sought to share in the prosperity ? The word ἐνεπαίχθη depicts what was to be expected of the lower type of mage [100]). Herod thought they were of the lower while they were (says Matthew) of the higher type: but such confusion was perpetual. The period during which Jesus was born was one of violent apocalyptic and messianic expectations; they were even inveterate by that time, as we find from the Qumran material. Political unrest, and the impending advent of Rome as master, will have stirred people to zeal for the independence of a true theocratic state, the state whose ruler is depicted in Jesus's parables as an absent landed proprietor and slave-owner. Messianic calculations are known

---

[98]) NELLESSEN, 120, brilliantly calls up Matt. viii 11-12 (Nur dürfte ihr Bezugspunkt weniger in Ereignissen der frühen Kindheit des Herrn liegen als viel mehr im Erfolg der urchristlichen Missionspredigt bei den Heiden)! Could he not have cited, in this connection, Matt. xxviii 17-18 (προσεκύνησαν, cf. ii 2, 8, 11) ? If Clement of Alexandria, Origen and Tertullian (adv. Marc. III c. 13) took the Magi as eschatological proof of the universality of the Christian gospel of the incarnate logos, could not the gospel story be an assertion of the predestined success of the missions ? Prof. Dr E. BENZ recommended the study of the hymns of Epiphanius in this connection: the question is postponed.

[99]) NELLESSEN, 122 (Glaubenszeugnis).

[100]) ʾamgûšāʾ (JASTROW, Dictionary, 75a); megûšāʾ (b. Soṭ. 22a = Sonc. trans. 110) (q.v.). Wisd. Sol. xvii.7, xviii.13. NOCK, Essays, I, 315, 318 notes the evidence for the 'lower' meaning of magos ('quack', already known in the 5th cent. B.C., so that Plato, Alcib. I, 112A instances a favourable use of the word accompanied by an explanation). Christianity was in stark contrast with magia: Acts xiii 6-12.

to have wasted many a learned man's time, to the despair of later rabbis. False prophecies of the coming of the Messiah are known to have been able to rouse multitudes, and were so taken for granted in that atmosphere that it was said Jesus foretold the continuance of this plague (Matt. xxiv 24 par.). On this aspect of Jewish history BRANDON has been eloquent, and the mere mention of Bar Kokhba is sufficient. Horoscopes of the Messiah were certainly possible, because traces of such have actually been found [101]). That foreign astrologers took advantage of this as of other more temporary enthusiasms to make their so-called calculations for gain is highly likely. Keen on astrology, the Jews yielded to Babylonians[102]), from whom both Greeks and Indians learnt that profitable trade. The Davidic family, identifiable from the pedigrees kept by the many interested in such matters, will have been alert to expectations. Girls married into such families will have been expected to think on the subject. Is it impossible that amongst the earliest Christians there were some who remembered its being asserted that the family of Jesus were, whether manipulated by others or not, themselves messianically-conscious people with naive political awareness and some keenness to further hopes of a rebellion ? And could not some mages, of less than utter holiness, actually have sought for Davidic families, and even gone to Bethlehem for the purpose (since contemporary scholars will certainly have counted it as one of the most likely places), to draw up horoscopes of likely people, and look for auspicious signs, such as are looked for up to our own times when a new Dalai Lama has to be identified ? Some such memory, loosely cherished by the earliest church, even founded on some more or less picturesque remarks of Jesus himself, could well lie behind both Luke and Matthew. If this could be so—and who can say that it is not?—it is wrong to dispose of the Magi (as of the shepherds) as mere fabrications. JEAN DANIÉLOU's conclusion that the Magi were an invention of Matthew and that they are merely a figuration of the admission of the gentiles into the church, may well have gone too far. The strong irony which pervades these tales supplies an aroma of truth, which the obviously secondary character of the composition does nothing to stifle.

---

[101]) A. DUPONT-SOMMER, *C.R.A.I.* (Paris, 1965), 239-53. J. DANIÉLOU, *Infancy Narratives* (1968), 76 n. 3.

[102]) GAECHTER, 281 n. 83 cites Cicero, *De Divinatione* I.41 (90): in Syria Chaldaei cognitione astrorum sollertiaque ingeniorum antecellunt.

FURTHER ANNOTATIONS

p. [85], l. 25. It deserves to be placed on record that at b.B.B. 91a, on Jdg. xii.8-9, Bethlehem near Nazareth and Bethlehem of Judaea not only could be but were midrashically confounded when it suited the exegete.

p. [85], n. 16. b.Sanh. 98b.

p. [98], n. 71. F. F. Schwarz draws my attention to A. J. Festugière, 'Trois rencontres entre la Grèce et l'Inde', in *Études de philosophie grecque* (Paris, 1971), 157-82; id., *Grecs et sages orientaux*, ibid., 183-95; G. Dumézil, 'Alexandre et les sages de l'Inde,' in *Scritti in onore di G. Bonfante* II (Brescia, 1976), 555-60; J. W. De Jong, 'The discovery of India by the Greeks,' *Ét. As.* 27 (1973), 115-42. Ap. Zosimus (M. R. James, 1893; A. Vassiliev, 1893) X, read in a pre-A.D. 70 version later adapted to Christian use (Brit. Lib. Ms. Add. 10073, fol. 202) proves the age of gymnosophist fantasies in a Jewish setting.

p. [104], l. 7. See Is.xl.11, xlix.22!

p. [105], l. 23. Herod was φίλος of Augustus up to 8 B.C. and ὑπήκοος thereafter (Jos., *Ant.* 16.290) : E. Bammel, 'Die Rechtsstellung des Herodes,' *Z.D.Pal.Ver.* 84 (1968), 73-9.

La nascita di Gesù ∗
Storie patristiche e *haggadot* ebraiche

Si va ristabilendo, un tratto dopo l'altro, il contatto fra la Chiesa primitiva e la vita e il pensiero ebraici, con processo dolorosamente lento che implica un certo scetticismo verso le idee tradizionali (elleniche), ma insieme dà a sperare di poter scorgere i discepoli col Maestro alla luce d'un giorno reale e non immaginario. È un processo a dir poco controverso e non è gradito negli ambienti avversi ai concetti giudeo-cristiani, naturalmente.

Il tema presente è soltanto un frammento, ma quale frammento e come suggestivo!

I cattolici sanno che Maria era vergine (cioè le era propria una condizione fisica particolare) alla vigilia della nascita di Gesú altresí dopo ed in perpetuo [1], benché non esistano prove nel Nuovo Testamento a favore della verginità perpetua di Maria, e questa affermazione contrasti con l'esperienza umana. La Chiesa ortodossa accetta del pari questa concezione: la *Theotokos* è una vergine perpetua. Si è suggerito in un articolo recente che la verginità perpetua, la quale, con l'eccezione di Tertulliano [2], è sostenuta da tutti i Padri del tempo di San Girolamo e dai posteriori, trovi una prova indiretta nel tema della nascita indolore [3]. Anche questo tema, diffuso ugualmente nella patristica greca e latina, sarebbe, secondo l'autore, coerente con la misteriosa persistenza della verginità dopo la nascita del bambino [4]. Di dove sorse

il concetto extrabiblico del parto indolore di Maria? Ritengo
che ci fosse una tradizione originaria intorno alla nascita di
Gesú la quale includeva la verginità di Maria al tempo del parto,
cui si accompagnava il racconto della sua gravidanza ante-
riore al momento in cui Giuseppe tentò di consumare il matrimonio [5]. In opposizione a molti studiosi considero le reminiscenze come la fonte della tradizione. Le ricerche sui concetti
ebraici di « verginità » [6] (di cui alcuni forse furono aguzzati dalle
affermazioni riguardanti Maria!) varrebbero la pena di essere
svolte, purché in uno spirito di reverente indagine, bilanciando
lo zelo di stabilire la verità e la preoccupazione di non varca-
re futilmente i limiti della fede. In breve: le menti giuste trove-
rebbero un alimento fascinoso nei materiali che gl'indotti fareb-
bero bene a non accostare senza una buona guida. Ma tutto ciò
ci allontana dal nostro fine specifico.

Come sviluppo collaterale la meditazione pia poté ben collegare Maria a Eva (e alla maledizione di Eva). Il parto senza dolore era sintomo atteso per gli Ultimi Giorni.

Pare che l'autore di *I Tim.* 2,15 (le cui traduzioni non con-
cordano) fosse dell'avviso che il parto, lungi dall'essere una maledizione, sarebbe stato un mezzo di salute nel Mondo Nuovo
che l'avvento della Chiesa annunciava. Ritengo plausibile suggerire che, su tale base, il parto di Maria fu riferito *come* se fosse
stato indolore, sussistessero o meno le prove relative.

Non nego che una giovane in attesa d'un bambino miracoloso
(di cui era rimasta incinta, secondo il suo convincimento, in modo
soprannaturale) possa, in Asia, dove la mente domina la materia
in misura assai maggiore che ordinariamente nell'Occidente mo-
derno, non accorgersi della sofferenza durante il parto e in seguito
affermare che esso fu indolore. Ma nego che abbia importanza,
ai nostri fini, che Maria facesse o meno questa affermazione e
che, in caso positivo, la si ricordasse. Non dubito per un istante
che la notizia della ininterrotta verginità *usque ad partum* prove-
nisse da fonti autentiche, cioè da Giuseppe e Maria, specie dal
momento che, lungi dall'essere contraria a natura per essenza, l'asserzione poteva risultare sí di somma rarità, ma, date le circo-
stanze, plausibile [7]. Ma, s'è detto, questa è un'altra questione.
L'asserzione del parto indolore non ha fondamento scritturale.

San Matteo tace; *Mt.* I 18 e 25 sono del tutto silenziosi
in merito, eppure suggeriscono che il concetto fantastico del *Pro-
toevangelium Jacobi* [8] — secondo cui Gesú non era nato nel modo
normale, ma anzi era apparso del tutto padrone dei suoi movi-
menti, e la sua comparsa era stata una sopresa per tutti — fu
basato sull'idea d'un parto non normale, ancor piú lontano dal

normale d'un semplice parto indolore. Tuttavia San Matteo non
suggerisce che la nascita fosse un evento normale. San Luca dà
ragguagli piú ampi. Ma poiché la conoscenza della legge rituale
ebraica andò svanendo dalle tradizioni della Chiesa, si è trascurato di osservare che in *Lc.* 2, 21, 23-24 ci è data un'indicazione
della normalità genetica di Gesú (altrimenti non sarebbe stato
circonciso), che avrebbe aperto il grembo normalmente (cfr. *Esodo*, 13, 2, 12-13, 15). Gli Ebrei, che praticavano il taglio cesareo,
sapevano che non andava pagato alcun riscatto (né poteva essere
accettato dai sacerdoti), salvo per il primogenito nato normalmente[9]. Non c'è prova che Gesú nascesse per parto cesareo, anzi
il racconto di San Luca lo escluderebbe.

Ma il tema della nascita indolore ha dalla sua una rispettabile
antichità nel mondo ebraico ed è basata sulla Scrittura. Dopo aver
maledetto il Serpente, Dio maledisse Eva dicendo (*Gen.* 3, 16):
« Moltiplicherò grandemente il tuo dolore e la tua concezione;
nel dolore partorirai i figli ». Isaia afferma che la redenzione ri-
pristinerà la vita quale fu prima della maledizione: « Una voce
di tumulto dalla città, una voce dal Tempio, una voce dal Signore che ripaga i suoi nemici. Prima del travaglio partorí; prima
che giungesse il dolore si sgravò d'un maschio. Chi ha mai udito
una cosa simile? Chi ha visto tali cose? Nascerà una terra in un
giorno? Sarà prodotta in un istante una nazione? Non appena
cominciò il travaglio Sion partorí i suoi figli. Porterò alla nascita per poi non far partorire? dice il Signore: io che feci partorire
chiuderò forse il grembo?, dice il Signore » (*Is.* 66, 6-9). Il passo
continua descrivendo i discendenti di Gerusalemme confortati come un bambino confortato dalla madre.

Esso fu interpretato messianicamente, e questo è ben noto,
almeno dal tempo di Edersheim[10].

Sarebbe ragionevole dunque ravvisare nel parto indolore il
simbolo della redenzione. Ma il pensiero ebraico andava oltre.

È certo che il simbolo era associato alle nascite dei bam-
bini la cui concezione fosse stata particolarmente decretata da Dio.
Naturalmente, coloro la cui nascita Egli ha voluta specificamente
non faranno soffrire le madri venendo al mondo, e queste madri
(cosí pare) erano esenti quanto Eva dalla maledizione. Filone,
la cui conoscenza della *haggadah* era assai vasta, ci informa che
Sara diede alla luce senza avvedersene e senza bisogno d'una levatrice. Sara concepí e portò Isacco quasi senza intervallo (pren-
dendo alla lettera *Gen.* 21, 2). Filone connette la storia del *Genesi* a quella del tutto diversa dell'*Esodo* (cfr. *Es.* 1, 19 e 2, 2),
Le Ebree, madri della generazione della prima redenzione, die-

dero alla luce all'improvviso e senza travaglio, e cosí frustrarono il Faraone. Con Sara non poteva essere diversamente[11].

Jocheved, ci si dice, partorí Mosè senza dolore[12]. Quale contrasto con Rachele che ebbe un travaglio dolorosissimo partorendo Beniamino e morí a Efrath (Betlemme) (*Gen.* 35), un luogo ovviamente significativo per le puerpere.

Il tema della nascita indolore era già conforme all'idea delle Cose Ultime, dell'era messianica.

Le disposizioni del *Genesi* erano contraddette da *2 Baruc* 73, 7; « le donne allora non soffriranno piú nel parto e non sentiranno tormenti quando daranno il frutto del grembo »[13]. I santi dotti della Chiesa primitiva attribuirono a Maria i caratteri già conferiti a Sara e a Jocheved, essendo Gesú il Messia. San Luca ci dice che Maria stessa fasciò il bambino (*Lc.* 2, 7), come Jocheved (evidentemente) che la *haggadah* rappresenta come levatrice; questo passo potrebbe legittimamente essere usato per provare che San Luca presumeva che i suoi lettori riconoscessero subito da quella vivacità di lei la grazia particolare predestinata alle madri dei grandi di Israele e a quelle dell'era messianica (da notare il preferito dei verbi in *Lc.* I 68 ecc.) nell'assenza di una levatrice (cfr. *Mc.* 4, 10).

Ci sono passi dove i Padri applicano delle ricostruzioni congetturali alla storia di Gesú: il loro contatto con la Chiesa primitiva era scarso o malcerto.

In altri casi, come quello in esame, riprodussero correttamente la *haggadah*, che poté soltanto formarsi quando la Chiesa era in modo predominante ebrea, e la continuità con la prima generazione cristiana risultò preservata. Tali prove non dovrebbero forse essere benvenute?

---

1   Greg Nys. *Nativ.* (Migne, *P. G.* 46, 1136 A, B) e altri riferimenti in G. W. H. Lampe (curatore), *Patristic Greek Lexicon*, Oxford 1968, vd. *parthenos* a 1039 IV A. Non fu mai sul letto del parto: Clem. *Str.* 7, 16 (*P. G.* 9, 529 B), ps. Cyr. *Trin.* 14, e altri riferimenti in Lampe, op. cit., 1036 P. Cfr. ps. Epiphan. *Hom.* 5 (*P. G.* 43, 500 A). H. Daniel-Rops, *The Book of Mary*, Kingswood - New York 1960, p. 86. J. Guitton, *The Blessed Virgin*, London 1952, pp. 81-82.
2   *Non virgo quantum a partu* (*De carne Chr.* 23 = II 461 Oehler).
3   Il parto indolore è affermato dogmaticamente da F. J. Melvin, *Mary and Christian Life*, New York 1958, p. 95. Nel Medio Evo (*sine dolore peperit*) fu generalmente accettato: S. Brunone, *ep. Sign., Comm. in Lucam* I 1 (*P. L.* 165, 341). San Brunone morí nel 1123. Notiamo che cita *Gen.* 3, 16.
4   J. C. Plumpe, *Testimonianze precoci poco note della* « *virginitas in partu* » *di Maria*, « Theol. St. » 1948, pp. 567-577.

5 *Prin* e *syneltbein autous* (*Mt.* 1, 18). Dobbiamo tentar di capire che cosa sta tentando di dirci San Matteo. Egli intende che Giuseppe si accostò realmente come uno sposo a Maria; non dice né sottintende che egli portò a termine il suo proposito perché qualunque Ebreo sapeva che i segni della gravidanza rendevano illecito l'amplesso. I grammatici ritengono concordemente che le parole greche equivalgono a *pro tou syneltbein* nel senso di « prima che si congiungessero » e non di *hoste me syneltbein* « sicché non si congiunsero », che sarebbe stato possibile qualora la frase avesse seguito il verbo principale. Che *syneltbein* abbia implicazioni sessuali è comprovato da passi e letterari e papirologici, e fu notato da San Severo (V secolo) anche se fu pervicacemente per lo più negato dal *Prot. Jac.* in poi. W. E. W. Carr, *Gregory abu'l Faraj*, London, 1925, p. 9.
6 *Talmud Bab.*, Hagigah 14 b (trad. ingl. Soncino 92). b. Yev. 59 b (Sonc. 397); b. Nidd. 7 b (Sonc. 40), 8 b (Sonc. 52); b. Yev. 59 a (Sonc. 395); J. M. Ford, *The Meaning of Virgin*, « N. T. S. » 12 1965-66, pp. 293-299 (affronta l'argomento). P. Saintyves (alias E. Nourry), *Les vierges-mères et les naissances miraculeuses*, Paris 1908, non tocca i corrispettivi ebraici della storia di Gesù (quelli che contano).
7 Mi limito al puro rinvio a F. H. A. Marshall, *An Introduction to Sexual Physiology*, London 1925, p. 39, e al mio (incompleto in certo modo) *Virgin Birth in the Gospels*, « Man » 2 1971, pp. 289-293.
8 XVIII-XX. M. R. James, *Apocryphal New Testament*, Oxford 1924, pp. 46-47; C. Tischendorf, *Evangelia Apocrypha*, Leipzig 1853, pp. 32-38; W. Bauer, *Das Leben Jesu im Zeitalter der neutestamentlichen Apokryphen*, Tübingen 1909, pp. 29, 58, 67, 69; Plumpe, op. cit., pp. 570-571; E. Stauffer, *Jeuschu ben Mirjam*, in E. E. Ellis e M. Wilcox, *Neotestamentica et Semitica Studies ... M. Black*, Edinburgh 1969, a p. 125 (una induzione dubbia). Anche R. H. Charles, *Ascension of Isaiah*, London 1901, XI 8-11, pp. 74 e 77; e J. R. Harris e A. Mingana, *Odes of Solomon*, Manchester 1916-20, XIX 8-9; H. Daniel-Rops, op. cit., pp. 66 e 76. Una posizione scettica è assunta da G. Miegge, *The Virgin Mary*, London-Toronto 1955, p. 48.
9 *Mishnah*, Bekh. II 9, VIII 1,2. *Lev.* 12,2 non si applica alla madre il cui figlio non è nato normalmente.
10 A. Edersheim, *The Life and Times of Jesus the Messiah*, London 1906, vol. II, p. 730. Vd. M. Kasher *Dictionary of Biblical Interpretation*, New York 1953, ad loc. per i commenti a *Gen.* 33, 1. Il passo di Isaia è riferito a Maria da Ireneo (*Demonstration of the Apostolic Preaching*, trad. di J. A. Robinson, London 1920), p. 117 ss.
11 Filone, *De migr. Abr.* 140-142; *De fuga et inv.* 167-168; *De ebr.* 60.
12 Giuseppe Flavio, *Ant.* II 218 (ed. Thaekeray, vol. IV, p. 258); B. Beer, *Leben Moses nach Auffassung der jüdischen Sage*, Leipzig 1863, p. 31; L. Ginsberg, *Legends of the Jews*, Philadelphia 1909, vol. II, p. 264; C. Perrot, *Les récits de l'enfance dans la haggada antérieure au IIe siècle de notre ère*, « Recherches de Sc. Relig. » 55 1957, p. 502; *Midrash Rabbah Escod.* I 20 (Sonc. 26); b. Sot. 12 a (Sonc. 61); R. Bloch, « Quelques aspects de la figure de Moïse dans la tradition rabbinique », in *Moïse, l'homme de l'Alliance*, Paris 1955, p. 113. Rabbi Yehudah disse che questo comprovava che le sante donne non avevano parte nel destino di Eva.
13 R. H. Charles, *Apocrypha and Pseudepigrapha*, Oxford 1913, vol. II, p. 518.

FURTHER ANNOTATION

Tit. Granted that continuity between the Judaeo-Christian custodians of the materials out of which the gospels are made and their Hellenic and other pagan coreligionists and converts was not perfect, as may be seen from the puzzle of the Unjust Steward (see *LNT*) and the charade of the Footwashing in John xiii (see *Rev. Int. Dr. Ant.*, forthcoming), not to speak of other *aporiai*, nevertheless there remain traces of notions alive in the early churches which have a clear Jewish origin of a comparable kind. This example, the myth of the painless birth, common to Sarah and the mother of Jesus, is particularly striking, since it is impossible to suppose that its relatively late appearance in Christian apocryphal texts derives from an equally late recourse to Jewish midrashim, in view of the peculiar slant, in this respect, of St. Luke's account of the Nativity. The bearing this myth has on the equally interesting myths of the perpetual virginity of Jesus's mother hardly needs to be emphasised.

The Manger at Bethlehem: Light on St. Luke's Technique from Contemporary Jewish Religious Law

The discussions about Luke's infancy narrative and its relation to the remainder of the gospel[1] have shown the strong Hebraic influence. Much research into the subject proceeds on broad lines, and there is no reason why it should not. But this paper is intended to show that concentrated analysis at a deep level, perhaps on a cooperative basis, would be necessary before any broad propositions would have hopes of success. Too much is still too hastily proposed, while for the method Luke adopted, and the details he chose to provide, no sufficient explanations are offered. Here I am concerned with Lk. 2. 1–20. The manger is as yet unexplained, and that is symptomatic of the position[2]. The Manger is quite obviously (and indeed explicitly) a ṣiymān, a symbol, almost a slogan, a catchword – but a symbol of what? Sentimental modern notions have no anchorage in contemporary Jewish ideas. A host of questions are raised by the narrative, and to solve them we must recognise a number of facts normally ignored. Once we have done this we have come nearer to knowing what Luke's technique was, and we can dispose of the assertions often met in conversation, though less often in print, namely that Jesus was probably born at Nazareth and that

---

[1] P. Winter, "Some observations on the language in the birth and infancy stories of the third gospel", N. T. S. 1. 2 (1954) 111–121. N. Turner, "The relation of Luke i and ii to Hebraic sources and to the rest of Luke-Acts", N. T. S. 2. 2 (1956), 100–109. P. Winter, "On Luke and Lucan sources ...", Z. N. W. 47 (1956) 217 ff. R. Laurentin, Structure et Théologie de Luc. I–II (Paris, 1957). M. D. Goulder and M. L. Sanderson, "St. Luke's Genesis", J. T. S. 8 (1957), 12–30. R. McL. Wilson, "Some recent studies in the Lucan infancy narratives", Studia Evangel. (1959), 234–253. R. Leaney, "The birth narratives in St. Luke and St. Matthew", N. T. S. 8 (1961), 158–166. H. H. Oliver, "The Lucan birth stories and the purpose of Luke-Acts", N. T. S. 10 (1963), 202–226, P. S. Minear, "Luke's use of the birth stories", in L. E. Keck and J. L. Martyn, Studies in Luke-Acts (P. Schubert Volume) (Nashville, 1966), 111–130.

[2] The classical studies have a painfully negative sound. M. Dibelius, "Jungfrauensohn und Krippenkind ..." in Bornkamm and Kraft, edd., Botschaft und Geschichte (Tübingen, 1953), 1–78. D. Völter, Die evangelischen Erzählungen von der Geburt und Kindheit Jesu kritisch untersucht (Strassburg, 1911). H. Gressmann, Das Weihnachts evangelium auf Ursprung und Geschichte untersucht (Göttingen, 1914). Worthy of note are H. Sahlin, Der Messias und das Gottesvolk ... (Uppsala, 1945), 207–8, 220–1; K. Bornhäuser, Die Geburts- und Kindheitsgeschichte Jesu (Gütersloh, 1930); M. S. Enslin, "The Christian stories of the Nativity", J. B. L. 59 (1940), 317–338; K. H. Rengstorf, "Die Weihnachtserzählung des Evangelisten Lukas" in Hoffmann and Rengstorf, edd., Stat Crux dum Volvitur Orbis, Festschrift Hanns Lilje (Berlin, 1959), 15–30. See below, p. 94.

there was no manger, that the manger was a pastoral myth, a myth more germane to pagan mystery than to Christian history.

In order to understand the manger it is desirable to understand the nineteen or twenty themes which Luke weaves into the story. To deal with them here would be impossible, but it is desirable to state which they were, and to give important references to show their verity, so that we may see not only where the manger fits in, but also how the historical tradition of the manger must have been so unquestioned when the gospel narrative was compiled that the entire function of the passage rests upon it and is authenticated by it.

The Themes in the Narrative of the Nativity in Luke

I. *The Virgin Birth:* (1) The divine marriage is at last fruitful. The Jewish people is fructified by God as promised in Ezk. 16. 8 and foreshadowed in the related passage in the book of Ruth[1]. The Jewish people spread and came to 'ornaments of ornaments' (M. T.) or 'cities of cities' (LXX) (hence the repetition of 'city' at Lk. 2. 3–4). A pregnant woman is a symbol of Redemption. The Redemption is referred to in Ezk. 16. 6[2], and its double promise refers to two redemptions, and to two births. The angel Gabriel, concerned with girls, pregnancies and children[3], tells of the 'word': Lk. 1. 37 refers to the 'word' which 'happened' at Lk. 2. 15 — and that word is the same as in Ezk. 16. 6.

(2) The biblical story of the birth of Moses, relied upon heavily in the Matthaean narrative, possesses a haggadah abundantly utilised here. Miriam is a quasi-mother to Moses, and Jochebed bears Moses as a quasi-'firstborn'[4].

(3) Joseph is a suitable father for the Messiah, to provide for the second 'Exodus'. The Messiah is called 'Son of Joseph' as well as 'Son of David[5].'

II. *The Census:* (4) The possibility of verification of Joseph's registration establishes questions of descent. (5) Augustus was *de facto* ruler. (i) He was

---

[1] With Ezk. 16. 3 cf. the origin of Ruth. Ezk. 16. 8 = Ruth 2. 12. Ezk. 16. 9 is to be compared with Ruth 3. 3. *kānāf* is (1) wing, (2) border (cf. the woman with a flux). Shadow of wings: Ps. 63. 7 (cf. 17. 8, 36. 7).

[2] Targ. ad loc. Passover Haggadah: Ezk. 16. 7 is a midrash on Dt. 26. 5; in many editions Ezk. 16. 6 precedes. The blood at Ex. 12. 23 was that of Isaac (Mekilta ad loc.). See also Mekilta, Pisha 5 on Ex. 12. 6, also Pisha 16. B. S. Childs, "The birth of Moses", J. B. L. 84 (1965) 109—122 at p. 177 connects Ex. 2 with Ezk. 16 (rightly). If we read Is. 41. 9 with Ezk. 16 *ad sensum* it is the Servant who is chosen and not cast away.

[3] Pal. Targum, Ex. 24 (Etheridge, I, 526). Midrashim and haggadot at Ginzberg, Legends of the Jews, vol. 2, 264, 267, 274 and notes thereon in vol. 5. 'Watchers' (cf. Dan. 4) cause pregnancies: Gen. Apocryph. II (Vermes, Dead Sea Scrolls, 1966, 216).

[4] Pal. Targ. ad loc. Yalḳūṭ Shim'oni ad loc. Ginzberg, op. cit., vol. 2, 258ff., 262—4.

[5] Bab. Tal. Sukk. 52a (Edersheim, Life and Times, 2, London 1901, 717) commenting upon Zch. 12. 10.

a wicked king, and an oppressor like Nebuchadnezzar. (ii) Jerusalem now had a king, to fit the obscure words of Mic. 4. 9. 'Counsellor' in that passage is needed: it is a Messianic title (Is. 9. 6); a counsellor is required in Jerusalem before the 'good tidings' are brought (Is. 41. 27–8); and this is why the synoptics show Joseph of Arimathaea as a 'counsellor'[1], for the parallelism to which we shall return below. (6) The first actual enrolment must have taken place by divine permission. False prophets are to be excluded from enrolment in the house of Israel (Ezk. 13. 9); thus the prophetic characters of Lk. 2 are trustworthy. (7) The Messiah will come from Rome. 'Edom' in Is. 63. 1 means (or includes) Rome. Rome rules the actual Edom. The Roman[2] provided that the Messiah came to Bethlehem and thus prophecy and haggadah were fulfilled.

III. *Bethlehem:* (8) Bethlehem was traditionally the birthplace of the Messiah (Mi. 5. 1/2), and his Redemption is concurrent with the giving birth of a woman in labour (see the Micah passage). (9) Females and the kingdom are referred to again by Micah at 4. 8, the obscure reference to the Tower of the Flock (hence Luke's shepherds are concerned with a flock), which is near Bethlehem. It is because of Migdal/Magdala that Mary of Magdala is distinctly referred to (see below), her geographical origin would not otherwise be significant. (10) The fields around Bethlehem contain the 'threshing-floor of Boaz'. The connection between Ruth and the story at Ezk. 16 is noted above[3]. They were also the scene of Rachel's death in childbirth and the sin that cost Reuben his primogeniture, and thus made Judah the ancestor of the Messiah (Gen. 35. 11–22, 48. 5, 49. 8ff.). (11) The fields around Bethlehem constitute the Open Field for midrashic purposes. The Temple is alluded to vaguely (cf. Gen. 27. 27), another threshing-floor. The field in Mi. 4. 10 is conceivably the Temple, or at any rate the Presence[4]. The daughter of Sion is in travail, goes out into the field (and enters the Presence?), entering the sphere of Babylon (Rome?) and gains Redemption.

IV. *The Open Field:* (12) The abandoned infant of Ezk. 16 was found in the open field. Jesus was buried in such a place (see below). (13) 'There was no room for them in the Inn' recalls the divine marriage of Ezk. 16. 8, which occurred at a time when travellers disrobe at a guesthouse[5]. Inns were

---

[1] The Old Testament passage which is alluded to principally by the intervention of Joseph of Arimathaea is Is. 22. 16–22. See Rev. 3. 7–9, the comments of Cornelius à Lapide thereon, and the antiphon O Clavis David (immediately before Christmas), discussed by C. Callewaert, Sacris Erudiri (Steenbrugge, 1940), 405–18.

[2] But (as the western mind has failed to grasp) the omission of the obligatory "Basileus" with "Caesar Augustus" (Moulton and Milligan, Vocabulary of the Greek Testament, 1930, 105, col. 1) has the effect of emphasising that Augustus's sovereignty was inferior to that of God. See the dictum of R. Simlai at Midrash Rabbah, Gen., VIII. 9.

[3] See p. 87, n. 1.

[4] Midrash on Psalms, Ps. 5, para. 7 (trans, Braude, I, 87), also Ps. 11, para. 3 (Braude, I, 160).

[5] Note LXX wording ibid.

dangerous for those bound for 'Egypt' in order to effect a Redemption[1]. The son of Moses redeemed by his blood his father, and by not putting up at the inn (the same spot?) the child's redemptive capacity was retained. The blood of circumcision connects the passage in Genesis with Ezk. 16. 6, as we have hinted[2]. (14) In the open field, that of the Presence, Jesus shed blood twice. The victim of the two great taboo experiences, birth and death, was twice promised Life *notwithstanding* his blood and *because of* his blood. That Jesus believed that the Holy Spirit gave life in the words of Ezk. 16. 6 is shown by the times when he used the anomalous formula 'I say unto thee'. The instances of the daughter of Jairus and the woman with an issue of blood, properly combined by Mark, show this, for there puberty and the perpetual (12-year) puberty of the woman are obtrusive and combine Ezk. 16. 6 and 8 dramatically and midrashically.

V. *The Manger:* themes I would number 15 and 16 are treated at length below.

VI. *The Shepherds:* (17) These are faithful watchmen over their flock, like the patriarchs and prophets (David is counted as a prophet), tested like Moses, for faithful shepherds can become faithful leaders of men[3]. They symbolise the true Israel. (18) They are keeping night watches. The watchman is a symbolic figure. There are three watches[4], divided by 'signs'. The last watch, the worst, is signalled by babies' crying[5]. The Dead Sea community, studying the Law and praying through the night, had one third of their number always on watch (1 QS VI. 7—8). Jesus says the master returns and the bridegroom comes late in the night[6]. Those who are on watch hear the good news and may communicate it. He that guards Israel neither slumbers nor sleeps (Ps. 121. 3—4), but in the last watch he takes counsel with angels who come on duty at that time[7]. (19) The detailed behaviour of the shepherds is to be studied along with the behaviour of the witnesses of the empty tomb. The result is that the shepherds do as the angels do[8]. The reason is their ocular observation, followed by communication to those who did not observe with inspired observation. Prior to the observation the shepherds were admitted to a theophany, for the angels at the third watch praise God[9], and in this case they greeted 'men of God's satisfaction', namely the small numbers of heroes (including Moses) in whom God had

---

[1] Ex. 4. 24—26 and Targ. thereon. Ginzberg, op. cit., 2, 295; 5, 423, n. 149.

[2] In citations at p. 87, n. 2 above.

[3] Ginzberg, op. cit., 5, 414. See Ezk. 34, Zch. 11, Lk. 12. 32, Jo. 10. 11—16, 21. 16—17, 1 Pe. 2. 25, 5. 2—3, Heb. 13. 20. I suggest that 'the shepherds' allude to the episcopate.

[4] See Bab. Talmud Ber. 3 a.

[5] Ibid. Watchmen look for the morning, or redemption: Ps. 130. 5—6 (cf. ψ 129. 6). On *ṣiymān* = mnemotechnical catchword, slogan see Mishnah, A. Z., I. 3, B. T. Ḥul. 46 a.

[6] Targ. Hab. 2. 1, cf. Lk. 6. 12. Mt. 14. 25, 24. 42—3; Mk. 6. 48, 13. 33—37; Lk. 12. 35—38.

[7] Pal. Targ., Ex. 14. 24. Midr. on Psalms, Ps. 106, para. 2 (Braude, 2, 189).

[8] Compare the vocabulary of Lk. 2, 14 and 20.

[9] See n. 7.

complete satisfaction[1], and, by double entendre, men who accepted the Redemption and so acquired God's satisfaction or approval.

It remains for us to study the Manger as the nucleus of this narrative, and also the subject of impurity and its significance for Judaeo-Christians about A. D. 70.

The Manger as the Counterpart of the Tomb

To use homely language, Luke provides the ramp up to the plateau of the earthly ministry of Jesus, from which we are led down another ramp in the story of the death and entombment, only to be led on the same up again into the post-Resurrection life, with its appendix the post-Ascension life. Parallelism required, it seems, that just as Jesus's rebirth in the tomb led to an activity leading on into the indefinite future, so Jesus's story cannot begin abruptly with a human birth devoid of significance as a purely human event. This 'leading' in the story of Jesus is itself a process of education and mental preparation for the proselyte, and it was (it seems) regarded as an error in Mark that he neglected to provide the spiritual background to the birth. Mark's great care about the deposition, entombment, and the finding of the empty tomb raises strong suspicions that Jewish teaching about the circumstances of the Resurrection, even polemics, were anticipated and met. The manger and the tomb provide an almost complete parallel: and the parallel and the quasi-completeness both indicate that the manger was known before the story of the entombment and the empty tomb was compiled as it now stands. Luke's story of the manger and his view of the shepherds (who represent the authors, the eye-witnesses, the foundation-stones of the faith) is a miniature restatement of the finding of the empty tomb and its sequel[2]. Following the shepherds we read the earthly ministry of Jesus with understanding; following the eye-witnesses we can understand the prophecy and believe it. Placing the two stories in parallel we can reveal the intention of the author.

Mary cares for Jesus at his birth (2. 7).	Two Maries, who served Jesus in Galilee, saw the crucifixion from a distance (Mk. 15. 40–1, Lk. 23. 49).
(Joseph provides accommodation.)	Joseph takes the body and places it in the tomb (Mk. 15. 42–7, Lk. 23. 50–4).
Mary hastily swaddled the baby.	Joseph (and/or his servants) wound the body in a linen cloth (Mk. 15. 46, Lk. 23.53) hastily as time was short (Lk. 23. 54).

---

[1] Ginzberg, op. cit., 2, 260; 5, 395.

[2] Compare the *ṣiymaniym* of the logos at 1 Cor. 15. 3–8. B. Gerhardsson, Memory and Manuscript (Lund and Copenhagen, 1961, reprinted 1964), 299–300.

The baby was placed in a rock-hewn manger.
(Mary watched the manger from a distance, like Miriam the ark.)

(The placing in the manger was only provisional until proper care should be forthcoming.)

The shepherds are informed in the last watch of the night.

The manger was open to view, but its depth was concealed.

The shepherds saw an angel and were frightened.
They are told news of *great joy*, and how to identify the saviour; and they establish the truth of this for themselves.

They explain to people what they have been told, and what they have seen, and the people wonder at it (Lk. 2. 17–18). Mary believes and understands (2. 19).

The shepherds turn away (from the cave) and praise God after connecting what they had been told with what they had confirmed by observation (2. 20).

Joseph's tomb was new, carved out of the rock (Mk. 15. 46, Lk. 23, 53). The Maries saw the tomb and how the body was placed in it (Mk. 15. 47, Lk. 23. 55).
The entombment, though apparently final, was only provisional (Mk. 15. 46; 16. 1; Lk. 23. 53, 56).

The Maries rise before dawn and prepare to visit the tomb (Mk. 16. 2; Lk. 24. 1).
The tomb was open (Mk. 16. 4; Lk. 24. 2). They enter the tomb (Mk. 16. 5; Lk. 24. 3).
They saw angels and were frightened (Mk. 16. 5; Lk. 24. 4).
"You seek Jesus . . . he has risen . . . there is the place where he was put" (Mk. 16. 6); "Why seek the living amongst the dead? . . . he has risen" (Lk. 24. 6). He is your shepherd; you will see him again: this is implied at Mk. 16. 7. "Remember what he foretold to you" (Lk. 24. 6–7).
They must tell others (Mk. 16. 7); they turn away from the tomb and explain everything to the others, who are incredulous (Lk. 24. 9–10). The Maries believe it all and are the source of the message and initial belief on the part of non-eye-witnesses (Lk. 24. 10).
The disciples on the way to Emmaus discuss what they heard; they had expected a redeemer; they had checked what the women said and found it true; their eyes are later opened and they return and tell the others who are watching late at night (Lk. 24. 13–35). After the last words and the Ascension, the disciples turn away with *great joy*, and bless God (Lk. 24. 52–3).

St. Gregory of Nazianzus describes Jesus as de-swaddled in the tomb[1]. The meaning of the manger was evidently lost by the time of Justin Martyr, who would certainly have explained it if he had known its point.

Impurity, purification, and Jesus as a purifier

Not to be prolix, the manger's explanation depends upon the timing of its use, and its own nature as a rock-cut receptacle. The interest in the tomb as a place of resurrection is the same as the interest in the cave where he was born as a place for his birth, and a hiding-place. I do not approve the scepticism held in some quarters as to the authenticity of the cave of the Nativity[2]. If it was not that cave it was some other cave in the vicinity of Bethlehem possessing a wall-cut socket intended from the first as a manger for asses and bovine cattle. The grounds for believing the cave now visited by pilgrims to be the authentic place are very substantial, and no grounds for doubting it can be substantiated. The *cave* is necessitated by the rock-cut socket, since no such socket would be cut in what was not actually or virtually a cave.

As to the time of its use, Jesus was dirty with blood and other fluids of parturition, unwashed, unprepared[3]. His swaddling was provisional dressing. He and his mother were impure, their impurity lasting for forty days[4]. The taboo condition of birth made them unsuitable for visits, let alone worship. Yet the angel did not wait for the forty days to be completed (Lk. 2. 22) before announcing the Saviour. It was the *parturition* which was important, blood, impurity, taboo and all! Western readers cannot grasp easily the anomaly which this involves.

It is certain that Jesus when placed in the tomb was a taboo object, being a corpse. The law relating to the defiling effect of corpse-blood would make it almost certain that the winding-cloth was highly defiling, and the blood congealed on to the stone would have rendered unclean the body when revived and brought back to life[5]! The anomaly is that the Holy

---

[1] Or. 29. 19 (A. D. 380). Migne, P. G. 36, 100 B.

[2] I am impressed by C. Kopp, The Holy Places of the Gospels (Freiburg and Edinburgh, 1963), 1–34, perhaps supplemented by M. Vionnet, "Les églises de la Nativité à Bethlehem', Byzantion 13 (1938), 91–128.

[3] Though he *was* swaddled, in opposition to Ezk. 16. 4, the general position indicated is of a hasty birth (cf. Ex. 1. 19, and Targ.), and (temporary) neglect conforming to Ezk. 16. 4–5. Had Jesus been born in the city he would have received normal treatment.

[4] But note that extreme impurity lasts for seven days (as with death impurity). Both mother and child are ritually impure (Lk. 2. 21–22). For the Jewish law see (Strack-) Billerbeck, Kommentar z. N. T., 3rd edn. (Munich, 1961), 2, 119–120; Mishnah, Kel. I. 8, Ker. II. 1, Eduy. V. 4, Nid. IV. 3. Danby, Mishnah, p. 695 n. 8 summarises the position. On touch see ibid., 803; Tah. V. 8.

[5] The discussions at Mishnah, 'Ahal. II. 2, 5; III. 2, 3, 5; cf. Yad. I. 1. A crucified corpse is specifically considered.

Spirit is active in contexts of impurity: yet it is clear that the Holy Spirit is not susceptible to impurity, just as the angels are not suceptible[1].

This is the point. Jesus, in his ministry until he took the Nazirite's oath, despised the taboo laws, virtually ignoring the menstruant's defiling effect, and completely ignoring the defiling effect of touching the bier of the dead son of the widow of Naïn. It is notorious how he disputed the validity of the hand-rinsing laws, and the basis of some at least of the dietary laws. This was a serious anomaly for a holy man. The only plausible explanation was that Jesus was an embodiment of the Holy Spirit, and this is evidently the explanation offered by the earliest church. Jesus could, and must, ignore the taboos and menstruation and death, since he is himself the bringer of life.

There is yet more. The re-birth of Jesus in the tomb is not birth *from* the rock in some pagan symbolism, but birth *in* a natural (miniature) cave. No interment had ever occurred in that space, and we can presume the same for the cave of the Nativity in its original condition at the time of the birth of Jesus. Caves in which no interment had ever taken place were the only places utterly free from suspicion of death-pollution, and in one such cave a succession of young boys were maintained in Jerusalem prior to A. D. 70 (after which time the basis for the system vanished) in order to provide the water for the Water of Separation (containing the Ashes of the Red Heifer). The mothers gave birth in the cave and the boys did not leave until their qualification was lost accidentally or they passed the maximum age for this purpose[2]. Anyone in Judaea, and especially in the neighbourhood of Jerusalem, in which Bethlehem is, would know that birth in a cave, in connection with a rock receptacle, symbolises purity from the pollution conveyed by death. Jesus was, though impure from the birth-pollution, qualified to be the means of cleansing from death-pollution. Jesus himself was likened (Heb. 13. 11−13) to the Red Heifer, and the reason is that the system of use of the ashes of the Red Heifer derives from a rationalized taboo.

Anthropologically, the taint of death is mere taboo, without moral significance. But by the time Num. 19 was compiled it was thought that the taint of death, which had become institutionalised and codified, was symbolic of sin, possibly the sin of Adam. The sprinkling of the water holding the ashes of the Heifer was a means of removing sin. A rational explanation was easy. The taboos of both birth and death involved cleansing, and both required an atonement[3]. A *haggadah* preserved in Josephus[4] shows that the

---

[1] Midr. on Psalms, Ps. 8, para. 2 (Braude, I, 122).

[2] Mishnah, Par. III. 2−3, Tosefta ibid. (ed. Rengstorf VI. 2, pt. 1, 24 ff.). Siphre ad loc. (R. Aqiba).

[3] The language of Num. and Lev. agrees: see Lev. 15. 30.

[4] Ant. IV. 4, 6−7.

Red Heifer was first slaughtered to provide an atonement for the death of Miriam [1].

The death of Jesus provided a perpetual atonement which rendered the sprinkling with the Water of Separation superfluous, and Jesus himself showed that for those in whom the Holy Spirit dwells the taboos of birth, menstruation, and death are at an end.

This argument, though not given *expressis verbis* by Luke, and perhaps more effectively given for that, would serve the needs of a Jewish community alarmed by the destruction of Jerusalem. The question is what is to be done now the Ashes of the Red Heifer cannot be found, or if found cannot be certified free from pollution, and there is no longer a child to make the water itself, nor the means to carry out the slaughter of another Red Heifer. What is the effect of pollution without hope of 'decontamination' until a Red Heifer can be slaughtered when the Temple is restored and ritual life re-established? The law relating to the Red Heifer continued to be studied amongst the Pharisees because one day the Temple would be rebuilt . . . Some argued that the ritual sprinkling was not necessary, except for those who wanted to enter the Temple area. When Jews were totally prohibited about A. D. 135 from entering that place, and when the possibility of rebuilding the Temple and re-establishing Jewish ritual life was at an end, concern about the provision for 'decontamination' faded away. Except amongst rabbis the learning conjured up by the word *Parah* had little or no meaning. But between A. D. 70 and 135 there was room for careful explanation that the basis of the ritual ordained in Num. 19 had been taken away by the death of Jesus, who was a perpetual substitute for this, as for so many other ritual provisions. After 135 an appeal to Num. 19 as an explanation for the significance of the Manger and the Resurrection in the cave-tomb became otiose and academic, and the secret was lost.

---

[1] Miriam's death was also an atonement: Yalḳūṭ Shim'oni ad loc.

The Manger: Ritual Law and Soteriology

Few readers of Lk. 2: 7, 12, 16 would guess that the thrice repeated reference to the manger in which Jesus was laid conceals references to the Fall of Adam, the birth of Moses, and the essential and perpetual purity of the Holy Spirit. Even after one has grasped that this is the case the natural reaction is to sigh over yet another demonstration that the Infancy Narratives are a pastiche of biblical and midrashic motifs, a work of art, and yet perhaps more artistic than true. That St Luke did produce a work of consummate skill, a kind of mosaic of Jewish religious poetry, is well enough known by now.[1] But to know it is not to accept, still less

---

[1] M. D. Goulder and M. L. Sanderson, "St Luke's Genesis", *J.T.S:* 8 (1957), 12–30; P. Winter, "Jewish folklore in the Matthaean birth story", *Hibbert J.* 53 (1954–5), 34–42; R. Laurentin, *Structure et Théologie de Luc. I–II* (Paris, 1957); J. Coppens, "L'évangile lucanien de l'enfance", *Ephemer. theol. lovan.* 33 (1957), 729–735; R. McL. Wilson, "Some recent studies in the Lucan infancy narratives", *Studia Evangelica* 1 (1959), 234–253; M. L. Bourker, "The literary genus of Mat. 1–2", *C.B.Q.* 22 (1960), 160–175; C. T. Ruddick, "Birth narratives in Genesis and Luke", *N.T.* 12 (1970), 343–348. The leading work, by an author whose untimely death robbed New Testament scholars of a most valuable helper, is Renée Bloch's, "Quelques aspects de la figure de Moïse dans la tradition rabbinique", in *Moïse, L'Homme de l'Alliance (Cahiers Sioniens, 2–4)* (Paris, 1955), 93–167, especially 102–119.

to digest it. What, after all, is the relationship between poetry and truth? Or is it not rather yet another case of As If? Are we looking, in our imaginations, upon the birth scene of Jesus, and, whatever the facts might have been, pretending that it had these features because the beginnings of a wonderful life must have been wonderful, even if wonderful only in terms of Jewish mythology, the imaginative recreation of bible stories in the light of the golden legend that is the *haggadah*?

Scepticism has played upon the Infancy Narratives. And the Virgin Birth, to which they relate more or less closely, has suffered in scholarly eyes because of its association with material which looks unashamedly legendary. In reaction to this a defensive strategy has developed: the Virgin Birth does not really matter, some say, or can even be regarded as contradictory of the doctrine of the pre-existence of Christ.[1] And the mystery of the Incarnation can get along, so to speak, the better if the proposition that Jesus was born of a virgin is jettisoned.[2] That subject deserves the closest scrutiny and reappraisal in the light of the psychological and gynaecological knowledge available to St Matthew and St Luke and their first hearers: but I cannot broach the topic here. If the manger is historically true, and the relationship between the manger as fact and the manger as Christian *haggadah* is understood, we are in a much better position to approach the other apparently legendary items in the Narratives, and to say to scepticism, "Wait a bit: perhaps there was more in this than you have realized!" And that can be said, as this very article has been written, in the spirit of enquiry and without apologetic or crypto-conservative motives.

No unprejudiced reader of the verses cited above can fail to notice that St Luke wishes the manger to be prominent, though he does not tell us why. His original hearers will have recognized, with a squirm of delight, what he was doing. But since the apostles died the clues have faded so badly that the words cannot convey what their author meant. To take the first instance, we are simply told that Mary swaddled Jesus and laid him (or perhaps propped him up) in a manger. In the second instance we are told that the angel told the shepherds that it was nothing less than a *sign*, that they should find a baby swaddled and lying in a manger. To complete the threefold announcement to the reader, we hear that they found Mary, and Joseph, and the baby lying in the manger.

It is a pity that she is not used in the study of Martin Rese, *Alttestamentliche Motive in der Christologie des Lukas* (Gütersloh, Gerd Mohn, 1969), 178–188. Rese does not deal with the manger.

[1] R. H. Fuller, "The Virgin Birth: historical fact or kerygmatic truth?", *Biblical Research* (Chicago society for biblical research) I (Chicago, 1956), 1–8. P. Althaus, *Die christliche Wahrheit* II (Gütersloh, 1948), sec. 43. E. Brunner, *Die christliche Lehre von Schöpfung und Erlösung (Dogmatik,* II) (Zürich, 1950), 413–422. W. Pannenburg, *Jesus – God and Man* (London, 1968), 141–150.

[2] Pannenburg, cited in last note.

This time it is "*the* manger". There have been several guesses, as that it was the shepherds' manger. But shepherds do not need mangers. The only manger likely to survive in a country short of wood and never short of pilferers would be a stone recess, cut from the living rock, at a height convenient for the smallish cattle, oxen and asses (Lk. 13: 15), whose valuable fodder is not spilt recklessly. The manger thus formed part, and, until pilgrims got out their knives, an immovable part, of a cave. The region had several caves, some intercommunicating.[1] In these there might have been more than one such manger. But the actual manger was identified with such certainty by the earliest church, obsessed with the theme of Davidic descent, and there was the hope of so certain a financial income from pilgrims from the very earliest times (to visit the places associated with the birth and, still more, the death and/or burial of the holy was a well-known means of obtaining their "blessing" and supernatural aid), that when the Romans felt it desirable to obliterate the shrine they were in no doubt whatever where the worship of Adonis should be instituted (or, perhaps, revived). This preserved knowledge of the exact site without fear of error, and so, in a manner strongly reminiscent of the identification of the Holy Sepulchre, a mixture of superstition and greed saved the two authentic Holy Places from oblivion.

But, whether or not the cave at Bethlehem is the actual cave in which Mary bore her child, we must put ourselves into a position to understand why the first hearers of St Luke's gospel were so thrilled by his allusions. To what theological doctrines was he drawing their attention in this attractive way? Fortunately, as knowledge of Jewish midrash spreads we become steadily more and more able to pick up those threads.

1. Mary swaddled the baby herself. This does not mean that she had a painless delivery, still less that the baby was born abnormally. St Luke himself shows us, in his account of the circumcision (2: 21), and the redemption of the firstborn (2: 23–4), that the baby was normal in every way, and that he opened the womb in the same way as any other normally-born child.[2] The mother's first baby can hardly have been a painless experience. But as she was able to swaddle him herself, without the aid of a midwife, in a cave outside the village, in an apparently deserted and neglected place, she was able to play a part known to prophecy and to legend. The people of Israel themselves were thought to have been castaways (Ezk. 16: 3–6), and the swaddling and feeding of the infants of the generation of the first redemption was done by angels.[3] Mary sat by the manger as Miriam watched over Moses, whose birth was likewise con-

---

[1] C. Kopp, *The Holy Places of the Gospels* (Freiburg/Edinburgh, 1963), ch. 3.
[2] *Mishnah*, Bekhorot II. 9 (Trans., Danby, p. 532); VIII. 1–2 (ibid., 539–40).
[3] The references will be found in "The Manger at Bethlehem: Light on St. Luke's technique from contemporary Jewish religious law", H. F. D. Sparks, ed., *Studia Evangelica* (proceedings of the New Testament congress at Oxford, 1969, to appear). I was not aware then of Adam's interest in the manger.

cealed, while he was in the little receptacle. Furthermore, there is a persistent legend that, improbable as it may seem from the biblical text (Ex. 1: 15–21), the two Hebrew midwives who were charged with the task of destroying the male children were none other than Jocheved, the future mother of Moses, and Miriam, Jocheved's daughter, who persuaded Amram and Jocheved to come together again and be the parents of the future redeemer.[1] They were expert midwives, though their customers apparently bore children too quick for them to use their skills often: but they certainly will have been provided with swaddling-strips. That would have been part of their equipment, and that is why we are told twice about the swaddling of Jesus. Here was a child of Israel who was *not* neglected, but swaddled by an expert, just like the generation of the first redemption in the land of Egypt.

2. Child of Israel, Jesus was also a son of Adam. No doubt this is not satisfactory to those who, supposing that Joseph played no part whatever in the conception of Jesus, wish to believe that that miracle was devised in order to exclude descent from Adam and Adam's tainted line. But Docetism awaits any that suppose Jesus not to have been a man, and, apart from the controversial question of Joseph's participation in the conception (which is universally, though I think mistakenly, denied in all the symbols of the faith), in so far as Jesus was born from Mary he was also descended from Adam on his mother's side. The Docetic view that Mary was merely a pipeline through which Jesus entered the world (a point of view gratuitously suggested by St Luke at 1: 35, which must be discussed elsewhere) is not accepted as representing the orthodox faith, and has nothing (Lk. 1: 35 apart) to support it in the gospels. Now it is well known that St Paul took it for granted that Jesus was a new Adam.[2] It could be regarded as a piece of theology without synoptic foundation. But here we have the foundation. Jesus as the new Adam, obedient as Adam was disobedient (Lk. 2: 49, 51; 22: 42), takes up the thread where Adam let it drop.

When Adam was cursed by God for his disobedience he was told (Gen. 3: 18) "thou shalt eat the herb of the field". Adam trembled, or sweated, or wept, as we are told in an ancient and persistent midrash upon this verse. "Lord of the Universe", he said, "Shall I be tied to the manger to eat with my ass?" God said no: "In the sweat of thy face shalt thou eat bread, till thou return unto the ground; for out of it wast thou taken: for dust thou art, and unto dust shalt thou return." The theme of the manger is a constant feature of the midrash.[3] So in being

---

[1] The midrash is available at several places, of which the most significant is the *Targum pseudo-Jonathan* on the place in Exodus.
[2] I Cor. 15: 22, 45.
[3] The word *'ebūs* occurs in all. *Midrash Rabbah*, Gen. 20: 10 (Soncino trans., 168). *Bab. Tal.*, Pesaḥim 118a (Soncino trans., 607). *Fathers according to R. Nathan* (a Minor Tractate of the Talmud), i (17b) (trans., J. Goldin, New Haven, 1955, 14); also in

put into the manger for a while Jesus was made, in the evangelist's eyes, to mime, as it were, the merited fear of Adam. And Golgotha was, as it were, the place of Adam's skull.[1] As Adam came, and as Adam went, he came from dust, and returned to dust: yet, says the irony of the gospel, it was not entirely from dust he came (there was the divine wind as well: Gen. 2: 7), and it was not entirely to dust that he returned. For what has no beginning has no end.

3. But we have not done with the manger. The stone receptacle is the abode of purity. Through stone no taint of death can penetrate. Into the manger he was put by a Mary, who watched over him there. Into the tomb he was put by two Marys, who watched the place where he was laid. A Mary took him out, we can be sure, from the first rock bed, and, irony again, Marys would have moved him in the second. The careful information that the tomb was cut from the living rock is of course valuable as it militates against grave-robbery as an explanation for the disappearance of the body. But it has a ritual significance.[2] The Holy Spirit is not susceptible of pollution. Throughout his life Jesus acted as if he were immune from ritual pollution. But the theme of the rock receptacle implies a concern with holiness in the ritual sense: the rock suggests the incorruptible, and like Adam, Jesus must pass through the cycle of emergence from it, and reconveyance into it. Gregory of Nazianzus saw the point, when he speaks of Jesus's being de-swaddled in the tomb.[3]

This elaborate construction could not have stood without a foundation in fact. In this case we cannot be in any doubt what it was. It was simply that Jesus as a baby was swaddled and placed in a manger. This information could have been obtained from Mary herself, and there is not the slightest reason to doubt but that Jesus knew of it and pondered on it. He may well have visited the scene, and grasped the point. Nothing happens by mere chance. A life which fitted into a pattern, filled with so many paradoxes and embarrassments, seemed to ask for verification in terms of scripture, the only anchor the culture had. The evangelist's

---

the translation of A. Cohen (London, Soncino press, 1965), 13. The idea is referred to at *Pirqe de Rabbi Eliezer* xiv (trans. G. Friedlander, New York, 1965, 100). Ginzberg's *Legends of the Jews* appears not to give an explicit reference to this midrash. J. P. Stehelin, *Traditions of the Jews* I (London, 1742), 23–4. The relation, if any, between this midrash and Is. 1: 3 is unclear. God's kingdom is still a *garden*, but one eats *bread* in it (Lk 13: 18–21).

[1] C. Warren at Hastings, *DB*, *s.v.* Golgotha. T. K. Cheyne and J. S. Black, ed., *Encyclopaedia Biblica* (1903), *s.v.* Golgotha.

[2] The particulars are noticed at the article referred to above, p. 568, n. 3. Use is made of *Mishnah*, Par. III. 2–3, and Heb. 13: 11–13.

[3] *Or.* 29: 19 (AD 380). See references in Lampe, *Patristic Lexicon*, *s.v.* σπάργανον, σπαργανόω, for confirmation that swaddling and wrapping in grave clothes were a similar process. It is of interest that the recognition that the manger in some way prefigured the tomb has occurred to many, including Kopp (cited above), though the connection was never evident. The poet George Mackay Brown's "From Stone to Thorn" (in *An Orkney Tapestry*) makes the same point.

informants, so we may suppose, told him what the significance of the little scene was: and he did the rest.

Luke, as we know, derives Jesus from Adam genealogically (3: 38). As if to confirm that Luke was aware of the notion of Jesus as the second Adam, perhaps consistently with Pauline ideas, we have the strange passage at Lk. 13: 10–17. The passage has no little medical interest, and perhaps this was intended. The woman's condition was susceptible of cure, not necessarily against the course of nature. Briefly, she had been bent down like an animal for eighteen years. It is the debate, not the "sign", which interests the evangelist. Jesus argues that anyone would loose from the manger, even on the Sabbath, his ox or ass; and surely *a fortiori* a daughter of Abraham (i.e. a Jewess to whom salvation should come) is entitled to be loosed from Satan. The Targums on the Pentateuch which unquestionably derive from midrashic material commonly known in Jesus's time tell us at Gen. 3: 18 that Adam prayed in particular not to have to eat bent double, but to stand upright, to work with his hands, and *not* to be confused with animals (at the trough, as it were). Luke's *anorthothe* is related to that. In his view Jesus arrived, and was the woman's saviour from a condition from which God released Adam (and his issue) at Gen. 3: 19. Now the Targum of pseudo-Jonathan and the so-called Palestinian Targum (the Neofiti Targum has nothing special to add here) do not especially mention the serpent in this connection, but it is evident that the serpent (*alias* Satan) very much wanted Adam to be like the animals (Satan was originally four-footed, in his appearance before Eve), and, though the curses of Gen. 3 constitute in some measure a victory for Satan, he must have been disappointed at the promise of an upright stance contained in verse 19. To clinch the matter we have the reference (which most probably was to a known fact) that the woman's condition had endured eighteen years. The numeral eighteen derives from Jdg. 3: 14, 10: 8 (with 11).[1] We are told in those passages that as a penalty for forgetfulness of God and disobedience to him the children of Israel were enslaved (i.e. bound) by Eglon the king of Moab and later the Philistines. At Jdg. 3: 13 and 10: 12 we are told that the children of Amalek were in part responsible for this. Now we know for certain that "Amalek" represents the "evil inclination", Satan.[2] These figures were taken allegorically. From those two enslavements the children of Israel were saved by God by means of two saviours respectively. The first, Ehud, is actually called a saviour (*moshiy'a*) and in the Targum the word used is *pāriyq*, which means "redeemer". The second was Jephthah. We need be in no doubt but that the idea was that eighteen years was a period after which God would give a particular generation freedom from the machinations of Satan. Thus Jesus is seen enacting the work of the second Adam, and once again the manger figures in the story.

[1] Josephus, *Antiquities*, V, 186–7, 263.
[2] *Law in the New Testament* (London, 1970), index, "Amalek".

Il significato della mangiatoia*

Per ripugnante che paia a molti la ' decifrazione ' d'un passo del Nuovo Testamento, cioè la riscoperta delle sue allusioni a noti temi biblici o haggadici, essa talvolta è l'unico modo di cavarne un senso.

Spesso gli esegeti moderni ricorrono a interpretazioni razionalistiche ed anacronistiche, essendo riluttanti a impegnarsi in esercizi di decifrazione midrascici, ai quali per istinto e per educazione sono inetti. Perciò la mangiatoia si è rivelata del tutto intrattabile. San Luca la menziona dapprima a II 7 dove φάτνη significa appunto una mangiatoia, e come tale riappare a II 12, sempre come una mangiatoia, ma in qualità di « segno »; e ciò che era un segno per i pastori era un segno « occulto », appena velato, per i lettori di Luca. A II 16 è diventata « la mangiatoia ». Perché mai? Il solito riferimento (a Is. I 3) non spiega molto, salvo si colleghi la questione del mangime (come metafora del cibo); ma era ben difficile capire come lo si potesse collegare, nei termini specifici del racconto di Luca.

Il metodo razionalistico « anglosassone » spiega la mangiatoia di Lc. II 7-16, in base al semplice fatto che Gesù vi fu deposto e che in seguito, dopo la Resurrezione, ad essa fu data una importanza simbolica forse in virtù di un'analogia forzata con Is. I 3. Il fatto che Gesù fu messo in una mangiatoia sarebbe l'unica spiegazione razionale dell'improvviso accenno di Lc. II 7, dei ripetuti riferimenti e della mancanza totale di spiegazioni in questi testi.

Una sfida che provenga dalla cultura « materiale » è esasperante. Due idee in proposito, che furono proposte in passato, hanno destato il mio interesse. L'una è che i pastori avrebbero riconosciuto la *loro* mangiatoia, ma purtroppo le pecore brucano a un'altezza ben diversa da quella del bestiame da stalla, anzi esse si cibano al pascolo, all'aperto. Φάτνη designa una conca, un incavo nella rupe, e non possiamo raffigurarci, nella storia di Luca, altro che una concavità scavata nella parete della caverna. Mangiatoie di legno mobili sono impensabili data la località, la mancanza di legno e il problema costante del mio e del tuo [1]. L'altra idea che mi ha interessato è che la mangiatoia fosse un'allusione alla costellazione omonima, e questo sarebbe stato significativo per un popolo di osservatori del cielo e per dei pastori in particolare; inoltre, benché la storia della Stella nelle narrazioni della natività da parte degli altri Evangelisti abbia rapporto con concetti differenti, ci potrebbe essere un arcano motivo per riunire questi diversi filoni [2].

Ma nessuna di queste idee mi ha fatto un'impressione favorevole.

Ne offro due mie. Nessuna delle due è discutibile, essendo entrambe ben documentate, ciascuna a modo suo.

(A) Una mangiatoia che sia un incavo nella roccia, è un luogo di purità rituale, appropriato, in modo un po' forzato, a una persona destinata a incarnare la purezza non ritualmente contaminabile [3]. La gente di Betlemme e di tutta la regione gerosolimitana sapeva che i fanciulli nati nelle caverne avevano certe prerogative rituali. Ho spiegato questo rapporto a proposito della Vitella Rossa [4].

(B) L'idea di essere messo dentro o vicino ad una mangiatoia implica che si divida il mangime con gli animali. C'è una formidabile *haggadà* secondo cui Adamo, dopo la Caduta, pregò Dio di non farlo mangiare coi quadrupedi alla greppia [5]. È certo che Gesù sapeva del diritto degli uomini a stare eretti e non curvi come i quadrupedi, e quale Secondo Adamo affrancò da tale condizione un Israelita [6]. Inoltre la *haggadà* sul passo del Genesi era abbastanza antica da poter essere nata da un racconto delle esperienze di Nabucodonosor (Dan. IV 15, 25, 32, 33; v. 21). L'episodio della mangiatoia mostra dunque che Gesù aveva sperimentato veramente la Caduta dell'Uomo e che, sia pure momentaneamente, entrò (e uscì) da una mangiatoia [7].

Se accostiamo il concetto dell'impurità di qualsiasi posto, a confronto della purezza d'una caverna, come luogo di nascita e d'una conca nella roccia in particolare, associata alla nascita, all'idea che il Secondo Adamo provi lo stesso timore del Primo, non sarà difficile ravvisare nella natività di Luca una riproduzione in miniatura della storia della sepoltura, che egli trasse da Marco. Il parallelo è manifesto [8]. Anzi, esso suggerisce che le stranezze della storia della sepoltura in Marco sono da mettersi in connessione con il ricordo della mangiatoia da parte di Marco stesso.

L'idea sottintesa sarebbe che ci furono due nascite, entrambe in un luogo scavato nella rupe e la seconda nascita, cioè la Resurrezione, fu prefigurata dalla prima e che lo Spirito Santo non agì soltanto promuovendo la generazione ma anche infondendo la purezza. Tutto ciò colpisce per la sua artificiosità, sia pure, ma questa non è un'obiezione, trattandosi di una letteratura di squisito artificio, d'altronde certamente il fatto nuoce al pieno godimento della composizione di Luca.

La presente nota vorrebbe attrarre l'attenzione su *Mishnah, Ned. IV 4* e sulle implicazioni della presenza in quel passo della parola *'ebūs* [9].

Un operaio aveva fatto voto di non trarre beneficio da un altro, e si poneva il quesito se ciò davvero inibisse ogni relazione sociale fra i due. Il parere adottato fu che, generalizzando, i rapporti e le esperienze comuni erano proibiti a chi aveva fatto il voto soltanto se la sua presenza accanto al ' nemico ' faceva sì che questi gli conferisse un beneficio. I due potevano mangiare allo stesso desco senza tema che l'uno aiutasse l'altro; ma non potevano attingere mangiando dallo stesso vaso e da un piatto fatto girare fra i commensali perché c'era il sospetto che l'uno si servisse più di quel che sarebbe stato altrimenti il caso. Qui la casistica dei rabbini si mostra alla perfezione.

Chi aveva fatto il voto poteva bagnarsi nella stessa vasca con l'altro purché essa fosse ampia, perché, fosse stata piccola, il livello dell'acqua sarebbe stato sollevato dalla presenza di quest'ultimo, ed egli ne avrebbe avuto un beneficio.

Incontriamo quindi nel testo l'espressione *lo' yo'kal 'immō min hā-ēbūs šelifnēy ha-pō'ªlīm*, da cui appare che *ēbūs* era un termine ben noto per designare un ricettacolo comune in cui si disponevano le vettovaglie per il pasto meridiano d'una compagnia di operai, che se le portavano sul posto di lavoro in modo da potersi concedere il rinfresco senza tornare a casa e senza interrompere per più del necessario il lavoro.. Non c'è dubbio che fra i pastori fosse familiare un *'ēbūs* (lo possiamo forse chiamare un cestino), dato che le loro ore di servizio, i loro turni, imponevano dei rinfreschi fuori casa, e che essendo in compagnia, essi consumavano i loro rinfreschi in comune. Una compagnia di pastori era dunque un gruppo di persone che lavoravano, sorvegliavano e mangiavano insieme.

Così la menzione improvvisa di una mangiatoia avrebbe richiamato alla mente i mezzi coi quali si provvedeva al cibo comune lontano da casa. La parola greca φάτνη vuol anche dire, un po' spregiativamente, greppia, un luogo dove la gente mangia non saggiamente, ma troppo bene [10]. Poiché la parola significa mangiatoia e per estensione lo scomparto dov'è sistemata, non si applica al luogo dove consumino il pasto degli uomini se non spregiativamente.

Sarebbe diverso se φάτνη andasse intesa come una traduzione di 'ēbūs. In greco è difficile far intendere che dei pastori vengono mandati a vedere un fanciullo in una mangiatoia con la speranza che questo venga inteso come « segno ». Ma le cose stanno diversamente se si tiene a mente Is. I 3. Il popolo d'Israele doveva, ad un certo momento conoscere « la culla del suo signore ». Se il pasto in questione era quello delle greggi dei pastori, non si potrebbe connettere la nostra φάτνη a Is. I 3. Ma non sarà invece possibile considerare i pastori come Israele che mangia, con la umiltà degli animali, un pasto comune fornito dal suo Signore? L'idea fantasiosa che Gesù bambino nella mangiatoia potesse essere un pasto (con la congiunzione inaccettabile di carne viva e di sangue) si volge in una direzione meno sgradevole, più plausibile se la paragoniamo a Gio. VI 51-6. San Giovanni insiste che il credente deve mangiare la carne del Cristo e berne il sangue in modo tale che doveva trattarsi di un concetto già generalmente accettato al tempo di san Giovanni.

Concludo proponendo le ipotesi seguenti.

(A) San Luca ricevette la tradizione secondo cui Gesù fu posto in una mangiatoia dopo la nascita, nonché tradizioni che consideravano in funzione simbolica questo ricordo. (B) Egli espose questo racconto simbolico in modo da suggerire varie proposizioni implicite: (I) Gesù era il Secondo Adamo e seguì il destino del Primo, spartendo per un istante il luogo del pasto con il bestiame (non con le pecore). (II) La nascita di questo Adamo ebbe luogo nella stessa assoluta purezza di quella del Primo Adamo (nel cui mondo la morte era sconosciuta). (III) La prima nascita di Gesù fu simile alla sua ri-nascita (nella tomba); (IV) come Gesù prima di morire sulla croce si diede, carne e sangue, da consumare, ingerire ai suoi umili seguaci (con tutto ciò che magicamente consegue: l'unione dell'offerente, di chi dà il pasto a coloro che lo ingeriscono e di tutti costoro l'un con l'altro secondo uguaglianza e di ciascuno con lui [11]); così sua madre subito dopo che egli nacque (a specchio degli eventi futuri) lo espose come fosse per essere il pasto comune dei poveri fedeli. Quest'ultima implicanza ha una sua logica e plausibilità poiché il concetto di un cibo celeste che sostituisca e renda superfluo quello terreno è attestato frequentemente (il Pasto dei Cinquemila ecc. e Gio. IV 31-34) e il tempo naturale di questo pasto è quando i doveri del giorno e della notte sono adempiuti, il turno è terminato e il « compenso » dovuto.

È vero che nessun commentatore di Gio. VI 51-6 ha additato un corrispettivo in Luca, a parte l'Ultima Cena, e il figlio dell'Uomo non è stato identificato con il Secondo Adamo; ma non c'è motivo che non lo debba essere.

L'importanza di 'ēbūs, se l'ipotesi regge, è che deve trattarsi di un cestino per la merenda comune, la fonte comunitaria di un cibo che sarà spartito soltanto da coloro che formano un'unità sociale e che è un'alternativa rispetto ai loro pasti domestici. In una sovrimpressione caratteristica e a volte sorprendente di praticità quotidiana e di immagini poetiche, il « segno » della mangiatoia pone in stretto accordo la vita ordinaria e gl'inizi della vicenda cristiana.

Naturalmente è impossibile immaginare che questa elaborata struttura in filigrana potesse essere costruita senza delle prove fededegne dell'esistenza di una mangiatoia comunemente considerata come quella effettiva. E tanti altri elementi fantasiosi delle storie dell'infanzia, anche i Magi, poterono avere un qualche nucleo di ricordi fededegni abbastanza saldo da fornire l'abbrivo a questo processo.

---

* Cfr. « Conoscenza religiosa » 3 1972, pp. 221-25.

[1] Non reparto di stalla, come in Gius. Antiq. III 4, poiché esso è chiamato φάτνη dalla mangiatoia che vi si trova. Così S. M. Creed, The Gospel According to St. Luke (London 1950), p. 34. Il riferimento a H. J. Cadbury e ad A. van Veldhuizen si trova in Bauer-Arndt-Gingrich, A Greek-English Lexicon of the New Testament (Chicago-Cambridge 1957). Studi più recenti non risolvono il nostro problema: L. Legrand, R. B. 72/2 (1968), pp. 161-87; C. H. Giblin, C. B. Q., 29/1 (1967), pp. 87-101; M. Bailey, Theol. der Gegenwart, 9/4 (1966), pp. 97-200.

[2] Vd. H. A. Blair, c. 2 di A Stranger in the House (London, Darton, Longman & Todd, 1963).

[3] The Manger: Ritual Law and Soteriology, in Theol. 74 (1971), pp. 566-71.

[4] Ibid., ultima nota. Cfr. Mishnah, Parah, III 2-3.

[5] Theol. 74 (1971), p. 569 n. 3. Vi ho fatto riferimento in Jesus's Audience (London 1973), p. 108, basandomi su Targ. ps. Jon., Gen. III 18, oltre che sulle fonti della nota precedente.

[6] Lc. XIII 10-17. Occorre paragonare Lev. XXVI 13 e Ps. CXLV 14; CXLVI 8.

[7] R. Scroggs, The Last Adam (Oxford, Blackwells, 1966).

[8] Il mio The Manger at Bethlehem... in Studia Evangelica, VI, pp. 94-102, ed. H. D. Sparks (di prossima pubblicazione).

[9] S. Krauss, Talmudische Archäologie, II (Leipzig 1911), p. 104.

[10] Filone, Spec. leg. I 148 (Loeb, VIII 182-4) parla del ventre come 'mangiatoia' d'una creatura irrazionale mutuando da Platone, Tim. 70 E

(Loeb, VII 152), dove c'è il quadro famoso delle parti dell'anima soggette agli appetiti, attaccate a parti del corpo corrispondenti all'addome che serve da ' mangiatoia ' per il nutrimento del corpo. È evidente che già al tempo di Platone φάτνη era suscettibile d'essere usata metaforicamente come luogo dove ci si nutra animalescamente. Filone non usa altrimenti la parola.

¹¹ Gli esegeti di I Cor. XI 23-30 si rendono conto di due correnti di opinione intorno all'effetto del sacramento eucaristico, secondo san Paolo, su chi vi partecipa. Secondo la prima opinione (cfr. J. C. Hurd, *Origins of I Corinthians*, London, S. P. C. K., 1965, pp. 135-36) gli elementi hanno un valore magico. Senza un'indagine psicologica o antropologica questo argomento non si può adeguatamente trattare. Ma il mangiare con qualcuno (nei tempi antichi e tuttora nei paesi sottosviluppati) implica la mutua fiducia; e mangiare delle provviste di qualcuno vuol dire mettere chi mangia a disposizione di colui che gli fornisce il pasto, e pertanto può esercitare magia su di lui. A sua volta chi mangia, ricevendo qualcosa che è appartenuto all'altro può danneggiarlo.

Questo è un motivo della benedizione o *eucharistia*, la quale, attribuendo tutti i cibi a Dio, Padre comune, reagisce alle virtualità magiche e ai timori che circolano fra chi dà e chi mangia. In questa luce il dono del donatore stesso come cibo (e tutto di lui, perché tanto la carne quanto il sangue sono offerti) prende un significato del tutto nuovo.

FURTHER ANNOTATION

Tit. The burden of this article is the explanation how φάτνη (*aliter* πάθνη) is also a picnic basket, in which the shepherds recognised the snack which they would share. This very extraordinary glimpse of St. Luke's intellectual equipment, at which even I was offended, has become less objectionable to me as I discovered that in St. Luke's eyes the Holy Eucharist was an immortality-specific. The juridical explanation of the Last Supper which had retained my attention in *LNT* perforce blinded me to this other aspect of which there are many traces, outspokenly in St. John. Once one has seen that Jesus, the Great Shepherd (the Great Fisherman theme [Mk.i.16-20] is neglected for the moment), is on watch when the others have come off watch, and that he meets them at 'picnic-' or 'snack-' time (!), the oddity of the story ceases to prejudice its beauty.

"The Stone that the Builders Rejected"

Cryptic, the quotation (Mt. 21,42; Mk. 12,10–11; Lk. 20,17) from Ps. 118 (Ψ 117), is often supposed not to have had any original connection with the parable of the Wicked Vinedressers, to which all the three gospels (and Thomas also: §§ 65–66) attach it ("the missing reference to the Resurrection"?). By many its context is despaired of. An important study of the saying would support the genuineness of the Matthaean sequel to the saying (Mt. 21,43–44) and would develop the allusions to the old testament[1]. It is important to observe those allusions, for otherwise we are open to the sarcasms of C. G. Montefiore (on Lk. 20,16)[2], who would see Jesus' words as an un-Christian (if traditionally Jewish) attack on his enemies. A thorough survey of the parable and the saying by Fr. Gozzo supports the originality of the connection between parable and saying[3]. No study has explained what was meant by the quotation of the Ps. and that is the task of this paper[4]. First we see what was the literal meaning of the verse in its original setting, next its metaphorical meaning there. From this we proceed to the significance of the verse for the theme of the Messiah and the redemption. We are then ready to examine the midrash, or explanation, of the verse which is actually provided for us by Luke, and we can then consider whether that midrash is likely to have been genuine. The effect and implications of that midrash form the conclusion of the study.

The Literal Meaning

One must study not the Greek version which appears to follow the LXX, still less the other versions which insert a relative pronoun not present in

---

[1] R. Swaeles, "L'Arrière-fond scriptuaire de Matt. xxi. 43 et son lien avec Matt. xxi. 44", N.T.S. VI (1960), 310ff. He points in particular to Theod. Dan. 2,44, and notes that at 43 we are told of a kingdom to be given to others (cf. the parable). I owe the reference to Prof. C. F. D. Moule's Birth of the New Testament (London, 1962), p. 41, n. 3, which contains some comment on the article. The prophetic allusions (long known) were previously handled by, *inter alios*, Loisy, but, as Fr. Swaeles says, the implications were not worked out. So Jeremias, cit. inf. (p. 181, n. 1) at p. 68. P. Sciascia, Lapis Reprobatus (Romae, 1959).

[2] Synoptic Gospels II (London, 1909), p. 1036.

[3] S. M. Gozzo, Disquisitio Critico-exegetica in Parabolam N. Testamenti de Perfidis Vinitoribus, Studia Antoniana 2 (Romae, 1949), pp. 142–179. Is. 8, 14 is referred to at p. 184.

[4] J. Jeremias at ThWNT 4, 279–80 suggests a combination of the Dan. passage with a proverb.

the Hebrew, but the Hebrew original. This says: אבן מאסו הבונים היתה
לראש פנה "A stone the builders rejected: it became the head (or at the
head) of the corner". Attribution of this curiosity or miracle to God's
work follows immediately. The picture which is brought to mind is of a
stone which was unsuitable for its position, and which specialists in the
craft would not have allowed to obtain that position, being somehow placed
there. There has been debate about the 'head of the corner'[1]. The metaphor
from daily life cannot refer to anything rare or obscure. The final stone
which serves to complete the corner of the house, binding two walls together, and which serves also as an ornament, a shelter on the roof[2], and a
part of the parapet which every Jewish house must have[3], is called the
'head of the corner'. A house would have not less than four. City walls and
the Temple would of course have more. The top of the (exterior) staircase
would have one. Naturally, for a people who spent much of their lives on
the roof, the stone in question was not only a sign that the building was
auspiciously completed and still structurally sound, but also a safety-factor.
Once the stones are in position the house is finished and the owners would
be congratulated. But such a stone should be obviously fitted for its many
duties, both in point of weight and otherwise.

The Metaphorical Meaning

The psalm is about David, and therefore inferentially about the Messiah[4].
It is a passover psalm and therefore relates to the redemption theme[5]. David

---

[1] Gozzo collects texts relating to the object at pp. 153—5, op. cit., the conclusion being
correct: lapis coniungens duos perietes angulares in summitate aedificii ut eiusdem per-
fectio et corona. The fullest treatment is at H. Gressman, "Der Eckstein", in Palästinajahr-
buch VI (1910), pp. 38—46. J. Jeremias seems wrong in his supposition that the stone (Bau-
schlußstein) occupied a position in the Temple, above the gate, for this would be an unnecessary limitation of a general term, though the psalm would seem to look to the Temple
particularly. However the term is a common metaphor. The references in Jeremias' article
are invaluable: "Der Eckstein", Angelos. Archiv f. N. T. Zeitg. u. Kult. k. I (1925),
pp. 65—70. Also at ThWNT 4, 277—8. For the roof and building and the stone generally see
L. Oliphant, Haifa or Life in Modern Palestine (Edinburgh/London, 1887), p. 166. G. Dalman, Arbeit und Sitte in Palästina VII (Gütersloh, 1942), pp. 48, 66, 67, 84 is valuable:
Der Eckstein ist es, der die Mauern des Hauses zusammenhält, auf den gebaut wird
(Eph. 2,20f.); so Augustine, De civit. dei, c. 28 (Gozzo, op. cit., 157, n. 128).
[2] Cf. Job 38,6; Is. 28,16; Jer. 51,26; Prov. 21,8; 25,24.
[3] It is part of the ma'akeh, 'railing'. Deut. 22,8 (Blood on the house . . .). Maimonides'
184th affirmative commandment. All parapets must be ten hand-breadths = 40 inches high,
and must withstand the pressure of the human body. The rule covers, by analogy, all traps,
such as defective ladders, pits, etc.
[4] See Midrash on Psalms, Ps. 31, para. 7, trans. W. G. Braude (New Haven, 1959),   *
I, 398. David too was anointed: 1 Sam. 16,12. Note that at Zech. 10,4 (MT) the 'corner-
(stone)' is promised, who is undoubtedly the Messiah.
[5] Naturally it is equally a Tabernacles psalm, and to that extent not peculiarly appropriated to Passover. But the verse we are concerned with figures to this day in Jewish

is the pattern of the Redeemer. The Philistines prefigure the Romans and the 'fellow-travellers' of the latter. David, though a younger brother and lacking in prestige, was chosen to effect that ancient redemption[1]. The specialists, even Samuel, David's own family, Goliath, then Saul and others rejected or overlooked him[2]. Yet he was chosen, evidently by God. David was also the *real* builder of Solomon's Temple[3], and in a real sense the completer of the Jewish state. He was political chief and spiritual leader in one. His eminence was the work of God. The psalmist emphasises that the junior and the unlikely can (as frequently in Jewish history) be the means of God's purpose. "It is wonderful in our eyes." The Hebrew for 'wonderful' is נפלאת which is pointed in the MT as *nifᵉlā't* and in other readings presumably *nifᵉlē't*. The sense is of the great, difficult, wonderful, miraculous. 'Hard', 'difficult to *believe*', is also a possible translation, the notion of joy being possible, but not essential.

The Messianic Aspect

The many instances of junior persons (Abraham, Isaac, Jacob, Joseph, Gideon, etc.) acting as God's chosen instruments lead to a plausible hypothesis that the Messiah will be such as the 'specialists' might reject[4]. The psalm would be attractive to sectarians and others who looked for the redemption of Israel from another quarter than orthodox Judaism or the rulers of Jerusalem. Even our gospel parable of the Prodigal Son may be

---

Passover services. The pains of the Messiah are celebrated in Ps. 116, equally part of the 'great Hallel' (Pss. 113—118): B. T. Pes. 118 a (C. Schoettgenius, Horae Hebraicae et Talmudicae, Dresden/Leipzig, 1733, 311). Ps. 116 is unquestionably the redemption psalm par excellence. On the Hallel and the phrase "Blessed is he that comes . . ." see J. Lightfoot, Hor. Hebr. on Lk. 13,35 (Works, London, 1823, XII, 137 ff.). Rashi (on Mi. 5,1) says that the Messiah is the corner-stone (Schoettgenius, op. cit., 173—4. Jeremias, op. cit., ubi cit.)

[1] This forms a smaller feature of K. Galling's Die Erwählungstraditionen Israels (Beih.Z.A.W. 48: Gießen, 1928) than one could wish, having in view the theme plainly relied upon in 1 Cor. 1, 20. 23—30.

[2] 1 Sam. 16,6 (cf. 7); 17,28.33.42; 18,9.

[3] Thus the Midrash on Psalms explains references to the Temple in the psalms of David, who of course did not build it.

[4] The vocabulary is important. At Acts 4,11 *mā'aṣu* is translated not ἀπεδοκίμασαν but ἐξουθενηθείς, (Delitzsch naturally retranslates as *mᵉ'aṣᵉtem*). At Mk. 9,12 ἐξουδενωθῇ or ἐξουδενηθῇ is read. Yet at Mk. 8,31 = Lk. 9,22 and Lk. 17,25 ἀποδοκιμασθῆναι is used. The two verbs are not found together, for each is a translation of the Heb. *mā'aṣ*. The latter appears at ψ 117,21 and seven times in Jeremiah; the former at 1 Sam. 16,1 (a relevant passage) and ten other times including 1 Sam. 10,19 (where God is rejected) and ψ 52,6 (Ps. 53,5) where God rejects the enemies of the Messiah. See also ψ 88,37 (Ps. 89,38) where God (appears to) reject the Messiah. ἐξουθενέω, a by-form of ἐξουδενόω, translates mā'aṣu (the same word as at Ps. 118,22) at 1 Sam. 8,7 (where the people reject God). ἠρνήσασθε may also translate *mᵉ'aṣtem* at Acts 3,13—14 (cf. LXX Is. 31,7).

seen as a praise of the Church in contrast with the unredeemed Jewish synagogue represented in the guise of the elder brother[1].

The Midrashic Explanation

What did the verse mean if the messianic theme is uppermost? The key is the word 'stone'. In the psalm the stone is David, therefore the Messiah is also the stone. The early Church saw Jesus himself as represented by the stone[2]. Jesus was not, in that image, seen as a foundation stone[3]. He is at the top of the corner, part of the parapet. Why should the Messiah be likened to so unpromising an object? What happens when an unsuitable stone is in that position? There are two possibilities. A recent commentator on Luke says, "the stone which becomes the head of the corner was hardly likely to fall on anyone or to be fallen on . . .", but in fact the unwary may trip over it, because (for example) it is too low, and fall off the roof. Or those who lean against it (as is usual) will push it off (because it is too light) and it will fall on innocent passers-by. Of course if the stone were the key-stone of an arch (which it is not) these things could not happen: but, as it is the stone well-known as *rosh-pinnāh*, either disaster or both can assuredly happen.

This, in dramatically exaggerated language[4], is what is said at Lk. 20,18, our surviving midrash. Peter expounds it at 1 Pet. 2,6–8[5]. The unpromising picture of the Messiah thus offered to us would be unacceptable, had not midrashic technique come to our aid. Because the Holy Spirit describes David as a "stone" who occupies a, shall we say?, mobile situation, we are entitled to look at other mobile stones which do God's work. Is. 8,14–15 is the parallel for the first half of Luke's midrash and Dan. 2,31–45; 7,13–27 for the second. Is. 8 has obviously alarmed Jewish readers. The LXX and the MT are opposed[6]. Yet the result is similar. The possibility that, through

---

[1] A study of the parable is being prepared by the present writer. Note at 1 Pet. 2,10 a 'no people' become the elect.

[2] Acts. 4,11; 1 Pet. 2,4–5.7; Eph. 2,20. From this paper the rabbinical skill of Peter will become evident (n. 5 below).

[3] An additional image, it has served to confuse. Jeremias and Dalman rule out this idea from Ps. 118,22. But *pinnāh* (without ro'sh) may well be a foundation-corner (Is. 28,16; Jer. 51,26: Job 38,6 is ambiguous). See n. 5 below.

[4] συνθλασθήσεται seems too strong, but looks to συντριβήσονται at Is. 8,15. It is curious that *shābar* is not rendered by θλάω in LXX. λικμάω (see Bornkamm, ThWNT 4, 283), apart from Dan. 2,44, alludes to scattering as in the dispersion, a fact that will have been significant after the Roman wars.

[5] Rejection and election are opposites (1 Sam. 16,6–10). At v. 4 Peter shows that Jesus was rejected as a 'living stone', and the preciousness of such a stone is alluded to at v. 7; then comes the citation of the psalm, and then the citation of Is. 8,14, so that the midrash needs only Dan. In the DSS (1 QS VIII, 7) Is. 28,16 is applied to the Council of the Community.

[6] The texts of the MT and the LXX should be compared. The Targum (J. F. Stenning, Targum of Isaiah, Oxford, 1953, 28) wanders between them with adaptations. It contains the woeful prediction at the end of the passage as in the MT. See also Jer. 6,21.

God's action, Israel and the inhabitants of Jerusalem shall stumble, fall and be broken[1], and thereupon be snared and taken, is admitted by both readings. The MT prophesies ruin; the LXX hopes for better: both contain the same notion. In Daniel the stone which is to break the kingdom of iron and clay (surely as good an image for the Roman-Jewish *de facto* condominium as one could have devised?) will be a stone cut out without hands, which ultimately becomes a mountain and fills the earth[2]. The midrash therefore runs as follows: 'the stone which is praised in Ps. 118, and which is David or the Messiah, behaves as a faulty corner-stone will, for those that stumble upon it will be broken (as Is. says) and those upon whom it falls down will be crushed (as in Dan.).' The Messiah will cause people to stumble, and he will be the destruction of the earthly kingdoms (including that of the Jews): it is inevitable.

Some readers might object: midrashic techniques will bring together very diverse scriptural passages, and a far-fetched allusion is tolerated if it will produce edifying or technically plausible results. But to liken a corner-stone on a parapet to a stumbling-block (which is naturally placed in or upon a path or passage) is to stretch the imagination too far. On the contrary, the two objects belong together, and for a most edifying purpose. We have seen that the parapet is the subject of the commandment at Deut. 22,8. If one places the parapet securely one complies with the commandment and has, in this regard, done one's duty by oneself and one's fellow-men. Not to place the parapet, e.g. to place faulty stones where good stones should be, is to be guilty of the same delict as he who places a stumbling-block before the feet of the blind (Lev. 19,14). The lawyers developed a number of propositions for the safety and welfare of the public out of these two texts. The positive commandment, to take care for one's self and others, is Deut. 22,8; the negative commandment, not to be negligent, is Lev. 19,14, and upon these two hangs the whole law of what we would now call negligence. Maimonides' *Mishneh Torah*, Book. XI (Torts), V 11–12 is, because it is translated (New Haven 1954), a convenient example of the technique. Thus, even at a most worldly and everyday level a corner-stone which builders would reject or have rejected presents the same risk or prospect as a stumbling-block.

But we must note the triple pun latent in the verse itself. The word בונים (*BWNYM*) is only the *plene* spelling of *boniym*. *Boniym*, 'builders', from בנה, 'to build', meant (i) actual builders, (ii) metaphorical builders, namely the workers in the Torah, builders in the Torah, the scholars. *Boniym*, an unusual formation from בין or בונ can also mean 'understanders', in the sense of 'interpreters'[3]. Thus the word *boniym*, apart from

---

[1] MT *nishbārū;* Targum *ytbrwn;* LXX συντριβήσονται.

[2] L. Sabourin, Rédemption Sacrificielle (Brussels, Desclée de Brouwer, 1961), 273–4. Dan. 2,34 ff. messianically interpreted in first-cent. Judaism: Jeremias, ThWNT 4, 276.

[3] In Deut. 32,10b *yᵉbonᵉnehū* "cared for" is construed in Siphre as meaning that the people shall watch, look into the Torah for all possible midrashim. In Neh. 8,8 *va-yāviynū*

its context, could mean 'scholars' by two independent derivations. And so the verse is actually taken at Acts 4, 5–11 (. . . the stone which was rejected *by you*, i. e. the rulers and elders and scribes, the builders . . .). There is a famous pun on *BNYCH* at Is. 54, 13. Contemporaries of the apostles were prepared to read not *bānayich*, 'thy children', but *bwnych* (*bonayich*), 'thy builders' (as the context allows)[1] in the sense, not of literal builders, but 'scholars'. *Boniym* as it stands in Ps. 118, 22 can therefore mean, 'builders', 'understanders', 'scholars'. David, of course, had been the object of multiple rejections of various sorts, including rejection by 'understanders'.   *

Yet if we read the verse immediately after the parable of the Vinedressers another possibility clamours for attention. The word *pinnāh*, 'corner', can refer to the princes, rulers of the people[2]. The metonymy is simple and obvious. David was ultimately a leader, but that was because God rejected Saul, who himself repeatedly (afterwards) rejected David and in fact tried to kill him (1 Sam. 16,1; 18,12.29, etc.). David's story involves the rejection of David's enemies by God. Let us render the verse, "The stone the builders (i. e. God) rejected, that has (somehow) become the head of the corner (the governing clique)". The government has been condemned by God. The result is a double rejection: the 'understanders' reject Jesus and God rejects them. The stone must fall! This is entirely justified by Ps. 118,8–9: 'It is better to trust in the Lord than to put confidence in man . . . than to put confidence in princes (or nobles).' Of course in the normal way one puts confidence in the parapet, most of all in the top corner stone. But in this case it does not deserve confidence, for very special reasons.

The Parable, the Saying, the Midrash and the Sequel

The coincidence of the text of the psalm in its natural meaning and its metaphorical meaning with the prophecies of Isaiah and Daniel, all con-

---

means "interpreted". In the DSS *heviyn* is used to mean "interpret". See also Midr. R. on Gen. § 34 on 8,20. I am obliged to Dr. M. Gertner for an explanation of these terms. He refers me also to Siphre p. 133 where the phrase *boniym ba-Torah*, "builders *in* the Law", occurs.   *

[1] R. Eleazar b. Azariah would read the text thus to make it certain that scholars are intended. B. T., Tamid 32b = Sonc. trans., 29. This Eleazar was head of the school at Jabneh alternately with R. Gamaliel II (c. A. D. 90–130, earlier period). His life therefore overlapped with the apostles. The same dictum is attributed at B.T., Ber. 64a to R. Eleazar in the name of R. Ḥanina (ben Dosa), a contemporary of Joḥanan ben Zakkai. The pun is therefore of very respectable age. Another example, also justified by the immediate context, occurs at Is. 49,17 (cf. the DSS reading: D. Flusser at Textus, Heb. Univ. Bible Proj., 1962, 140–142; Bible de Jérusalem ad loc.). The Targum has "children" at Is. 54,13, but must have read "builders" at 49,17 (Stenning, op. cit., p. xix). See Jastrow, Dict. (New York, 1950), 176.

[2] *Pinnāh* absolutely as a battlement or parapet of a tower or housetop: Zeph. 1,16; 3,6; 2 Chr. 26,15; Gesenius compares Sir. 1,2. *Pinnāh* as a chief or leader: Jud. 20,2; 1 Sam. 14,38; Is. 19,13; cf. Zech. 10,4 MT (cited at p. 181, n. 4 above). DSS: p. 188, n. 5.

nected with the Messiah, would suit Jesus' situation well. At a passover time he is rejected by the leaders of the people, who are the 'understanders', the 'scholars' of the time. The psalm, as it were, proves that the Messiah will be rejected. But those who reject him and their kingdom are themselves rejected and will be swept away by him. Paradoxically the people must rejoice! Not at the removal of the Romans, leaving the 'understanders' in full possession, but a total removal of an altogether unexpected character. The verse 'this was the Lord's doing', etc. (Mk. 12,11) need not actually have been quoted, unless it was to give an especial edge to that passage. In ordinary circumstances, the psalm being so well known, the quotation of v. 22 would have implied the remainder. One perhaps ought to add that in view of the prophetic overtones and the irony of the scene it is not an inappropriate citation or allusion, whether as a quotation or a reference in the mouth of Jesus, as some have supposed[1].

The parable of the Vinedressers has been studied juridically elsewhere[2]. The implications are evidently wider than direct references to Jesus, but the Church has naturally seen, or imagined it saw, the son in the parable as Jesus[3]. In any event those who reject God God himself rejects. The replacement of the Vinedressers is the direct result of their disobedience and fraud. The saying about the stone fits, taken in both ways, and better in both ways than in either separately. The parable is thus applied to the coming of the Messiah. He will turn the 'specialists' out, because of the pattern of David's triumph over his rejecters and also because the scribes and priests were guilty of disobedience and fraud.

Luke and Matthew agree that it was because of the quotation from the psalm, sharpened and pointed by some interpretation which is partly revealed to us in Luke only, that the Jewish leaders knew that the parable was aimed at them.

Luke emphasises that from that moment, when a direct attack was made upon them, they determined to make away with Jesus. The irony is striking. The scholars must at that moment reject Jesus because at that moment he applies the scriptural prophecies to that effect. The prophecies, the psalm, the occasion and the situation all converge. He knows that they reject him, and they thereupon reject him. It is foretold that the Messiah functions when he is rejected by the 'builders-understanders'. And they have no choice but to be rejected by God, because that stage must occur before the reign of the Messiah may commence.

---

[1] D. E. Nineham, The Gospel of St. Mark (London, 1963), 313.

[2] Rev. Int. Dr. Ant., 3rd. ser., 10 (1963), 11—41.

[3] Note the sketch of the parable by Prof. J. Blinzler, Der Prozeß Jesu, 3rd edn. (Regensburg, 1960), 321—2.

FURTHER ANNOTATIONS

p. [181], n. 4. Ps. cxviii.22 was recited by Yishai (Jesse): b. Pes. 119a.

p. [185], l. 8. On the ambiguity of sons/builders see the text of Is. lxii.5. It is of interest that even the feminine form of this pun is evidenced. Midr. R. Exod. XXIII.10 = Sonc. 288, and Midr. R. Cant. I, §5 (p. 53) show that at S.S. i.5 for $b^e not$ (daughters) we should read *bānôt* (builders). J. M. Ford, *NT* 9 (1967), 111.

p. [185], end of n. 3 on p. 184. 'Builders' (*bannā'îm*) means disciples or scholars (Danby, 'edifiers'; cf. Matt. xvi.18, 2 Cor. x.8, xiii.10): Mishnah, *Miqwaot* IX.6. See b. Shab. 114a, Ber. 64a.

"You build the Tombs of the Prophets"
(Lk. 11,47—51, Mt. 23,29—31)

This sadly cryptic passage abounds in difficulties, but in this short paper some of them it is my hope to remove. At first it should be noted that the Matthaean version constitutes an obvious attempt to make intelligible some sayings of Jesus which could, perhaps, only be clarified by conjecture at his time. It may be however that Matthew has preserved not only a possible but also a sound understanding of the saying.

A literal translation of the Lucan passage reveals the problems without comment: 'Woe to you, for you build the tombs of the prophets, but your fathers slew them. Therefore you are witnesses and you approve the works of your fathers, for they killed them, and you are building. This is why the wisdom of God said . . . in order that the blood of all the prophets poured out . . . may be required from this generation. Yes, I say to you, it shall be required from this generation.' There is apparently no logic in these statements.

To obtain light it is necessary to know something about tomb-building and the implications of it, about the blood-feud, and about midrashic interpretation and puns. As for the latter, we have already[1] seen that puns in connection with the Hebrew root *BYN* were matter for serious thought.

Building tombs

There is no doubt but that Jews believed that building monuments over the graves of the pious was in itself sinful[2]. The Hellenistic world would of course take another view of tombs and monument-building, and spending

---

[1] Above pp. 184—5.
[2] Pal. T., Sheḳ. II, 47 a (M. Schwab trans., V, 275). R. Nathan. At Midr. R. Gen. LXXXII, 10 = Sonc. trans. 760 the saying is referred to R. Simeon b. Gamaliel (c. A.D. 140—165). One notes its Heb. form which looks old: אֵין עוֹשִׂין נְפָשׁוֹת לְצַדִּיקִים דִּבְרֵיהֶם הֵם לְכָרוֹנֵיהֶם non exstruunt μνημεῖα ((nᵉfāshot)) justorum nam dicta eorum sunt memoria eorum. Note that Matthew's addition (?) καὶ κοσμεῖτε τὰ μνημεῖα τῶν δικαίων coincides partially with לְצַדִּיקִים at v. 29 c. The rule is still part of Jewish law, Maimonides, Mishneh Torāh XIV (Judges), IV 4,4 (trans., Hershman, New Haven 1949), 174. The point escaped even Origen, In Matth. Comm. Ser. §§ 25—7, Migne, P. G. 13, coll. 1630—6. The saying is noted by T. Keim, Hist. of Jesus of Nazara, trans. Ransom, V

money on tombs was an example of cultural awareness as well as conspicuous consumption. Those who would have liked to see Jerusalem adorned
like a Hellenistic city would have approved of schemes to build tombs for
the heroes of the nation, the prophets[1]. But at the same time it would be
accepted that in building tombs to righteous people one was as it were
denying their sanctity, for the deeds of the righteous are their memorial.
In a sense construction of tombs of prophets is not so much, as is usually
said, worship of the dead while one neglects the living word, as denial of the
importance of that word, which after all is the prophets' 'deeds'.

But the saying of Jesus, though it clearly condemns such building, does not
turn upon a rational reflection of this character. The topic is vengeance, God's
vengeance for the blood of all the prophets, and the interjection of Lk.11,51
and Mt. 23,35b–c, is evidently intended to show that by prophets is meant all
those (including Abel) whose blood *so far* cried out to God for vengeance.

Oriental nations were familiar with the notion of 'blood', i. e. guiltiness
of someone's murder, passing from one person to another[2]. One could accept
responsibility, an altogether unseemly notion, for the death of someone
whose murder one was urging upon the actual doer, who might or might not
suppose that thereby his own guilt was eliminated[3]. One might become
vicariously liable for the death of another person by actions admitting
liability. To the subjects of blood-guiltiness and the blood-feud we return.
Meanwhile it will be accepted that vengeance would fall, if fall it must, upon
those who have meanwhile accepted liability.

A key to the thread of ideas is certainly asked for. Two statements are
made, which the scribes and Pharisees would not hesitate to accept. First
that they are building tombs, one motive for which we have guessed, and
another we shall conjecture presently. Secondly that they are the sons of
those who committed the murders. That prophets were murdered seems to
have been an article of belief[4], independently of any actual proof of such
murders, and no doubt there was haggadic material to support the notion

---

(London 1881), 215 n. 2; also I. Abrahams, Studies in Pharisaism and the Gospels, II
(Cambridge 1924), 29 n. 5; and set out at P. Billerbeck, Kommentar z. N. T. aus Talm. u.
Midr. I (München 1926/1961), 938. The practice was certainly known temp. Chr.: Jos.,
Con. Ap. II, 26/27, 205. The Hellenistic fashion was objectionable by reason of inscriptions
(cf. 4 Macc. 17,8–10) and other adornment. Typical is the quandary of W. Beilner, Christus
u. die Pharisäer (Wien 1959), 22–4.

[1] J. Jeremias, Heiligengräber in Jesu Umwelt (Mt. 23,29; Lk. 11,47) (Göttingen 1958).
Buildings of the time of Herod the Great were monuments, not graves. On Herod's honour-
ing the patriarchs at Hebron see pp. 92 ff. On Herod's ἱλαστήριον μνῆμα see Jos., Ant. 16,182
and here p. 121. Jewish 'graves of saints' are dealt with at p. 49.

[2] E. g., 1 K. 2,32; 33,37; Jer. 26,15; Acts 5,28. K. Koch, ZThK 52 (1955), 1–42;
V.T. 12 (1962), 396–416; H. Graf Reventlow, V.T. 10 (1960), 311–327.

[3] E. g., Mt. 27,25; Acts 18,6. Cf. 2 Sam. 3, 26–31.

[4] 1 Thess. 2,15; Acts 7,52; Mt. 5,12; 1 K. 19,10; Jer. 2,30. For an instance: Jer. 33,22
(LXX). H. J. Schoeps, Die jüdischen Prophetenmorde (Uppsala, 1943). For its significance
to the church see R. Schippers, N.T. 8 (1966), 230–4.

which is now out of sight. As for the persons addressed being 'sons', this would not be disputed, since the word only means membership of the same clan, company, or ethnic group. Naturally there are overtones of 'like father like son', but this need not be stressed (as it usually is) at this point in the argument. Now, after passing from the statements which Pharisees would accept, we come to statements which *we* at any rate cannot accept at first sight: *therefore*, the text says, they are witnesses and approve the works of their fathers. By implication they are not approving the deeds of the righteous who have been slain, but that is a side-implication and need not detain us. Why should *builders* be witnesses, and approvers?

It is obvious that by merely building a tomb one neither bears witness to the death or the manner of it nor approves of it. Matthew has stumbled, it would seem, at the suggestion, and turns the expression in a vain attempt to make it digestible. But if we look at the expression in Hebrew, *boniyn lahem nᵉfāshot*, 'We build tombs for them', the ill-omened words immediately bring numerous ideas to mind. The meaning amounts to this: – by saying that they (the collectors of funds for this pseudo-charity?) are building the tombs of persons admittedly murdered they reveal, unawares, their own predicament.

The puns hidden in the expression

The word *boniyn* (*boniym*), 'builders' can be read equally 'understanders'. This was explained above[1]. *Boniym*, 'understanders', includes scholars, especially in the Torah. *Boniym*, 'we understand', 'we know', can also mean 'we know all about it'. Thorough comprehenders are also *boniym*. *Bāniym* would be more acceptable grammatically: see below. There are degrees of knowledge and comprehension, from mere witnessing (for example) to deliberate contemplation, or to full approval. The saying attributed to Jesus, not content with drawing out the *witness* element, insists on the objectionable type of witness, i. e. the silent participator who consents by being a passive spectator[2]. But, beyond this, the word *boniym* is made to produce independently the *two* ideas, because the word *nefashot* does not mean so much *tombs*, as corpses, i. e. murders! *Nefesh*, as is well known, means (i) a tomb (presumably because the dead is supposed to inhabit it), and (ii) the spirit or the blood that is the life, and also the formerly live body when dead[3]. *Nefesh* means blood in a living person, and the corpse of a dead

---

[1] At pp. 184—5.

[2] By-play with μάρτυρες, so that μάρτυρες ἔστε = *atem boniym* (as if from *BWN*) becomes μαρτυρεῖτε ἑαυτοῖς (dativus incommodi) = *meʿiydiym* may have been justified by the form of the saying; but note that *boniym* does not suggest evidence (as does μάρτυρες), and οἰκοδομεῖτε certainly = *boniym*

[3] Jastrow, Dict., 926—7. *nefesh* = tomb explains the use of ψυχή in the same sense: B. Lifshitz, Zeits. d. Deut. Palästina-Vereins 76 (1960), 159—60. Gesenius, Dict., 17th edn., 515 col. 1: *nefesh* 4 d), esp. Lev. 19,28; 22,4; Num. 5,2; 9,6. 7.10; 19,13.

one. A witness of a *nefesh* is a witness in a capital case, because the defendant's life is in issue.

The ill-fated admission, 'We are building tombs for them', which sounds an indication of piety, is in fact a bundle of dreadful admissions. First it shows that the builders *knowingly* do what is in any case wicked (building tombs of the righteous); secondly they know all about the deaths of the persons commemorated with a knowledge which they could only have in a spiritual, but none the less effectual sense; thirdly, because they *contemplate* those deaths they accept them and do not repudiate them.

Blood-guiltiness

The concept of 'seeking-out', i. e. 'requiring' blood is too well testified to need comment[1]. It is to this that Luke refers at 11,50–51, and the idea in Matthew, that the blood 'comes' upon someone (23,35–36) is not different in essentials[2]. There is no doubt that if a servant of God is put to death, or anyone belonging to God for that matter (hence the reference to Abel, in whose case the 'crying out' of blood arose for the first time and is memorably documented)[3] God will 'require' the blood, or he must be appeased. Failing appeasement, sooner or latter the vengeance will fall. Between men vicarious punishment is deprecated (Deut. 24,16) but God's vengeance reaches far into the generations (Ex. 20,5; 34,7; Num. 14,18; Deut. 5,9). The generation of Jesus might or might not be able to take advantage of Jesus' atoning sacrifice, depending upon individuals' response to the occasion. No doubt the Church saw all these prophecies of doom as pointers to the Jewish War. But in fact the comment on the tomb-building might have arisen without any such allusion or prophetic vision.

The rules of the blood-feud are very well known, as the institution is abundantly documented in the bible itself[4] and is a living institution capable of being investigated and described[5]. Some of its notions seem immortal. The loss of a blood-brother creates an obligation in his kindred to seek a life from (it makes little difference) the killer or one of the killer's kin-group. If the latter do not hasten to make composition during the time when the blood 'boils' the victim's kindred are entitled to take vengeance without more ado. This relationship can be cemented by mutual killings and the

---

[1] Gen. 42,22; Deut. 32,43; 2 Sam. 4,11; 2 K. 9,7; Ps. 9,12; 79,10; Ez. 3,18 ; 33,6.8.

[2] Deut. 21,8–9; 22,8.

[3] Gen. 4,10 (with 11 — blood on the ground — cf. Mt. 23,35 a ἐκχυννόμενον ἐπὶ τῆς γῆς: Num. 35,33; 2 Chr. 22,8). Heb. 12,24. Job. 16,18.

[4] E. Merz, Die Blutrache bei den Israeliten (BzWAT. 20: Leipzig 1916) is the leading work. S. Jampel, "Blutrache", Jüd. Lex. 1 (1927); J. D. Prince and L. Ginzberg, "Avenger of Blood", Jew. Encyc. 2 (1925); G. Schrenk, ἐκδικέω etc., ThWNT, 2 (1935).

[5] M. J. L. Hardy, Blood Feuds and the Payment of Blood Money in the Middle East (Leiden, 1963) and biblio. there given.

affair can drag on until the source of the dispute is forgotten. Jewish orthodox theory deprecated the exaction of 'blood-money'[1], but there can be little doubt but that the practice continued and was well known in the time of Jesus as it is today in the Islamic world. The person entitled to reparation is of course the owner, as it were, of the victim, viz. his tribe, or his patron. A wretched situation develops when one brother kills his only brother, whereupon the parents could be rendered childless[2]. That God would require the blood of his murdered servants was known by putting together three pieces of information, namely that God will require blood, that God sent to the Jews all his servants the prophets (Jer. 7,25b), and that prophets had been murdered. Exactly this combination of ideas occurs at 2 Esd. 1,32, and the notion of sending the servants, namely the prophets, who have not been listened to, appears again at 2 Esd. 2,1; 7,60. The fact that the Ezra Apocalypse is Judaeo-Christian in inspiration does not deprive it of value as evidence of early Christian midrashic technique, and, as we shall see, it can afford some check upon the Matthaean version of the saying. 2 Esd. leaves us in no doubt, for example, but that God will require the blood of the ancient (not specifically Christian) "servants" presently, as it were. Since the blood of those servants could not be required from the guilty persons themselves, according to the traditions of the blood-feud the descendants of the guilty parties, if they were still members of the same tribe, as it were, must pay the penalty. If they *truly* repent they will not bear their ancestors' iniquity (Ez. 18,13−20).

The words of Jeremiah mean that because the Jews did not listen to the prophets they will be killed (by their enemies) and driven away (into exile). In fact a serious misunderstanding has arisen[3]. It has been assumed that the Matthaean version at Mt. 23,34 with its difficult sequel was more original than the Lucan counterpart. The Matthaean version of Jesus' saying raises difficulties which seem insurmountable without either the removal of the passage as an interpolation or the discovery of a hitherto unknown Jewish midrash: whereas, on the contrary, the Lucan version makes sense. The ἐξ αὐτῶν in v. 49c refers back to the εἰς αὐτούς of 49b. Jesus' saying is apparently a midrashic combination of Jer. 7,25 with Jer. 29,18−20 (cf. the same phrase at 2 Chr. 36,15ff.; LXX Jer. 33,5). Whereas we have supposed that the persons to be killed and persecuted would be the prophets, etc. (so Mt. 23,34b), in reality what is meant is that Jer. 29,18 will be

---

[1] Num. 35,19−27.31.32−4 (the basic provision being Gen. 9,6); Deut. 6,12; Josh. 20; 2 Sam. 14,11 (below).

[2] 2 Sam. 14,5−7.11 is valuable. They would have been bought off but for the hope of an inheritance.

[3] All trans. except the Vulg. suppose that ἐξ αὐτῶν = ἐκ προφητῶν καὶ ἀποστόλων and that αὐτούς provides the subject of ἀποκτενοῦσιν. But this is an impersonal construction, the unexpressed subject being God, as at Lk. 6,38; 12,20; 16,9 (Blass-Debrunner-Funk, Greek Gramm. of the N. T., Cambridge/Chicago 1961, § 130(2)).

worked out on the Jews of Jesus' generation, because, as Jeremiah says, they did not listen to the prophets sent to them. The Jews of this (*sic*) generation join with the murderers of the prophets in their actions (which conform to their scholarship), and in their doom!

The blood-guiltiness could have been avoided had the scribes and others so acted as to repudiate their 'parentage'. But, just as *boniym* means 'builders' and 'scholars', so the similar-sounding word *bāniym*, written identically, means 'understanders' or 'scholars' (from the root בין), *and* 'sons'. We have seen the pun at Is. 54,13, discussed above[1]. The double-reading, known in Jesus' time, of children/builders at Is. 49,17[2], justified Professor M. Black[3] and A. R. C. Leaney after him[4] in suggesting that there is a pun of Jesus' making here between *boniym* (builders) and *bāniym* (sons). As we *
shall see, it is not quite certain whether the pun is strictly speaking of Jesus' own making. However all three claims, to be builders, scholars and sons are figuratively appropriate, for the following reason.

The context

After prophets had ceased to come, or, for a different reason, when John the Baptist came, fear of divine vengeance for the murder of prophets must have arisen. As Matthew seems to have had reason to believe (though, as usual, he is glossing the text in front of him), people professed to deplore what had happened. But, if one cared to see their action in that light (and one must remember that admissions by actions told heavily in those legally-minded days), they spent on tombs, as if they were the representatives of the victims, money which tribesmen would have paid as compensation to an 'avenger of blood'. Those who do not repudiate admit. Those who stand by a crime assume responsibility (they stand by the blood: Lev. 19,16), as did Paul[5]. To spend money on a tomb, when that money was incapable of being paid as compensation, would have been correct practice at Jewish law[6]. The actions therefore confirmed the unconscious admission concealed in the description of themselves by the learned as 'builders'.

The context deals with hypocrisy. Perhaps this Hellenistic activity of tomb-building, a cultural aberration, was hypocritical. It seemed to bear

---

[1] At p. 184.

[2] Above, p. 185, n. 1. But see also H. M. Orlinsky, "Qumran and the Present State of Old Testament text studies", J.B.L. 78 (1959), 26ff., where Tarbiz 24,1 (Oct. 1954), 4–8 (Eng. summ. at pp. i–ii) is cited. Cod. Petrop. does not read (i) *bonāyich* as Kittel suggests at Is. 49,17 but in fact (ii) *bānāyich* as does the M. T. Theod. and Aq. read (i), Symm. (ii), and the Targ., in the author's view, shows both traditions (*sed quaere?*).

[3] Aramaic Approach, 2nd edn. (Oxford, 1954), 11–12.

[4] Comm. on the Gospel acc. to St. Luke (London, 1958), 194.

[5] Acts 7,58; 8,1; 22,20.

[6] Mishnāh, Sheḳ. II 5 (Danby, Mishnah, Oxford, 1933, 154. Billerbeck, ubi cit.). *Nefesh* is distinguished from *ḳever:* Jastrow, op. cit., 926, col. 1.

out the scriptural prophecy that the blood would be 'required'. It could naturally be required only from the descendants of the killers. If the Jews had ceased to rely upon the tradition of their 'fathers' (cf. Jer. 7,26; 16,12), they could have averted the vengeance. The rabbinical mind, fastening upon the ill-omened coincidence of 'building', 'understanding' and 'sons' in the word *boniym/bāniym*, has devastatingly coped with an aspect of 'respectable' Jewish activity.

But it may be asked, in Is. at two places we have found *boniym* treated punningly, in each case with the evident permission of the immediate context. The sacred text permits such treatment. Given the word in an authoritative place, no doubt such interpretations are open to a scholar. But can one play in this fashion with a casual self-description by, shall we say, people coming round with a collecting-purse? The objection would be valid but for a suspicion that the original proposition was not quite as we find it in either Luke or Matthew. The scholars of Jesus' time and later called themselves 'builders', 'builders in the Torah'. They applied to themselves, one may suspect, the passages in the prophets which speak of the builders of Jerusalem. They were certainly proud of their scholarship, as if it were constructive as well as laborious. Perhaps Jesus said something like this: "You say you are the builders (and I am knocking down your structure with my unexpected interpretations of the Torah . . .). Of what are you the builders? You are building the tombs of the prophets . . ." This by no means rules out the likelihood that such tombs were being constructed or that collections were being made for such work. On the contrary, these would add point to the saying[1].

---

[1] I am obliged to Prof. J. Jeremias for suggestions during a correspondence of April, 1964. He wrote, "Ich würde meinen, da Matthäus 23 Vers 32 von entscheidender Bedeutung ist und überhaupt erst den Schlüssel gibt: die Angeredeten stehen selbst im Begriff, den letzten Gottes-Propheten zu morden." On whether the attack was on Pharisees or scribes see Jerusalem z. Z. Jesu, 3rd. edn. (Göttingen, 1962), 287–8. Did Jesus' words acquire a new sense when he himself became mankind's *go'el*? The question must be left over.

FURTHER ANNOTATIONS

Tit. S. *R.E.J.* 62 (1911), 201-15. On the murders of the prophets : H. J. Schoeps, *Die jüdischen Prophetenmorde* (Uppsala, 1943). Slaying prophets : Neh. ix.26. On the tombs of the prophets : M. Goulder, *Midrash and Lection*, 427. On the cult of tombs : J. Jeremias, 'Drei weitere spätjüdische Heiligengräbe,' *ZNW* 52 (1961), 95-101. The balance of the phrases in this accusation is pointed out by O. Linton, 'Le parallelismus membrorum dans le N.T.,' *Mélanges B. Rigaux* (Gembloux, 1970), 498. The want of logic (apparently!) in the accusation was pointed out long ago by Scultetus : *tu sepeliisti ergo occidisti : imo si occidissem non sepeliissem.* The present article intended to refute that. H. Cousin, 'Sépulture criminelle et sépulture prophétique,' *RB* 81/3 (1974), 375-93, is important for the question of the prophet's tombs, and the burial of martyrs generally. S. T. Lachs, 'On Matthew 23:27-28,' H.T.R. 63 (1975), 385-8, referring to b. Ber. 28a, surmises that whitewashed ossuaries are what is intended, and this is an interesting but inconclusive use of a doubtful apothegm.

p. [187], n. 2. Conspicuous monuments were not acceptable : Jos., *c.Ap.* ii, 205. For the righteous no monument need be erected : Maim., M.T. XIV.iv.4,4 (trans., p. 174). The Greek interest in monuments is reflected in Megasthenes' comment that the (righteous?) Indians knew no monuments : Arrian, *Ind.* x (trans., 209).

p. [189], n. 3. Cf. Hag. ii.14 LXX.

p. [192], l. 12. Such punning is not foreign to the literature : see *ro'îm/rā'îm* at Is. lvi.11.

Gesù maestro della legge   *

1. L'idea corrente vuole che Gesù non fosse maestro di legge
e nemmeno un avvocato o giurista, in breve, che si interessasse di
questioni morali e non giuridiche. Critico questa idea. Anzitutto
spiegherò donde essa nasca e che cosa la conforti. Dopo una pre-
messa metodologica porrò la domanda di che cosa fosse la legge nel-
l'ambiente ebraico al tempo di Gesù, per tentar di spiegare quindi
quale fosse in esso il ruolo d'un maestro religioso. Il carattere del-
l'insegnamento di Gesù è esaminato di seguito, per proporre il
quesito: fino a che punto si aspettava egli d'esser preso sul serio?
in qual misura va inteso alla lettera? Concludo con un commento
alle cosiddette antitesi del sermone della montagna, affermando che
esso costituisce un programma giuridicamente intelligibile, con in-
trinseche implicazioni e conseguenze nelle due sfere della politica
interna e delle relazioni internazionali.

A. L'idea che Gesù non fosse un giurista

2. Certi passi del Nuovo Testamento sono contrari all'idea
che Gesù si interessasse della legge, sia di quella del suo tempo
e dell'epoca sua, che in generale. Ricusò di fare da arbitro, essendo l'arbitro uno che « divide » (in Lc. XII 13-14: « Gli disse uno
della folla: – Maestro, di' a mio fratello che divida con me l'ere-

dità. – Ma egli rispose: – Uomo, chi mi ha costituito giudice o arbitro sopra di voi? – »).

Allorquando fu accostato in qualità di giurisperito, trascurò la questione legale (cfr. il mio *Law in the New Testament*, 1970, c. 7) e fornì una risposta puramente morale (Gio. VIII 11: « Disse allora Gesù: – Neppure io ti condanno: va' e d'ora innanzi non peccar più – »). Gesù giunge come giudice soltanto in un senso escatologico (Gio. VIII 15-16: « Voi giudicate secondo la carne, io non giudico nessuno; e anche se giudico, il mio giudizio è vero, perché non sono solo, ma io e il Padre che mi ha mandato »). Gesù tratta la legge mosaica come se le fosse estraneo (o così ci indurrebbe a credere San Giovanni): « ... nella vostra Legge sta scritto... » (VIII 17). Da San Paolo apprendiamo che Gesù, a differenza dei rabbini o dei farisei, faceva scarsa attenzione alla casistica (I Cor. VII 10,25). San Giovanni prospetta Gesù che rivendica decisamente i diritti del Padre sfidando il mondo, che per lui è legalmente nel giusto, moralmente nel torto: « ... chi non entra per la porta nell'ovile delle pecore, ma vi sale da qualche altra parte, questi è un ladro e un predone » (X 1).

Gesù è sarcastico nei confronti degli avvocati (« Guardatevi dagli scribi che amano passeggiare in lunghe vesti, esser salutati nelle piazze... », Mc. XII 38) e addebita loro ipocrisia e dolo (« ... che divorano le case delle vedove », Mc. XII 40; cfr. *Novum Testamentum*, 14, 1972, 1-9). La chiesa primitiva era sicura che Gesù fosse indifferente allo stato mondano, cioè al sistema giuridico in cui gli uomini vivono, rispettandolo soltanto quale strumento di punizione divina: « Ogni persona sia sottoposta alle podestà superiori: perciocché non v'è podestà se non da Dio; e le podestà che sono da Dio ordinate. Talché chi resiste alla podestà resiste all'ordine di Dio e quelli che vi resistono ne riceveranno giudizio sopra loro » (Rom. XIII 1-2; vedi anche I Pet. II 13-15).

3. Tanto la Chiesa cattolica che le protestanti si accontentano di ravvisare in Gesù l'elargitore della grazia di Dio e non il mediatore della legge, quale che questa sia: « Perché la legge fu data per mezzo di Mosè; la grazia e la verità son venute per mezzo di Gesù Cristo » (Gio. I 17). La legge, anche quella divina, è del tutto inflessibile, e quanto meno ne troviamo nella Cristianità, con tanta più libertà la Chiesa può offrire di epoca in epoca, le sue soluzioni ai problemi umani. È storicamente noto che allo Spirito Santo si affidarono in vasta misura i primi cristiani per giustificare i loro contegni antinomiani, e lo Spirito Santo è un mezzo fortemente autenticato di oltrepassare la teologia ebraica tradizionale basata sulla Torah, la legge di Mosè. La Chiesa ritiene di possedere lo Spirito Santo e d'esserne guidata, e non c'è numero di con-

traddizioni fra i pretesi possessori che li possa rendere meno avversi ad un'interpretazione giuridica del Vangelo. I teologi protestanti sono particolarmente ostili a questa possibilità, poiché per loro lo Spirito Santo non è di fatto attribuito ad un'istituzione, la Chiesa, bensì al corpo attuale dei teologi (per diversi che siano tra loro) e la fonte dell'ispirazione è per loro il solo testo scritturale; la « giustificazione per fede » significa giustificazione per la fede nelle interpretazioni contrastanti che del Vangelo dànno i teologi. Se il silenzio di Gesù risulta comprensivo, totale e (almeno) ambiguo, resta loro spazio sufficiente alla loro abilità e intelligenza. Inoltre i teologi, benché ci tengano ad avere una legge ecclesiastica chiara e definita per le loro questioni interne, sono gelosi della legge come fenomeno esterno, dato che i suoi presupposti restano incompatibili con quelli della teologia e coloro che la praticano sono un polo rivale di potere e prestigio. Gli atteggiamenti degli avvocati verso la teologia inclinano allo scetticismo, perché la flessibilità e fecondità pregiate fra i teologi, i giuristi sono portati a considerarle una fonte di insicurezza e d'errore.

B. Metodologia

4. È arduo discutere dei testi che lumeggiano il pensiero di Gesù senza stabilirne l'autenticità. I critici della redazione evangelica sono ossessionati dall'idea che, se le parole non possono essere ricondotte positivamente a Gesù, debbano attribuirsi alla (cosiddetta) Chiesa primitiva. Essi ignorano che così si attribuisce alla Chiesa delle origini una abilità ed una forza mentale pari alla loro, se non maggiore, e non indugiano a fornirne la prova. I critici della redazione testuale sostengono che ciò che i critici delle forme chiamano « detti dichiarativi » nonché il sermone della montagna furono composti in una temperie ellenistico-ebraica o perfino pagano-ellenistica nella quale ben pochi detti sapienzali di Gesù sarebbero stati tramandati per tradizione. Gli argomenti a pro di tale ricostruzione sono essi stessi ipotetici, come ad esempio che San Marco scrivesse a Roma o che tutti gli scontri coi farisei nei Vangeli non riflettano la vita reale di Gesù bensì i problemi insorti fra i primi cristiani e gli ebrei ortodossi (e naturalmente i critici li attribuiscono a una data eccessivamente tarda). Non c'è dubbio che occorre dar ragione delle discrepanze fra i Vangeli; ma non ne consegue che la loro chiave sia nel vario grado d'ignoranza d'una Chiesa storicamente lontana dalle reminiscenze degli alunni di Gesù: c'è una altra possibilità, cioè che i detti, i dibattiti, gli atti ricordati, erano, nel tempo in cui ebbero luogo, deliberatamente ambigui e aperti a varie interpretazioni.

5. Gli argomenti a pro delle opinioni dei critici della redazione testuale trascurano certi fatti che riducono la loro ricostruzione a qualcosa di soltanto possibile (ho trovato *Die Gesetzeauslegung Jesu* di Klaus Berger una guida preziosa alle loro idee). I fatti sono i seguenti: (a) l'importanza data a taluni dei dieci comandamenti negli ambienti ebraici ellenistici non era necessariamente esclusa in Israele; (b) l'importanza notevole data nella diaspora all'apocalittica non era esclusa in Israele; (c) l'autorità personale di Gesù è rilevata in tutti i Vangeli, negli Atti e nelle epistole di San Paolo e non può essere un'invenzione delle chiese cristiane gentili; (d) per quanto la combinazione di questi temi possa campiacere o risultare adatta all'ebraismo della diaspora ed ai suoi convertiti gentili, su tutti i suoi piani la letteratura neotestamentaria mostra Gesù che attua da solo questa combinazione nel Suo primo ministero. Inoltre i rotoli del Mar Morto comprovano che l'ebraismo non-rabbinico, il fervore apocalittico ed un ritorno millenaristico antigerarchico alla « vera » Torah di Mosè, erano tutti ben impiantati nel cuore della Giudea. Si sono scoperte a Qumran copie della versione dei Settanta e ciò prova che gli aspetti midrascici di essa ed il suo vocabolario specializzato erano tesoreggiati anche dai puristi dell'ebraismo. Gli errori dei critici della redazione testuale (i quali psicologicamente sono mossi dal desiderio di allargare la sfera della loro libertà nel mediare al loro gregge i Vangeli) risalgono (a) alla loro formazione culturale prevalentemente greco-romana, (b) alla loro ignoranza dei concetti orientali salvo nella loro apparenza letterale, dunque irreale, nell'Antico Testamento, e pertanto all'importanza eccessiva da loro data ai materiali rabbinici farisaici nella valutazione dell'ebraismo contemporaneo in Giudea e in Galilea; e infine (c) al loro procedere circolare dalle ipotesi agli esempi e dagli esempi alla prova delle loro ipotesi.

6. Per affermare il mio punto di vista ai fini di questo studio, noto che consegue che, per quanto il quadro, la dizione e la tendenza di molti passi evangelici fossero determinati dagl'interessi e dalle speranze delle prime chiese, per le quali scrivevano gli evangelisti, resta da dimostrarci che i loro materiali fossero limitati a qualche detto sapienziale arido e staccato. Come che sia, questo studio dipende assai poco dal presupposto che i passi siano storicamente autentici. Le sue illazioni sono fondate sul nocciolo della tradizione, a parte la sua ambientazione drammatica o retorica in San Marco, in « Q » o in « L ».

C. La legge nell'ambiente di Gesù

7. Si è largamente ignorato il sistema di governo del tempo di Gesù. Ho tentato di chiarirlo in qualche modo in *Law in the*

New Testament e ulteriormente in « New Testament Studies » 18
(1972), pp. 178-191. Ma ci sono dei particolari da aggiungere.   *
Ciò che denominiamo « legge » era amministrata in vari modi, e
non esisteva una giurisprudenza generale. Forse essa non era mai
esistita. C'erano almeno due generi di tribunale con rispettive suddivisioni. Le corti statali ellenizzate applicavano la legge statale ellenistica secondo una procedura ellenistica, fra gli Ebrei c'erano i
tribunali consuetudinari di due specie: (a) i tribunali di villaggio
o, nelle città ellenistiche, di ghetto, che amministravano leggi lo-
cali non scritte, consuetudinarie, e (b) i tribunali rabbinici, ai quali
non possiamo dare se non questo nome. Esistevano suddivisioni
ulteriori. C'erano la corte sacerdotale di Gerusalemme, che era un
organo prevalentemente amministrativo, le corti dei farisei che amministravano tutto il complesso della legge mosaica (tanto le questioni religiose come le « secolari ») secondo principi farisei per
coloro che volontariamente si sottomettevano o che per qualche
motivo non si potevano sottrarre alla loro giurisdizione; in terzo
luogo c'era l'autorità giudiziaria suprema dello Stato ebraico, a
Gerusalemme, comprendente i rappresentanti delle famiglie po-
tenti e studiosi di grido, sadducei, farisei o altri che fossero, ed essa
esercitava poteri di revisione di fatto rispetto ai casi difficili emer-
genti nei villaggi e aveva il diritto di accertare la legge ebraica au-
tentica in qualsiasi materia religiosa secondo la loro interpretazione. Il rapporto fra questo Sinedrio e la corte sacerdotale ci è
sconosciuto. Come fra le tribù africane d'oggi, non è probabile che
sussistesse una costituzione fissa e definitiva, fornita di poteri legali,
e la mancanza di stabilità nelle faccende ebraiche, testimoniata
dal Nuovo Testamento stesso e da Giuseppe Flavio, aggiungeva una
ulteriore complicazione e un elemento d'imprevedibilità al lavoro
di qualsiasi maestro.

     8. In un tale ambiente nessun maestro poteva spiegare la leg-
ge in maniera moderna con la speranza che i suoi insegnamenti fossero per essere applicati con una qualsiasi regolarità. Ai farisei spesso non dovette riuscire d'applicare le loro regole. I loro insegnamenti, quelli dei maestri della setta di Qumran e quelli di Gesù,
come quelli di Giovanni Battista (ad esempio: « Non vessate né de-
nunziate falsamente nessuno, e contentatevi delle vostre paghe... »,
Lc. III 4) avevano la validità d'un precetto rivolto a una persona.
Si riconosceva che la legge sacra fosse racchiusa nella Torah e nel
resto della Bibbia ebraica e in qualche misura nelle opere apocalit-
tiche e sapienziali che erano extra-canoniche, nonché in tradizioni
trasmesse di lunga mano e orali, non scritte. Una vita santa, la
devozione a Dio e lo studio protratto, originale della Scrittura
qualificavano a insegnare la religione e anche la legge, poiché la
legge ellenistica e i regolamenti amministrativi non si potevano

imparare dalle Scritture e non possedevano un'autorità soprannaturale: tuttavia erano le norme dalle quali di fatto era regolata
buona parte della vita quotidiana.

9. Confinandoci alla legge di Mosè, riconosciamo subito che,
essendo il testo quasi inflessibile, la sua interpretazione doveva
essere flessibile per forza. Era opinione universale che la « vera »
legge fosse quella di Mosè che si poteva intendere soltanto attra-
verso i sermoni o le spiegazioni di studiosi versati nell'ermeneu-
tica. Le loro argomentazioni però non avevano mai altra forza che
persuasiva, sia che fossero totalmente originali, sia che fossero tradizionali, come quelle che andavano svolgendo i farisei. Il senso
della dirittura dettava ciò che era il diritto, se mai questo aveva
qualche probabilità di applicazione. Così tutto l'insegnamento,
anche se prospettato come ciò che gli uomini facevano, era rivolto
all'individuo. Che egli fosse membro della nazione ebraica era significativo, ma valeva soltanto ad accrescere l'importanza del suo
dovere di comportarsi rettamente, obbedendo alla volontà di Dio
rivelata con una certa ambiguità e perfino contraddittorietà a Mosè
ed ai padri (cfr. Gio. VII 22). Il fatto che nessun giudice ammini-
strasse ed applicasse poi gli insegnamenti d'un maestro, non to-
glieva al loro valore, alla loro giustezza, alla loro verità e alla loro
convenienza. I suoi discepoli non lo stimavano meno per il fatto
che non aveva potere né giurisdizione.

D. I ruoli di un maestro religioso

10. Non conviene considerare i pronunciamenti legali o appa-
rentemente legali di un maestro (come il « Non ti è lecito tenere
la moglie di tuo fratello », Mc. VI 18) senza porli in relazione agli
altri e diversi suoi ruoli. Egli predicava su passi dei cinque libri
di Mosé, citando i profeti e usando massime della letteratura sapienziale. La parabola era uno strumento importante dell'insegnamento, poiché essa ricorre alla conoscenza popolare della vita quotidiana e dà per scontato che tale conoscenza sia una chiave per
capire la natura divina e la divina volontà. Le parabole ebraiche
preservate (e ne restano parecchie) sono in genere più facili di
quelle di Gesù ma mostrano che il pubblico, non essendo molto
colto, preferiva le illustrazioni concrete alle proposizioni astratte.
I maestri religiosi erano consultati intorno a problemi morali o
religiosi (ad esempio: « ... che cosa devo fare per ottenere in sorte
la vita eterna? », Mc. X 17) o di natura meramente giuridica (così:
« È lecito ripudiare la propria moglie per un motivo qualsiasi? »,
Mt. XIX 3) o tali che richiedevano una penetrazione sopranna-

turale particolaggiata (così: « Rabbi, chi ha peccato: quest'uomo o i suoi genitori, perché sia nato cieco? », Gio. IX 2).

11. Un maestro religioso era anche un guaritore, un arbitro morale e risanatore di anime («Ecco, io scaccio demoni e opero guarigioni oggi e domani, e il terzo giorno sarà la mia fine », Lc. XIII 32). Lo accostava anche gente strana, come la donna sirofenicia (Mc. VII 24-30).

Mi sovviene un mio collega. È birmano e fu uno dei primi, nel suo remoto villaggio, ad andare all'Università. Quando vi fece ritorno, a piedi, dopo la laurea, lo avvicinò un vecchio che aveva in mano un orologio rotto. « Puoi ripararlo? » egli domandò. Il mio collega rispose che non sapeva riparare orologi. « Perché? » domandò il vecchio, « hai una laurea e sai tutto ».

12. Il maestro religioso operava sugli individui, ed anche se era un messia orientato verso la politica (e Gesù non lo era) mirava a dirigere e a migliorare il cuore. Convertendo l'individuo se ne convertiva la società, essendo la solidarietà un principio instrinsecamente ebraico. Anche nella Mishnah, il maggior repertorio di legge ebraica farisea del primo e del secondo secolo, la legge era esposta in termini di ciò che uno dovrebbe fare, di ciò che l'individuo è obbligato o non è obbligato a fare. I termini ebraici costantemente usati sono *asūr* (vietato) e *muttar* (lecito), *hayyāv* (tenuto) e *patūr* (esente). È vero che vigeva un sistema raffinato per amministrare questi principi in seno alle comunità ebraiche della diaspora e anche in certa misura in Israele al tempo dei Talmud, ma ciò implica che la società sia già autosufficiente, formante un ghetto, del tutto conformata alla scuola farisea nel pensiero e nella pratica religiosa. Ma questo non valeva ancora al tempo di Gesù, quando la terra d'Israele somigliava all'Israele odierno, che è ben lungi dall'essere schiettamente ebraico ed ortodosso. Perciò ogni maestro, appartenesse o no ad una scuola o a una setta affermate, parlava all'individuo con parole che avevano una forza persuasiva e non coattiva.

E. Il contenuto dell'insegnamento di Gesù

12. Gesù chiede all'individuo di eliminare la bramosia di possesso: « Guardate gli uccelli del cielo: non seminano né mietono né raccolgono in granai, eppure il Padre vostro celeste li nutre! » (Mt. VI 26) e « Farò così: demolirò i miei granai... » (Lc. XIII 18). Chiede di abbandonare il desiderio di riconoscimenti sociali: « Quando, dunque, fai elemosina, non farla... come... fanno gl'ipocriti per aver gloria dagli uomini »; « E quando pregate, non imitate gl'ipocriti, i quali amano... star nelle sinagoghe... per

esser veduti dagli uomini » (Mt. VI 2, 5). Chiede di cercare la situazione più umile: « ... quando sei invitato, va' ad adagiarti all'ultimo posto, in modo che... colui che ti ha invitato ti dica: – Amico, vieni più su, – » (Lc. XIV 10). Chiede che sia il servitore degli altri: « ... e chi tra voi suol esser primo dovrà esser servo di tutti » (Mc. X 4). Che sia il primo a chiudere, a sanare una disputa: « Mettiti d'accordo con il tuo avversario mentre sei in cammino con lui... » (Mt. V 25) e, nel versetto precedente: « lascia la tua offerta là davanti all'altare, e va' prima a riconciliarti con il tuo fratello! » (Mt. VII 1). Che sopporti la persecuzione pazientemente, aspettando che il Signore vendichi i torti: « Io vi dico che renderò loro giustizia ben presto » (Lc. XVIII 8). Che non si preoccupi delle pratiche socialmente imposte né dei tabù, concentrandosi invece sull'eliminazione dei pensieri malvagi e dei loro effetti palesi... « Queste son le cose che contaminano l'uomo; ma mangiare senza essersi lavate le mani non contamina l'uomo » (Mt. XV 20).

13. Gesù insegnò ai suoi discepoli a gradire la calunnia: « Beati siete, quando vi oltraggeranno e vi perseguiteranno e diranno, mentendo, ogni male contro di voi per causa mia. Gioite ed esultate, perché la vostra ricompensa è grande nei cieli... ». Ad aver fede nella prossimità dell'èra messianica, nel suo primo inizio; essi non debbono attendere un segno palpabile della presenza di Elia: « ... infatti, vi dico: – Se avete fede grande come un granello di senapa, direte a questa montagna: ' Spostati di qui a là ', ed essa si sposterà... – » (Mt. XVII 20). Per attingere la giustizia essi debbonυ rinunciare ai vincoli familiari, alla proprietà, facendo a meno dei compensi mondani: « Se uno viene a me e non mi preferisce a suo padre, alla madre, alla moglie, ai figli, ai fratelli, alle sorelle e alla sua stessa vita, non può essere mio discepolo »; e: « Non crediate che io sia venuto a metter pace sulla terra; non sono venuto a metter pace ma spada » (Mt. X 34). Non solo debbono amare il prossimo come se stessi (Lc. X 27), ma anche amare i nemici: « Amate i vostri nemici, fate del bene a coloro che vi odiano... » (Lc. VI 27). Come Peter Noll ha dimostrato in una preziosa conferenza (*Jesus und das Gesetz*, 1968) questo limita strettamente gli effetti dell'amor del prossimo. Infatti ridefinisce il « prossimo »: « Quali di questi tre ti sembra che sia stato il prossimo per colui che s'imbatté nei briganti? » (Lc. X 36-7). Il dottore della legge rispose: « Quello che gli usò misericordia ».

14. Tutto ciò costituisce un'etica individuale dotata di implicazioni etico-sociali. Sta al di sopra della legge, ma si può forse dire che escluda la legge? Vieta le liti fra individui e fra gruppi, ma non esclude la giurisdizione (quale la esercitò San Paolo sui Corinzi) *pro salute animae*.

F. Quanto seriamente va preso Gesù?

15. È forse necessario detestare i genitori ecc. (Lc. XIV 26 citato dianzi)? Confidare in Dio soltanto, è forse possibile in pratica (Mt. VI 34; Lc. XII 28)? forse che i missionari non devono portar denaro, né cambio di abiti (Mc. VI 8-9 e passi paralleli)? Viene raccomandato di tagliar via la mano, il piede e di estrarre l'occhio (Mc. IX 43-45)? Poiché gli scandali debbono avvenire (Lc. XVII 1) è forse questo il modo di affrontarli? Sono peccaminosi i pensieri colpevoli anche se non comportano nessuna azione (Mt. V 28)? Che magia risiede nel lavare i piedi? L'inferno di fuoco è sicuramente un'applicazione del passo di Isaia (LXVI 24), ma è davvero la destinazione di coloro che chiamano gli altri « sciocchi » (Mt. V 22)?

16. Come facciamo a decidere se Gesù vuole essere preso sul serio? L'esagerazione dopo tutto è dello stile drammatico orientale. Di certo tutto ciò si può considerare un'esagerazione, ma in tal caso, che cosa resta? Se non si allontanano i propri congiunti (cfr. I Re e Mt. VIII 22), ci si può forse dedicare alla giustizia? San Paolo dà una risposta negativa: « ... questo dico per la nostra comodità... per quello che è decente, è convenevole da attenervi costantemente al Signore, senza esser distratti » (I Cor. VII 32-5). Il detto « lascia che i morti seppelliscano i loro morti » è prova ottima che Gesù prese il « mondo » seriamente, quale opposto costante ai « figli della luce »; egli dice: « Se il mondo vi odia, sappiate che ha odiato me prima di voi. Se voi foste del mondo, il mondo amerebbe ciò che è suo... » (Gio. XV 18-19), ed anche: « ... voi siete di questo mondo, io non sono di questo mondo », parlando agli « Ebrei » (Gio. VIII 23). I suoi discepoli debbono essere distinti dal mondo, non una sua componente benevola e civile. Se non si è pronti ad amputarsi (come in Giuseppe Flavio Vita 170-3; Bell. Jud. II 642-4) non si eviteranno veramente le occasioni di atti e desideri peccaminosi: questo è il senso del dialogo fra Gesù ed i discepoli: « ... – Se questa è la condizione degli uomini, non conviene sposarsi –. Egli rispose loro: – Non tutti comprendono questa parola, ma soltanto coloro ai quali è dato – » (Mt. XIX 10-11). Così se non si lavano mai i piedi degli estranei non si può amare l'estraneo (ebbi qualcosa da imparare somministrando clisteri durante la guerra!). L'idea di Gesù è che la consueta solidarietà con gli « amici » deve cedere il posto ad una solidarietà religiosamente imposta con tutti gli uomini, semplicemente in ragione della loro umanità.

16. Gesù opera sulle disposizioni dell'individuo chiamandolo alla giustizia. L'ascoltatore è al centro dell'attenzione, come punto focale di ogni obbligazione. E se l'individuo risponde alla chia-

mata, non c'è più un gruppo particolare di individui che possa essere governato da un'etica diversa e continuare a considerarsi fra i discepoli di Gesù.

G. Le antitesi del sermone della montagna come progetto giuridico

17. Veniamo al complesso problema del sermone della montagna. Taluni lo ritengono un programma per il mondo a venire, e non già un insieme di norme per noi. Si dà (comicamente) un consenso generale sul fatto che non si tratta per niente di norme. Taluni l'hanno presa per un'etica provvisoria. L'opinione più popolare è che esso ci fornisca dei criteri impossibili su cui saggiare la nostra debole devozione, che sarebbe l'etica dell'impossibile, la sfida dell'irraggiungibile. Durante la guerra apparve una dichiarazione degli aspetti positivi di questa ricerca senza speranza, a mia cognizione: *The Relevance of the Impossible* di H. C. McGregor (1941). Molti hanno tentato di ravvisare nel sermone della montagna una visione di perfezione che la persona ordinaria non deve sforzarsi di raggiungere (« voi dunque, siate perfetti come il vostro Padre celeste è perfetto », Mt. V 48; « Se vuoi essere perfetto va', prendi ciò che possiedi e dàllo ai poveri... » XIX 21). Ma l'opinione favorita oggi è che Gesù c'insegni a mirare costantemente a ciò che non raggiungeremo mai. Questo non mi è mai sembrato razionale, se lo inquadriamo sullo sfondo delle idee ebraiche, che sono sempre pratiche.

18. Le antitesi vanno esaminate nel loro contenuto e significato letterale. Ma su di esse è sospesa la questione generale cui anzitutto dobbiamo rivolgere la nostra attenzione. Quale era l'atteggiamento di Gesù verso la Legge di Mosè, verso i costumi e le tradizioni del luogo e del tempo suoi? Su tali problemi le opinioni divergono in misura sorprendente. A questo proposito mi sono stati d'aiuto la tesi, sostenuta a Cambridge, di Robert Banks e il suo articolo nell'« Expository Times » 84/9 (1973), pp. 265-269. C'erano un tempo tre tesi sull'atteggiamento di Gesù verso la Torah. (a) La sua opera ne era un'esposizione e un completamento; (b) egli la radicalizzò e acuì (e in entrambe queste tesi, si presuppone la sua accettazione della validità della Torah); e infine (c) egli l'abrogò totalmente. Secondo il Banks a e b sono insufficienti e c è improprio. Sono d'accordo con lui. Banks scopre che restano tre soluzioni alternative, ciascuna delle quali individua il tratto di discontinuità rispetto all'Antico Testamento nell'unicità dell'insegnamento di Gesù, e che tuttavia fra loro differiscono per il peso che dànno alla continuità fra i due. Esse interpretano le esigenze di Gesù come l'espressione della volontà immediata

di Dio nella nuova situazione prodotta dalla sua venuta, e ne deriva: (a) il trascendimento di tutte le leggi dell'Antico Testamento, senza che si definisca ulteriormente il rapporto fra l'antico e il nuovo (secondo Banks questa è l'opinione di E. Percy e di P. J. Verweijs); (b) la « legislazione » di una nuova Torah mosaica o messianica che sostituisce cronologicamente l'antica (tale l'opinione di B. W. Bacon e di W. D. Davies); e infine (c) d'adempimento della Legge mediante l'obbedienza alla Croce (l'opinione di Lyungman).

19. Dobbiamo scegliere fra queste alternative ultime o esiste forse una quarta possibilità? Nel suo studio degli atteggiamenti di Gesù verso la consuetudine, Banks suggerisce che egli fosse indifferente e che egli non si pronunciasse sulle tradizioni degli anziani fra i Farisei, ma assunse un atteggiamento *ad hoc* verso ciascuna, secondo che la sua missione esigeva. Possiamo noi dire che Gesù non ebbe un atteggiamento costante verso la legge e la consuetudine ebraiche e che non esiste un tema sottostante a tutti i suoi atti e detti? Questo è invero possibile, ma è stolto rifiutare a priori un principio intelligibile quando lo si può discernere. La nostra risposta è un rinvio a dopo l'esame delle antitesi stesse del sermone della montagna (Mt. V 21-48). Superfluo dire che il nostro trattamento dev'essere del tutto sommario. Esiste in ciascuna delle sei antitesi un elemento comune, che è facile notare.

(1) « Avete udito ciò che fu detto agli antichi: – Non ucciderai... – ». Anche nelle fonti rabbiniche è noto che questo comandamento fu esteso a comprendere casi nei quali fosse stato inferto un danno meno grave della morte. In certi ambienti il Decalogo era interpretato assai estensivamente e analogicamente. Gesù dice che per evitare il giudizio escatologico non basta essersi limitati a evitare l'assassinio: non solo un'offesa alla fratellanza, ma anche l'aver trascurato di ristabilirla è un peccato per analogia con l'assassinio. Questo cancella chiaramente la distinzione fra gli atti apertamente criminali e la mancata ubbidienza al comandamento d'amore fondamentale.

(2) « ... – Non commetterai adulterio –. Io, però, vi dico: Chiunque guarda una donna desiderandola, ha già commesso in cuor suo adulterio con essa ». Nelle fonti rabbiniche un'applica-   *
zione analogica del comandamento di non commettere adulterio si può pure rintracciare. Gesù ha combinato con essa l'errore dei rapporti sessuali illeciti documentati negli apocrifi e nella letteratura di Qumran. Ancora una volta non gl'interessa tanto che sia evitato passivamente il peccato quanto che ci sia una presenza a se stessi positiva, attiva tale da impedire che il movimento peccaminoso non si profili nel cuore. Non ci interessa ora discutere il fon-

damento psicologico o la convenienza sociale di questa concezione, allora o oggi.

(3) « È stato anche detto: Chi vorrà rimandare la sua donna, le dia un atto di divorzio. Io, però, vi dico: Chiunque rimanda la sua donna, eccettuato il caso di concubinato, ne fa un'adultera... ». È naturale, avendo definito conseguenze peccaminose dei desideri sregolati al di fuori del matrimonio, che si passi ai problemi della coppia sposata – i problemi più sgradevoli, poiché tutti gli altri dolori si possono reggere se li condivide una coppia unita da un mutuo affetto. L'insegnamento di Gesù, come ho spiegato (*Law*, c. 16), è che non ci dovrebbe, non ci deve essere il divorzio, e che il risposarsi è impensabile finché vivono entrambi gli sposi. Ogni divorzio e ogni risposarsi hanno perciò soltanto un'esistenza di fatto e peccaminosa (per quanto comprensibile) a meno che, causa l'inverecondia della moglie, il pericolo morale nel cacciarla di casa sia minore di quello che si corre nel tenervela. Gesù non poteva dire e non dice che i divorzi nel « mondo » sono invalidi. Ma il criterio di validità mondana è il criterio del mondo, i discepoli di Gesù debbono comportarsi altrimenti. « Se mi amate, osservate i miei comandamenti » (Gio. XIV 15).

(4) L'antitesi seguente concerne il giuramento. Il comandamento di non spergiurare è interpretato da Gesù come un ordine di non giurare affatto. Questo si spiega facilmente come un consiglio di cautela. Uno studio attento di questi versi (Mt. v. 33-37) rivela che Gesù proibisce soltanto i giuramenti preliminari e testimoniali. Certamente nella vita sociale che egli conosceva l'abolizione dei giuramenti avrebbe danneggiato il commercio ed i rapporti internazionali. Su questo punto tornerò fra breve. Ma tutti converranno che da questa antitesi risulta una radicalizzazione del comandamento dell'Antico Testamento, per cui si converte in una misura profilattica che garantisce da ogni offesa, anche accidentale, dell'onore di Dio.

(5) « Avete udito che fu detto – Occhio per occhio e dente per dente –. Io però vi dico di non resistere al malvagio... ». La storia della cosiddetta legge del taglione nella storia del diritto è abbastanza nota ormai. Lo studio di Bernard Jackson *The Problem of Exod. XXI 22-5* (in « Vetus Testamentum » 2 1973, pp. 273-304) fornisce una guida essenziale. Al tempo di Gesù c'erano dei partigiani della tesi per cui la ritorsione precisa sarebbe la legge di Dio, ed i mussulmani vi si sono attenuti per quanto hanno potuto, in base alla legge coranica, fino a tempi recenti. Ma i farisei avevano adottato la tesi secondo cui i testi veterotestamentari esigevano cinque tipi di risarcimento da liquidarsi alla vittima che li chiedesse in giudizio. Gesù mostra l'impossibilità della compensazione esatta. Ancora una volta, non gl'interessano

l'omissione di ogni danno ad altri, la disperazione a non saper risarcire esattamente chi è stato danneggiato per negligenza o addirittura volontariamente, ma gli preme piuttosto che non si richiedano risarcimenti e che non si metta nessuno in condizione di restarci debitore d'un risarcimento. Il che si riduce alla fine all'ordine: « Non dare in prestito, regala! ». Noi non possiamo risarcire e gli altri non ci possono risarcire pienamente: Dio solo vendica, solo Lui dà il giusto compenso. La resistenza al male accresce l'altrui debito e non vi si ha diritto!

(6) L'ultima antitesi era fonte di perplessità per i teologi, dato che non esiste nell'Antico Testamento l'ordine di odiare i nemici; ma la scoperta delle opinioni della setta di Qumran al riguardo ha chiarito la situazione. Essi erano tenuti a odiare i figli della Tenebra. Va osservato che l'odio dei presunti nemici di Dio è certamente testimoniato nell'Antico Testamento (cfr. Salmo V 5; XXVI 5; e XXXIX 21-22). Gesù addita che l'amore del prossimo, se è reciproco, non produce nessun merito soprasensibile. Il comandamento d'amare, per produrre effetti nel mondo a venire, deve includere l'amore senza reciprocità. Perciò si esige l'amore perfino dei nemici e non nel senso negativo di non lederli, ma in quello positivo, di favorirne il benessere. Questa è un'interpretazione perfettamente intelligibile del testo veterotestamentario ed è analoga alla teoria rabbinica delle esigenze supererogatorie del comandamento di cercare la pace.

20. Molte idee di Gesù si possono riscontrare particolareggiatamente nelle interpretazioni ebraiche della Scrittura a noi pervenute, e che restano marginali, ma avrebbero potuto diventare principi direttivi se l'insegnamento di Gesù fosse stato accolto. Una fra esse è il principio per cui colui che porta qualcuno al peccato è colpevole lui stesso della violazione del comandamento in questione.

21. Il programma proposto dalle antitesi è palesemente morale, e opera soltanto nel foro interiore. Ma è pur sempre altresì un programma giurisprudenziale. Quando i cristiani formino un corpo autosufficiente possono anche mettere in atto queste norme. San Paolo era dell'opinione che questa fosse la norma cristiana fin dal 53-4 della nostra èra: « Ma ora ecco coloro coi quali vi ho scritto che non vi mescoliate, cioè, che se alcuno, che si nomina fratello, è fornicatore, o avaro, o idolatra, o maldicente, o ubriaco, o rapace, non pur mangiate con un tale. Perciocché che ho io da far a giudicare anche quelli di fuori? Non giudicate voi quelli di dentro? Or Iddio giudicherà quelli di fuori. Togliete il malvagio d'infra voi stessi. Ardisce alcuno di voi, avendo qualche affare con un altro, piatire davanti all'indegni, e non davanti ai santi? Non sapete voi che i santi giudicheranno il mondo? E, se il mondo è giudicato

per voi, siete voi indegni dei minimi giudizi? Non sapete voi che noi giudicheremo gli angeli? Quanto più possiamo giudicar delle cose di questa vita? Dunque, se avete dei piati per cose di questa vita, fate seder per giudici quelli che nella chiesa sono i più spregevoli. Io lo dico per farvi vergogna. Così non vi è un savio fra voi, il qual possa dar giudizio fra l'uno dei suoi fratelli e l'altro? Ma fratello con fratello piatisce, e cioè davanti agl'infedeli. Certo dunque già v'è del difetto in voi, in ciò che voi avete delle liti gli uni con gli altri: perché non soffrite piuttosto che vi sia fatto torto? Perché non vi lasciate piuttosto fare qualche danno? Ma vi fate torto e danno, e ciò a fratello. Non sapete voi che gl'ingiusti non erediteranno il regno di Dio? » (I Cor. V 11-VI 9).

22. Una comprensione letterale del passo di San Matteo (V 17-20) che precede le antitesi, è a parer mio la migliore: « Non crediate che io sia venuto per abolire la Legge o i Profeti: non sono venuto per abolire, ma per compiere... Poiché vi dico che se la vostra giustizia non sorpasserà quella degli scribi e dei farisei, non entrerete nel regno dei cieli ». Questa è sicuramente una difesa successiva di Gesù (e dei suoi seguaci) dall'ostilità delle sinagoghe, ma anche se fu scritta dopo il tempo di Gesù è tuttavia, a mio avviso, esatta. Il programma di Gesù era un programma come quello dei farisei, ma comportava la distinzione dal mondo, mentre la « distinzione » dei farisei era soltanto una forma di compromesso col mondo abbinata alla loro propria auto-esaltazione.

H. Le implicazioni sociali, politiche ed internazionali

23. Un programma giurisprudenziale che renda superflui gli avvocati, che proibisca ogni lite e neghi l'importanza secolare del risarcimento dei danni, sarebbe unico nel suo genere: l'Età dell'Oro, senza dubbio, ne sarebbe l'unico precedente, semmai. Certo, il diritto consuetudinario di natura non contestativa era dato per scontato e non abrogato. La legge sui gradi di parentela impedenti il matrimonio non era ovviamente abrogata! Ma la normativa fiscale ed amministrativa era considerata irrilevante.

24. Presa alla lettera, una società dove non si possa ottenere l'esecuzione coattiva dei contratti è una società basata su un'economia di sussistenza. Essa non ha motivo di temere un attacco dall'esterno. Ma se questo si produce, secondo la dottrina, non si deve opporre resistenza nel senso attivo. Si obietterà che una popolazione di questo genere sarà ridotta in servitù. Nel mondo di Gesù gli schiavi c'erano, ed erano spesso ben curati. Ma la risposta a tutti questi dubbi è semplicemente questa: l'insegnamento di Gesù non privilegiava la sopravvivenza. La sopravvivenza come

tale era uno scopo secondario. Una volta che si sia capito ciò, tutto il programma va a posto. La vera vita è per dopo la resurrezione: « Io sono la resurrezione e la vita » (Gio. XI 25). Per entrare nella vita si debbono osservare i comandamenti: « Uno solo è il Buono. Ma se tu vuoi entrare nella vita eterna, osserva i comandamenti » (Mt. XIX 17). « Poiché chi vuol salvare la sua vita la perderà, ma chi perderà la sua vita per causa mia e del vangelo, la salverà » (Mc. VII 35) « Chi ama la sua vita la perde, e chi odia la sua vita in questo mondo la conserverà per la vita eterna » (Gio. XII 25).

25. L'intenzione è che interiormente tutte le perdite e i danni siano assorbiti e che esternamente la chiesa tratti col mondo in base a principi del genere, per glorificare il nome di Dio. Questa è una superlegge che fa sembrare puerili e buffi i sistemi giuridici vigenti. Peter Noll ha mostrato che i due principi, l'amore del prossimo e l'amore del nemico, distruggono con un colpo solo tutti i progetti di ingrandimento personali e collettivi. La classe e il credo, il colore e la razza, la religione e la politica scompaiono quali mezzi per classificare e svantaggiare gli uomini a proprio favore. Tutte le ineguaglianze scompaiono salvo quelle dovute alla crescita morale e alla salute. San Paolo lo chiarisce nei suoi rimproveri ai Corinzi. Non soltanto la non violenza, ma anche la cura attiva dei bisogni degli altri, cristiani o non cristiani che sieno, è un dovere. La giustizia personale essendo il primo scopo, tutte le direttive collettive vanno subordinate ad essa. Essendo eliminata la bramosia di possesso, l'aggressività e la gelosia sono sradicate. La prospettiva politica in vista della quale il programma è formulato è più plausibile e razionale perfino dell'*Utopia* di San Tommaso Moro.

26. Gesù era un maestro della legge e basava l'insegnamento sull'Antico Testamento, leggendone i testi nel loro complesso ed estraendone un sistema che provvedeva ai bisogni spirituali dei seguaci. La scuola, che consisteva in una disciplina di tutta la vita esercitata sugl'istinti ereditati dai nostri antenati subumani, e, in senso poetico, in un ritorno al Giardino dell'Eden, mentre albeggia l'èra messianica, era la scuola d'un unico Maestro. Unico quesito che ci si pone è se ne siamo davvero i discepoli. « Quanto a voi, non vi fate chiamare Rabbi; uno solo, infatti, è il vostro maestro e tutti voi siete fratelli » (Mt. XXIII 8).

FURTHER ANNOTATION

Tit. The burden of this article (sup., viii) is that, taken literally, the society Jesus planned placed survival of the individual second, and his righteousness first. The justification for such a scheme was derived from a new view of the Hebrew Bible. Putting it into operation would mean abandoning the expectation, but not necessarily the hope, of a highly integrated, advanced, technological civilization such as that of the modern West. Where no sanctions operate against a workman for inadequate work neither a railway timetable nor a telephone directory can be produced accurately or on time, not to speak of the railways themselves, etc. The teaching of Jesus placed legal rights second to moral obligations, but this did not mean that a social organization of a distinctive type was not to be envisaged.

To complete the article two concepts could usefully have been developed. The Jewish background cannot be visualised correctly without knowledge of the standards of the *ḥasîdîm* (the pious) (inf., p. 117), who are not content with the Torah's requirements, or without imagining the Men of Sodom (who have already figured in LNT). The Men of Sodom ignore the injunction 'thou shall do what is right and good' (Deut. xii.28). They not only object to a man's using his legal rights when it would inconvenience them, but they also make their own convenience the touchstone of all claims whatever: Maim., M.T., XII.iii. 7, 8; 12, 1.

While the standards of the *ḥasîdîm* are recognisably in the same category of the idealistic as Jesus's Utopia, the Men of Sodom are too overdrawn even for the World which Jesus understood to be in need of redemption.

p. [53], ll. 1-2. S. sup., SNT I, 32 ff.
p. [59], ll. 37-8. Now see Haacker's discovery, sup., p. viii.

ALLEGORY AND THE WICKED VINEDRESSERS

THERE is a trend, at least in England, to dispute the 'entrenched position' regarding the absence of allegory in Jesus' parables, and to suggest, on the contrary, his use of allegory, whether or not the early church continued or elaborated allegorical elements in the tradition they received.[1] The trend is advanced if we gain further light on Jesus' raw material, i.e. parabolic patterns known in his day. An example has now come to hand. It enables us, after some thought, to do more, viz. to answer

[1] J. Drury, 'The Sower, the Vineyard, and the Place of Allegory in the Interpretation of Mark's parables', *J.T.S.* n.s. xxiv (1973), pp. 367–9, refers to C. F. D. Moule's article in the Black Festschrift, *Neotestamentica et Semitica* (1969). There is also M. Black's excellent 'The parables as allegory', *B.J.R.L.* xlii (1960), pp. 273–87 (apropos of the Sower): cf. also C. H. Cave, *N.T.S.* xi (1965), pp. 374–87.

objectors who doubt whether any first-century Jewish scholar could have told stories laced with allusions (as opposed to quotations) from the Old Testament. A Jewish parable containing such allusions, with a tannaïtic application of it containing overt and covert biblical allusions, takes us a long way towards defending a position sometimes reprobated, viz. that Jesus' material (however subsequently worked over by the church) was inherently allusive and thus capable of allegorical interpretation from the first. Below I give an English translation of the critical text of an ancient Jewish parable, followed by an obviously less ancient,[1] but still very old rabbinical application of it. Since the parable is, to my mind, related as uncle or cousin to the raw material taken up by Jesus, a worthwhile comparison is possible. After the English version I note the textual history of this material and explain its neglect. My comments on the rabbinical application are necessary to show the techniques involved. We can consider the various scopes of intrinsic meaning, the potential (as it were) of the parable as it stood without any application. Jesus appears to have taken up its close relative for his own purposes; we can tell his meaning much more closely than we could previously, and in the sense of humour revealed one can detect the bitter flavour we have found elsewhere already.

Sifre on Deut. § 312 (p. 134*b*) runs:

'But the Lord's share was his own people; (Jacob is the lot of his inheritance)' (Deut. xxxii. 9). This is like a king who owned a field and consigned it to tenant-farmers.[2] The tenant-farmers began to steal (from) it. He took it away from them and gave it to their sons. These then began to be worse than the first. *He took it from their sons and gave it to the sons of those sons. They, in their turn, were worse than the previous.* A son was born to him. He said to them, Go out from that which is mine: you can no longer remain in it. Give me my share, so that I may acknowledge (and look after) it!

'Thus when Abraham our father came into the world there arose from him unworthy (offspring), Ishmael and all the sons of Qetura. Isaac came into the world. There arose from him unworthy (offspring), Esau and all the princes of Edom. They began to be worse than the first. And when Jacob came there did not arise unworthy (offspring) from him: but all the sons born to him were fit, like himself, as it is said, "Jacob was a simple man and dwelt among tents" (Gen. xxv. 27). Whence did the Omnipresent recognise his share? From Jacob, as it is said, "The Lord's share was his own people . . ." (Deut. xxxii. 9), "For the Lord hath chosen Jacob unto himself, (Israel for his peculiar treasure)" (Ps. cxxxv. 4) . . .'

---

[1] On the dates of these sources see the sage words of an expert, Morton Smith at *J.B.L.* xcii (1973), pp. 112–13.

[2] On the status and rights of these see Derrett, *Law in the New Testament* (London, 1970), pp. 291–4.

The words printed in italics above correspond to Hebrew words that were omitted by scribal error (homoeoteleuton) in several manuscripts. The critical edition (Finkelstein, 1939, reprinted 1969, p. 353) notices faulty specimens. Unfortunately, when Ugolinus published the text of the whole of Sifre with a Latin translation in 1753 he used the defective text, and Christian scholars have followed him in this. The threefold dissatisfaction of the owner was thus lost. Ziegler,[1] (Strack–) Billerbeck,[2] and Bonsirven[3] thought the parable (in its defective state) worth noticing. Lightfoot, Schöttgen, Jeremias, Kümmel, Bammel, and Linnemann preferred not to use the rabbinical material lying here in their own studies of the parable, and it is obvious why. For my part I neglected to check back Grotius's reference,[4] to my regret. Now we have the complete text we can see what the respective authors were about.

The parable is about God's relationship to those who exploit, for him (as it were), the world and its assets. He is like an owner of a piece of land who is necessarily absent, and, for the time being, not very concerned about the public notoriety of his rights or their observance. As in Jewish law, the title to land cannot theoretically be lost, so long as the owner, or an appropriate agent, can assert the ownership in time. Typically, in the Jewish parable the hero is a king ('of flesh and blood', as they usually say). His tenants 'steal', i.e. cheat him in respect of the produce or rent. Their successors behave progressively worse, obviously by refusing rent altogether and defying the owner in various ways which we are left to imagine. The theme 'they did worse than their fathers' is certainly biblical, and is an allusion to Jer. vii. 26, xvi. 12. They do so because each successive predecessor was not appropriately punished. Thus it is a parable about divine patience. The unsatisfactory tenants are merely removed, and a new set are instated. We notice that there is a hereditary continuity between the sets. There are three, as is appropriate in a Jewish story—the threefold character of the incidents implies its indefinite persistence. Yet the owner's patience has a theoretical limit. An occasion arises when he needs his rights and title to be put beyond anyone's doubt. A son is born to him, obviously not merely an only son, but a son about whose endowment the father is deeply concerned. Then he ousts the tenants, and, we are to understand, he makes other arrangements altogether.

---

[1] I. Ziegler (who did not write primarily for Christians), *Die Königsgleichnisse des Midrasch* (Breslau, 1903), pp. lxxxix–xc follows the version at B. Ugolinus, *Thesaurus Antiquitatum Sacrarum*, xv (Venice, 1753), cols. 889–90.

[2] P. Billerbeck, *Kommentar zum Neuen Testament* (Munich, 1926, 1961), i, 874m.

[3] J. Bonsirven, *Textes rabbiniques* (Rome, 1955), § 355.

[4] Ubi cit., p. 291, n. 2.

The application in Sifre, is at first sight, inappropriate. The hereditary link between the generations is retained prominently. What was perhaps not so prominent in the original parable is now articulate in the story. Abraham is the first generation, but *some* of his issue were unsatisfactory; Isaac was the second generation, but *some* of his issue were unsatisfactory; Jacob was the third generation, and it is said that his issue were satisfactory—they are the fourth generation. Yet the story would require that Jacob and his issue (jointly) represent the ultimate 'good' tenants. It plainly does not fit. Moreover, many of Jacob's issue were not satisfactory: Reuben was no model, and what of those that sold Joseph? The fact is that the rabbinical author of the application could not get away from the idea that Israel was the Lord's inheritance (Isa. xix. 25), that Jacob was 'unlike (unsatisfactory) others', and Israel was the tribe of God's 'inheritance' (Jer. x. 15–16). The images of the 'inheritance', viewed as a plot of land, and the 'inheritance' as the Jewish people, have been allowed to overlap, though they are intellectually quite distinct. Further, the rabbinical scholar was aware that, whatever might be said of other issue of Jacob, 'the sceptre shall not depart from Judah, nor the ruler's staff from between his feet, until Shiloh come . . .'[1] (Gen. xlix. 10). This is the reason why there are only three patriarchs and the series does not end with Judah. Judah and the Messiah are included within their 'father' Jacob. Thus he wishes to utilize the parable not as evidence of God's patience, but as an explanation why the promise of the Messiah, not limited to Abraham, lay behind a fresh sign of approbation when Jacob 'came'. The parable was awkwardly adapted as a midrash on Ps. cxxxv. 4 and Deut. xxxii. 9. Authors of sermons need not be too scrupulous or logical.

What *authority* did the original author of the parable have, upon which to build his little story? An authority is available if we bear the 'third-generation' motif in mind. It would be wrong to presume that he must have begun with his mind a blank. The three generations are at one and the same time a family-solidarity group, and an instance of three chances. A point raised by Canon Drury[2] is well illustrated by the homely arrangement of the realistic with the remarkable. It is realistic for the owner to insist on his rights being established rather than allow the tenants to acquire ownership adversely to him. It is, however,

---

[1] That the mysterious word 'Shiloh' was interpreted by some as the Messiah has been clear since the publication of the Blessings of Jacob: G. Vermes, *The Dead Sea Scrolls in English* (London, 1966), p. 224; E. Lohse, *Die Texte aus Qumran* (Munich, 1964), pp. 246–7; D. C. Duling, *N.T.S.* xx (1973), pp. 64–6.

[2] Ubi cit. above, p. 426, n. 3, at p. 374: 'In a detective story the piece of evidence which does not fit is of the greatest interest to the detective.' I should say the piece of evidence which stands out, anomalous without being impossible.

remarkable for a king to beget a son so late in the day that he ousts, for the latter's sake, the *grandchildren* of the original tenants! It could happen, but its very singularity points to the religious overtones of the whole tale.

In its raw state the parable takes for granted a sensible resolution of the apparent contradiction between Exod. xxxiv. 7, Num. xiv. 18, and Deut. v. 9 on the one hand (God visits iniquity on the third and fourth generation) and Deut. xxiv. 16 (related at 2 Kings xiv. 6), Ezek. ii. 3 and xviii. 2–21 on the other hand (vicarious punishment is unlawful and God rejects it in moral contexts). Guilt is not, indeed, punished promptly. Opportunities exist for each generation to repent. There is no fate which obliges the sons to be worse than their fathers (note the progression in Jesus' version of the parable, and compare the Jeremiah passages cited above with Matt. xxiii. 32). There is a limit to divine patience. Thus the parable is a midrash on two sets of verses. If that is so, there is no emphasis on the 'thirdness' or the 'fourthness' of the generation: the point is that guilt will find retribution eventually. Consequently the specific generations can be left out, as is the case in Jesus' version.

It may be asked whether the 'son' originally implied the Messiah. The story in the bare form available in Sifre does not suggest this. On the contrary it suggests something quite different. God will be worshipped and obeyed, the only question is when and by whom. No usurping worldly power can obliterate his eventual assertion of his rights. If one must ask for an appropriate allegory it is as between the Gentiles and the Jews. God put up with Adam and Cain, with the generation of the Flood, then with Noah and his descendants, and only when the Jews accepted his sovereignty did he find an acceptable people. Certainly the Bible equates the Jews with God's inheritance, in contrast with the Gentiles.[1] Hence, no doubt, the way in which the compiler of Sifre attached the parable to his midrash on Deut. xxxii. 9. For it is a biblical theme that Israel is not only God's chosen, his inheritance, but also the one *entitled* to the inheritance. Israel is God's son: Exod. iv. 22, Hos. xi. 1.

Hos. xi. 1 is adopted at Matt. ii. 15 as a messianic allusion. In that view the Messiah is the ideal Israel. We have seen a covert allusion to the Messiah in the rabbinic author's identification of Jacob and his perfect issue as the 'share'. Thus at one and the same time the original parable was capable of being used to indicate (1) that God will redeem

---

[1] Exod. xxxiv. 9; Deut. iv. 20, ix. 26, 29, xxxii. 9; Ps. xxviii. 9, xxxiii. 12, lxxviii. 62, xciv. 14, cv. 6, cxxxv. 4; Jer. x. 15–16; Zech. ii. 12. See also Ps. Sal. xiv. 5, xvii. 23!

the world from those who hate him; (2) God takes or chooses Israel as his 'share' because only in that generation did he find satisfaction; and (3) (Jesus' version) if the son too is defied by the tenants, and it is the fourth occasion of downright refusal of the owner's rights, the tenants, i.e., as the gospel text makes very clear, the Jews themselves, will be ousted. The parable is capable of passing through several stages, a vague one which presents a general principle in story form, an allegory in which the same form is used to predict the coming of the Messiah from amongst a chosen generation of Jews, and a further allegory in which that very generation is rejected because it rejected the Messiah. Mark xii. 12c is reasonable: ἔγνωσαν γὰρ ὅτι πρὸς αὐτοὺς τὴν παραβολὴν εἶπεν.

It is already clear[1] that Matthew and Luke, independently, thought it essential to alter the text of Mark in order to show that the owner's son was killed *outside* the wall. I have dealt with this,[2] to show that his being killed inside the wall was not impossible, but was remarkable and intrinsically improbable. Canon Drury's approach is enlightening here also. Matthew and Luke require the son to be killed outside the wall in order that it may be made plain that the son is to be understood as Jesus.[3] They did not impugn the accuracy of Mark, but they thought him insufficiently pointed. Mark, on the contrary, seems to have insisted on the remarkable and improbable fact just because an additional point of an allegorical nature could be made by it. The Vinedressers pollute the inheritance itself.

We have seen the overt and covert biblical allusions in the parable in its original form; we have seen the motives of the rabbinical editor adapting the parable to his immediate purpose, with his own covert biblical allusions beside the actual quotations; we have seen that Jesus' use of the parable seems to take the Jewish sense, ironically, one stage further. Is it all a Heilsgeschichte? It does not need to be. Exact correspondence with the Passion story, for example, was not as necessary as Matthew and Luke seem to have supposed. It is all about God's patience, and its limit, as it was from the beginning, and all layers of the parable's message coexist and cohere.

Postscript. It is often said that the sending of the son was implausible. Canon Drury's point arises again. A risk, but not an absurd one: the parables do not have impossible, or unreasonable features; they have

---

[1] C. S. C. Williams, *Alterations to the Text of the Synoptic Gospels and Acts* (Oxford, 1951), p. 37.

[2] Op. cit., pp. 306–7.

[3] And, one hesitates to add, a scapegoat (Lev. xvi. 21–8)?

remarkable ones, to call the hearer's attention to the allegorical point. The repeated sending of messengers, who are quietly done away with by the recipient, who is afraid of the consequences of acknowledging the orders they carried, is a secular theme set down as history by Josephus. What was done by Varus, viceroy of Agrippa, about the year 66 was remarkable, but not implausible, still less impossible.[1]

As for the doubt whether a first-century rabbi might *allude to* scripture, as opposed to quoting it, an excellent example of just such a procedure is available in the Mishnah. At *Avot* iii. 9 (10 in Danby's translation) R. Ḥanina b. Dosa's saying[2] is based upon Prov. ix. 10, Ps. cxi. 10.

---

[1] Josephus, *Vita*, §§ 50-2.
[2] See G. Vermes, *Jesus the Jew* (London, 1973), p. 78.

THE RICH FOOL: A PARABLE OF JESUS *
CONCERNING INHERITANCE

Lk 12: 13—21 has not been handled well since Jülicher,[1] and the general ignorance concerning it is astounding. In fact it contains the second part of an intellectual diptych, pairing with the logia on divorce. Alluding plainly to Ex 2: 13—15, 2 Sam 15 and 2 Chr 31 it proves once again the function of allusion in such compositions. Moreover I do not recollect a case where the *aroma* of the vocabulary is so well chosen. It evidences once again Jesus's love of puns. The 'treasure-in-heaven' motif proves that at vv.16—20 a genuine teaching of Jesus barely survives the retelling in Greek. The questions whether 15 is more than Lucan paste between 14 and 16, and whether 21 is his unaided composition, whether Luke really knew what Jesus meant, or to what extent he adapted the parable to his favourite theme of poverty,[2] all bear reinvestigation. It will be found that 13—21 is a unit: perhaps it is its hinge with 12: 1—12 (legal proceedings in the nature of inquisition) which is rather insecure.

THE QUESTION

'Teacher, tell my brother to divide the inheritance with me!' An ill-omened petition, as we shall see. The inheritance was probably their father's. There are many possible reasons why the brother should be reluctant. Perhaps there was a disposition by the father in his lifetime which the brother (*was* he the eldest son?) neglected to implement,[3] since no *diatiki* was automatically valid against the scriptural rights of male issue.[4] Hence he might well lis-

---

[1] A. Jülicher, *Die Gleichnisreden Jesu* II (Tübingen, 1910), pp.608—17. J. Bligh, *Christian Deuteronomy* (Langley, 1970), sec.15, has a correct approach.

[2] See W.G. Kümmel, 'Der Begriff des Eigentums im Neuen Testament', in his *Heilsgeschehen und Geschichte. Gesammelte Aufsätze 1933—64* (Marburg, 1965), p.273 (Luke sharpens Jesus' words on complete renunciation: Lk 14: 21/Mt 22: 9). Luke's peculiar passages are 1: 53; 3: 11; 4: 18; 6: 24—5; 12: 13—21; 14: 12—14, 33; 16: 1—13, 19—31.

[3] On the whole subject of dispositions and attempted dispositions, and the lameness of the Jewish law in this regard relative to Roman law, see R. Yaron, *Gifts in Contemplation of Death* (Oxford, 1960).

[4] G. Horowitz, *Spirit of Jewish Law* (New York, 1953), pp.402, 405—6, for a succinct explanation. Obedience to the oral commands of an ascendant was a high moral duty, but not necessarily enforced at law.

ten to a religious teacher! A 'saint's' arbitral award is acceptable in societies (e.g. pre-revolutionary Russia, China, Taiwan) where litigation is costly and unpredictable. To place embittered relatives at peace, and especially where they quarrel (as ever) over an inheritance, should seemingly be a religious teacher's prerogative and pleasure (as indeed it was: see below). A problem which would not yield to precept of the Law might well, by give and take, find a compromise. Such reconciliations are performed by many a judge even today: Jesus might have helped the pair, and if thereby they avoided recourse to a hellenistic state court, so much the better.[5] *Actually he did help them,* precisely by refusing the petition as made to him!

THE ANSWER

This falls into three parts: the refusal of jurisdiction, the moral warning, and the maxim. The brothers were quarrelling. The speaker asked Jesus to enjoin a partition, a separation of their co-tenancy, sharply separating warring parties as Moses tried to do at Ex 2: 13. Partition is a seemingly final thing, but it always leaves loose ends. What a way to frame the petition! Jesus is to be deprived of the spiritual gain he would make by 'making peace between man and his fellow'.[6] This was one of the acts of charity which were believed to win for the doer imperishable reward in the World to Come.[7] The petitioner assumed too readily that 'peace' was achieved by severance, whereas it might have been better for them to live in amity and unity (*ameristoi,* Ephr.3.xxv) (see Gen 13: 8, Ps.133: 1; everlasting life is associated with the latter!). In the Golden Age boundaries were unnecessary and partition unheard-of.[8] Claiming to be brothers (cf. 1 Cor 6: 5–6, Heb 13: 1), one of them wanted a partition, ill-omened since the true 'inheritance' (Mk 10: 17/ Lk 10: 25, 18: 18; 1 Cor 6: 9, 15: 50; Tit 3: 7, Justin, *Dial.* 119,5) is impartible (Gal 6: 9; Acts 20: 32, 26: 18), for only the outcasts are divided

5 Derrett, 'Law in the New Testament: the Parable of the Unjust Judge', NTS XVIII (1972), pp.178–91.

6 $h^a v \bar{a}'at \ \check{s}\bar{a}l\hat{o}m \ b\hat{e}n \ '\bar{a}d\bar{a}m \ lah^a v\bar{e}r\hat{o}$ (Mishnah, Peah I, 1). This function is very important: b. Yev.109a. Ta'an.22a. Peace must be brought about even at the cost of truth: b.Yev.25b, j.Sot.I.4,16d., cf.b.Ber.64a. Mishnah, 'Eduy,VIII.7, 'Avot I.18. Aaron was peacemaker while Moses was justice-giver (!) b.Sanh.6b, 'Avot I.12,cf.b. Yoma 7lb. Praise of him who makes peace: Mekilta, Ba-Hodesh 11 (tr.Lauterbach, ii,p.290; StrB I, p.215). Blessed are the peacemakers: Mt 5: 9 (cf.1 Chr 22: 9–10), Heb 12: 14. Philo, *Spec.Leg.* II.192 (a divine attribute). Foerster, TWNT II, 408. G.F. Moore, *Judaism* II (1927), pp.195–7. H. Windisch, 'Friedensbringer – Gottessöhne', ZNW XXIV (1925), pp.240–60 at 244 (cf. Foerster, TWNT II, 418 n.2).

7 See below, note 70.

8 So also ancient Indian tradition: see W.W. Rockhill, *Life of the Buddha* (London, 1884), pp.5–6.

(Lk 12: 46).[9] A demand for partition is what the selfish Sodomites would seek (Gen 13: 11–13).[10] Stupidly, since everyone could call to mind[11] instances where brothers took their legal shares and in no time one was in poverty and the other had an abundance: the virtues of remaining joint were by no means inconsiderable.

If Jesus is another Moses, about to effect the final Redemption, he must do better than Moses who, before he had effected the first Redemption, failed to reconcile two warring Hebrews (Ex 2: 13–15), not only incurred the wrath of the heathen power but proved his own want of natural leadership. The two men, Dathan and Abiram,[12] were not only unaware of Moses's status as a *vindicator,*[13] redeemer, but were notorious trouble-makers who went, eventually, alive into Hell. Saying, 'Man, who appointed me judge or divider over you?' Jesus disclaimed authority (from God) to impose a legal decision upon them both, either in the quality of judge (which he will have after the Redemption!)[14] or as divider (instead of healer!).[15] Even Moses, when he was asked to handle a *partition* problem (Num 27: 1–7, 36: 2–10), went direct to God for an oracle – *and it is striking that the actual decision never represented Hebrew law as it developed,* it was an *ad hoc* provision.[16] Jesus disclaims Moses' role, for reasons which will soon appear.

A peacemaker, which, taking the long view, Jesus was, a judge and redeemer at an abstract level which the brothers could not comprehend, will

---

9 If we exclude the peculiar example of Mk 12: 7/Lk 20: 14, there is no literal example of *klēronomeō* and cognate words in the N.T. except Lk 12: 13!

10 R. Ze'era in Pirq e: de R. Eliezer 25 (tr. Friedlander, p.181): Ps 52: 9 and 49: 6 so read. Cf. C. Schöttgen, *Hor. Heb.,* p.883. Luke knew the myth of the Sodomites: see Derrett, *Law in the New Testament* (London, 1970), p.87 (hereafter *Law*); to the references add *Mart. Is.* 3: 10.

11 E.g. Xenophon, *Symp.* 4, 35 (Loeb ed., 1969, p.428); Philostratus, *Apoll.* 1, 13.

12 Midr. R. Exod. 1, 30 (Sonc. tr., p.38): 'Tale-bearing is rife amongst them. . .'; Sir 45: 18, Jude 11; Philo, *Mos.* I, 46; b. Sanh. 109b, Meg. 11a; Yalqût Šim. § 167; b.M.Q.16a; Midr.R.Num.18, 10; J. Lever, 'Korah, Dathan and Abiram', *Scripta Hierosol.* VIII (1961), pp.189–217. The connection is Num 16: 13.

13 *Sofēt* means judge and vindicator: see 1 Sam 24: 16, 2 Sam 18: 19, 31 and other references in BDB, *Lexicon,* s.v.,3b. This is the midrash at Acts 7: 35 (cf. Lk 24: 21). I believe the point was seen by the gifted A.R. Habershon, *The Study of the Parables* (London, 1904), p.42.

14 Believers knew that Ps 72 depicted the Messiah as judge, but the question was 'when?'.

15 There is no reason to believe that the *Gospel of Thomas* retains pre-synoptic material. However it is significant that G. Thom 92 (= 94, 1–6) and 106 (= 98, 18–22) show the gnostics correctly retaining the idea that Jesus insisted he was a uniter (restoring the great Unity!). So correctly identified by E. Haenchen, *Die Botschaft des Thomas-Evangeliums* (Berlin, 1961), p.53. W. Grundmann, *Das Evangelium nach Lukas*[2] (Berlin, 1964), pp.255–8. My own suggestion is that the admittedly very rare word *meristēs* is a translation of *gozēr* (for which v. inf.).

16 Cf. N.H. Snaith, VT XVI (1966), pp.124–7; J. Weingreen, ibid., pp.518–22.

not take anyone's part in a quarrel, however justified he might be in inter-
fering. To court popularity by deciding people's disputes was not an auspicious notion, as the story of Absalom shows.[17] Even the son forgot that it is
the true king who awards decrees, and presumption is tantamount to
rebellion. To remind litigants of their religious duty is another matter.
Absalom's mistake reminds us of Solomon, himself king and paragon of
wisdom, a practical man if ever there was one. 'Divide the living child. . .! –
palm-tree justice? Hardly. The word translated here, exceptionally, 'divide',
means literally cut, and, as is well known,[18] *decree*. Attempting to provide a
practical substitute for the fine scales of divine justice, one may indeed play
with partition as a means to an end, but it is not necessarily the answer. The
followers of the Messiah might well expect him to deal out justice according to the messianic psalm 72: 1–4, but in vv.13–14 of the same psalm his
assignment is more general.

'Watch and guard[19] yourselves from every (scintilla of) greed (or
appetitiveness)'. 'Covetousness' is a little too narrow, since one cannot covet
that to which one has a right. But greed is another matter. *Pleonexia* is one
of the sins, one of its characteristics being that one *encroaches* on one's neighbour's share (hence Deut 19: 14).[20] Jesus is concerned with the moral condition of the man before him; the other brother has not submitted to his
advice. If it would be wrong to connive at *his* unlawfully detaining assets, the
petitioner could have been actuated by desire for that to which he had no
natural title by labour and which was superfluous to his needs: one cannot be
greedy in respect of one's 'necessaries'. This was not a dispute about maintenance, on which subject Jesus could, of course, be sarcastic.[21] Inheritance
is another matter. The heirs and dependants were up to that moment being
maintained, in part at least, out of it. Partition could have been desired to

17 2 Sam 15: 4. A Schlatter, *Das Evangelium des Lukas* (Stuttgart, 1931), p.317,
discovered this. As so often, he was ignored. For *katestēsen* as the correct word for
'appointement' see Jos., B.J. II 571; Ant. IX, 4, XVI, 203; Vita 49.

18 Heb. *gāzar*, Aram. $g^c z\bar{a}r$. *Gozēr* is (1) a splitter (e.g. circumciser), (2) author of
a decree having the force of law. See Jastrow, Dict., s.v. The suggestion of G. Maier,
'Verteilt Jesus die Güter dieser Erde. . .', *Theol. Beitr.* V (1974), pp.149–58, that Jesus,
contrasted with Moses, refused earthly justice, is attacked (rightly) by R. Weisskopf,
ibid. VI (1975), pp.23–7, and U. Eibach, ibid. pp.27–30. Maier's reply is ibid.,
pp.72–4.

19 Philo, *Spec. Leg.* IV, 149 (Colson, VIII, p.100); Test. Jud. 18: 2.

20 The verse refers specifically to *inheritance* in this world and by interpretation in
the World to Come. See Philo, quoted above. G.B. Caird, *The Gospel of St Luke*
(Harmondsworth, 1963), p.163, rightly points out that those that have entered the
Kingdom have no use for litigation.

21 Mt 15: 4–6/Mk 7: 9–13 (see Derrett, 'Korban. . .', NTS XVI (1970), pp.364–8:
add to the references Prov 28: 24 and Philo, *Hypoth.* VII, 3–5).

clear off, or reduce, such claims. As *teacher* Jesus warns him of the dangers of greed, for the *greedy* will not *inherit* the World to Come (1 Cor 6: 9—10). If they can avoid greed they may spontaneously avoid a partition. I have been observing partition actions for about 30 years and none favoured economy. 15a flows well from 13—14. Now for the intriguing 15b.

The maxim has some disagreeable implications. With practically no exceptions[22] the widely divergent translations[23] agree in failing to see the point. No wonder. It is a cross double paradox. The sustained paronomasia is marvellous. ὅτι οὐκ ἐν τῷ περισσεύειν τινὶ ἡ ζωὴ αὐτοῦ ἐστιν ἐκ τῶν ὑπαρχόντων αὐτῷ. Here *perisseuein* must mean to be present in superfluity.[24] The person has more than he needs. Translate. 'For it is not at the point where he has a superfluity that a person lives on his assets (such as they are)': Awkward Greek, and impossible to translate back into Aramaic or Hebrew, but evidence that Luke wanted to allude to Aristotle.[25] The temporal usage of *en* with the articular infini-

---

[22] Knox and Rieu come very close, though they differ. A.T. Cadoux, *The Parables of Jesus* (London, n.d.), p.204, was near to the point. No one has observed *both* that *perisseuein* implies surplus *and* that the *huparchonta* are indeed means of life.

[23] For the older efforts admirably summarized and juxtaposed see M. Polus, *Syn.* (1669) IV ad loc. With their aid I can manage an improvement: read *nec enim cuiusquam vita, quae ex eis quae ipsi suppetunt tenetur, in eo sita est ut redundent.* The ironies of C.C. Tarelli, JTS XLI (1940), pp.260—2, are understandable, but his solution, to alter the text, is unnecessary. B. Weiss correctly identified *einai ek*. (*Die Evangelien des Markus und Lukas* [Göttingen, 1901], p.488). Winer-Moulton *Treatise on the Grammar of New Testament Greek* III § 47 (ed. 3, p.460) cite 1 Cor 9: 14, Arist. *Pol.* 3,3; Lk 16: 9. See Gal 3: 10, Rom 3: 26; 4: 14—16: *ek tinos einai* = depend from. Contra, Bauer-Arndt-Gingrich, s.v. *ek* 3f. (because of). Tarelli thought the meaning was that it was foolish to trust to a superfluity for one's maintenance. So also Klostermann. Moffatt: a man's life is not part of his possessions because he has ample wealth. Fitzmyer favours, 'even if one is in abundance one is none the more secure as a result of one's wealth'. Rengstorf likewise, but, 'one does not derive one's life from one possessions', citing Sir 15: 1 (one is not secure with a sufficiency). J.A. Findlay, *The Gospel according to St Luke* (London, 1937), p.147: 'when a man has more than enough he does not get his true life from his possessions'. W.O.E. Oesterley, *The Gospel Parables* (London, 1936), p.170, 'it does not depend upon the abundance of things that a man possesses as to whether he leads a profitable life', citing Ps 49: 6—10.

[24] Contrasted with sufficiency: Xen., *Symp.*4,35; Jos., Ant.XVI,19. To have a superfluity: Polyb.18,18,5. Cf. esp. Philo, *Re.div.her.*191 (ad Ex 16: 16—18). On *perissos*, P. Joüon, 'Marc 14.31', RSR XXIX (1939), pp.240—1. The allusion is to Tob 4: 16 (so Jülicher).

[25] The comparison with Arist., *Ethic.Nic.* X,8,9—10 was suggested by M.—J. Lagrange, *Evangile selon Saint Luc* (Paris, 1921), p.358. 'Self-sufficiency [which has a particular evaluation in the system] does not depend upon a superabundance of means, nor does conduct [i.e. moral achievement], and a man may perform noble actions without being master of land and sea'. See J.A.K. Thompson, trans., *The Ethics of Aristotle* (Harmondsworth, 1959), p.308: the whole chapter is relevant, and throws light on Luke's intention.

tive[26] occurs no less than 26 times in St Luke alone, not to speak of Acts. Cases where it can mean 'in that', or 'because' are not rare in classical Greek and occur in the literature of our period.[27] But the temporal use fits our context. An effort must be made to envisage a Hebrew original and I suggest: *kî hayê hā'ādām 'ênām t'lûyîm b'môtrôtāyw.* This makes good sense. 'For the life of man does not depend from his superfluities (or luxuries)'. Students of Jesus who seek after the life to come can hardly claim to be concerned with superfluities in specie (*ad possidendum*), for such concern is greed. To this statement the words *ek tōn huparchontōn autō* have been added. They were thought necessary, apparently, in order to make it quite clear that *perisseuein,* which is an ambiguous word in Greek, means, here, the fact that a man *has* his assets and more than enough. The result is that though one's life depends from that which is available to one, including the beggars' bowl, pouch and stick, it can never depend from what is superfluous to one's needs. Food is for life, and vice versa (Lk 12: 22). Moreover, the phrase *ek tōn huparchontōn autō* (v.l. *autou*) bears a very significant aroma for a Greek; he wrote it when he pledged his assets to secure a loan.[28] Even when one has a superfluity one's life is not a charge (as we say in English) on one's assets. Superfluity does not make life *exigible* from them. The legal twist to the saying makes the point obvious. Yet the truism takes on a new meaning when one tries to work out the paradoxes. Hebrew, like English, has only one word for life, but it is conveniently plural. Greek has two: *bios* is nearer to livelihood, means of living; *zoe* (the opposite of death) is adopted for true life, the Life to Come.[29] The Hebrew pun is in danger of being lost.

Four meanings are to be elicited: (*a*) a man's daily life depends from the essentials (and is not the poorer for want of superfluities), (*b*) the individual's true (eternal) life depends from his spiritual assets (see below) which can never be superfluous; (*c*) a man's life in the World to Come does not depend on his worldly assets, however numerous, but from his otherworldly assets

---

26 Winer-Moulton III, § 44.6; Blass-Debrunner-Funk, § 404. Jülicher, p.615, refers to Lk 10: 35.

27 Heb 8: 13; 1 Clem 10,1; Pap. Oxyr. IV, 734.35 (2nd c. B.C.); other examples in Blass-Debrunner-Funk, § 404(3).

28 R. Taubenschlag, *The Law of Graeco-Roman Egypt in the Light of the Papyri* (New York, 1944), pp.230, n.5, 402, 408; J. Modrzejewski, *Tijdschrift voor Rechtsgeschiedenis* 31 (1963), p.114.

29 R.C. Trench, *Synonyms of the New Testament*[9] (London, 1880), § 27; id., *Notes on the Parables* (London, 1898), p.339; D. Hill, *Greek Words and Hebrew Meanings* (Cambridge, 1967), ch.5. J. Dillersberger, *The Gospel of Saint Luke* (Cork, 1958), pp.327–8: the man did have a living, but not the means of Living. Note that the talmudic word for alimentation (maintenance), the equivalent of *bios,* is *m'zônôt.*

(however exiguous); and (d) there *is* superfluity in the World to Come,[30] but man's life in *this* world does *not* depend on what causes it (i.e. his spiritual assets). There is a paradoxical balance between the superfluity in this life and the superfluity in the life to come: the latter can be literally acquired by the way one handles one's *total* assets in this life: render as much as possible superfluous to you here, and dispose of it in obedience to the commandments, and it will purchase for you a true and lasting abundance hereafter. If you assess what is superfluous to you at a generous rate here (by allowing yourself luxuries at your option) you diminish your stock hereafter! Gospel instances of superfluity bear out these intriguing notions. Superfluity was gathered in baskets,[31] which had been blessed (see below): yet it was not superfluous. At Lk 15: 17 the labourers have a superfluity, out of which the *prodigal* can be fed (!): the eldest brother was jealous of the use of an inherited means of production!

Most significant of the instances is Mk 12: 44/Lk 21: 4, the glorious paradox asserted by Jesus himself and not recognized for what it is, a careful pun on 'treasury' and depositing in it.[32] The rich threw their copper coins[33] into the earthly treasury for the relief of the poor.[34] The widow who was herself an object of charity[35] believed, in strict accord with Jewish piety,[36]

30 LXX, Amos 9: 13, Isai 65: 17—25; Ezek 47; Joel 4: 18. For rabbinical references see Hauck in TWNT VI, pp.58—9. Hauck thought Lk 12: 15 and Mt 12: 44 the *only* uneschatological instances of *perisseuein*, but he was mistaken: all references are!

31 Mt 14: 20/Lk 9: 17 (Q)/Jn 6: 12—13.

32 Mk is heavily semitic, Lk modifies and weakens the force of the pun. Mishnah, Šeq.6,5 is irrelevant. *Gazophulakeion* is (*1*) the Treasury and (*2*) the safe-deposit of heaven! For *ebalen* cf. Mt 25: 27. See Lev 11: 1, MT. M. Dibelius, *From Tradition to Gospel* (London, 1934), p.261 and R. Bultmann, *History of the Synoptic Tradition* (Oxford, 1963), pp.32—3, doubt whether anything more than a parable or a biographical apophthegm lies behind the story. F. Hirsch, *Frühgeschichte des Evangeliums* I (Tübingen, 1951), pp.137—8, is unacceptable.

33 *Chalkon* can indeed mean 'cash' (Liddell-Scott-Jones, *Greek-English Lexicon*, s.v., II.4) (Grundmann, *Markus*, p.257), but surviving papyrus cheques invariably use it of copper as such. Here the point of copper donations was clear: they could be given to the poor in specie without the loss which would have been sustained (to the donors!) by changing gold and silver into small change. *Dora* is *qorban*, which was certainly used for relief of the poor. This is why those objectionable vows came into vogue: the votary assigned his assets to the use of the poor including his parent (whom he could not exclude). Note Tob 4: 11. On the actual coinage itself see D. Sperber, NT IX(1963), pp.178—90 (he perceives a pre-Greek source, correctly).

34 See last note. Not the temple service (as Grundmann, ibid.).

35 *Ptōchē* (Jesus himself so identified her according to Luke) means 'down and out'. (Cf. G. de Sainte-Croix, 'Early Christian Attitudes to Poverty and Slavery', in *Church, Society and Politics*, ed. D. Baker (Oxford, 1975), [pp.1—38], p.11.

36 b. Gitt. 7a (Soncino tr. p.24): 'if a man sees that his daily bread is meagre (has run out: Goldschmidt, *Bab. Tal.* V, p.380, n.146), out of that he should still give alms; even more so if his daily fare is abundant... Said Mar Zutra, 'A poor man who is supported by ha-ṣadaqa should still give ṣadaqa himself' (ibid.7b). Alms was greater than

that what was *on that day* superfluous to her should be given for the relief of others. Jesus knew that she had a right to keep for the next day what might have turned out to be her livelihood. The rich, seemingly enlarging the earthly treasury of the Lord, did not proportionately enlarge their 'treasure in heaven'. Even the pagan world was aware that the gods weigh the sacrifice of the sacrificer in the scales of his ability.[37] But Jesus announces that her treasure is greater than that of all the rich collectively since they gave from their superfluity and thus their sacrifice was more nominal than real. To the theme we shall return. One scholar has observed that the Widow's Mites are the essential clue to the Rich Fool and his context.[38] No doubt the church, even then seeing Christ as a priest, accepts his authentic pronouncement to the advantage of even modest donors' contributions, but this must not distract us from the fact that biblical learning and ideas current amongst pious Jews not less than two centuries before Jesus's day (see the whole of Tob 4) agree that alms and offerings must be given out of one's capital (like *zakat* in Islamic law) and not out of the net balance left when one's expenses have been met. The Vow of Jacob runs (Gen 28: 20—22): 'If God will be with me... and will give me bread to eat and clothing to wear, so that I come again to my father's house in peace, then the Lord shall be my God, and this stone, which I have set up for a pillar, shall be God's house; and of all that thou givest me I will give the tenth to thee'. There might be discussion about what the exact proportion should be,[39] one might begrudge all but *perisseuma* (2 Cor 8: 14), and a Pharisee might believe that only income needed to be tithed (Lk 18: 12); but it is clear that only food, clothing and shelter are necessities,[40] and of the *total* assets whatever corresponds to a 'tenth' is owed to comply with the commandments relative to the poor, etc. Righteousness and charity, alms, are interchangeable terms, as is well known,[41] for to give in alms is to obey commandments. 'Both riches and honour come from thee... For all things come from thee, and of thy own have we given thee... our days on the earth are like a shadow, and there is no abiding' (1 Chr 29: 12—15).

---

sacrifices: b.Sukk.49b (R. Elazar). S. Krauss, *Talmudische Archäologie* III (1912), p.71. Midr. R.Lev. 3,5 (Sonc.tr, pp.39—40), a story of 10 B.C. to 40 A.D.; ibid.,34.2 (Sonc. tr., pp.427—8); b.B.B.10a (Sonc. tr., p.49).

37 Euripides, *Danaae* fr.327.4—7 (A. Nauck, *Trag. Gr Frag.*, 1964, 458).

38 K. Bornhäuser, *Studien zum Sondergut des Lukas* (Gütersloh, 1934), pp.81—93.

39 b. Ket.50a (Sonc. tr., p.286), the ruling at Usha: a tenth plus a tenth.

40 Sir 29: 21. 1 Tim 6: 8.

41 D. Hill, *Greek Words...* (n.29 above), ch.4; Ps.Sal. 9: 5 (9: 9 in Ryle-James, 1891); Prov 11: 4, but illustrations are endless.

THE MAXIM AND THE PARABLE

The story of the Widow's Mites proves that Eternal Life may well arise (Lk 12: 33, 16: 4,9) from superfluities as well as 'essentials'. In the World to Come all enjoyable superfluities will abound. This bears on an inheritance dispute between hearers of Jesus, in a manner which strikes the student of canon law and its history from Constantine onwards as deeply ironical.[42] The parties in Lk 12: 13 were in dispute about a margin superfluous to both of them; they were jeopardizing an opportunity to dispose of it charitably. If their present income was 800 den., and partitioned, less expenses of building and fencing, with separate living costs and marketing costs, it would bring in a total of 700 den., the lost 100 den. could have been devoted to charitable purposes, *to their spiritual profit*. The petitioner called him 'teacher'[43] and here was teaching indeed! If, on the other hand, what was in dispute was a capital estate from which father and two sons had drawn their living, say a total of 3 den. a day, and after the father's death those 3 den. became available for two persons alone, this would leave them with an annual amount of 365 den. for charity! To remain undivided would leave them better off in this world and richer in the world to come.

The Mosaic law of inheritance[44] has no bearing on this situation. The Torah operates unexceptionably as to means of subsistence. 'Righteousness' and alms are not less enjoined.[45] The obligation to provide for the disposal of assets over and above one's barest needs for one's soul's health is a fundamental rule which Moses's oracles on inheritance cannot modify. The two ideas runs concurrently. The maxim about superfluity is illustrated by the very funny story in the parable.

THE PARABLE

The word *agatha* in 18 proves that we have an authentic Hebrew or Aramaic story in front of us. Greek was barely capable of using it to mean 'benefit'. No doubt good deeds counted in pagan notions of the last judgement, and deities took notice of good deeds. But 'good', meaning the fact of A having benefited B, is confined to such restricted usages that they are

---

[42] See Hugo Grotius' once celebrated, succinct and pungent comment on our passage, reproduced in M. Polus, *Syn.* IV (1669), pp.1014–15.

[43] F. Hahn, *The Titles of Jesus in Christology* (Eng. tr., London, 1969), pp.73–8.

[44] Mishnah, B.B. 8–9. Maimonides, *Mishneh Torah* (Code) XIII ('Civil Laws', i.e., 'Judgments'), V (tr. J.J. Rabinowitz, New Haven, 1949).

[45] See below, p.141, n.60. K. Berger, 'Almosen', *NTS* 23 (1977), pp.180–204.

barely a precedent for our purpose.[46] The Hebrew *tôvâ* and its Aramaic equivalent *tevutā'* provide a notorious double meaning.[47] The pun is written out at large in Tobit.[48] The good deeds A does to B are benefits from B's point of view,[49] but coincidentally *assets* to the credit of A.[50] The pious do good with their assets and make God grateful, as it were, where there is no reciprocity in this life. Such gratitude is capital. One's worldly treasure is underground, one's spiritual capital in the vaults of heaven.[51] Tobit's Hebrew and Aramaic versions, which must have some close relation to the
*   original,[52] actually use the very vocabulary. We find the word 'barns'![53] If non-human creatures require no barns it is presumably because they require no merit, as they require no store.[54] The Palestinian Targum uses the word barns on Deut 32: 34 for the acts done secretly.[55]

The intriguing and beautiful idea, 'treasure in heaven', undoubtedly part of Christ's teaching,[56] does not derive from the Old Testament. It was, however, part of Sirach's thought-world,[57] and therefore was acceptable piety by 180 B.C. It was very well accepted by A.D. 50, since it is utilized in the

---

46 Thuc. III, 52.4, 54.2 (the Plataeans), 68.1; Lysias 13, 92; benefactors: Aristophanes, *Aves* 1706; the usage *ep' agathō*, to the advantage of, opposite to *epi kakō;* Xen., *Cyrop.* VII, 4.3 Aristoph., *Ranae* 1487–8; *ouk ep' agathō*, Thuc. I, 131.1, V,27.2. Xen., *Hist. Gr.*, V, 2,35. The meaning 'good deeds' *is* found at Jn 5: 29 and
*   Hermas, *Mand.* 10: 3,1.
47 See BDB, *Lexicon*, s.v., 2,3(a), 3(b); Neh 6: 19. *Tôv* itself means 'good things', ibid., s.v., 2 and 3; benefit: Prov 30: 12, Gen 26: 29, Prov 14: 22, etc. For the Aramaic see Jastrow, *Dict.*, s.v.
48 Tob 4: 21f.
49 Jastrow, *Dict.*, s.v. *tôvâ* (2), citing b. Sot 47b., Ibid., s.v., *tivu*.
50 Ibid., *tôvâ* (2) citing Mishnah, Sev. 4, 1, 2 and b. Pes. 46b. Likewise s.v. *tivu.*,
51 Tob 4: 9. A deposit with a bank: Plut., *Consol. ad Apoll. 28.*
52 F. Zimmermann, *The Book of Tobit* (New York, 1958), pp.68–70. The book was composed in Hebrew about 160 B.C. (ibid., pp.24, 37–8).
53 A. Neubauer, *Book of Tobit* (Oxford, 1878), xxxii, 1; the Aramaic actually cites Gen 28: 22! Neubauer read the equivalent of *hupothēkē*, Nöldeke *apothēkē*. R. Charles, *Apocrypha and Pseudepigrapha of the Old Testament*, I (Oxford, 1913), p.211.
54 Lk 12: 24. Pursuing their instincts the creatures live on a hand-to-mouth basis, and show no consideration for each other. Man's complex and refined development requires as well as permits accumulation, but subject to God's coefficient requirements.
55 Deut 32: 34 (Pal. Targ.: *'apôtēqayī*). Job 14: 17. Hos 13: 12. Note the reverse of the 'treasure in heaven' idiom at Rom 2: 5–6. On barns and that which is hidden from sight see the reference to Deut 28: 8 at b. Ta'an.8b (Sonc. tr., p.36), B.M. 42a (Sonc. tr., p.250).
56 Mt 6: 19–21, 19: 21/Mk 10: 21, Lk 12: 33–4, 18: 22. Bo Reicke claims this is an exception to the 'new direction' in the Christian theory of reward: 'The New Testament concept of reward', *Mélanges Goguel* (Neuchâtel-Paris, 1950), pp.195ff., at p.205.
57 Sir 29: 11 (q.v.): The Peshitta is particularly helpful here (see Charles, *A.&P.*I, 411).

widespread legend of the historical character Monobazus II,[58] convert to Judaism and holy prodigal. The texts which he cites to justify his conduct,[59] viz. dissipating his assets amongst the poor, etc., attempt to attach the idea to scripture, occasionally plausibly. The idea itself persisted for long in Christian and Jewish circles.[60] It was the fruit of a marriage between the hellenic taste for paradox and Jewish piety. Jews knew that God prepared treasures for his elect,[61] and that he rewarded those that did his will.[62] The acquisition of merit was a Jewish concept of indefinite age. The hellenic contribution arose in a different way. Reciprocity was a fundamental maxim of life: *do ut des*.[63] Gifts to friends not only secured their friendship but secured, literally, their generosity in future. The best treasure was the gratitude of (benefited) friends.[64] In *that* sense friends themselves were treasures. In the absence of hotels, and with the limited range of banking facilities until quite late in history, friends were literally assets upon which one could draw (but not overdraw, I suppose). These are commonplace ideas of the hellenic

---

58 *Der Kleine Pauly* III(2), 1412. King of Adiabene from c.59. Became a Jew: Jos., Ant.XX, 17–53, Midr. R. Gen. 46,10; associated with Palestinian Judaism: Jos., B.J. V, 252. Mishnah, Yom. 3, 10. H. Grätz, 'Zur Anwesenheit der Adiabenischer Königin in Jerusalem und des Apostel Paulus', *Monats.f.G.W.Jud.*XXVI (1877), pp.241–55, 289–306; N. Brüll, 'Adiabene', *Jahrb. J.G.L.* I (1874), pp.58–86; J. Neusner, 'The conversion of Adiabene to Judaism, a new perspective', JBL LXXXIII (1964), pp.60–66. Tos.Peah 14,18; j. Peah 1,15b,533: Schwab II, 7–8; b.B.B.11a (Sonc. tr., pp.52–3); Pes. Rabb.25.2 (tr., W.G. Braude, 1968, II, 515). A. Marmorstein, *Doctrine of Merits in Old Rabbinical Literature* [1920] (New York, 1968), p.21.

59 Ps 85: 12, 89: 15, Is 3: 10; Prov 11: 30; Deut 24: 13; Is 58: 8. Alternatively Ps 97: 2 and Prov 10: 2. or 8. Ps 31: 20 (31: 30) is much favoured: Midr.R.Lev.3,6 (Sonc. tr., p.41); Midr.R.Deut.1,19 (Sonc. tr., p.21). Note how Aquila and Symmachus translated *ṣāfantā*.

60 2 Cor 8: 7–15; 1 Tim 6: 6–10, 17–19. The date of the latter is disputed: see W.G. Kümmel, *Introduction to the New Testament* (London, 1966), p.272. Cf. C.F.D. Moule, *The Birth of the New Testament* (London, 1962), pp.220–1. R. 'Aqiba at Pes.R.25.2 (Braude II,516), citing Ps 112: 9 and Prov 3: 9,10. Test. Levi 13,5. Cf. Test. Napht.8,5. Philo, *Praem.* 104; 4 Ezra 7: 77, 8: 33, cf.8: 36. Apoc.Bar.14: 12 (Charles, 1896, p.27). S1. Henoch 50: 5 (Charles, *A.&P.* II,400), b.Šab.31b. Midr. R.Exod.45,6; Midr. R.Gen.9,5 = (Sonc. tr., p.67), ibid. 9–10 (Sonc. tr., pp.68–9); 39,3 (tr., p.314); Midr. R.Lev. 28,1 = (tr., p.358): Midr.R.Qo.I,3,1 (Sonc. tr., p.7); Yalq. Šim. § 966. Ibid. § 784: R. Jehuda said, 'Sin is barren and produces no fruit, but righteousness/charity does produce fruit (*pērôt*).

61 Ps 31: 20. Cf. Deut 32: 34.

62 Deut 28. Ps 73. Of particular value is Sir 11: 21–28.

63 H. Bolkestein, *Wohltätigkeit und Armenpflege in vorchristlichen Altertum* (Utrecht, 1939), pp.157–9.

64 (Ps.) Isocr. *Ad Demonic.*29 Libanius, *Epist.*728 (817) (R. Foerster, 1921, p.738) a reminiscence of Isocrates. Philostratus, *Soph.*II.547 (W.C. Wright, 1952 , pp.138–40). Phalaris, *Ep.*12 (2nd cent.A.D.). Agapetus, *Diac.cap.*38 (PG 86,1176). Xenophon works out the 'friends' treasure' theme at length at *Cyr.*8,2,15ff. (Miller,II,338ff.). Ibid. § 22 is very like Mt 6: 20.

world.[65] In Lk 16:9 we see the Greek concept neatly married to the old Jewish concept.[66] He who gives to the poor lends to the Lord (Prov 19:17). Opened out with an adaptation of the Greek fancy the doctrine is this: the Lord (how Jewish!) is banker for the pious and stores up their good deeds for them, to collect the capital in the World to Come. This concept emerges in the New Testament with assurance and an abundance of imagery.[67] The idea, returned into Greek garb would occasion no surprise. The words for *treasure*, though they apply to an individual's hoard or even cash balance, are very happy in connection with deities' temple-deposits.[68] Yahweh was no exception. His temple too held deposits not only for religious purposes but also for individuals' convenience. That was not the only culture that utilized the deity's superior buildings and staff for purposes of simple security. The metaphor was therefore a happy one; human friends surely would reciprocate if you did them a good turn; the poor who could not reciprocate and those whom you benefited in secret and without your or their identities' being known will be represented by Yahweh, who will also surely compensate in secret.[69] Reward there must be for the selfless deed, and it is obviously in heaven.

On the other hand, a theory of greater sophistication made itself felt before Monobazus' time (we cannot say that the theory as we find it in the Mishnah [70] was so systematized in Jesus' time): this was that certain good deeds, including respect for parents, acts of loving kindness, making peace, and so forth, which cannot be reciprocated in this life, are *not only* rewarded in the World to Come, as an imperishable treasure, but that reward (again in the metaphor of the divine bank!), whilst remaining undiminished, produced fruit (*pêrôt*), i.e. interest (!) in this world.[71] God rewards, in this life

65 An absolute truism: Pap.Bour.1 (3rd—4th cent.A.D.) E. Ziebarth, *Aus der antiken Schule*[2], Bonn, 1913, p.23, no.46 item 21 (= *Gnoma: Monostichoi* 526; *Erotemata Chrysolarae*, ed.Aldus, 1549, p.262). Menander (ed. Sandbach, 1972), *Dys.* 797—812, deals with the folly of hoarding for you know not whom.

66 Derrett, *Law*, p.75, n.2, also Mic 6:10, Prov 11:18, Targ. Ex 18:2, Targ. Isai 33:15.

67 Rom 2:5, 1 Tim 6:17—19, Jas 5:3.

68 Dittenberger, *Syll.* 954.80 (1st cent.B.C.). The incidence of the word and cognates in Josephus produces a similar impression. For the Temple's local branch banks: Philo, *Spec. Leg.* I,78.

69 Mt 6:1,18. See above, p.140, n.55, also b.B.B.10a (Sonc. tr., p.48).

70 M. Peah I.1. Midr. R.Deut.1,15 (Sonc. tr., p.16). Midr. Ps., Ps.31 § 7 (trans. W.G. Braude,I, p.398). 'Study of the Law' as an item is illustrated by a tradition of c.150 at b.Qid.4, 14 (StrB I,439). StrB ibid.IV/1,491, b.Šab.127a (Sonc. tr., pp.632, 632—3).For another list see Mt 25:31—46. That the fruit/capital theory and treasure-in-heaven theory go back to c.180 B.C. at the latest is proved by Sir 3:3—4. We note other instances of *apothēsaurizō* and recognize it at 1 Tim 6.19.

71 J. Jeremias, *New Testament Theology* I (London, 1971), p.148. Jn 4:46 seems to reflect the theory.

itself,[72] perhaps in quite unforeseeable ways, the one who performs such acts of piety. One who is rich in piety is rich indeed.

A *rich* man's lands brought forth copiously: as did the land of Egypt under Joseph (Gen 41:47).[73] He was already rich, so the divine bounty was all superfluity. The word *chōra* suggests the open country, almost a district, in any case a region far from cities and their non-Jewish or cosmopolitan culture.[74] This unusually large harvest, for which existing accommodation was insufficient, implied provision for a coming scarcity and for a present piety. The Joseph story, while emphasizing the virtue of storage facilities,[75] shows that lean years follow fat years. The Seventh Year[76] is connected, via the Sabbath, with the provision of manna in the wilderness,[77] and with the everlasting felicity of the World to Come which is all Sabbath. The pious were preoccupied with preparations for the Seventh Year (see *Mishnah*, tractate *Sevi'it*). In the sixth year (as on Friday in the wilderness) extra stocks were stored up, and surpluses were retained instead of being sold. A bumper year suggests a sixth year: God had said so.[78] If it was not a sixth year it was as if it was. Since the Seventh Year gave a Sabbath to the ground, all produce actually arising in that year belonged to the whole people, particularly the poor. No seventh-year produce may be garnered or traded with. *
Normal barns were therefore large enough to contain a sixth year's crop.

'He calculated what he should do in view of his not having space to accumulate his produce in'. The word 'calculated' inevitably suggests a misguided contrivance of some kind.[79] *Sunagein* is the correct word for garnering crops,[80] but 'produce' of course suggests, comically, the *pêrôt*, the 'income' from one's heavenly capital, to store which there can be no shortage of space, whereas, in fact, the man's plans reveal that he will spend so little of his fortuitous gains in charitable acts that he will need little room 'up there'! Precisely because he needs more room 'down here'. Now we go back to the plain meaning of 'produce'. A miraculously large harvest (*karpos*) welcomed, on a famous occasion, the reform of the services to God. We recollect that the

---

72 Mt 6:33, Mk 10:30, Lk 18:30.

73 *Euphorēsen hē pedias:* Philo, *de Jos.159.*

74 G. de S. Croix, 'Early Christian attitudes' (n.35 above), pp.1, 2, 3, 9 (wholly Jewish); Qoh 2:8.

75 Gen 41:35–36, 48–49, 56.

76 Exod 23:10–11; Lev 25:1–7, 20–22; Deut 15:1–3, 9–12.

77 Ultimately because of the structure of Exod 16:22–27.

78 Lev 25 18–22. The reference to sowing automatically requires us to envisage barns.

79 Though in papyri the word means 'disputed, debated' the verb in the LXX almost always has the significance of a plot, etc. Both in the LXX and the New Testament *dialogismos* has negative implications.

80 Num 11:32 (quails); Gen 41:35, 49; 47:14; Jer 47:10 (LXX); Qoh 2:8.

Vow of Jacob contemplates the divine service. The provision for priests and their function is implicit in it: the shewbread and the priestly robes were amongst the items Jacob stipulated for.[81] On the occasion to which I allude the provision for the divine king's ministers was superabundant: the priests ate and drank and left over (2 Chr 31: 10 LXX) and critical difficulties arose with the heaps of tithe. So the righteous king ordered the building of go-downs to accommodate the non-perishable tithe. These were, according to the appropriate source (Jos. *Ant.*IX.274), no other than the very same structures which figure in Lk12: 18,24. In other words, admitted that both *tam(i)eion* and *apothēkē* have metaphorical usages (more the latter than the former),[82] Jewish hearers would be amused to see that instead of putting his accommodation problem into the hands of the trustees of national charities, it is the owner himself who retains this quite unnecessary embarrassment to himself.

Now God promised to bless barns and baskets, if men were obedient to him.[83] There would be no poor; and yet, due to disobedience, poor would not cease.[84] To *pull down* barns suggests contempt for God's promise, distrust for the future, and absence of concern for his ministers and services, whether ritual or charitable. It was an inopportune notion (cf. Joel 1: 17), 'I shall destroy my barns (or go-downs)[85] and build larger ones, and gather there all the corn[86] and my good things'. Will his good things be buried

---

81 In view of Gen 28: 15 (Midr.R.Lev 35,2 Sonc. tr., p.447). Jacob's vow, the first, deserves close scrutiny as it is associated with the Redemption: Tos.A.Z.IV,Sifre Deut.31, Midr. R.Gen. 70,6 (Sonc. tr., p.639), Zech 14: 8, Isai 7: 21, 11: 11, Joel 4: 18, Isai 27: 13 are associated. The food was shewbread (Ex 25: 30), the raiment the priestly garments (Ex 40: 13–14: Midr. R.Exod.19,4 (Sonc. tr., p.745), Midr. R.Lev. 37,1 (Sonc. tr., p.465). For full references see M.M. Kasher, *Encyclopedia of Biblical Interpretation* IV (New York, 1959), pp.80–83.

82 See the lexica. Metaphorical references for *tam(i)eion* can be seen at Philo, *Det. Pot.*68, *Quod Deus* 42; Themistius, *Orat.*6 (84a) and ibid.79c.

83 Prov 3: 10; Deut 28: 8 (cf.Lev 25: 21, Ps 133: 3); Deut 28: 5, cf.17. Note how 'baskets' at Deut.28: 5, 17 is rendered by the LXX. Cf. Aquila, Symmachus, and the Targum *'ōsārôt* with the LXX.

84 Deut 15: 4, 11.

85 Jer 41: 8. Storehouses (in 'towers' or underground) are really necessary for any crop to be stored in specie (Midr.R. Exod.30,14, Sonc. tr., p.362) particularly *sitos.* Gen 41: 25–31, etc. Cf. MT. Pal.Targ., LXX, Vulg. ibid. It seems that *ʾsāmê har* was the original (for *'ašerbāhem*) at Gen 41: 56 (LXX *sitobolōnas,* Vulg. *horrea,* Targ.Onq. *'ōṣāraȳā'* [so at 47], Pal.Targ. *'ōsrîn* (ditto). Kittel suggests *'oṣrôt har.*

86 It is usually thought that the man's repeated *mou* is a sign of egoism. possibly, but it catches up a *sou* elsewhere. See *corn* at Prov 3: 10 (sup.), which is God's gift: Deut 11: 14. Cf. Deut 28: 51, Isai 62: 8, Jer 31: 12, Hos 2: 8–9, Joel 2: 19, Zech 9: 17. However, the act of 'gathering the corn' into the or my barn was a metaphor for *God's* harvest: Mt.3: 12/Lk 3: 17, Mt 13: 30. The origin of this metaphor (cf. Jer 23: 28–9, Mal 4: 1) remains unknown. The idea is attractive if the souls of the righteous are, like seed-corn, (1 Cor 15: 37) awaiting the Resurrection.

with him in the tomb – for that is one of the meanings of *apothēkē*? He proposes, he who, we shall find out, needs no more than six feet of ground, a significantly larger space (mostly underground), contrived at great expense, in order to retire. Comically he wishes to have a pause, whereas what is coming is a dead stop.[87] He is to perform no services, divine or human, yet he will eat, drink and enjoy himself (cf. Sir 31: 8–11). 'Enjoy' strongly suggests the enjoyment *before the Lord* of those that honestly tithe all their produce and set aside that which is to be spent in holy joy in Jerusalem.[88] The author of this parable is an artist: he links Sir 11: 19 with the inauspicious words of Is 22: 13, 56: 12–57:11.[89] The *psyche* to which this soliloquy is addressed is the earthly, not to say earthy person made, like Adam, from clay.[90]

Any farmer, even in the relatively dependable climate of Palestine, would laugh at this man. Blight, locusts,[91] enemies, the king's troops, thieves: so many hazards lie between cup and lip. Crops to be stored must indeed be kept in the cool and the dry, but his plans sound speculative. Moreover, it is labour, even the somewhat abstract labour of the rich farmer-employer, which justifies consumption, and he plans to put a stop to it while no true farmer ever retires (Sir 11: 20). He piles up as an insurance what may be needed by poorer people immediately. The parable shows that, insurance being in fact for his heirs, or those to whom God destines all the wealth of those who accumulate assets,[92] its moral justification was negligible compared with the claims of instant need. A man who neglects, instinctively, systematic concern for the poor is suspected of evading the commandments relating to relief of the same; one will readily suspect him of lending his surplus at usury (as well he might)[93] and of keeping the corn, for example (which he goes out of his way to specify separately), until a year of scarcity has driven the price right up. Moral indignation at such behaviour is not

87 See Philem 7; Sir 31: 3–4.
88 References under *šāmaḥ*, especially in Psalms. Qoh 8: 15, 11: 9; Prov 14: 10. Deut 14: 26 offers a pattern.
89 b.Ta'an. 11a (Sonc. tr., p.48; StrB II, 190); Sir 18: 32.
90 *Psuchē* (see Deut 14: 26) is the live person as a whole (Prov 19: 12, 15) and *also* his tomb (whither the spirit will return) (hence the comedy of the form of address): B. Lifshitz, Z.D.P.V.LXXVI (1960), 159–60. Gesenius, *Dict.*, ed.17, p.515, col.1: *nefeš* 4d. The flesh is weak: see Mk 14: 38 par., Jn 12: 27. In Luke see 9: 24, 12: 19f, Acts 11: 27, 20: 10, 27: 22f. E.E. Ellis in F. Neirynck, ed., *L'Evangile de Luc. Mémorial L. Cerfaux* (Gembloux, 1974), p.146, n.14. Midr. R.Gen. 82,10 (Sonc. tr., p.760), *'ōšīn n^efāšōt l^eṣaddîqîm*, building the tombs of the just.
91 Locusts arrive in March/April, but their larvae do their worst in May/June. G. Dalman, *Arbeit und Sitte in Palästina* I/2 (Gütersloh, 1938), pp.393–5.
92 Ps 89: 11, 50: 10–12, 14. Prov 8: 21, 28: 10. See below, p.146, n.97.
93 Derrett, *Law*, pp.60–1, 65, 66, 72. Neh 5: 10. For our man see 1 Jn 3: 17.

confined to Jews.[94] An opportunity to cancel shortcomings and silence suspicion was neglected. Had he merely *intended* to distribute his surplus *before his death* he would have gained merit (Prov 11: 26, b.B.B.8*b*) whether or not he had time to implement the intention. 'This very night your life will be taken from you:[95] and who will have (even) the valuables which you *have* managed to accumulate?' The word 'Fool' is taken from nowhere but Ps 48. 11 (q.v.). In other words, it is a time of accounting (for the word 'accumulate' has an aroma of preparation for a visitation),[96] but your assets will be distributed by those to whom God assigns them (not necessarily the lawyers who will deal with a disputed *diatiki*),[97] and your few merits (he can hardly have none) are beyond your power either to bequeath or augment. From the parable of the Virgins we know[98] that the account-books of heaven are closed and that merit cannot be acquired vicariously, or too late.

    The great pun, upon which the parable turns, which secured, in fact its longevity and its appeal, lies in the 'good things', and in the double meaning of 'produce'. He thinks of piling up (not consuming) his fruits (cf. Jn 4: 36, and the fruits of the spirit: Gal 5: 22; i.e. the fruits belonging to him, not the fruit he could have produced for God, see v.21, also Rom 7: 4, Lk 3. 8–9, 13: 6–9, 20: 10, Mt 21: 41, 43, Jn 15: 2–8), in a worldly treasury, when all superfluities could have been used to create for him wealth 'with God' i.e. credit to his spiritual account.[99] Even where the ground brings forth fruitfully without the 'owner's' meriting such 'fruit' by reason of his good deeds (see above), that fruit must still be disposed of in favour of God's dependants, if anything like a corresponding capital is to be acquired in the heavenly

94 Julian, *Misopog.* 369D (Wright, II, 506); Philostratus, *Apoll.*I, 15.

95 The plural means God: Lk 6: 38, 16: 4 and perhaps 14: 29 (God laughs at the neo-Babelites?). StrB II, 221. Jeremias, *New Test. Theol,* p.9 (cat.4). Cf. Arrian, *Epict.* IV,1,172. For the idea: Ps 119: 109(?), 140: 29, Qoh 12: 7, Sap.Sal. 15: 8. All things are lent by God: Philo, *Cher.* 108–9.

96 Job 27: 16. See Moulton-Milligan, *Vocabulary,* s.v.

97 Manson was wrong to suggest the man was friendless in his wealth (a most unusual thing!). Menander (342–293 B.C.) had already commented on the risk involved in accumulating with a view to leaving an estate: Fr.250 (Koerte), 7. The same idea is echoed at Qoh 2: 18–21, 24–26. The heir will be a stranger: Qoh 6: 2. Derrett, '"Eating up the houses of widows": Jesus's comment on lawyers?', NT XIV (1972), pp.1–9, also Z.W. Falk, *Rev.Int.Dr.Ant.* XVIII (1971), pp.11–23 (on the *epitropos*). On accumulations see Prov 28: 8 and Prov 13: 22. On the foolishness of contemplating even *children* as heirs: Rab at b.Er.54a (Sonc. tr., p.375). On God's disposing: Qoh 9. 11, 1 Sam 2: 7, Job 27: 13–17, 19; cf. Ps 39: 6, 49: 6, Qoh 2: 18–23. Midr. R.Num.22 (Sonc. tr., p.860).

98 Derrett, 'La parabola delle vergini stolte', *Conoscenza Religiosa* 1971, pp.394–406.

99 As usual, Grotius saw the point. On 'rich towards' see Rom 10: 12, Prov 19: 14, Lk 12: 33, 1 Tim 6: 18f (Jülicher).

accounts, where an unobjectionable compound usury can take place! Had he pursued that kind of profit-making he would indeed have 'many good things' 'laid up' (deposited, the word is quite technical in banking)[100] for 'many years', i.e. eternity. A good depositary will sow the deposited wheat, reap, garner, and sow again, for a long period till the depositer appears,[101] and God can do no less.

Whereas the owner, by outright gifts, by interest-free loans, and by investment in partnerships[102] could have done, even in a selfish way, a good deal of good for deserving people (taking a tip from Tobit to avoid encouraging rogues),[103] he preferred to plan an accumulation which could at any time leave a burden and a trap for the undeserving heirs.[104]

'THUS HE WHO TREASURES UP. . .'

V.21 is generally thought to be a Lucan transition-verse. It looks like a comment by the evangelist; if so it brings out the point. One must look carefully at the *kai*. As very often in New Testament Greek the conjunction[105] suggests consequence and even implies (as consequences do) intention. The treasurer or trustees of a heathen temple 'treasure up' donations, votive offerings, income voted to it by assemblies. Here an individual piles up treasure (stock) for his own ease, *thereby* cumulatively failing to acquire credit to his account with God. Called suddenly to account he is bankrupt 'up there' precisely to the extent that he is rich 'down here'. Luke goes on to thrash the problem out uncompromisingly in the rest of the chapter. The Golden Age fantasy is ubiquitous,[106] and is a reflection of man's perennial expectations of justice. In the Golden Age, when there were neither lawsuits nor lawyers, subsistence was free and abundant, and crops were not

---

[100] See Liddell-Scott-Jones, *Lex.*, s.v. *keimai* III.

[101] Midr. R. Deut.3,3 (Sonc. tr., p.70) (R. Pinchas b.Jair). From the faithfulness of man (sowing, reaping, hoarding in storehouses) we can learn the faithfulness of God.

[102] Derrett, *Law*, p.20 and n.4. Add Pirqe d^cR.Eliezer 33 (tr., Friedlander, p.239). Doles are known to be pernicious.   [103] Tob 4: 17.

[104] Cf. Meishu-sama, *Fragments* (Atami, 1965), p.20: 'There are many instances of prodigal sons who squander huge legacies. Unconsciously they are atoning for the spiritual "clouds" accumulated by their forefathers'. H. von Campenhausen, *Die Askese im Urchristentum* (Tübingen, 1949, = *Tradition and Life in the Church* [London, 1968], ch.4), p.15, places Lk 12: 13−21 beside Mt 13: 22; 22: 5.

[105] E.g. Mk 10: 11/Mt 19: 9; Lk 8: 16/11: 33; Lk 11: 5ff; Jas 4: 7; Rev 14: 15. One may also see Blass-Debrunner-Funk, § 442 (16), taking our participles as mere nouns.

[106] B. Gatz, *Weltalter, Goldene Zeit und sinnverwandte Vorstellungen* (Hildesheim, 1967).

stored because one harvest came on the heels of the previous.[107] Barns belong to the Age of Iron in which seed has to be kept for sowing in good, and bad, years. In Luke's Christian variant stress is laid on man's susceptibility to elaborate hoarding (cf. Mt 6: 26), thus overlooking his opportunity to become (if he is a good steward: Lk 12: 42, 48b, 16: 1ff, 8—12) the guest of his own master at the eternal banquet (Lk 12: 37, b. 'Er.54a), where indeed the blessed eat, drink, and make merry (Ex 24: 11, b. Ber.17a).

ACCUMULATIONS, SUPERFLUITY AND JUDGEMENT

To confirm the connection within vv.13—21 we must retrace our steps. The dispute is about an inheritance. Jesus could not, consistently with his teachings about property,[108] have awarded *shares* to the brothers. Judgement of earthly problems is in any case spiritually perilous for the judge. We cannot imagine that Jesus never settled squabbles between his disciples. that stretches credulity. But Jesus's teaching on property is uniform: it is necessary in order to live (Ps Sal 16: 12—13), and one may ask God to provide one's daily living (Lk 11: 3). Where one has both the duty and the means to maintain another person one may not escape that duty by subterfuges. But accumulations are owed to no one. If they chance to accrue one must divest oneself in the interest of all, particularly the needy. The collection of manna in the wilderness provided a pattern and indicated God's will (2 Cor 8: 15). If what arises as a subject of dispute is what affords or will afford superfluities, no award is conceivable which connives at an unrighteous application of assets.

There is a parallel in the Mishnah which has not attracted the attention which it deserves. Where a man inherits produce of the Seventh Year (ownership of which could be litigated in a pagan, but not a Jewish, court) the rabbis say he must *sell* it, and **distribute its price**. If the *sinner* (i.e. the hapless heir!) were to have distributed the produce in specie he would have taken a benefit from it, since the donees would have been grateful to him and he would have acquired *tôvâ*, which as we have seen, is a credit, by the use of Seventh Year produce, which is a forbidden benefit. If however he distributes the pur-

---

107 Philo, *Praem.* 99—104. Cf Lev 26:10 (cf.25: 22). In the Age which is withering away barns are a necessity: in the Kingdom they will be superfluous.

108 F. Hauck, *Die Stellung des Urchristentums zu Arbeit und Geld* (Gütersloh, 1921), esp. pp.70—93. Cf. W.G. Kümmel, 'Der Begriff. . .' (n.2 above), pp.271—7 (not a burning problem; property individual and unequally distributed); M. Hengel, *Property and Riches in the Early Church* (London, 1974), pp.23—30 (in drawing attention to injustice Jesus made no social protest but demonstrated God's will in respect of his coming kingdom).

chase price, even to the very same people who have bought from him, he could conceivably obtain their gratitude, but it would be for a cash gift, and not for transfer of the produce itself, to which the negative commandments attached. This is the authentic Hebrew hairsplitting mind at work, and no student of our passage, or of Lk 12:33 or 18:22, can afford to neglect Mishnah, Šev. IX.9.

In the world we know no actual court will pass a decree in favour of a litigant whose claim cannot be substantiated without a breach of public policy or the law.[109] Well-known maxims illustrate this position,[110] even though as a result rogues are sometimes left in possession of what is not justly theirs. A religious teacher can surely be expected to eschew the position of arbitrator when the relief asked for is a partition of that which, in the eyes of the religion, better fits the public utility than private enrichment. The rule 'Thou shalt not put a stumbling block before the blind' (Lev 19:14) is used by the rabbis to enjoin *referees* not to give misleading advice unsuitable for the enquirer, especially if it would aid or abet a transgression on the part of a man blinded by passion.[111] The *ḥasidim* and men of whom the Sages approve would have their own rigorous standards which the merely learned will not attempt to achieve.[112] Their own rabbis would not permit a scintilla of consent to a transgression. To the generality the scrupulous award of property to which legal right can be proved is a would-be imitation of the divine quality of Justice; to the ultra-pious it is more wicked to further, e.g., covetousness in the plaintiff than to leave the defendant to his conscience.

109 G.C. Cheshire and C.H.S. Fifoot, *The Law of Contract*[4] (London, 1956), pp.272–3, 275 n.1. O. Kahn-Freund and others, *A Source Book on French Law* (Oxford, 1973), pp.213ff. Code Civil (France) artt.1131, 1133, 1382; Z.G.B. (Switzerland), art.2; Civil Code of Japan of 1948, art.1. The ethical element is more obtrusive in Jewish than in English law: I. Herzog, *Main Institutions of Jewish Law*[2] I (London, 1965), pp.381ff. A rabbinical court will not decree a claim based on a usurious contract, nor a contract in respect of produce of the Seventh Year.

110 *Ex turpi causa non oritur actio. Melior est conditio possidentis vel defendentis.* For these maxims one may consult H. Broom, *A Selection of Legal Maxims* (many editions).

111 Lev 19:9–15 deals with property. There is a connection with Ex 23:2–3, 6. Ex 23:7 reads, 'Keep thee far from a false matter. . .' On Lev 19:14 see b.Šev. 30b–31a. Maimonides, *Mishneh Torah* (Code), XIV (Judges), I,xxiv, 3 (tr., Hershman [New Haven, 1949], pp.72–3): 'He should withdraw from the case and let another judge, who can without qualms pronounce judgement, handle it. . . 'For the judgement is God's (Deut 1:17)'. Id., *Commandments* II (ed. C.B. Chavel, London-New York, 1967), pp.277–8. Help may not be given to them that commit transgression: Mishnah, Sev. V.9. Witness, sureties, and the like break the law of Ex 22:24 as they assist in a usurious transaction: b.B.M.70b–71a. Maimonides, op.cit., XIII,III,iv,2 (tr.,J.J. Rabinowitz, p.89); id. *Commandments* II, no.237, pp.225–6.

112 Herzog, ubi cit., p.384–5 (*middat ḥasidut*)., Mishnah, Sev.9,9,cf. ibid.8,11.

As the parable shows, the right use of the fruits of the soil, assuming a virtually self-governing Jewish community, is to spend a high proportion of them in good works, retaining a modest amount for daily expenses and the needs of agriculture: barns as such are not reprobated! Amongst the followers of Jesus there is scope for inheritance, which indeed operates relative to items of consumption. Means of production pass indeed by the law (whichever *de facto* applies) to heirs but the law of the Kingdom requires that superfluous fruits be spent in ways beneficial to the poor, whereby the charitable obtain assets in heaven. Thus disputes about an inheritance are to be seen as virtually disputes as to who will direct the superfluous fruits into which channel of benevolence. Labour to earn one's own keep is right: to desire more is covetousness (Acts 20: 33–4). The high evaluation of personal labour for necessaries is scriptural.[113]

Thus Jülicher was wrong in suggesting that the parable was a story to inculcate the futility of worldly endeavour in the face of the fugitiveness of life, while Luke, interested in holy poverty, adapted it to a setting in which wealth is shown at a disadvantage,[114] and Jesus is depicted as indifferent to secular practicalities.[115] On the contrary the traditional elements – here combined – attacked the concept of accumulation, whether for the self or the heir(s). It was against righteousness. Here we have a concealed parallel with the law of divorce. One might use one's legal right to divorce one's wife: this would be secularly valid but religiously invalid, except in one context in which reason, and perhaps piety suggested the reverse. The provisions promulgated by Moses, apparently *ad hoc,* could not undermine the nature of the husband-and-wife relationship. similarly here the law of inheritance could not sanctify short-sighted secular arrangements which disregarded the heirs' spiritual health; and still less could it act *proleptically* as an excuse for accumulating surpluses and thus violating commandments binding upon the acquirer!

Now marriage and succession to property are related subjects: in fact they interlock. Succession is one of the reasons for legitimacy and therefore for marriage as opposed to concubinage. From the Hong Kong and Indonesia

---

113 Qoh 5: 11–12, 17–19. Qoh 5: 18, 8: 15, particularly pertinent to our passage (cf. Qoh 6: 2). Lk 5: 1,6; Jn 21: 1. Mt 25: 14f, Mk 13: 34f., 2 Thes 3: 10, Eph 4: 28. Hauck, *Die Stellung,* pp.11ff., 70ff.

114 Jülicher, *Die Gleichnisreden,* pp.615–17.

115 Rengstorf rightly denies that Jeses was reluctant to handle legal matters: *Das Evangelium nach Lukas* (Göttingen, 1962), p.159. J. Klausner, *Jesus of Nazareth* (New York, 1959), pp.374–5, thought Jesus disregarded justice generally, and so did not belong to civilization at all. Kümmel, 'Der Begriff. . .', p.274: Jesus is not concerned with property questions.

of today to the Prerogative Courts in England prior to 1857 any territory knowing personal or religious laws invariably retains a religious law of marriage and succession, perhaps (as in the Palestine of Christ's own day) alongside a state secular law on the same topics.[116] This is no accident. So far as succession was concerned Jesus did not regard the disposal of such accumulations as of any religious concern in comparison with the duty of the proprietors to distribute, from their assets as a whole, and in particular from their superfluities, in the service of God, whose is the land and its produce.[117] The dynastic view of marriage, which depends on inheritance, functions through arranged nuptials. When any powerful lineage's accumulations are dissipated (as was Monobazus's) the dynastic aspect vanishes. If religiously inclined heirs take Jesus seriously their own marriages are quite another affair. Marriage becomes a means of populating the earth with faithful subjects of the heavenly king: it has other hopes entirely. It is exempt from the strains which in ancient times vitiated betrothals, encouraged polygamy, or, as an alternative to the latter, fostered divorces. The teaching of Jesus on marriage and divorce cannot be understood without his teaching on accumulations and in Lk 12: 13–21 we have it.

---

116 See M.B. Hooker, *Legal Pluralism. An Introduction to Colonial and Neo-Colonial Laws* (Oxford, 1975), for the information in detail.

117 Ex 9: 29, 19: 5, Lev 25: 23, Deut 10: 14, 2 Chr 7: 20, Job 41: 11, Ps 24: 1, 50: 12, 89: 11, 104: 14, 136: 25, Isai 34: 1, Jer 8: 16, 47: 2, Ezek 19: 7, 30: 12, Mic 1: 2, Hos 9: 3, Joel 3: 2. Gen 48: 15. Qoh 5: 18 (sup.). 1 Cor 10: 26. Midr. Ps., Ps.89 § 3 (tr., Braude II, p.83). I believe it significant that *melô'*, fullness, can also mean the fullness of a building, and its contents: Num 22: 18, 14: 13.

FURTHER ANNOTATIONS

Tit. F. W. Robertson (a celebrated preacher of his day), 'Christ's judgment respecting inheritance' (a sermon [1851] based on Lk. xii.13-15), *Sermons on Religion and Life* (London, 1906), 31, acutely identified our parable as an attack on inheritance. In 'Reflections on biblical understandings of property,' *Int. Rev. Mission* 64, No. 255 (1975), 354ff., at 359, W. Brueggemann takes the view that Jesus explores the *potential for life and death* in the handling of property, which can easily give a vain hope of securing one's existence : the faithful community is left to wonder at Christ's proclamation of the security of living without anxiety for the assets *per se*.

p. [133], n. 15. On the relation of the Gospel of Thomas to the synoptics in the area of parables see G. Menestrina, 'Le parabole nell' "Evangelo di Tommaso" e nei sinottici,' *Bibb. Or.* 17 (1975), 79-92 (Thomas has many sources and where he keeps strictly to tradition he may give a better version in some instances than the synoptics).

p. [140], l. 9. Pesiqta Rabbati at Pis. 25, §2 (trans. Braude, ii, 516) says plainly that when Prov. iii. 10 (inf., n. 83) says 'Thy barns should be filled with plenty' what is meant is barns in the world to come.

p. [140], n. 46. *agatha* in our sense *does* appear at *Ap. Bar. Gr.* ed. Picard 1967 (a Jewish work), xi.9, xii.6!

p. [143], l. 19. Seventh Year produce is *kerdos adikon* : Philo, *Spec. Leg.* iv, 218.

p. [146]. Modern printed texts read τὸν σῖτον καὶ τὰ ἀγαθά μου, and as to τὰ ἀγαθά there is no dispute. However the Textus Receptus reads τὰ γενήματα μου καὶ τὰ ... This is almost certainly right for reasons of textual criticism given by G. D. Kilpatrick at *Essays ... G. H. C.* Macgregor (Oxford, 1965), 190, 202 (σῖτος was a stylistic improvement on γένημα). The pun on the man's produce is clearer with the T.R.'s reading.

The Good Shepherd: St. John's Use of
Jewish Halakah and Haggadah

The most beautiful and moving piece of St. John has remained a puzzle to commentators,[1] though in it the centuries have heard the living voice of Christ.[2] Some suggest that the order of verses should be changed, and even

---

[1] C. K. Barrett at *J.T.S.* XLVIII (1947), 163–4; the same, *The Gospel according to St John* (London, 1955), pp. 304–17. C. H. Dodd, *The Interpretation of the Fourth Gospel* (Cambridge, 1968), pp. 57, 135–6, 358–61; the same, *Historical Tradition in the Fourth Gospel* (Cambridge, 1965), pp. 382–5. The major study is A. J. Simonis, *Die Hirtenrede im Johannes-Evangelium* (Rome, 1967) (not referring to rabbinic learning). A good study of the text: A. Schlatter, *Der Evangelist Johannes* (Stuttgart, 1948), pp. 233–9. J. de Zwaan, 'John wrote in Aramaic', *J.B.L.* LVII (1938), 155–64. J. A. T. Robinson, 'The parable of John x. 1–5', *Z.N.W.* XLVI (1955), 233–40 (now in *Twelve New Testament Studies* [London, 1962], pp. 67–75) is highly regarded by Dodd and Jeremias. It suggests the fusion of two parables (of the watchman and shepherd respectively). It contains excellent points, but illustrates the difficulties presented by the want of adequate biblical foundation to the study. Robinson does, however, cite Isa. lvi. 9–12 appropriately and calls attention to Rev. iii. 3, etc. J. Wellhausen, *Der Ev. Johannis* (Berlin, 1908), pp. 47–50. A. Schlatter, *Die Sprache und Heimat des vierten Evangelisten* (Gütersloh, 1902), pp. 392–5. K. Bornhäuser, *Das Johannesevangelium, eine Missionschrift für Israel* (Gütersloh, 1928), pp. 58–9, fitted Ezek. xxxvii. 20 ff. (one nation) with *Mishnah,* Shev. VIII (H. Danby, *The Mishnah* (Oxford, 1933), pp. 420–1) and *B.M.* VIII, 9–10 (*ibid.,* 360). H. Odeberg, *The Fourth Gospel* (Uppsala/Stockholm, 1929), pp. 313–28. E. Hirsch, *Studien zum vierten Evangelium* (Tübingen, 1936), pp. 82–6. W. Jost, ΠΟΙΜΗΝ. *Das Bild vom Hirten in der biblischen Überlieferung und seine christologische Bedeutung* (Diss. Giessen, 1939). J. Quasten, 'The parable of the Good Shepherd', *C.B.Q.* X (1948), 1–12, 151–69. H. Strathmann, *Das Evangelium nach Johannes* (Göttingen, 1959), pp. 164–7. S. Schulz, *Komposition und Herkunft der Johanneischen Reden* (*B.W.A.N.T.,* 5th ser., 1) (Stuttgart, 1960), pp. 76–9, 103–7 (Schulz, like Bultmann, attends too much to Mandaean material). J. Jeremias, ποιμήν etc., *T.W.N.T.* VI (in the Eng. trans. of 1968, at pp. 485–502). E. C. Hoskyns and F. N. Davey, *The Fourth Gospel* (London, 1947), pp. 366–81, rightly deprecate 'general mysticism' as the background to our chapter.

[2] W. F. Howard, *The Fourth Gospel in Recent Criticism and Interpretation* (London, 1931), p. 227.

many conservative scholars believe that some verses are 'secondary'.³ The commencement seems abrupt, and, in spite of εὑρὼν αὐτόν at ix. 35 (cf. Luke xv. 4–6), it has never been certain what connection the passage has with the elaborate and prolonged story of the man born blind.⁴ Imagination has forcibly connected the dispersed sayings, and there are different ways of attempting to reconcile the 'shepherd' with the 'door', and the door *to* the sheep with the door *for* the sheep. Apart from the occasional phrase, the only Old Testament passages to be recognised as being behind John x have been Ps. xxiii; Isa. xl. 11; Jer. xxiii. 1–8; 1.6–7; Ezek. xxxiv;⁵ and Zech. xi.⁶ For the 'door' or 'gate' Ps. cxviii. 20 is cited as a pattern, or even the source.⁷ No attempt has ever been made to reconstruct the parable lying behind the catena of sayings (though the presence of a parable is generally admitted), and when the Old Testament documentation has been found, that, of course, cries out to be done. W. Tooley, however, has correctly identified 'shepherd' as meaning 'teacher' (in the oriental sense of a teacher of law as well as morals) besides meaning 'leader', and sheep as meaning the people to be taught (citing Matt. x. 6; xv. 24).⁸ The disciples

³ R. Bultmann, *The Gospel of John, A Commentary* (Oxford, Blackwell, 1971), pp. 358–91 (his rearrangements have not been generally accepted). E. Schweizer, *Ego eimi* ... (Göttingen, 1939), pp. 141–2. In his view *vv.* 7–9 are secondary ('gate' should be eliminated). J. Jeremias, *ubi cit.*, 494–7; the same, θύρα, *ibid.*, III (Eng. trans., 1968), p. 178. So (unfortunately) Schulz also. W. G. Kümmel, *Introduction to the New Testament* (London, 1965), p. 146.

⁴ Schweizer, *ubi cit.* A. Guilding, *The Fourth Gospel and Jewish Worship* (Oxford, 1960), p. 129.

⁵ K. Berger, *Die Amen-Worte Jesu* (Berlin, 1970), pp. 14, 103, 116, 128. Dodd places great emphasis upon the Ezekiel passage.

⁶ Ever since John Lightfoot the importance of Zech. xi for our chapter has been notorious. It would be easy to link up other passages with the present exposition, e.g. ix. 11–12 (prisoners, want of water, and, especially double requital, which appertains to the thief), 16 (flock, and stones?), also x. 8 (hissing for, increasing). But the amateur midrashist must curb his imagination or the technique will fall into disrepute.

⁷ W. F. Howard, *Christianity according to St John* (London, 1943), p. 138. A. Schlatter, *Der Ev. Johannes, p.* 235, was right to see that the gate was the main feature of the allegory. Odeberg, *op. cit.,* p. 313. Simonis' most interesting experiment with πρὸ ἐμοῦ as 'before me' *in space* rather than in time (*op. cit.,* p. 208, cf. Acts v. 9) occupied me, but in sum I reject the textual objections to those words, and to their being taken temporally. The prophets *before* Jesus also tried to rescue the people by force (as it were) (see the covert midrash below), but they were not the Messiah, *opus non potuerunt operare.*

⁸ 'The Shepherd and sheep image in the teaching of Jesus', *N.T.* VII (1964), 15–25. The theme of teacher and student (ποιμένας καὶ διδασκάλους, Eph. iv. 11) runs through John ix–x. Cf. *Damascus Document* XIII. 9. Apollonius of Tyana in Philostratus, *Vita,* VIII. 22 (Barrett). Wolves are false teachers: Matt. vii. 15; x. 16; Luke x. 3; Acts xx. 28–30 (cf. Jude 12).

were in this position: Mark x. 32; xiv 28 (cf. Zech. xiii. 8ff.).[9] And that the Messiah was a shepherd was known from Ps. Sal. xvii. 40, and from the LXX rendering of Ps. ii. 9, which is striking.[9a]

Existing studies of John x antedate the renaissance of targumic and midrashic research. The instinct to look for Torah and prophetic foundations first before looking for non-Jewish parallels has all but died out. The artistry of St. John has here escaped everyone since the church became hellenic. The rediscovery of living Jewish learning and piety in the fourth gospel at this place will support the view that, contrary to so many supposed indications, it is a Palestinian production[10] aimed at an audience still in easy contact with *halakah* and *haggadah*. Further, the surprising conclusion emerges that even in our hypothetical parable, as with actual Lucan parables, the *Heilsgeschichte* pervades the traditional theological-moral propositions, without actually being their root or starting-point. The present purpose is to show the scriptural background to the Good Shepherd, to restate the factual and metaphorical meanings of the passage, and *in order to direct the mind better to what is intended,* to offer a hypothetical parable, similar to synoptic parables (with all its vocabulary taken from biblical precedents!), upon which St. John might have based his chapter. Such a start must be made, since it is so much easier to correct another's *praelusio* than to initiate a better one oneself. I assume that the reader has the text open in front of him, and shall save space by not reprinting any part of it except where essential. I warn the reader that here again he finds the sharp, but apparently idle Jewish mind at work, with its needless 'rabbinifications', so contrary to modern taste, its confusion between embellishment and creation, which we instinctively resent, and its insistence upon minute accuracy where a warmer style of poetry would have more easily drawn our applause. But he will find the case stated, the gauntlet flung down: Jesus's own interpretation of his function is stated in terms requiring a detailed familiarity with the synoptic story of the Passion and its purpose: and in recreating yet another contact between St. John and the synoptics we are in fashion indeed.

For the first time no emphasis is laid upon the figure of God as the Shepherd: Joachim Jeremias correctly adverts to the paucity of this image in the

---

[9] C. F. Evans at *J.T.S.* V (1954), p. 11.

[9a] W. Jost, *op. cit.,* p. 37. MT: t͏eroᶜēm (Syr. and Jerome tirēᶜēm) rāᶜaᶜ. LXX: ποιμανεῖς αὐτοὺς ἐν ῥάβδῳ (shēveṭ, staff, Ezek. xx. 37; Ps. xxiii. 4) σιδηρᾷ. 'Α. προσρήξεις. Σ. συντρίψεις. Micah vii. 14 has ποίμαινε λαόν σου ἐν ῥάβδῳ σου πρόβατα κληρονομίας σου (i.e. the shepherd is, as it were, heir, son). Cf. Ps. Sal. xvii. 24.

[10] Jeremias, *T.W.N.T.* VI (Eng. trans., 1958), p. 496. On St John's access to the Hebrew Old Testament rather than to the LXX see C. F. Burney, *The Aramaic Origin of the Fourth Gospel* (Oxford, 1922), ch. 8.

New Testament and divines the reason, but the explanation is implicit in what comes below. God is, in fact, the owner of the sheep (as anyone familiar with the practical background would have realised long ago).

John x. 1 tells us where to look for our material. A catena of texts emerges, upon which, along with Num. xxvii, our chapter (x. 1–18, 25–30) is virtually a midrash. It is proposed to take it as one suggested by the parable, written out in full by St. John in his usual explicit style. There is no superfluous word, the biblical texts being exploited in two commentaries simultanously, what we shall call the overt and the covert midrash. It is an oriental concept of the exquisite to tell two stories at once. A text is much more enjoyable, in their eyes, if its surface meaning contains, without explicitly stating, more than one hidden meaning. The quaintness of some of the applications of the biblical texts certifies that here we have authentic ancient sermon style. A modern translation of the Old Testament does not permit us to view the Hebrew as did Jesus and his contemporaries.

Now the words 'He who does not enter the sheepfold by the door but climbs in by another way, that man is a thief and a robber' are a clear statement of civil law, accurately reproducing a leading aspect of Exod. xxii. 1 (MT) (*v.* 2 in the LXX and modern versions), unquestionably referring us to it. The *haftarah* belonging to this passage from the Torah was Isa. lvi. 1 to lvii. 19, perhaps with the omission of some verses.[11] That lection, pregnant with relevant themes, has a verbal connection with Micah (a book which is especially important for us), for Isa. lvi. 12 ('wine and strong drink') is reminiscent of Micah ii. 11. Micah ii. 12–13 is (as we shall see) the basis of the abundant figurative detail of John x. 1–18.

The risk in burrowing through a wall

Normal Jewish preaching does not hesitate to derive a spiritual lesson from a legal text. The *Mishnah* says (B.Q. VI. 4 (mid.)), 'If a man caused fire to break out and it consumed wood or stones or dust, he is culpable, for it is written, "If a fire break out and catch in thorns ..." (Exod. xxii. 6).' R. Samuel b. Naḥmani said that R. Joḥanan said: 'Calamity comes upon the world only when there are wicked persons in the world, and it always begins with the righteous, as it says: *If fire break out and catch in thorns.* When does fire break out? When thorns are found nearby. It always begins with the righteous, as it says: *so that the stack of corn was consumed*' (b. B.Q. 60*a*). Thus 'thorns', even in the most prosaic legal context, is a symbol of righteousness, and righteousness suffering for the wicked.

[11] J. Mann, *The Bible as Read and Preached in the Old Synagogue* I (Cincinnati, 1940), p. 469.

Now Exod. xxii. 1 (MT) follows upon xxi. 37, and relates to a man's burrowing through a wall, so as to make a breach, the wall being that of a compound in which cattle or sheep are penned.[12] This appears from the 'thief' appearing as 'the thief' (not 'a thief'). It is convenient to read xxii. 1 and 2 together, but according to midrashic technique a reader of *v.* 1 might construe it in isolation, and then reconstrue it in association with *v.* 2. As we shall see when we come to the covert midrash, the latter part of *v.* 2 can even be taken separately as well as in conjunction with the earlier part of it. Small wonder that modern scholars have wanted to rearrange the words – though their results must be ignored here, since they defeat the method of this study! We shall find it convenient to take the verses apart, not forgetting that the Mishnaic law takes them firmly together (as is natural).

ɔim-bamaḥteret yimṣeɔ haganāv we-hukāh we-mēt ɔēyin lw dāmiym.

'If in the breach (i.e. digging-through, excavation)[13] the thief is found, and is struck,[14] and dies, there is no blood (i.e. no right to blood-vengeance or blood-money) on his behalf.'

The law implies that anyone who, ignoring the normal entrance, enters a sheepfold by making a breach in the wall, or enters by any method other than the legitimate one, is presumed to be intending to attack and perhaps kill anyone who challenges him. Unless there were evidence to the contrary, the presumption of *justification* would protect the occupier of the sheepfold (or any inmate)[15] if he slew the would-be thief in the act of entry or within the enclosure.[16] This was a commonplace rule.[17] Nothing is said here about night-time.[17a] But the practical law (like any reader from biblical times on-

---

[12] H. M. Orlinsky, *Notes on the New Translation of the Torah* (Philadelphia, 1969), p. 180. B. Jackson, *Theft in Early Jewish Law* (Oxford, 1972), pp. 49–50. Guttmann (1949) cited by Jackson at p. 50 n. 1.

[13] LXX: διορύγματι. *ḥātar,* 'to dig into houses', Job xxiv. 16; Ezek. viii. 80; xii. 5, 7, 12. Jackson, p. 205. The important Targum ps.-Jonathan says 'If the thief be found *in a window* of the wall . . .' (to which he has climbed up?).

[14] Cf. *mukēh* (Isa. liii. 4), 'struck' (by God).

[15] So all sources of law from talmudic times, and the *Midrash Haggadol.*

[16] Josephus, *Ant.* iv, 271. Philo, *De Spec. Leg.* IV, 7–8 (ed. Colson, viii, 426). *Mishnah,* Sanh. VIII. 6. b. Sanh. 109a, Yoma 85a. Ch. Tschernowitz, 'Der Einbruch nach bibischem und talmudischem Rechte', *Z.V.R.* XXV (1910), 443–58. b. Sanh. 72a (Soncino trans., 491–5). L. Goldschmidt, *Babylonische Talmud,* VII (1902), 307–311. B. Jackson, *Theft,* pp. 41, 49, 203–6.

[17] The easy allusion at Jer. ii. 34.

[17a] Cf., in Roman law, the XII Tab. (5th cent. B. C.), tab. 8 (*FIRA.* I. 57): si nox furtum faxsit, si im occisit, iure caesus esto.

wards) must read *vv.* 1–2 together, and it originally confined the privilege, and its corresponding risk for the in-breaker, to a housebreaking *by night*. Jewish law holds, however, that attack is a means of defence, so that one may, without sin, slay an assailant or anyone who is evidently about to kill one, or even about to commit such a crime as he should be protected from committing at the cost (if need be) of his own life.[18] The right of self-defence is traced to this verse.[19] Further, in all cases where a person within would be entitled to slay the intruder without warning, that intruder, if he escaped with his life, would not be bound to recompense the householder or owner for any damage caused in the process of entry.[20] This curious, but characteristic Jewish rule is notorious, [21] and is explained simply: he risked his life for the enterprise, and a lesser (e. g. a monetary) penalty is out of the question should the crime of burglary ever be brought home to him.

So, to proceed, Exod. xxii. 2 (MT) forces us to ask, in a legal context, whether the intruder was found at night time. It is not an exception to *v.* 1, but is to be construed with it.

ɔim-zarḥāh hashemesh ᶜalayw dāmiym lo . . .

'If the sun has risen upon him, there shall be blood for him . . .' What follows appertains to our covert midrash (see below) and must be ignored for the moment to avoid confusion. So far we learn that if he is caught in the daytime, and slain, his relatives may demand compensation; and it follows that the slayer is a wrongdoer, and if the system of sanctuary were not in operation he could be convicted of murder. One must not, if one obeys the biblical law, slay even a housebreaker if he breaks in in the broad light of day. A common-sense result is, indeed, achieved in talmudic law. If it is clear that the in-breaker's intention is only to steal or do damage, and not to slay an inmate, the latter could have no justification in killing him, when-

---

[18] b. Ber. 58 a (Sonc. trans., 362). *Mekilta* on Exod. xxii. 1–3 (Lauterbach, iii, 1935, pp. 101 ff.). *Midrash on Psalms,* Ps. 56, § 1 (trans. Braude, I, 496–7) (citing I Sam. xxix. 19, 23; Lev. xix. 16). One who breaks in by night is as good as dead (Rashi).

[19] D. Daube, *Studies in Biblical Law* (Cambridge, 1947), pp. 101 n. 30, 207. B. Cohen, *Jewish and Roman Law* II (New York, 1966), pp. 628–9. M. Sulzberger, *The Ancient Hebrew Law of Homicide* (Philadelphia, 1915), pp. 23, 34.

[20] Tschernowitz, *op. cit.,* p. 454. b. Sanh. 72 a (Sonc. trans., 489, 491–5; see note at p. 490); *B.Q.* 114 b (Sonc. 680). Raba lost some rams because thieves broke in: he refused to accept them back (they belonged to the thieves!). L. Goldschmidt, *Bab. Tal.* VI (1908), p. 431.

[21] H. E. Goldin, *Hebrew Civil Law and Procedure* (New York, 1953), pp. 175–7. It is profitable to study the general principles explained by Maimonides, *Mishneh Torah* (Code of Maimonides), XI (*Book of Torts,* trans. H. Klein, New Haven, 1954), II, ch. iii, pp. 67 ff.

ever he appears. Indeed if the thief is actually armed, and still more if there are more than one thief, the fear that resistance would end in the occupier's own death will justify the slayer; though it was daytime it was not 'clear as the day' that the intruders had no intention to slay the occupier should he resist.[22]

Another ancient way of taking the verse was that 'if the sun has risen' means that witnesses must be available to certify what were the actual circumstances of the slaying.[23] If there were no witnesses it was the same as if it were night time. The whole point was that proof of the in-breaker's intention must be forthcoming before his killer can claim to be guiltless. The Jews were familiar with housebreaking and theft by burrowing through walls, or entry over walls (events of everyday occurrence).[24] They knew that when a man entered a compound otherwise than through the door (which would rouse the watchman and his dog) he did so absolutely at his own risk. But if there were witnesses, and if his action was bold (John vii. 26), in the broad light of day, the occupiers, however much they resented his conduct and might try to prevent the escape of their flock, could not lawfully slay him. On the other hand, if his method was secret, unexpected, as in the dead of night, it was quite natural to presume his action to be hostile. In the breach itself his head could be cut off by the light of the watchman's lamp: and apart from sanitary arrangements and repair of the wall, that was all there was to be considered! The reader will have grasped that we have crossed into the area of redemption-theology, to which I shall return.

Meanwhile we must study, briefly, further portions of Exod. xxii, viz. *vv.* 8–12 (MT). Verse 1 is a catch-passage automatically calling up what

---

[22] *Mekilta,* and *Babylonian Talmud,* cited above. The summary by Maimonides, *op. cit.,* II, ix, 7–13 (pp. 87–8) is extremely useful, especially when considering the covert midrash (below). b. Pes. 2*b* (Sonc. 3). Jackson, *Theft,* p. 209 for references. Cf. b. Sanh. 71*a* (*ibid.,* p. 210). The rights of the owner were extended as time passed. In the time of Jesus the occupier was protected only in the night time, and in the daytime only where there was no doubt but that the intruder was prepared to make an attempt on his life. Consider Mark xiv. 49, improved upon in Luke xxii. 53 and explained in John xviii. 20. Yet it was dark when Jesus died: Luke xxiii. 44,46.

[23] *Mekilta* on Exod., xxii. 2 quoted by Jackson, p. 212. Maimonides also incorporates this opinion, *ubi cit.,* para. 11.

[24] Josephus, *Ant.* XVI. 1. S. Belkin, *Philo and the Oral Law* (Cambridge, Mass., 1940), p. 209. Luke xii. 39; Matt. vi. 19–20. *Mishnah, B.Q.* VI. 1 (Danby, 339). An actual breach made by a nocturnal thief, patched (presumably) soon afterwards may be seen in the photo at plate 13 in N. Glüeck, 'Tell el-Khileifeh inscriptions', at H. Goedicke, ed., *Near Eastern Studies in Honor of W. F. Albright* (Baltimore and London, 1971), 239. The building is Edomite, 6th–5th cent. B.C. Since the hole is fairly high in the wall, the thief would spring up into it after he had made it (an effort of *climbing*).

follows. Verse 8 explains the general proposition that a Jew must pay double the value to a fellow-Jew when he is unable to restore a valuable article entrusted to him. The normal penalty for theft is the same. If, however, he successfully takes an oath, he is believed in his explanation that his failure to restore is not due to wrongdoing on his part.[25] Dealings with things entrusted to one (sheep are mentioned) are a matter of conscience; either double compensation must be paid or the explanation for failure to restore intact must be certified by an oath; and now we come to particular rules. The same oath exculpates a herdsman when an animal entrusted to him is hurt, driven off (as by robbers), or dies (as at the hands of a hunter or through wild beasts), and he has no witnesses to testify to his probity. The owner must accept the oath, even though everyone knew that shepherds, men of suspect morality,[26] might take oaths rather readily. Further, 'If it (i.e. the sheep) is stolen from him he shall make restitution to its owner.' Therefore there was an absolute liability to restore the value of all sheep taken by thieves (but not by *robbers,* brigands: Exod. xxii. 9, 11 MT), and a shepherd knew that if he failed to protect his flock he must make good the loss out of his pocket. He could be excused if there were many thieves.[27] Otherwise the loss would be deducted from his wages, and he might even be sold for the debt, an eventuality contemplated in *v.* 2 of this same chapter. A thief can certainly cause a shepherd the loss of his livelihood and so virtually of his life (Ecclus. xxxiv. 21–22).

The liability of the shepherd where an animal is killed by a wild beast is absolute unless he can produce the carcass (Amos iii. 12). Thus where a wolf makes off with the entire carcass the shepherd is liable. In many ancient systems of law the position is similar. It is difficult to see how anyone could make a profit out of sheep-keeping without such a law or custom.

The sheep-owner tries to protect his sheep by penning them securely in, if possible, a walled enclosure, perhaps with a thorn fence on top, and, best of all, adjacent to his own dwelling house. His servants will sleep nearby, the watchman (who probably counted the sheep on egress and ingress) would sleep across the doorway,[27a] his dog beside him. A sword would be near at hand. When the sheep were taken off to pasture he who took them accepted liability for them, and, with carefully limited exceptions, was an-

---

[25] *Mishnah,* Shev. VIII. 1 (Danby, 420).

[26] Jeremias cites *B.Q.* X. 9; Billerbeck, *Kommentar zum Neuen Testament* II, 114; III, 108. Maimonides, *op. cit.,* II, vi, 1–2 (trans., p. 78) puts it very shortly. One shepherd would readily accuse another: Test. Gad I. 6.

[27] Jackson, *Theft,* p. 39.

[27a] E. F. F. Bishop, 'The door of the sheep', *Ex. T.* lxxi (1959–60), 307–9, is interesting, but I do not apply it literally.

swerable to the owner for them ultimately to the extent of his own freedom. He not only protected them, and took them to such sparse pasture as the region afforded, keeping them off strangers' property (Mishnah, B.Q. VI. 2), sometimes staying away for long periods from home;[28] but also had to exert himself personally to defend them from animals and thieves, quick with his sling and staff;[29] and he had to risk his safety in meeting wild beasts, single-handed perhaps (for his boy might run off), and in beating off thieves, casual or organised. Shepherds were tough people; small wonder they were likened to kings and leaders, and the latter to them.[30]

The peoples of Yahweh

The ancient Sabbath lections are not known for certain. But known lectionary systems had great continuity. It was always an advantage to know in advance what passages from the Law and the Prophets would be read throughout the Jewish world. We may trust evidence of sermons noted from the first century onwards. Fixed lections from the Law and the Prophets listed in documents surviving from an early period in our era can be relied on to indicate the combination of concepts available to the preacher, texts upon which his imagination and literal knowledge of scripture could embroider, even as early as the time of Jesus.[31] Yet there is no proof that lections known to St. John, and familiar in the synagogue of Christians, were known in that very sequence in Jesus's time and place. It is likely that a synagogue with many gentile members would adjust its lectionary, and there might be almost as many lectionaries as there were such synagogues. But the best evidence lies in the results. In this case the traditional (not the modern)[32] arrangement of the lectionary produces impressive data.[33] Exod. xxii. 1 is in the Mishpaṭiym section commencing at xxi. 1 (the sixtieth *seder*

---

[28] Test. Gad, I. 4.

[29] Test. Gad, I. 2–3. The exploits of David, I. Sam. xvii. 34–7; II Sam. xxiv. 17, as explained by *Mekilta* on Exod. xv. 1. amount to a pledging of life for the sheep.

[30] There is the interesting case of a shepherd who actually aspired to the throne (along with four brothers): Athrongaeus, who carried on guerila warfare against all parties. Josephus, *B.J.* II. 60–5 (Loeb ed., ii, 347).

[31] The classic illustration is Luke iv. 16–22 (not necessarily reflecting practice anterior to Luke's source). Exod. Rabbah XXX. 24 shows an early combination of Exod. xxi. 1 with Isa. lvi–lvii.

[32] The modern annual lection for Exod. xxii. 1 is Jer. xxxiv. 8–22 ending with Jer. xxxiii. 25–6. It has no bearing on our questions.

[33] In connection with Guilding's treatment of this chapter, which does not answer our questions, one may note L. Morris, *The New Testament and the Jewish Lectionaries* (London, 1964), pp. 64, 66. W. A. Meek, *The Prophet-King* (Leiden, 1967), p. 92 n. 2.

of the triennial cycle). The ancient *haftarah* was Isa. lvi. 1–lvii. 19, or extracts from it. The nominal connection is Isa. lvi. 1, which puts a complexion on the Mishpaṭiym section, as indeed does the rest of the chapter: – 'Thus says the Lord: "Keep justice and do righteousness, for soon my salvation will come, and my deliverance be revealed."' Obedience to the Law relates to the speedy coming of Salvation. It is a redemption theme. It is not surprising that the chapter is traditionally Messianic,[34] and that Jesus himself is represented as quoting it. Passing through the chapters we notice topics throwing light on Exod. xxi–xxii, and linking up with John x.

Foreigners and eunuchs figure largely; the theme is that Jewish law exists also as an attraction for pagans, who, if they are willing to adhere to Yahweh, and to obey his commandments, will not continue to be outside the circle of Judaism, will not be separated from the Jews, whatever they think on that subject. The harsh distinctions between Jew and gentile will disappear (a theme figuring in the synoptics especially in the episode of the Syrophoenician woman). The first century, too, regarded eunuchs as privileged persons because of their awesome, enforced chastity.[34a] Eunuchs, nominally excluded from the congregation, [35] because of the peculiar Jewish horror of them, will be brought in, and, on a spiritual footing, be relieved of their disability. It was believed by some in the time of Jesus that in the Messianic age eunuchs would indeed have posterity.[36] At any rate such exclusion was at an end. Verse 5 promises eunuchs posterity within the house of Yahweh and *within his wall*. At *v.* 7 Yahweh brings (or leads) the foreigners to his holy mountain. The 'house of prayer' theme is repeated at the end of the verse: even offerings of pagans will be accepted. Verse 8: 'Thus says the Lord God, who gathers the *outcasts of Israel,* I will *gather yet others* to him besides those already gathered (or 'his gathered ones').' Who, we may ask, is the person referred to in 'his'?

Immediately after the shepherd metaphors, with the adding of *others* to 'him', we come to explicit references to our present advantage. In *v.* 9 the wild beasts are invited to devour the flock. The watchmen are blind (*v.* 10, cf. John ix. 39–41), and their blindness amounts to want of understanding. They are like dogs which are too well fed, liking to sleep: only their appetite is strong (they work only for the meals!). Everyone knows that sheepdogs are not to be fed too well. In *v.* 11 the shepherds themselves appear; again

---

[34] A. Edersheim, *Life and Times of Jesus the Messiah* (London, 1901), II, app. ix, p. 728.

[34a] A study of eunuchs is amongst the early works of A. D. Nock, *Essays on Religion and the Ancient World* (Oxford, 1972), vol. 1.

[35] Lev. xxi. 20; Deut. xxiii. 1.

[36] Josephus tells of Pharisees misleading a eunuch on this basis: Ant. XVII, 45.

they have no understanding; they wander pursuing selfish interests; they do not choose a route taking their flocks to pasture. Their object (*v.* 12) is luxury, and they care nothing for the future. Chapter lvii begins with a lament over the self-sacrifice of the righteous man (who is this?), whose death signals a great calamity,[37] and continues with an eloquent attack upon the illegitimate and the adulterous, manifestations of unfaithfulness to Yahweh: the butts of this attack are accused of deriding the speaker or those with whom he sympathises (*v.* 4). They belittle him, but what, he asks, are they? After this long harangue the lection ends on a happy note – peace is promised to the far (the rebellious, or the pagan) and the near (the obedient and the Jew).

Professor B. Gerhardsson once suggested that R^c could be read as neighbour (*re^{c}a*) or as shepherd (*ro^{c}eh*).[38] However that may be, in Isa. lvi. 11 the words translated 'and these are shepherds (corrected misleadingly to 'the shepherds *also*'), they have no understanding' (*whmh r^{c}ym l$^\partial$ yd^{c}w hbyn*) are correctly pointed in the Masoretic Text. 'Shepherds' are needed after 'dogs' (a favourite term of abuse). But in Palestinian dialects *ro^{c}iym* could sound the same as *rā^{c}iym* (wicked ones). A preacher would say that the 'shepherds' in the figure were the evil ones of Israel, who of course did not look after their sheep. Both the Targum and the LXX read the word as *rā^{c}iym* and so translate 'the wicked have no understanding'. Aquila and Theodotion return to what became the Masoretic reading. But Symmachus stubbornly retained 'wicked'. Isa. lvi. 11 referred to wicked shepherds, not merely because the sense requires this, but because current readings produced this paronomasia. It does not follow that all shepherds are wicked (any more than all lawyers are liars), but it was a curious coincidence that a favourite word for 'the Wicked' was written identically with the word for 'shepherds'.

God appoints ΙΗΣΟΥΣ *a shepherd over all flesh*

The metaphor of stealing into a sheepfold, and the risks involved in this, is obtained from Exod. xxii, as we have seen. But we have not yet noticed

[37] The Targum to Isa. lvii. 1 (of early second century or earlier) explained by P. Churgin, *Targum Jonathan to the Prophets* (New Haven, 1907 [for 1927]), p. 104. See b. Sanh. 113*b*, *B.Q.* 60*a* (it is more than a mere atonement for the wicked: see *Law in the New Testament*, London, 1970, pp. 418–9). A different use of the same verse is evidenced at Enoch lxxxi. 9 (the righteous are taken away [to bliss] on account of the deeds of the godless). Isa. lvii. 1 gave the Greek translators acute trouble. One marvels at the revisers' zeal to 'correct' the LXX.

[38] B. Gerhardsson, *The Good Samaritan – the Good Shepherd?* (Coniectanea Neotestamentica XVI) (Lund/Copenhagen, 1958), pp. 19–20.

the extreme relevance of Num. xxvii. 15–20 to the theme of the divinely chosen and appointed leader who is not merely the shepherd of Israel but is also the accredited leader of the one flock (ʿēdāh) of Him who is the God of the spirits of all flesh. Once the appointed shepherd is seen to be Joshua the relevance of the passage is plainer. Our elaborate parable must have been hung from two Torah passages, Exodus and Numbers. Neither have been exploited before to explain John x. It was with the LXX that St. John expected his hearers to be familiar (there is little difference of substance between the LXX and the MT in this case).

15 καὶ εἶπεν Μωυσῆς πρὸς κύριον: 16Ἐπισκεψάσθω κύριος ὁ θεὸς τῶν πνευμάτων καὶ πάσης σαρκὸς ἄνθρωπον ἐπὶ τῆς συναγωγῆς ταύτης, 17 ὅστις ἐξελεύσεται πρὸ προσώπου αὐτῶν καὶ ὅστις εἰσελεύσεται πρὸ προσώπου αὐτῶν καὶ ὅστις ἐξάξει αὐτοὺς καὶ ὅστις εἰσάξει αὐτούς, καὶ οὐκ ἔσται ἡ συναγωγὴ κυρίου ὡσεὶ πρόβατα οἷς οὐκ ἔστιν ποιμήν. 18 καὶ ἐλάλησεν κύριος πρὸς Μωυσῆν λέγων Λαβὲ πρὸς σεαυτὸν τὸν Ἰησοῦν υἱὸν Ναυη, ἄνθρωπον ὃς ἔχει πνεῦμα ἐν ἑαυτῷ, καὶ ἐπιθήσεις τὰς χεῖράς σου ἐπ' αὐτὸν ... 20 καὶ δώσεις τῆς δόξης σου ἐπ' αὐτόν, ὅπως ἂν εἰσακούσωσιν αὐτοῦ οἱ υἱοὶ Ισραηλ ....

The Targum to this passage relates the movement of the sheep to going out to and returning from war (cf. Targ. Micah ii. 13, below); the purpose of the appointment of Joshua is said to be that the congregation (i.e. the flock) shall never be without the wise, nor go astray among the nations as sheep go astray without a shepherd. For that idea see 1 K. xxii. 17; Mk. vi. 35!

To 'go before' the people, and other themes familiar to us, the line of David and even the Crucifixion would seem, to the Christian midrashist, to be present in Zech. xii. 8–10 (false prophets figure at xiii. 2–3) – and this brings us to the prophetic *Hintergrund* of our parable.

The In-breaker and the compound in Micah

Hearers of Exod. xxi, xxii followed by Isa. lvi–lvii will have grasped that those technical rules of law are not for the Jews alone perpetually. If the Jews are faithfully led gentiles will be brought to join them in obedience to Yahweh. Their offerings will be accepted on the holy mountain. Micah, to which we turn, is connected with Isaiah by 'wine and strong drink' and is connected with Exod. xxii. 1 by the very rare idea of a 'breach'. Since St. John utilises every word we must examine the text carefully. The ancient translations assure us that here, as often, the text is obscure and quaint, the delight of the preacher. It is desirable to print it without vocalisation.

11. lw-ᵓysh hlch rwḥ wshqr kzb ᵓṭf lch lyyn wlshkr whyh mṭyf hᶜm hzh.
12. ᵓsf ᵓᵓsf yᶜqb klch qbṣ ᵓqbṣ shᵓryt ysrᵓl yḥd ᵓsymnw kṣᵓn bṣrh kᶜdr btwch hdbrw thymnh mᵓdm.
13. ᶜlh hprṣ lpnyhm prṣw wyᶜbrw shᶜr wyṣᵓw bw wyᶜbr mlkm lfnyhm wyhwh brᵓshm.

'If there were a man who went about in a spirit and deceived with lies, "I shall distill for you about wine and strong drink", he would be a distiller for this people (cf. Isa. xxviii. 7) (i.e. he would be the appropriate sort of prophet).'

'I shall surely assemble, O Jacob, all of thee; I shall surely gather the remnant of Israel. I shall set them together like sheep of Bozrah, like a flock in the midst of its pasture:[39] they shall be in commotion [40] from a man (or from Man).'

'The breaker-in has ascended [41] before them. They have broken through, and they have passed through the gate, [42] and they have gone out by it. And their king has passed before them, and the Lord at their head (cf. Isa. xlv. 2).'

We are not asking what was the original text or meaning of Micah. We are interested in the potentialities of the unpointed text prior to the preaching of Jesus. [43] The drift is not easy too catch. Micah complains of the people's complacency, and the repute in which false prophets are held (Micah iii. 5-6, etc.). He ridicules their confidence that Yahweh will not take vengeance on them (ii. 7). The modern suggestion that ii. 12-13 did not belong where we find them need not detain us, for they were there in the time of Jesus. Much is known of the ways in which the verses were taken. First, two flocks are mentioned in *v.* 12, one gathered in one place, and one apparently on the mountains at pasture. The word Bozrah is now

---

[39] ΣΘ. ὡς βοσκήματα ἐν ὀχυρώματι (reading *bᵉṣārāh*), ὡς ἀγέλη ἐν μέσῳ τῆς ἐρήμου.

[40] *tᵉhiymenāh* might come from *hum, hiym* (to murmur in discomfort) or *hāmāh* (to be in commotion, murmur). The idea is resolved at Zeph. iii. 13 c.

[41] Θ. ἀνέβη. Σ. ἀναβήσεται ὁ διακόπτων.

[42] *ᶜāvar* means to go to and fro at Exod. xxxii. 27. It is the action of the redeemed at Isa. lxii. 10.

[43] Fragments of a commentary or commentaries on Micah treasured by the Qumran community exist: D. Barthélemy and J. T. Milik, *Discoveries in the Judaean Desert* I (Oxford, 1955), pp. 77-80; J. Carmignac, 'Notes sur les Pesharîm', *R. Qum.* III (1962), 515-9. J. M. Allegro, *Dis. J. Des.* V (Oxford, 1968), p. 36. For *ṣon* meaning Israel see H. Stegemann at *R. Qum.* IV (1963), 262, 263 n. 165. Micah ii. 6, 11 have influenced the Damascus Document, VIII. 13, cf. XIX. 25 f.; I, 14; IV, 19 f. (J. T. Milik at *R.B.* LIX, 1952, 412-8).

always replaced with a hypothetical word meaning 'fold' (be-ṣirāh, 'in the fold', for 'of Bozrah'). I doubt if this was known to contemporaries of Jesus, for the word was read beṣārāh, 'in straits', i.e. in distressful confine-ment or restraint. The LXX took it so (ἐν θλίψει) and the revisers do not seem to have 'improved' upon it. The word would thus be read alternatively 'of Bozrah' or 'in straits'. Bozrah is a foreign place, and thus the sheep would be foreign sheep; and to dispose of the things of Bozrah is to do the action of the Messiah, for Isa. lxiii. 1 ('Who is this that comes from Edom, with dyed garments from Bozrah ... marching in the greatness of his strength? I that speak in righteousness, mighty to save.') and the succeeding verses were taken as messianic in the early centuries of our era, if not earlier.[44] If we read the word as 'in straits' it fits the idea of the sheep being in confusion, waiting for release, and v. 13 tells us of their release, and sub-sequent progress. One word can raise the idea of foreigners' being herded with Israel's remnant and the former's being in need of deliverance. More-over the word ᶜBR, normally 'to pass', 'to exceed', has reminiscences of 'entrance into a covenant' (Deut. xxix. 11). Modern editors cut out 'they shall be in commotion from a man' in v. 12 as a gloss. The whole virtue of the sheep's 'passing' lies in the condition they were in previously. The words were in situ in the time of the LXX, who supposed they meant that the sheep 'rush forth' away from men (who frighten them? cf. Ezek. xxxiv. 28), and the NEB, true here to the MT, restores the words, rendering them 'which stampedes at the sight of a man'.

The breaker-in in v. 13 must first ascend in front of the sheep; and it is left to our imagination whether he is the same as the 'king'; we cannot tell whether the Lord and the king are different persons, or the same person in two guises. These ambiguities are a preacher's joy. Further, will the 'breaker-in' be responsible for their breaking out? Pereṣ (διακοπή) is a breach in a wall or fence, such as must be repaired if the enclosure is to keep animals in, or intruders out. [45] Moses stood in the breach, and defended Israel with his own person.[46] Yahweh, and the Messiah, will make breaches in the course of punishment and redemption, if several texts are to be read

---

[44] Edersheim, ubi cit., p. 730.

[45] Gen. xxxviii. 29; Isa. v. 5; xxx. 13; lviii. 12; Ezek. xxii. 30; Ps. lxxx. 12 (13); Ecclus. xxxvi. (27) 30 (Vattioni, p. 190). False prophets do not stand in the breach or build up the wall: Ezek. xiii. 5. The barrier between God and man: Exod. xix. 22, 24. Eccles. x. 8: 'a serpent will bite him that breaks through a wall'. Breaking into a house: II Chron. xxiv. 7.

[46] Ps. cvi. 23. Mekilta on Exod. xii. 1 ('offered their lives'); Ruth Rabbah proem. 5 (Soncino trans. VIII, 8). Cf. Ezek. xiii. 5.

with sufficient latitude.[47] Moreover *poreṣ* (the breaker-in) is exactly the word to describe a robber breaking into a sheepfold to steal sheep or to *let them out* (*lisṭiym peraṣūhā:* Mishnah, B.Q. VI. 1).

Verse 13 is taken in several ways. The 'breaker-in' is the Messiah, and the verse foretells the redemption of the remnant.[48] This is so though the word *poreṣ* often has a bad sense (the action metaphorically is ambivalent).[49] A king may make a breach in any fence to make a path for himself.[50] When the flock have emerged through the breach, they will spread abroad and become numerous. [51] Next the prophecy is of punishment, or of conquest. Breaking a breach is an allusion to God's retribution (because of Micah iii. 1).[52] Yet the same idea suggests a breach to enable prisoners to get out (Zech. ix. 11–12 and Isa. xlii. 7; Ps. cxlii. 7, cxlvi. 7), and form a triumphant army (on the Way of Holiness: Isa. xxxv. 8–10?), to breach in turn the enemies' walls and triumph over the heathen (cf. Isa. xxviii. 6). The Targum[53] interestingly shows two interpretations; the 'interpolator' of the second took his cue from Micah iv. 11–13. The Messiah's salvation is alluded to, then conquest of the heathen is added. Their king is he who is inspired by the Word of the Lord. Other imaginative interpretations of the 'in-breaker' (e. g. that he is Elijah) need not detain us. Nor need we pause over the halakic midrash of the same verse which uses it to prove that, 'first things first', the mention of the 'king', i.e. God, must precede other elements in a blessing, and the blessing itself comes first. The word 'gate' is thus taken twice

---

[47] Amos iv. 3; Ps. lxxxix. 41 (40); II, Sam. v. 20; vi. 8; I, Chron. xiii. 11; xiv. 11.

[48] *Yalqūṭ Shimᶜoni* on Micah (A. Wünsche at *Vierteljahrsschrift für Bibelkunde* . . ., I (1903), 256 ff., 260–2): the *poreṣ* is Jacob or the Messiah (see Gen. xxviii, 14). Genesis Rabbah XLVIII, § 10 (Sonc. trans., 412); LXXIII, § 11 (Sonc. 675); LXXXV, § 14 (Sonc. 799); XLVI (Sonc. 923); Exod. R. XXIII, § 5 (Sonc. 283); Lev. R. XXXII, § 8 (Sonc. 417); Eccles. R. IV, § 1 (Sonc. 112; IX, 11, § 1 (Sonc. 244). The Shekinah: Cant. R. IV, § 2 (Sonc. 221–2). So *Pesiqta Rabbati* XXXIII, 13 (trans. Braude, II, 658), XXXV (p. 675). So *Midr. Mishley,* ed. Limberg (1850), 4b, lines 4–3 from bottom (the Messiah will lead Israel). Perez is the Messiah: L. Ginzberg, *Legends of the Jews* V (Philadelphia, 1925), 336 n. 92. M. N. Kasher, *Encyclopedia of Biblical Interpretation* IV (New York, 1959), 112–3; V (1962), 81. Targum to Micah ii, 13 (Churgin, *cit. sup.,* 109) resembles Gen. R. LXXIII, § 3.

[49] Exod. xix. 22, 24; Judg. xxi. 15; Ps. xvii. 4; Jer. vii. 11.

[50] b. Pes. 110b.

[51] Midrashim in references cited at n. 48 above. The idea is already suggested at Isa. liv. 3; Jer. xxiii. 3.

[52] Most modern commentators express amazement how these lines could be taken in the sense of a threat; but it is significant that they also doubt the originality of them, and their correct location. Ancient commentators made the most of the context as they found it.

[53] Churgin, *op. cit.,* pp. 126, 140.

over by the targumist, once to mean a regular way out, which they (the sheep) use freely[53a] after the breach has been made for them, and the second time to mean the gates, the strongholds of the enemy. Further essential references to Ezekiel and Zechariah will be drawn in shortly.

The structure of John x. 1–18, 25–30

In an elaborate allegory at 1 Enoch lxxxix. 12–41, the story of the first redemption, in which blindness figures repeatedly, is taken up with a metaphor of sheep, wolves, and shepherds as an indication of right thinking leading to a good polity. St. John, by contrast, will have worked up a parable which, like many of Jesus's parables, will have had an allegorical aroma, without one-for-one correspondences such as can be traced in the Enoch allegory. The great parables are loaded with allusion to the Old Testament, not seldom hinting at the *Heilsgeschichte*.[54].

The man born blind, having obtained earthly sight, receives spiritual insight and becomes Jesus's pupil.[55] His expulsion from the fold of the synagogue[56] immediately precedes his reception, once he has really 'seen', into Jesus's group of students, his 'little flock'.[57] Students were like sheep, and that flock was led like sheep.[58]. Teaching students was like feeding sheep.[59] Jesus spoke of them as sheep entrusted to him by his Father, and claims not to have lost any,[60] though a scattering took place at Gethsemane. The question whether Pharisees are blind, i.e. their complacent suggestion that they are *not,* introduces Jesus's long reply, explaining that they are sinners and why,[61] and what they risk by misusing his 'sheep', and what is the contrast between him and them. This is the overt midrash of the texts I have adduced.

[53a] See below, p. 42 n. 72.

[54] Studies of the Prodigal Son, Good Samaritan, and the Wicked Vinedressers illustrate this (see *Law in the New Testament*), also the Unjust Judge (*N.T.S.,* XVIII, 1972, 178–91).

[55] ix. 34–8.

[56] ix. 34. The technical expression is used, and is taken up quaintly at x. 4: they expel into, they suppose, darkness; he expels into the way of life – the boundary across which the subject passes is the same.

[57] Luke xii. 32.

[58] See above, p. 26 n. 8.

[59] The Injunctions to Peter in John xxi.

[60] John xviii. 9.

[61] x. 1–5, 7–18 are presented as successive attempts to explain the point made in ix. 41. x. 18–21 prepares the hearer for the crisis which will have to be met at x. 31. The hearer (now, reader) must make up his mind whether *for him* the claims (perhaps preposterous claims) of Jesus really convict his opponents of sin. If they do, the hearer knows his own path.

x. 1: The sheepfold must be entered through its gate (legitimately); one who 'ascends' (ἀναβαίνων = ᶜālāh)⁶² before the sheep by any other path is readily presumed to be a thief, or a robber.⁶³. A *thief* in Jewish law is a fellow member of society liable to make restitution (unless he is, or might be, killed in the breach).⁶⁴. A *robber* is a stranger, perhaps an outlaw. The intruder does this at the risk of his life, for he may be killed with impunity unless the intention of the intruder can be proved *to the occupier's satisfaction* to be innocent (e.g. if the occupier illegally detains *his* sheep) – but in practice it is difficult to visualise the occupier, sword in hand, listening to the intruder's arguments relative to title in the sheep! That such claims could, however, be made by robbers is envisaged by the rabbis.⁶⁴ᵃ

x. 2: The one who enters through the gate is usually the shepherd. He has access to the sheep in the owner's interest. Exod. xxii. 1 tells us that an intruder risks his life; and indeed God looks after his own.⁶⁵ The shepherd is, as against all intruders, privileged. But who is entitled to use the gate?

x. 3: The watchman opens readily, for he is a fellow-servant;⁶⁶ he wakes up in time to hear the shepherd's call. ... καὶ πρόβατα χειρὸς αὐτοῦ. σήμερον ἐὰν τῆς φωνῆς αὐτοῦ ἀκούσητε (ψ. xciv. 7). The sheep hear the voice of the shepherd (John viii. 43, 47) and he calls them by name (Isa. xl. 26; xlv. 3–4; cf. John xviii. 9). This is the new name of the elect (Isa. lxii. 2, lxv. 15) and is an eternal name (Isa. lxvi. 5). He leads them.

x. 4: The shepherd's own flock follow him, as they are accustomed to depend upon him. They know his voice; obedience to him is profitable for them.

---

⁶² R. Schnackenburg, *The Gospel according to St. John* (London, 1968), pp. 553–4, is amongst the few who have boldly grasped that 'ascends' here is a deliberately quaint expression. The verb is not used of mere motion, it is used of entry into a boat, but the element of climbing is needed there too. The τοιχωρύχος by no means necessarily climbed or ascended.

⁶³ The tannaïtic distinction between *ganav* and *gazlan* seems already to have existed: *Mishnah, B.Q.* VII, IX–X; Hag. I, 7 and other sources cited by B. Jackson, *Theft*, p. 26 nn. 1–2. As Moulton confirms, καὶ is never used for ἤ except in negative clauses, and to speak of an individual as a thief and a robber is like saying he is a bull and a donkey (a common factor is indicated, presumably).

⁶⁴ *Mishnah, B.Q.* VII, 1–6. See above, Maimonides cited at p. 30 n. 21.

⁶⁴ᵃ A robber says 'it is mine that I snatched!' at b. Shev. 32b = Sonc. 183.

⁶⁵ Philo, *Leg. Alleg.* III, 32 (ed. Colson i, 320). The editor's amazement at Philo's 'perverse allegory' might have abated had he known the midrashic penumbra of the passage from the Law.

⁶⁶ Who is the watchman? Isa. xxii. 22 seems inadequate. Also Isa. lvi. 10. The angelic 'watchers' did not really watch. Ps. cxxi. 4 would be too far-fetched, perhaps. But to watch is to be, as it were, a shepherd: Hos. xii. 12.

x. 5: He is entitled to use the gate not only because of the watchman's recognition but also the sheep's (John xii. 19). He may get hold of the latter (ἐκβάλῃ) detaching them from the rest of the animals.[67] Their recognition of him enables him to select them. They do not know the voice of strangers, whose unauthorised approach automatically confuses them (Micah ii. 12).

x. 6: So far we have a cryptic saying, further developed below.

x. 7: Jesus himself is the sheep-gate[68] in Micah ii. 13.

x. 8: There was no means of getting out prior to Jesus; previously[69] thieves and robbers had access to them,[70] but that was not taking them to pasture. There is no direct reference to Zealots, etc., but a covert allusion to the precursors of that bane is not to be ruled out. Jesus is the Messiah, and only when they go out through him do they obtain the Life to Come. Previous attempts to lead them had come to nothing. The sheep had not followed the would-be leaders: they had been no one's true students, no one had effectively taught them.

x. 9: Jesus is the gate, or rather gateway, itself.[71] Micah ii. 13 shows the sheep passing the gate, to and fro (Num. xxvii. 17, 21; cf. Mark vi. 34). This means living and moving[72] by means of Jesus. As sheep find pasture daily or periodically, so the followers of Jesus will find salvation exclusively through him, for he is their way (John xiv. 6). Improving upon a hint from J. A. T. Robinson,[73] I suspect that at Rev. iii. 20 we have an independent tradition of a saying of Jesus about the gate between man and his Redeemer.

x. 10: The thief's (but not necessarily the robber's) object is to do harm,

---

[67] See below, p. 44 n. 84, for a comment on the implication of this term. On shepherds' ability to call out their own sheep see E. F. F. Bishop, *Jesus of Palestine* (London, 1955), 297–8.

[68] The Sheepgate of Jerusalem (Neh. iii. 1, 32; xii. 39; John v. 2; *Z.D.P.V.* VIII (1885), 269) seems to have been built over by Herod the Great, and it is not clear whether it was open *temp. Chr.* I cannot see any relevance between it and our chapter.

[69] See above, p. 26 n. 7. The words should be retained.

[70] Again the ambivalence of these words must be realised, as indicated in the last reference.

[71] B. M. Metzger, *The Text of the New Testament* (Oxford, 1964), cites a papyrus (bearing the no. 75) which reads ποιμήν instead of θύρα. The Sahidic version agrees. A misunderstanding, not a better text. So Schulz. C. C. Torrey's conjecture of a confusion of similar Aramaic words is unnecessary. J. N. Sandars and B. A. Mastin, *Commentary on the Gospel according to St. John* (London, 1968), p. 249. W. F. Howard, *Christianity*, p. 139.

[72] Deut. xxviii. 6; xxxi. 2; I, Sam. xxix. 6; II, Sam. iii. 25; II, Chron. i. 10; Ps. cxxi. 8; Acts i. 21. C. Spicq, *Théologie Morale du Nouveau Testament* II (Paris, 1965), p. 644 n. 1. A. Schlatter, *Der Ev. Johannes*, p. 236. E. Schweizer seems to have misunderstood the phrase.

[73] Above, p. 25 n. 1.

perhaps to the occupier, certainly to the sheep or some of them, for he is not able to tend them, he only wants to kill (as at Micah iii. 3) or sell them, certainly not to shear, milk (1 Cor. ix. 7), pasture and breed them, as a shepherd would.[74] Hence the intruder's peril. Jesus's coming (whether as shepherd or as gate) is in order that his 'sheep' (contrast John v. 40) might live on, of course in the supernatural sense of 'life'.

x. 11: Jesus is the good shepherd, antithesis to the evil shepherds characterised in Micah, Jeremiah,[75] Ezekiel,[76] and Zechariah.[77] The good shepherd is good, as was Moses.[78] He is faithful, and therefore 'good'. The evil shepherds cheat their masters (i.e. Israel's leaders defy the will of God), and it is characteristic of a good shepherd to pledge his life[79] for the sheep's safety. He does not *acquire* them at the risk of his life, but he certainly protects them and restores them at that risk.

x. 12–13: The hired man who is not the regular shepherd has no personal financial interest in the sheep, despite his greater liability to take care of them than a gratuitous bailee would bear;[80] he is suspected of abandoning the sheep whenever danger arises – and they would be scattered. This is because he is supposed to want only his wages, not the sheep's welfare. The figure of the 'hireling' is taken from that of the 'dogs' in Isa. lvi   from the corrupt officials and priests of Micah iii. 11, and from the figure of the hired shepherd in Zech. xi, who actually tells the sheep they can eat one another for all he cares (v. 9). A bad teacher will abandon his flock to the wolves: 2 Esdr. v. 18. St. John shows his knowledge of Jewish law by saying, correctly, 'a wolf' (singular) and not a robber: a robber or more than one wolf would have been *ones* ('inevitable accident'),[81] an invariable rule (Mishnah, B.M. VII. 9, 11), and the 'hireling' could not have been blamed.

---

[74] Jackson, *Theft*, p. 23 shrewdly says that John x. 10 does *not* imply that κλέπτειν normally implies violence. But see the 'covert midrash' below.

[75] Jer. x. 21; xxiii. 1–2; xxv. 34–6 (?); 1.6–7 ('we offend not').

[76] Ezek. xxxiv. 2–10.

[77] Zech. x. 2–3(?); xi. 4–5, 15–17. The metaphor became commonplace: II Esdr. v. 18 ('his flock in the hands of cruel wolves').

[78] *Mekilta* 13 d, 14 a reproduced at Odeberg, *op. cit.*, 138–9. P. Fiebig at *Angelos* I (1925), 57–8. Exod. R. II; Pes. Rabb. 26. Exod. iii. 1; Ps. lxxvii. 20. Isa. lxiii. 11. Exod. R. V. Pirqe de R. Eliezer XLII (trans. G. Friedlander, 1965, p. 333).

[79] Pledge himself utterly: J. Bonsirven, 'Les aramaismes de S. Jean L'Évangeliste?', *Bib.* XXX (1949), 431. Simonis, op. cit., p. 265. In practice a shepherd does not consciously throw away his life for the sheep, but he may well choose to risk it (*msr nfshyh*). Read carefully b. B.M. 93 b (bottom).

[80] b. B.M. 93 b (first half).

[81] For *onēs* see I. Herzog, *Main Institutions of Jewish Law* II (London, 1967), p. 182 and index, *s.v.*

x. 14: The good shepherd is recognised by the sheep because they know he leads them to pasture. Israel's leaders had led her to one disaster after another, in pursuit of personal gain. This is why they are disorganised, troublesome, disobedient to God and man. Whatever preaching might have been done previously, they never reached the true pasture.

x. 15: Mutual knowledge of sheep and shepherd, of Jesus and the Father:[82] they are alike in that each trusts and cares for the other (there is no question of Jesus's being submitted to an oath by his Father!). The sheep obey the shepherd; Jesus obeys his Father; they trust the one and he the other. Mutual knowledge explains leadership. Isa. xlv. 4: 'I have surnamed (LXX: προσδέξομαι) thee, though thou hast *not* known me ... (cf. *vv.* 5–6).' Isa. lxiii. 16: 'You are our Father, though Abraham does not know us, and Israel does not know us; but you are our Father. O Lord, Redeemer for ever is your name.' The LXX translate the last words 'Protect us, from the beginning your name is upon us', a phrase suggesting the marking of sheep. And his sheep know Jesus (John vi. 69), while John xvii. 11 can be traced back in part to Isa. lii. 5.[83]

x. 16: It is not enough that the remnant should be called forth through the gate (the gate, also, of death?, cf. Luke xi. 7, 9, 10)[84] by the good shepherd. He must also add to that flock by bringing in other sheep,[85] also entrusted to him, but not yet knowing his call. Once they are brought in they will obey. These are, according to Isa. lxiii. 1, lvi. 3–8 and Micah ii. 12, none other than the heathen, though John x neither says so nor requires this, and Jer. xxiii. 3, xxxi. 10 (the shepherd) suggest the recall of dispersed Jews. The nations are indeed sheep: Ps. ii. 9. Proselytes are to be visualised as joining, once they know the shepherd's voice. Proselytes do indeed join a 'flock'.[85a] They are encouraged to follow by the behaviour of the existing flock (especially if these keep to the pathway): it is the way of sheep. As

---

[82] C. Spicq, *Dieu et L'Homme selon le Nouveau Testament* (Paris, 1961), p. 99 n. 2. I. de la Potterie, 'οἶδα et γινώσκω', *Bib.* XL (1959), 709 ff., 721, 724 n. 1. B. E. Gärtner, 'The Pauline and Johannine idea of "to know God" against its Hellenistic background', *N.T.S.* XIV (1968), 209–31.

[83] F. W. Young, 'A study of the relation of Isaiah to the Fourth Gospel', *Z.N.W.* xlvi (1955), 215–233, notices this tenuous link.

[84] P. W. Meyer, 'A note on John 10:1–18', *J.B.L.* LXXV (1956), 232–5.

[85] R. H. Lightfoot, *St. John's Gospel. A Commentary* (Oxford, 1960), p. 206, says, 'it is not the duty of every shepherd ... to bring into the fold other sheep, not presently belonging to it'. True. This shows the want of appreciation of the Old Testament background of the parable behind this chapter. Tell-tale words, such as ἀναβαίνων, κλέπτης ἐστὶν καὶ λῃστής, and tell-tale ideas such as 'and other sheep I have' betray, and were intended to betray, a midrash upon scriptural texts.

[85a] Midr. R. Num. VIII. 2 (Sonc. 204).

in the case of Moses, shepherd of Israel, there will be one flock, one shepherd (Ezek. xxxiv. 23, xxxvii. 22, 24).[86] That, as we have seen, was exactly the point in Joshua's commission. That the nations shall follow sheeplike after Jews is picturesquely promised at Zech. viii. 23 (Jews first and then Greeks, as it were!).

x. 17: The Father's love of Jesus is connected with the fact that Jesus 'gives' his life for the sheep, on the basis that having pledged it, taken the risk, it is his again, the risk having (paradoxically) been successfully taken. There is no question, on this level, of a vicarious death.[87] The sheep are restored and, despite the dangers, the shepherd emerges ultimately unscathed.

x. 18: Voluntarily assuming this risk, he emerges triumphantly; the opportunity to do this is given him by the Father, who is the owner of the sheep. Moreover, though acting voluntarily he is enjoined so to act. Jews of the period understood that self-sacrifice in the service of God was only to reacquire life hereafter.[88] Such self-sacrifice is promised[89] and required in Isa. 1vii. 1–2.

The covert midrash

Μὴ λήψεταί τις παρὰ γίγαντος σκῦλα; καὶ ἐὰν αἰχμαλωτεύσῃ τις ἀδίκως σωθήσεται; ὅτι οὕτω λέγει Κύριος, Ἐάν τις αἰχμαλωτεύσῃ γίγαντα λήψεται σκῦλα· λαμβάνων δὲ παρὰ ἰσχύοντος σωθήσεται .... Isa. xlix. 24–5.

Collectively, the texts can be interpreted soteriologically. We have been alerted by the word 'ascended' in John x. 1,[90] which is eccentric unless one pictures the intruder climbing in through a window or aperture he has made high in the wall (the Palestinian Targum to Exod. xxii. 1 (MT) does indeed refer to a window).

Our texts must now be looked at in a different way. We have proceeded on the basis that the Jews wishing to kill Jesus (John v. 16, 18; vii. 1, 19, 25; viii. 37, 40; x. 31, 39; xix. 7) are acting sinfully in their treatment of Jesus's sheep: he alone is the shepherd and the way to pasture, and their dealings

---

[86] See Num. xxvii. 15–20. Eccles. xii. 11: 'like nails firmly fixed are the collected sayings which are given by one shepherd'. The Targum, and b. Ḥag. 3b, take this as referring to the teachings of Moses.

[87] Jeremias, *T.D.N.T.* VI (1968 trans.), p. 497.

[88] The attitude of the Essenes during the Roman war: τὰς ψυχὰς ἠφίεσαν ὡς πάλιν κομιούμενοι (Josephus, *B.J.* II. 153, Loeb edn., ii. 381).

[89] Churgin, cited at p. 35 n. 37 above.

[90] Above, p. 41 n. 62.

with his sheep, though ostensibly authorised and effective, are illegitimate. Now we must take account of the fact that the Pharisees were the erectors of a fence around the law,[91] and attempted to keep the public protected from such as Jesus. They actually *ejected* Jesus's students. The text of Micah could as easily be taken to foretell the 'breaker-in' as the saviour of the sheep, and, correspondingly the Pharisees and the priestly hierarchy as illegal detainers of the sheep. The maker of the breach could thus be none other than Jesus, and thus he was a kind of robber (see Jer. vii. 11, which Jesus quotes, MT and LXX). We must first satisfy ourselves that Jesus did think of himself as a thief or robber (or possibly both); then we must look into the Jewish law and note again its curious and relevant provisions.

Speculations whether Jesus actually *was* a robber in the ordinary sense are vain. Meanwhile the image of the Thief has been misunderstood. Rev. iii. 3, xvi. 15; I Thess. v 2, 4 and II Pet. iii. 10 have been construed only as indicating the unexpectedness of the Second Coming. One cannot know when the thief will come (Matt. xxiv. 43; Luke xii. 39; cf. Obad. 5). But the words can well be taken to refer to what seems to have been a well-known paradox, namely that Jesus was a good thief or robber (or both). He entered the house of his Father (Mark xi. 15–17 par.) and turned out the bad thieves (or robbers, predicted at Ezek. vii. 22); an ironical passage: Jeremiah, as we have seen, uses the word *pāriṣ*, a by-form of *porēṣ* as in Micah ii. 13. He speaks of burrowing into the house of the strong man (Satan), binding him and stealing the goods (Mark iii. 27 par. – note Luke xi. 21 says αὐλήν)[92], which can be taken very plausibly of taking back wrongfully acquired gains without intending to slay the occupier. He enacted the part of the 'wicked' (cf. Isa. liii. 12) in the Garden, so that the Two Swords were necessary (Luke xxii. 36–8) (sc. in order to be a *lisṭiym mezūyyān,* an 'armed robber' [b. B.Q. 57a, B.M. 95a, B.B. 92b]). They came out to him as against a robber (Mark xiv. 48 par.). He was virtually exchanged for a robber (John xviii. 40); and he finally turned on the cross (Mark xv. 27) a pair of robbers into what seemed to be a plurality of robbers. Was he not God's robber, like the thieves in Joel ii. 9?

---

[91] I must emphasise that the 'fence' of which the Pharisees themselves spoke was intended for a different purpose, namely to prevent them and their followers from breaking a commandment: *Law in the New Testament,* pp. 57 n. 3, 380 n. 3. The 'breaker-in' of Micah ii. 13 projects a metaphorical fence, and this is the one alluded to, not the well-known Pharisaic metaphor.

[92] Laudable self-help: Jackson, *Theft,* pp. 212–3 (citing *B.Q.* 27b, etc. on legitimate forcible 'recaption'!). On the Strong Man see Jer. xxxi. 11; Tobit viii. 3; Ps. Sol. v. 4 (3); I Enoch lxii. 5 ff.; lxix. 27.

No matter which their nation (John xviii. 37) all the sheep would be received in the Father's house. 'And not only on behalf of the Nation, but in order that he might lead together into one place the scattered children of God': John xi. 52. Those who do not grasp this message are not of his sheep. A son when given sheep to look after is in fact working without wages, tending his inheritance, in which he has almost a vested interest. Having risked his life for them (John xv. 13) Jesus restores them and they are safe for ever, beyond the reach of Satan (John x. 25–30).

'I and my Father are one' brings to mind St. Paul's quaint (and understandably controversial) expression at Phil. ii. 5–7: 'Have that bearing towards one another which was also in Christ Jesus, who, since he was in the form of God did not consider it robbery (cf. 1 Esdr. iv. 23) to be equal to God, but made himself nothing, taking the form of a servant, assuming the likeness of man.' The power of God being in Jesus there was nothing to which he could not aspire, but in spite of this chose to play a man's role. The amusing aspect (to offer light on only one aspect) of this pun[93] lies in the fact that the role Jesus *did* play was that of a robber, snatching men, like sheep, from the wrongful possession of rebels against God. Bauer–Arndt–Gingrich say ἁρπαγμός is 'next to impossible', 'the state of being equal to God cannot be equated with the act of robbery', and cite a large bibliography supporting the word 'prize' as the meaning of the word here (hardly less problematical).[93a] In fact the robber theme works out astonishingly well.

Thieves had the common characteristic of taking assets possessed by others (irrespective of title). *Robbers* would drive sheep away boldly, might even shepherd them through their employees. *Thieves* slaughtered or sold for slaughter (as in Zech. xi). Thieves were liable to make two-fold, or even four-fold restitution. Robbers were liable to none. Thieves did not acquire the sheep by mere taking; robbers *did,* for it was axiomatic that the owner would give up hope of recovering sheep from robbers.[94] Sheep could of course be detained by those who did not really own them. An interesting additional fact to be borne in mind is that sheep could (like other property)

[93] Jackson has shown, *op. cit.,* 23–4 that ἁρπάζειν etc. represent *gazal* (robbery, exploitation), which *in Greek* necessarily imply violence (open deprivation [p. 27] of property in broad daylight by an outsider to the society thus threatened [John x. 12, 28–9]). But the Hebrew word *gazlan* (robber) did *not* necessarily imply violence (Jackson, p. 28), but only an open taking with a high hand. Naturally in most cases force was involved.

[93a] J. Carmignac says we should read 'non-robbery' (i.e. by right): *N.T.S.* 18 (1972), 131–16. The curiosity of the word is not removed. Nock would have translated 'lucky find', *Essays* (Oxford, 1972) I, 87 (see n. 157).

[94] *Mishnah,* Kel. XXVI. 8; *B.Q. X.* 2.

be dedicated to the Temple, i.e. to God, and would then be *heqdesh*. To *heqdesh* none of the laws relating to theft and restitution applied. Theft or robbery *by way of self-help* was not frowned upon by society.[95] If the thief or robber was really entitled to the sheep he had nothing to fear but the possessors' resentment and retaliation. The Jewish community could conceivably flog an offender who stole or robbed *heqdesh,* but it could not enforce restitution – it was up to God to protect his own.[96] But the Roman *state,* which had an interest in preventing robbery in general, might well put to death a robber who retrieved his own or his friends' or comrades' sheep, or robbed sheep dedicated to the Temple; for it was the state's task (not the customary court's) to put down robbers.[96a] Robbery might be exercised under the shadow of a cross, but for the best of motives, and no civil restitution might be owed to anyone.

The Law *ought* to be enforced, and Jesus plainly saw himself as working within it, and under its protection. The Prophets, however, insisted that the Jews tampered with the Law in actual administration. Exod. xxii. 2b (see below) and even the Pharisees' oral law might not be applied, if the leaders were 'blind'. Even a thief caught in the act in broad daylight could lawfully be sold for his theft (since, not being liable to instant slaughter, he was not free from the normal duty to compensate for damage, under the notorious rule, if indeed title to the sheep lay with the possessor – which, in our metaphor, it did not). But he could not lawfully be put to death – as might certainly be feared if he had operated stealthily, without witnesses, in the dead of night. The thief who burrowed through at night did so absolutely at the risk of his life. Would this distinction be observed by an irate hierarchy, keen to apply the words of the Prophets to their opponents (Qumran fashion), and, if they were Sadducees, by no means impressed by metaphorical and fanciful applications of ambiguous prophetic texts? St. John seems to be telling us that Jesus knew well that his heroism was within the Law, but outside its practical protection. But when we turn to the story again, there is irony upon irony, for the Jews who 'sought to kill him' actually did not execute any Jewish sentence, and it was as a robber that he

[95] Jackson, p. 30, 35; Macmillan, 'The Roman concept of Robber-Pretender', *R.I.D.A.* X, 3rd ser., 1963, 221–5. It was a Jewish proverb that one should not even steal one's own thing from a thief (b. Ber. 5b): obviously it was often attempted. See. n. 64a above.

[96] *Mishnah, B.Q.* I. 2; b. *B.Q.* 62b (Sonc. trans., 364), 71b (Sonc., 411), 74b (Sonc., 427); Mishnah at B.M. 56a. G. Horowitz, *Spirit of Jewish Law* (New York, 1953), pp. 320, 603.

[96a] On the Romans' concern to put down robbers, and Jewish notions of robbers as potentially authors of an alternative kingdom, see E. R. Goodenough, *Jurisprudence* (1968), 146–51; Philo, *De decal.* 135, 136; *Spec. Leg.* IV. 2.

was 'punished'! Though no one could have foretold it, and none might have been aware of it, the formalities were accurately observed.

Two poetical views of Jesus's situation, assuming him to be a thief or a robber, seem to have existed before St. John, evidenced in different places. St. Matthew is interested in the 'sale' of Jesus, for a slave's valuation, to the priestly authorities, as if he were liable to be sold, in payment for what? He became, incidentally, *heqdesh* himself (but we should not pursue that far-fetched notion now).[97] The sale had to be taken seriously, since it was regarded as proving that the ambivalent shepherd of Zechariah had appeared. Jesus only *seemed* to have damaged the established 'shepherds' of Israel, he had not really done so, and therefore he was not liable to be sold. It is a fanciful concept: sold, handed over, he gave his freedom (in effect his life) in order to rescue (redeem) his 'sheep'. Could he both be 'sold' to the Jewish authorities 'illegally' *and* be punished as a robber? Certainly. The customary court normally inflicts its own penalties, and where it is powerless (as in the case of robbers) the state (under the control of pagans) fills the gap, and inflicts the appropriate robbers' punishment. The popularity of Jesus might well abstract the Jewish people from all rule, let alone Roman rule, and so Pilate's action was reasonable. St. John seems aware of all this, in his curious phrase 'a thief and a robber' (see above), since everyone knew that thieves and robbers differed in vital respects: Jesus was both the one and the other.

Let us take up Exod. xxii. 2 b (MT) at last:

dāmiym lo shalēm yeshalem ʾim-ʾēyn lo wenimkar bigenēvāto.

Let us re-translate:
'There is blood for him (a life is due for him, forfeit to him if he is killed),'
'He shall make a full satisfaction,'[98]
'if he has nothing (of his own),'
'and he shall be sold[99] in his theft' (cf. Mark xiv. 11).

St. Matthew linked the 'betrayal' with the story of the hireling shepherd of Zechariah xi. 12–13, whose resignation and pay (hire of services) were en-

---

[97] *Law in the New Testament,* p. 409. I am reluctant to pursue here the 'price of blood' theme à propos of *dāmiym lw* in Exod. xxii. 2. One must have a firm handhold while moving amidst hypothetical midrashim.

[98] The original meaning was simply that restitution in kind should be made: D. Daube, *Studies in Biblical Law,* pp. 133–9. But where *heqdesh* was concerned there could be no restitution, thus 'restoring he shall restore' hangs in the air and must have a figurative meaning.

[99] S. Belkin, *Philo and the Oral Law,* p. 207.

gineered by Yahweh to show the leaders of Israel what kind of shepherds they were, and to foretell a crisis when the evil shepherding will cease and a remnant of the flock (Jer. xxiii. 3) will be saved. 'Strike (*or* 'I shall strike') the shepherd and the sheep will be scattered (cf. Zech. xiii. 7)' recognises[100] (Mark xiv. 27; cf. John xvi. 32) that the process of Redemption requires the testing of the sheep by means of the temporary removal (and striking) of their shepherd. Those who remained faithful would be saved. Fortunately a saying from Q (Matt. xii. 30, Luke xi. 23) indicates that Jesus did not envisage himself as absolutely alone in the process of assembling the sheep:[101] 'He who does not gather-in with me scatters.'

The suggested parable behind John x. 1–18

The suggestion is that St. John had a parable, such as what follows, in front of him, 'decoded' it by tracing back the biblical allusions, and based his chapter upon it. The vocabulary is taken from Torah and prophetic material (utilising the MT and versions). Reference to Philo, *De agric.* 50–54 (noted by C. K. Barrett) is desirable and to Judith xi. 19. Moreover, a parable should contain an allusion to Wisdom literature also, and the needed link between Num. xxvii, Ezek. xxxiv. 23; xxxii. 22,24, and John xi. 52 appears at Sir. xviii. 13 (*q.v.*).

Ἄνθρωπός τις ἦν πλούσιος ὃς εἶχεν πρόβατα πολλά, ἃ μὲν συναχθέντα ἐπὶ τὴν αὐλήν, ἃ δὲ ἐν τῷ ἐρήμῳ. καὶ ἐξέβαλε τοὺς ποιμένας αὐτῶν ὡς σκορπίζοντας τὰς ποίμνας αὐτοῦ. καθεύδοντος δὲ τοῦ θυρωροῦ κλέπτης τις διώρυξεν καὶ ἔθυσε πρόβατον καὶ ἄλλα ἐξεφόβησεν. εἶπεν δὲ ἐν ἑαυτῷ ὁ κύριος, εἰ ἄλλον τινὰ ποιμένα μισθώσομαι ἵνα ταῦτα εὕρωσιν νομήν, φοβοῦμαι μή πως τὸ ποίμνιον ἀφῇ καὶ ἀπόληται τὰ πρόβατά μου. ἔγνων τί ποιήσω, ἵνα ἐξελεύσεται καὶ εἰσελεύσεται καὶ σωθήσεται. ἀποστελῶ τὸν υἱόν μου, ὅπως ἐξέλθῃ πρὸ προσώπου αὐτῶν καὶ προαγάγῃ αὐτὰ καὶ φυλάσσῃ ἐπὶ τὴν ποίμνην. τῆς γὰρ θύρας ἀνεῳγμένης ἡ μὲν ἀκούσει τῆς φωνῆς αὐτοῦ καὶ εἰδήσει αὐτόν, καὶ ἐξάξει αὐτήν. ἄλλα δὲ πρόβατα ἐκζητήσει ἃ ὄπισθεν τούτων ἐπακολουθήσει αὐτῷ..

---

[100] There could conceivably be an eschatological point here: Jer. li. 23. On the text see B. Lindars, *New Testament Apologetic* (London, 1961), 127–32; R. H. Gundry, *The Use of the Old Testament in St. Matthew's Gospel* (Leiden, 1967), 25–8. The optimistic (not pessimistic) implications of the quotation of Zech. xiii. 7 are well brought out by J.Jeremias, *New Testament Theology* I (London, 1971), 297–8.

[101] Bauer–Arndt–Gingrich agree that the word refers to sheep: σκορπίζω 1.

FURTHER ANNOTATIONS

Tit. O. Kiefer, *Die Hirtenrede. Analyse und Deutung von Joh. 10, 1-18* (Stuttgart, 1967). Whether the 'fold' really means Israel (the church is the New Israel) is discussed by S. Pancaro, 'The relationship of the church to Israel in the gospel of St John,' *N.T.S.* xxi (1975), 396-405.

p. [38], l. 31. Note Ezek. xii.5 : 'Dig thou through the wall in their sight and carry out thereby!'

p. [42], n. 72. Num. xxvii.17, Tob. v.17.

p. [44], n. 85. And it ignores the force of Gen. xxix.8.

p. [45], l. 21. There is a comm. on Is. xlix.24 (in another sense?) at Ps. Sol. v. 4.

p. [46], l. 6. I see 2 Tim. ii.26 as expressing this idea.

p. [46], l. 13. A. Smitmans, 'Das Gleichnis vom Dieb,' *Fest. K. H. Schelkle* (Düsseldorf, 1973), 43-68.

p. [47], n. 93. Robbers bring out a flock : Mishnah, B.Q. VI.1.

FIGTREES IN THE NEW TESTAMENT   *

The curious title corresponds to an unexpected question. Have the figtrees in the New Testament something in common? I shall contend that they have, and that the different passages, coming, as they do, from different strata in the gospels, produce a common factor of value to students of Jesus' conception of the End Time. We cannot begin to study this question without a tolerance of midrash. The popularity of targumic and midrashic studies increases rapidly. There was a time when a lone voice achieved no response.[1] Now we are flooded with studies.[2] Introductory works are available which go some way towards warning newcomers against over-enthusiasm,[3] and many specimens of the midrashic art are available which could well encourage the seeker after novelties to embark on research of a speculative nature.[4] Just as the eye often sees what it is predisposed to see, and the ear hears (or thinks it hears) what it expects to hear, so the untrained student of midrashim may find difficulty in knowing where the under-senses and overtones of the passage he is analysing rank in real importance relative to the superficial meaning. It is well to bear in mind, also, that unless a midrash can be traced in Jewish sources it is unwise to foist it upon Jesus or his interlocutors; for, although this caution might deprive Jesus of originality, and although it may be that the Jewish material which *is* available to us may actually have appeared after his day, there is no excuse for fathering upon him ideas which cannot plausibly be shown to have been his. It is up to each gatherer of midrashim to form his own opinion as to how far he can indulge in speculation.

Now if ever there were passages that called for the aid of the expert in

---

[1] A Guillaume, 'The Midrash in the Gospels', *Expository Times XXXVII* (1925–6), pp. 392–8.

[2] M. P. Miller, 'Targum, Midrash, and the Use of the Old Testament in the New Testament', *Journal for the Study of Judaism II* (1971), pp. 29–82 (an astonishing bibliography).

[3] Renée Bloch, 'Midrash', in DBS 5 (Paris, 1957), pp. 1263–81; A.G. Wright, *The Literary Genre Midrash* (Staten Island, N.Y., 1967, =CBQ XXVIII [1966], pp. 105–54, 417–57); R. Le Déaut, *Introduction à la Littérature Targumique* (Rome, 1966); id., 'Les Études Targumiques. État de la Recherche et Perspectives pour l'Exégèse de l'Ancien Testament', in H. Cazelles, ed., *De Mari à Qumrân* (J. Coppens Festschrift I [Gembloux/ Paris, 1969]), pp. 302–31; cf. also works reviewed by R. Murray, HJ XIII (1972), pp. 441–51.

[4] E.g. J. Bowker, *The Targums and Rabbinic Literature* (Cambridge, 1969).

haggadic midrashim, the episode of the so-called Cursing of the Figtree and the episode of Nathanael under a figtree cry aloud. Nathanael was a puzzle to which no convincing answer had been attempted. Uncontrolled guesswork even produced bizarre suggestions. On the other hand the beautiful and (if I may say so) first-rate article of R. H. Hiers explained the haggadic background behind the Cursing and led on to make very sensible and controlled suggestions as to what actually happened.[1] J. G. Kahn, upon rather more slender foundations, and motivated by a desire not to see Jesus cursing the Jews (!), produced a very short and poorly attested midrashic notion which, viewed more closely, supports Hiers's welcome thesis (of which he was unaware).[2] Kahn's study merits close attention, not only for its valuable information, but also for the amount of subjective exegesis, so easy to detect in a non-professional's work, so hard to detect in one's own!

When we put together the various passages in which figtrees figure, and take the hint which was published for the first time by Hiers, it is very striking how the theme of the Coming of the Kingdom fits the contexts in the gospels, different as these are, showing that, to understand the intention of the evangelists (if no more), the haggadot must be unravelled. My own recent adventure with the Palm Sunday Colt left the question open, whether Jesus was deliberately miming actions reminiscent of the Exodus, and combining these reminiscences with messianic prophecies, or whether others saw in his actions significant agreements with the Hebrew bible understood with the aid of Christian haggadot.[3] But when a number of episodes which are closely associated in St Mark are viewed together with the aid of midrashic technique it seems very difficult

[1] ' "Not the Season of Figs" ', JBL LXXXVII (1968), pp. 394–400. On p. 399 Hiers asks, 'Could it be that Jesus himself had led his followers to believe—and himself believed—that it [the Messianic Age] would indeed appear there and then?' 'If stones should not cry out to greet the Messiah, surely the figtree might bear fruit out of season. For in the messianic age should not all fruit be continually in season?' The 'stones cry out' theme, by the way, is midrashically attested: Midrash on Psalms, lxxiii. 4 (trans. W. Braude [New Haven, 1959], II, 4).

[2] 'La Parabole du figuier stérile et les arbres récalcitrants de la Genèse', NovT XIII (1971), pp. 38–45. Midr. Rabbah Gen., V.9 (Soncino trans., pp. 39–40) contains a comical exchange of guesswork as to why God cursed the earth (Gen 3: 17): were trees disobedient in not being edible themselves, or in bearing fruit indiscriminately? The allusion to the Messianic Era, however, is welcome, indirect as it is. Mention must be made of J. W. Doeve, 'Purification du Temple et Dessèchement du Figuier. Sur la Structure du 21ème Chapitre de Matthieu et Parallèles', NTS I (1954), pp. 297–308. This would reconstruct Mt and Lk as variant developments of themes derived from Ps 118: 22–26; Isai 62: 11; and Zech 9: 9. Alas, the starting point is not adequate to support all the structure, but the method is attractive.

[3] NovT XIII (1971), pp. 241–58. To the citations there add Josephus, Ant. XIII. ii, 3 (52) (Loeb ed., Josephus VII, tr. R. Marcus [1943], p. 251).

to believe that in his view Jesus was not deliberately miming biblical actions. Perhaps he did this upon a principle analogous to sympathetic magic, i.e. that if one performs the right actions in the right sequence nature responds, the supersensory world responds, with corresponding efficacy for man's benefit. The historical plausibility of such a conclusion is high. The Cursing of the Figtree is so written as if to emphasize that the actions were deliberately undertaken by Jesus, and were not mere coincidences. Whether the disciples understood them, or were convinced of their utility is quite another question. Participating in a drama, in the hope that so one may work out cosmic functions, did not require that the participants really understood what they were doing; and such a proceeding seems to breathe the atmosphere of the ancient world. In readiness to see traces of history in these stories we may now approach all the figtrees in succession.

THE SENTENCE ON THE FIGTREE

Quite apart from the question whether Mk 11: 14 = Mt 21: 19c is correctly translated from Aramaic[1] it has always been a gratuitous assumption that Jesus 'cursed' the tree. To go further, as Manson did,[2] and describe Jesus' behaviour as 'bad temper' is to compound ignorance with naïveté. Everyone has seen that the action is 'out of character' (for the general tendency of all accounts agrees in eliminating all question of spitefulness from Jesus' personality), and some would go so far as Kahn[3] in saying that the passage must be invented, as Jesus' humble philosophy could not extend to such conduct. The words, both in St Mark and in St Matthew, amount to a sentence (cf. God's sentence at Gen 3: 17), which must have been expressed in the imperfect tense: the reaction of Jesus to the want of figs on that tree at that place and time was to tell the tree that it would not bear fruit until the end of the Age; that is its punishment.[4] The tree has been judged. One knows a tree by its fruit.

[1] J. Jeremias, *The Parables of Jesus* (London, 1963), p. 228, n. 2.
[2] T. W. Manson, 'The Cleansing of the Temple', *Bull J. Rylands Lib.* (BJRL) XXXIII (1951), pp. 271–82. The pericope is regarded as unfortunate, and 'understandably omitted by Luke': B. H. Streeter, *The Four Gospels* (London, 1926), p. 178; J. M. Creed, *The Gospel according to St Luke* (London, 1950), p. 239. See also C. V. Jones, *Art and Truth of the Parables* (London, 1964), p. 112.
[3] See p. 250, n. 2 above.
[4] *Eis ton aiōna* can mean to the end of *this* age: Jn 8: 51–2; 12: 34; 1 Cor 8: 13; Heb 5: 6; 7: 17, 21, 24; 1 Jn 2: 17; 2 Jn 2: 2. Lk 1: 55 and Jn 4: 14 must mean to the end of *this* age. 'Ages' is more common for eternity. On *aiōn* see G. Dalman, *Die Worte Jesu* I (Leipzig, 1930), pp. 120–7. E. Schwartz, 'Der verfluchte Feigenbaum', ZNW V (1904), pp. 80ff., on p. 84 suggested 'till I come'. H. W. Bartsch, 'Die "Verfluchung" des Feigenbaumes', ZNW LIII (1962), pp. 256–60, on p. 258: the end is coming so soon that no more figs would be borne in any event!

This one should have had at least one fig and it had not. Talking to trees, which strikes us as absurd, is to be found in contexts familiar to the Jews of the period. In the haggadah concerning the scaffold of Haman,[1] in that concerning the trees of the Garden of Eden,[2] and that concerning the Messianic Era, trees and men communicate.[3] And one of the ways of getting barren trees to bear was (as we shall see) to talk to them,[4] or to have a conversation in front of them. Moses spoke to the rock: Num 20: 8!

Scholars reluctant to convict Jesus of spiteful behaviour towards a tree have suspected that the words 'for it was not the time of figs' (Mk 11: 13c), which do not appear in St Matthew, are an interpolation, or an addition by St Mark.[5] However, the point of the story is greatly enhanced by their presence, and since Hiers's study no one need doubt but that they are genuine. Several scholars have thought it absurd that Jesus should be hungry soon after leaving his lodging: one cannot take this seriously, for, apart from the relationship between the story and actual chronology (which is unknown), no one knows what arrangements were made for breakfast! The words however stand as they do in order to bring out the haggadic aspect of the story.

To the references assembled by Hiers a number can be added, but his reference to Billerbeck's enormous accumulation[6] absolved him from belabouring a point he had made so ably. When Adam sinned the trees of the Garden reacted. It must be remembered that the ancient world never lost sight of the fact that trees and animals 'know' more about what goes on in the world than humans do, i.e. the turning of the seasons, the weather, and so on, having powers (apparently) of predicting factors from which the agriculturalist draws his very livelihood. It is not surprising that trees were cross with Adam and Eve.[7] Until the Fall all trees bore fruit, including those that subsequently were non-fruit-bearing.

---

[1] L. Ginzberg, *Legends of the Jews* (Philadelphia, 1947) IV, p. 443; VI, p. 479.

[2] Ibid., I, p. 75; V, p. 122. Targ. Pal. on Gen 3: 17 says that the 'earth' did not warn Adam against his misdeed (and so it was punished).

[3] About work on the Sabbath (which will endure): Ginzberg, op. cit., V, p. 142; *Midrash on Psalms*, as above, p. 250, n. 1.

[4] b. Ta'an. 24a (Soncino trans., p. 122), on the pious employer's son's bidding.

[5] G. Münderlein, 'Die Verfluchung des Feigenbaumes', NTS X (1963), pp. 89–104, on p. 91. So C. W. F. Smith, 'No Time for Figs', in JBL LXXIX (1960), pp. 315–27.

[6] StrB IV/2, pp. 888–90, 949–54. Of interest is the *agraphon* reported as Jesus' word by John to Papias, quoted by Irenaeus, *Adv. Haer.*, V. 33, 3 (Harvey II, pp. 417–8) which relates passages from Isaiah to the Kingdom. Biblical authorities are Lev 26: 4–6; Jer 31: 12; Zech 8: 12 (see *Midr. Rabbah Gen.*, XII. 6, Soncino trans., pp. 92–3; *Midr. Rabbah. Num.*, XIII. 12, Sonc. trans., pp. 523–4); Ezek 34: 27; 36: 8–11, 30; 47: 9; Joel 3: 18; Amos 9: 13.

[7] Ginzberg, op. cit., I, p. 75; V, p. 122. They also reacted badly to Cain's killing Abel: ibid., I, p. 112; VI, pp. 141–2.

After the Fall barren trees came into existence, and a barren tree is a witness to the Fall of Adam.[1] In the Messianic Age the productivity of the earth will be prodigious. There will be no want of water. The Brook Kidron will be a huge river, from which unimaginable productivity will result.[2] Trees will not be barren; they will bear constantly (Ezek 47: 12!). Since the figtree has, normally, a long season,[3] and is a very satisfactory tree generally, it is not surprising that it will figure largely in this prosperity. In the Messianic Age the children of Israel, returning to their Home, with the Messiah at their head, will find a constant supply of fruit along the way, and shade also, for the trees will bend forward to give them shade, just as the low places will fill up, rough places will become smooth, hills will be levelled and the sea will become dry land over which the redeemed shall pass (Isai 40: 4–5; 45: 2; 49: 11; 51: 10; 54: 10; Ps. Sol 11: 4; 1 Bar 5: 7).[4] Does one take such fantasies seriously? Why not? That, perhaps, is the point. In the Messianic Age so many wonders will occur. The dead will be raised, and the crooked straightened.[5] John the Baptist was told that he could draw his own conclusions from happenings which, haggadically, testified to the beginning of that Age: or so the text tells us (Mt 11: 5; Lk 7: 22).

No doubt seeds planted in the Messianic Age (or planted in anticipation of its commencement?) will bear a hundredfold (cf. Mk 10: 30; also Lk 8: 8, haggadically better than Mt 13: 8?), but even after the Fall a supremely righteous person could obtain such results as testified by the experience of Isaac, who foreshadowed the Messiah (Gen 26: 12 with

---

[1] Ibid., I, p. 80; V, p. 28.

[2] *Pirke de R. Eliezer* (tr. G. Friedlander [New York, 1971]) ch. LI, pp. 416–8.

[3] Manson summarizes G. Dalman, *Arbeit und Sitte in Palästina* I (Gütersloh, 1935), pp. 331–79: 'A very late Passover (third week of April) might just see leaves and immature fruit. It would hardly be worth eating.' E. F. F. Bishop, *Jesus of Palestine* (London, 1955), p. 217, tells of an unripe fig quite large enough to warrant picking, fit to be eaten by 'hungry Palestinians', picked on April 16, 1936. But Jesus was, in biblical terms, looking for a 'first-ripe fig' at a time when no one could expect an eatable fig, ripe or unripe. He mimed Isai 28: 4 and Mic 7: 1.

[4] For shade see Isai 49: 10; Ps Sol 11: 5; 1 Bar 5: 8. Lohmeyer, after a careful comparison of 'mountain-moving' passages in the synoptics, came to the conclusion that Mt 17: 20 was based on Isai 54: 10; Mt 21: 21 on Isai 49: 11; Lk 17: 6 on Isai 51: 10; the idea going back to Isai 40: 4 and 49: 11; and Mt 21: 21 bearing the marks of greater originality (authenticity). This brilliant analysis, undoubtedly on the right lines (E. Lohmeyer—W. Schmauch, *Das Evangelium des Matthäus* [Göttingen, 1956], pp. 271–3), is doubted and rejected by W. Grundmann, *Das Evangelium nach Matthäus* (Berlin, 1968), p 454 n. 11, and sadly ignored by almost everyone. The further life of these apocalyptic ideas in Asia is commented upon by Derrett in *Zeitschrift für Religions- und Geistesgeschichte* XXIV (1972), pp. 153–5. Previous explanations of Mk 6: 48–49 could be discarded in favour of Mk 11: 23 understood as in this present paper.

[5] Isai 40: 4 (Lk 3: 5) possibly put into action in associating Ps 145: 14; 146: 8 (cf. Lev 26: 13) at Lk 13: 10–17: cf. Derrett in *Theology* LXXIV (1971), p. 571.

LXX and Targ. Pal.). As the story shows (Gen 26: 27–28) one who raises such a crop will not fail to attract 'friends'!

For the trees to produce the wonder-crop of the New Age they must be approached by one who is hungry: they must offer their crop not as a matter of biological cyclic action but in response to the need of the righteous. If it is the season for figs the crop is not that of which haggadah speaks. Hence such fruit must be looked for by one who is (1) hungry, (2) righteous, (3) applying out of season, (4) entering the New Age. Speaking in haggadic terms, why did the figtree not produce immediate figs, like the tree to which the pious employer's son spoke in the Talmud? Obviously because the Age had not commenced. But had it not? This might be a matter of opinion. If other signs signified that the Age had commenced the tree was wrong. Trees adopted attitudes at the time of Adam, and here was a tree adopting an attitude towards the Messiah. It would be really disgraceful if it should produce figs again until the Age, when, as I have said, either there will be no barren trees, or previously barren trees will bear prodigiously.

Peter interpreted Jesus' words as a curse (Mk 11: 21) whereas, as we have seen, the words need not necessarily have implied this. The tree had withered from the roots; obviously its leaves had shrivelled and some may even have dropped. It is absurd to rationalize this by assuming, as many have,[1] that the true season was the autumn, Jesus was not on his journey of Redemption, it had indeed been a season of figs, and a sudden frost, or the like, had caused the leaves to begin to drop. This destroys the story as St Mark conceived it. The sudden shrivelling of a substantial plant was a biblical theme, and Jonah was a biblical character in whom we know Jesus was interested. Jesus does not say that the withering was due to his sentence. The story as told by St Mark leaves it open for us to believe that Jesus accepted this as God's confirmation that the tree would remain dormant until the Age matured.

Now we are prepared to read Mt 21: 21–22 understanding, as one may always presume to be the case, that St Matthew aimed to make St Mark's story intelligible and meaningful in terms of what he conceived to be the gospel. St Mark simply says 'Have faith in God . . . believe that you have received it, and you shall have it.' Without the midrashic gloss this is a piece of primitive psychological self-therapy (not necessarily to be des-

---

[1] Manson, BJRL XXXIII (1951), p. 280; C. W. F. Smith, JBL LXXIX (1960), p. 324. R. Bultmann, *History of the Synoptic Tradition* (Oxford, 1968), p. 218, is refreshingly unsceptical. Only the apophthegm is secondary in his view. The instantaneousness of the miracle in Mt is due to St Matthew. Bultmann (ibid., pp. 230–1) is rightly doubtful whether the story could have grown out of a parable— the common view which this writer rejects (with Münderlein).

pised in its own right). St Matthew supplies a gloss (alas, too feebly for us until Hiers saw the midrashic background). A misunderstanding has evidently arisen. It may explain why scholars have supposed (V. Taylor, *St Mark*, p. 466) that Mk 11: 22–25 is inappropriate in the context and the arrangement artificial. As we shall see, πίστις (as at Mt 17: 20 and 1 Cor 13: 2) can very well allude to the eschatological words at Ps 46: 2. Jesus is not telling the disciples that, if they have enough faith, they will be able to go round cursing figtrees, but that they will lead the Messianic Age in by believing in it. Jesus is not saying that his experiment failed, and next time he (and they) might be lucky, but that the episode of this figtree is a practical example of the well-known haggadic midrash on Genesis, illustrated from the prophets, to the effect that when the Age commences nature will put herself at the disposal of the righteous. *In that nature man, in order to be righteous, must play his corresponding part.* Jesus, as Messiah, thought he was entitled to a fig on that occasion; the want of a fig seemed to prove that he was not Messiah; but there was another possible explanation, namely that the figtree was wrong. Paraphrase Mt 21: 21–22: 'Jesus answered them, "I tell you, if you have faith and do not waver, you will not only perform the action of the figtree [wherein the figtree failed] but even if you were to command this mountain to up and fall into the sea it would happen. And whatsoever you ask for in your prayer, with faith, you will receive".' Superficially it seems as if Jesus told them that they could achieve the wonder of cursing figtrees as a minor piece of magic, since even greater 'tricks' would be open to them; and the whole would be passed off as oriental exaggeration. But the other way of taking it makes better sense. 'When you are ready for the Age, figtrees will bear for you when you are hungry, or at your request; and as you move forward high places will be levelled, etc.' In other words the coming of the Messianic Era depends on the readiness of the righteous, and this expresses itself in the attitude to prayer, including the sincerity of prayer for the Kingdom to come.

That this is a correct interpretation is shown by Zech 14: 4 and Ps 46: 2, to which Jesus is made to allude. Even the Mount of Olives will part in two to make way for the Messiah and his 'holy ones' on the day which God alone knows (Zech 14: 7, alluded to by Jesus immediately after the figtree 'parable' according to Mt 13: 36). But the disciples must be prepared to *cause* the ultimate cataclysm by their prayers, without fear, for on the day when the mountains are removed into the depths of the sea, God himself is their shelter and strength, and, being king in their city, defends them, whatever happens to the kingdoms of the world. The connection between the immensely optimistic and trusting Psalm 46 and the strange saying about commanding mountains to be cast into the sea has not been noticed;[1] it would seem to be further proof that Jesus regarded the Day of Catastrophe as a day of joy. St Mark seems to point out that, when facing the Catastrophe, the disciple must not be dismayed (μὴ διακριθῇ) in his heart (ἐν τῇ καρδίᾳ αὐτοῦ: is there a verbal link with $b^e l\bar{e}\underline{b}$ yammim [Ps 46: 3], a phrase occuring in other passages which contrast God's might and men's vanity [Ezek 27: 27; 28: 8; cf. $b^e l\bar{e}\underline{b}$ yām in Ex 15: 8]?).

The moving of mountains seems to have appealed to Jesus as an indication of faith (cf. Mt 17: 20—the motif known to St Paul, 1 Cor 13: 2) and not in the rabbinical sense of prodigies of learning. St Luke, whose catenae of sayings are often suspected to lack authentic connecting links, most cunningly associates such transmutations of nature with a variety of fig which combines an abundance of fruit (on the bark itself) with a great abundance of shade and a frequent location by the roadside, imagining that this figtree will be planted in the sea and so, at one and the same time, celebrating the sea's drying and becoming a road for the returning 'holy ones'. The tree in Lk 17: 6 is *Ficus Sycomorus*,[2] and the fact that the NEB and JB render it 'mulberry' is a disappointment. *Ficus Carica* in the sea (salt water would do its fruit and its timber no good whatever!) would symbolize the beginning of the Age if ever a tree could. But so that the point of the relationship between faith and the Age should not be lost, Lk gives us the most amusing of the parables (Lk 17: 7–10). Granted that the faith *is* given, it does not follow that the Messianic Era will begin, in all its luxury, immediately. Those that yearn for the Messianic Banquet, and are qualified for admission by their doing all that is required of them (in the terms of their commission: οἱ ἀπόστολοι) may still have to wait in circumstances of tantalizing uncertainty—they must wait upon the Lord as well (Mk 15: 43; Lk 2: 25;

---

[1] The suggestion (R. H. Lightfoot, *The Gospel Message of St Mark* [Oxford, 1952], p. 78) that the mountain which is required to be sunk in the sea is the mount on which the Temple stood (relating Mk 11: 23 to Mic 4: 1) appears to have no midrashic foundation, since it is a plain (and senseless?) contradiction of scripture.

[2] So even Plummer, *St Luke* (ed. 4, Edinburgh, 1901), p. 400 n. 1, quoting Groser, *Trees and Plants in the Bible*, pp. 121, 123. Wetstenius was in no doubt on the subject; see ancient citations fully reproduced in his *Novum Testamentum Graece* (Amsterdam, 1751), ad loc. The equivocations in G. E. Post's articles 'Sycamine', 'Sycamore' in Hastings's *Dictionary of the Bible*, ed. 4 (1902), pp. 634–5, are due to the 'by consent of scholars', They have plainly consented in error; see N. McLean in *Encycl. Biblica* (1903), col. 4831–2. *Ficus Sycomorus* is described by the author of the Article 'Fig', *Encycl. Brit.* ed. 11 (1911), Vol. X, p. 333. If as is possible, St Luke distinguished between the true and the false fig, with unexplained vagaries of vocabulary, and was not referring to mulberry trees at all, we can guess why Zacchaeus was under such a figtree at Lk 19: 4, and an analogy between Zacchaeus and Nathanael emerges for the first time.

12: 36; 23: 51; Acts 10: 7, and consult the very large number of instances
in the Old Testament shown in concordances s.v. 'wait', beginning with
Hos 12: 6 and Prov 8: 34). The Kingdom may not come with being
watched for, in the sense of divined (Lk 17: 20), but the righteous must
wait for it with prayer.

This unexpected interpretation of several gospel passages is supported
by aspects of the 'cursing' to which Hiers did not apply his mind. It must
always be a question with every New Testament story, which biblical
characters are alluded to, and which prophetic themes evoked. A haggadist
familiar with the prophets would know what was meant by one of the
righteous going to a figtree and asking for fruit out of season, and he would
not at all be surprised to find the tree sentenced for disobedience. To
desire the first-ripe fig is a metaphorical way of searching for the
righteous![1] God wishes the righteous, on their journeys, to have fresh
fruit.[2] The righteous may search for figs, and may be searched for as
figs. If the righteous do not bear 'fruit' they will be made barren; the
fruit trees of the wicked will be made to dry up.[3] We actually find all
the themes combined in *Pesiqta Rabbati* XXXIII. 13,[4] where Braude
translates, 'They [sc. Adam] sinned at a fig tree: "As the first-ripe in the
figtree (Hos 9: 10)"; and they were smitten—snatched like figs from the
trees: "Nor figs on the figtree (Jer 8: 13)"; yet they will be comforted by
bearing fruit like figtrees: "The figtree putteth forth her green figs (S. of S.
2: 13)".' The theme of the whole passage is of the joy which the Messianic
Age will bring (Isai 62: 5; Mic 2: 13, etc. are cited).

Without question, the Marcan story evokes the idea that Jesus searched
for signs of the Age, and failed to find them, not because he was wrong,
but because the 'figtree' was wrong. From this his students must learn

[1] Isai 28: 4; Mic 7: 1 (the Targum takes *bikkûrāh* as 'good men'). A. de Q. Robin,
'The Cursing of the Figtree in Mark xi. A Hypothesis' (NTS VIII [1961], pp. 276–81,
on p. 280), thought Jesus quoted Mic 7: 1–6 and was misunderstood by his companions.
There is a useful comment by N. Birdsall in *Exp. Times* LXXIII (1962), p. 191. The
passage is a lament for sins according to *Midr. Rabbah S. of S.*, II, 15, 2 (Soncino trans.,
p. 137); Hos 9: 10 (MT and Targ.). The figs are the men who had merit, the patriarchs
(so Hos 9: 10—cf. 16!) (*Midr. R. Gen.*, I. 4, Sonc trans., p. 6; XLVI. 1, trans., p. 389;
LIII. 3, trans., p. 462; *Midr. R. Num.*, XVI. 24, trans., pp 693–4); Israel (*Midr. R.
Esther*, IX 2, trans., p. 111) or a great find (*Midr. R. Num.*, II. 6, trans., p. 27). J. R.
Michaels, *Exp. T.* LXXVIII (1967), pp. 182–3, links Hos 9: 10 with Gen 27: 35; 32: 28.
[2] Jer 8: 13 as interpreted at *Midr. R. Lam.*, I. 13–14, para. 42, Sonc. trans., p. 112.
[3] Ps 105: 33; Isai 34: 4 (had St Mark this in mind?); Jer 5: 17; 8: 13; Hos 2: 12;
9: 16; Joel 1: 7, 12. It is uncertain what relation, if any, the theme in Hab 3: 16–19
has to our passage (not to be cast down in misery: Abraham in *Midr. R. Gen.*, LIII. 3,
Sonc. trans., p. 462). According to Ps.—Severianus, *In parab. de ficu Hom.* (PG 59,
588) Jesus cursed the figtree because he put an end to the shame of Adam. St John Dama-
scene (PG 96,582) saw the figtree as the wicked nature of man.
[4] *Pesiqta Rabbati* II, tr. W. G. Braude (New Haven/London, 1968), pp. 656–7.

that if they have faith in prayer they will be God's crop, and, correspondingly, as he can come confidently to them in search of 'figs', they will, in the Age already, confidently find figs from every figtree, whatever the season. That Jesus failed to find the world ready for him when he came to his own (or seemed to do) had no bearing on the conditions required for the coming of that Age, except as a lesson that the celebrated haggadot were not merely wishful thinking and fantasy but held a profound truth, that the Kingdom was within them. The *faithful* are *fruitful:* Jer 17: 8!

This midrashic reading of the story is by no means self-evidently smooth and obvious. Could Jesus' failure to find the fig he wanted really be supposed to be, teleologically, a condition precedent to an important lesson for the disciples? In the ancient world such an idea would not dismay anyone but a confirmed sceptic. Today it is possible to believe with this, as with many curious combinations of narrative and midrashic allusion (such as the Colt and the Cleansing of the Temple),[1] that real events have been told with an eye to their spiritual, pedagogic value, not that a midrashic frenzy has upheld the evangelists or their sources in wholesale forgery and imposture. In my experience forgeries and frauds are neatly and unambiguously worked out, with few or no loose ends: it is not worth the immense pains required if the intended dupes are left in any doubt as to what is contended. The many loose ends and irregularities in New Testament stories, revealed when their midrashic content has been exposed, tell rather for their essential historical authenticity (within, perhaps, rather wide limits) than against it.

THE SIGNS OF THE END

We are now so well prepared to approach Mk 13: 28-32 that it explains itself, and Lk 21: 29-33 operates as a splendid gloss, showing that St Luke's Jewish advisers were anxious that midrashic points should not be lost, so far as could be achieved without tampering with the Marcan text. St Mark has been involved in an apocalyptic discourse containing many prophetic passages cited verbatim. He wishes to show that there is a parallel between nature as we know it and nature as it reacts to the Messianic Age. He chooses the figtree, perhaps partly because its dramatic annual cycle is best for his metaphor, and partly (as we shall see)

---

[1] J. W. Doeve, NTS I (1954), pp. 297–308, would make the purification of the Temple depend on Mal 3: 3 (refiner of silver!). The Cleansing should be studied with the aid of C. Roth, 'The Cleansing of the Temple and Zechariah xiv. 21', NovT IV (1960), pp. 174–81; E. Trocmé, 'L'Expulsion des Marchands du Temple', NTS XV (1968), pp. 1–22. There is also R. H. Hiers, 'Purification of the Temple: Preparation for the Kingdom of God', JBL XC (1971), pp. 82–90.

because the figtree has a special connection with the Messianic Age. But the haggadah about the fruit trees is not confined to the fig. It was thought that Adam ate of the fig, that it was the forbidden fruit.[1] In the Age to Come all trees will have edible fruit. Summer, in our age, is forecast by the opening of the leaves; when the disciples see 'all those things' to which Jesus has alluded they will know that something or someone is 'at the doors'. The ambiguity between Jesus' ministry as the beginning of the Messianic Age, and his Second Coming as the true commencement of that Age, is one from which these texts do nothing to release us. No doubt, whatever is 'at the doors' is already present, but present in an imperfect sense. What is the subject of *estin?* Jeremias suggests it is the Messiah himself.[2] I think it is the Age. St Luke says it is the Kingdom of God, which must be the same thing. Certainly, from Mk 13: 31b one can obtain the impression that there is a link between the present Age and the one to come: Jesus' 'words' are that link, and what is valid for his ministry is not invalid for that Age, in which the conditions of life as we know it cease to apply.

That Jesus originally mentioned only the figtree is indicated by the puns on *qyṣ:* 'time' (especially of Redemption), Heb. *qēṣ*, Aram. *qîṣâ*, *qiṣṣâ;* '(fig-) harvest', Heb. and Aram. *qayiṣ;* perhaps also *qṣ'* in sense of 'pluck'.[3]

THE PARABLE OF THE BARREN FIGTREE

The tale of the figtree at Lk 13: 6–9 has been recognized[4] as a version of a folk-remedy for barren trees.[5] This smart discovery adds a further touch of humour to an already charming story. The reader will be amused to know that I was taught by an old country person how to deal with barren fruit trees. I had a peartree which annoyed me by producing

---

[1] Ginzberg, *Legends*, I, pp. 75, 96–7; V, pp. 97, 98.

[2] Jeremias, *Parables*, pp. 119–120, referring to Rev 3: 20.

[3] M. Perez Fernández, ' "Prope est aestas" ', *Verbum Domini* 46 (1968), pp. 361–9. This would tend to emphasize the 'harvest' aspect of *theros.*

[4] W. L. Knox, *Some Hellenistic Elements in Primitive Christianity* (London, 1944), p. 19 n. 4. He relates this portion of the *Geoponica* to a pseudo-Zoroastrian *Peri physeōs* of about 250 B.C., relying on J. Bidez and F. Cumont, *Les Mages Hellénisés* (Paris, 1938), I, pp. 109ff., but the age of the notion, evidently timeless, cannot be located securely even in 'Zoroaster'.

[5] The story of Ahikar, VIII. 35 (R. H. Charles, *Apocrypha and Pseudepigrapha* [Oxford, 1913], II, p. 775) is useful as it shows the tree's fear of being cut down (not further). Cf. Jeremias, *Parables*, pp. 170–1. Since pagan sources strongly reminiscent of gospel passages may be suspected of influence from that quarter (Lk 7: 1ff. is compared with Apuleius, *Flor.* XIX and Philostratus, *Life of Apollon.* IV. 45) it is desirable to compare the wording and the ideas meticulously. From the Appendix below it will be obvious that the *Geoponica* owes nothing to St Luke.

nothing for several years. I was told to go up to the tree with an instrument capable of cutting it down, and to tell it that it was useless and would be cut down the following year. I had also to strike the tree vigorously several times so that it should not misunderstand my ability to carry out the threat. I carried out the instructions carefully, and since the tree bore the following year it is impossible to prove that the method was inefficacious. After all, I imitated John the Baptist (Mt 3: 10, Lk 3: 9)!

I do not think it out of the way to refer to the gospel's reference to pruning (Jn 15: 2) since the 'cure' alluded to must have arisen from the discovery, accidentally, that pruning improved a tree's capacity to bear, and, since humans are not the better for being pruned, primitive man must have thought the trees bore out of fear that they might be cut down altogether. It is noticeable that both in the folk-remedy and in our parable *manure* figures.[1] Whatever the rational meaning of manure in both, we still have to find the midrashic allusion; for the evident suggestion of humility and poverty does not seem to have any bearing on the story.

Why is the tree in a vineyard? Evidently because the vineyard is Israel, or God's world (Isai 5: 1–7; Jer 12: 10; S. of S. 8: 12). Who is the vinedresser, who, because the tree is in a vineyard, is the appropriate person to look to the trees? It is suggested that this is Jesus himself,[2] but it is not clear at once. The three years make sense, for after three years the tree could be presumed barren and might lawfully be cut down.[3] But the scriptural allusion must not be abandoned. It is not impossible that St Luke has in mind the vinedressers of Joel 1: 11–12. We find that appropriate action leads to fertility (Joel 2: 12–13, 23–26).

I should go on to suggest that the reason why the tree is a fig, and its location is a vineyard, is enhanced by the special meaning of vines and figtrees to which we shall come in reference to Nathanael. The position of this parable immediately before the story of the healing of the crippled woman suggests to me that originally this parable also dealt with the Coming of the End. Just as a barren tree is spared until proper treatment has been shown to fail, so the Age to Come, in which all trees and plants will bear prodigiously, is postponed until the immediately suitable 'treatment' has been applied to the existing Age, which is the precursor of the

---

[1] Lk: *kopria; Geop.: achyra kyamina.*

[2] Jeremias, *Parables*, p. 171.

[3] Interpretation of Deut 20: 19 given by a halakhic midrash evidenced in b. Baba Qamma, 91b, 92a; *Mishnah*, Baba Bathra, II. 11–13 (H. Danby's *Mishnah*, p. 368); Maimonides, *Code*, XIV (Judges), V (Kings and wars), vi. 8–10 (trans. A. Hershman [New Haven, 1949], pp. 222–23). One may cut it down, if its wood, or its room, is worth more than any crop from it.

next. Whatever the original meaning of the parable, St Luke links the last opportunity for repentance (Lk 13: 5) with the marvellous redemption of a daughter of Abraham from the curse of Adam by means of a story explaining that time has been afforded for the conditions to mature, and, as we have seen, for the righteous to manifest themselves and be available as 'fruit' for their 'owner'. That the gardener is the New Adam would, on that basis, be a reasonable conjecture, especially since Adam's curse figures in the woman's predicament.[1]

NATHANAEL'S FIGTREE

We come at last to the most puzzling of all the figtrees. It is clear that Jn 1: 35–51 is concerned with the assembling of the companions of Jesus, and the Wedding at Cana sees them involved in an action which, other things apart, establishes Jesus' disciples' faith in him (2: 11). Towards the end of Jn 1 the topic is the methods by which the first group were gathered, and no one can doubt but that St John wishes to reassure new Christians as to their status, though they have not seen Jesus personally, nor been initiated by Jesus' actual students. The importance of testimony, credibility, and personal relationships is emphasized in this passage. On the surface it seems as if the initially incredulous Nathanael, who may represent well-trained but sceptical Jews, was brought to believe in Jesus by the latter's testifying to Nathanael's having been under 'the figtree' when Philip called him.

It is possible to argue that we are not at liberty to go to haggadic sources for the explanation. St John is manifestly influenced by Hellenistic ideas, and the Jewishness of his background is not yet within sight of being estimated. It has been shown that the Wedding at Cana possesses intimate Jewish social ingredients,[2] but it could be argued that St John is working upon a story taken from a synoptic-type source. Further, it has recently been shown that the passage about the Good Shepherd, which hangs from an explicit citation of the Old Testament, makes much better sense with the aid of scriptural allusion and midrashic insight than it does when read with the superficial meaning alone.[3] But it could be argued that the whole was a characteristic elaboration of a parable, which

[1] See Derrett cited on p. 253 n. 5 above.

[2] Derrett, *Law in the New Testament* (London, 1970), ch. 10. The turning of static water into wine could conceivably represent the richness of the Messianic Age (cf. citations above, p. 252, n 6.) if the amateur haggadist read Isai 36: 16e with 36: 16c in the light of those citations (no other clue has yet been found), but the boldness of this would be breathtaking.

[3] Derrett, 'Law in the New Testament: the Good Shepherd', *Studia Theologica* 27 (1973), pp. 25–50.

might well have existed in a source resembling those from which the synoptic gospels were compiled: indeed that is often supposed to be the case. However, we are far from sure that St John did not utilize midrashic skills, and the figtree in Jn 1 seems a specially curious instance to test a hypothesis.

Those who study under the shade of a figtree were often students of the Torah,[1] but one can hardly say that to be under a figtree is to be a Torah-student, for at that rate sleepy Arab camel-drivers would be Torah-students. Under whose figtree was Nathanael? Philip came to him and invited him. Perhaps we are to visualize that it was under his own figtree. If we take Zech 3 we shall find material of great interest, if, as too often, of perplexing obscurity. The chapter is obviously messianic, and many themes fit the coming of the Messianic Age, in which God's servant, the Branch, comes forward and God will remove the iniquity of the land in one day. The relationship between Joshua (in the LXX this is 'Jesus'), the High Priest (Hag 1: 1, 12, 14; Sir 49: 12; Zech 3: 4 read with Isai 61: 10), and the Branch is not clear.[2] There is a stone, with seven eyes upon it which 'run to and fro through the whole earth' (Zech 4: 10). There are men who sit before this Joshua; they are men who are a sign, or men of, or fit for, a sign.[3] In some way they witness the coming of the Branch. On the day when this Joshua's obedience, and his companions' fitness, are fulfilled, 'In that day, saith the Lord of hosts, shall ye call every man his neighbour under the vine and under the fig tree'. The Targum plainly says here, as elsewhere where the vine and the figtree symbolize prosperity and peace,[4] under the fruit of the vine and under the fruit of the figtree. Correctly: the Messianic Age will see no vine and no figtree without fruit, whatever the season.

If Zech 3: 10 is the explanation for Nathanael's figtree, one might ask why he was not seen under both a vine and a figtree. The obvious answer is that, unlike modern Italy and even Palestine, vines were not normally trained over figtrees, and the presence of a figtree in a vineyard did not

[1] StrB II, p. 371.

[2] It is confusing that the Targum on Zech identifies him with the Messiah, so that the High Priest and the Branch (Isai 11: 1) (and, elsewhere, the Stone) are all one and the same. The Branch is the Messiah according to *Midr. Rabbah Num.*, XVIII. 21, Sonc. trans., p. 734 (citing Isai 3: 3) and *Midr. R. Lam.*, I. 16, para. 51, trans., p. 136. For C. H. Dodd's consideration of the 'Joshua' theme see p. 264, n. 2 below.

[3] Zech 3: 8, MT, LXX, and Targ. In b. Hor. 13a, Soncino trans., p. 97, the sign is referred to a prophet. Cf. *Midr. R. Num.*, VI. 1, Sonc. trans., p. 157.

[4] Zech 3: 10 (MT, LXX, Targ.) relate to Zech 3: 1, 8. Joel 2: 22 and Zech 8: 12 are read into the passage by the Targum. See also 1 Kgs 5: 5 (4: 25); Mic 4: 4; 1 Mac 14: 12; cf. Isai 36: 16. It is of interest that A. de Q. Robin in NTS VIII (1961), pp. 276ff, p. 279, suggested that the idea of every man sitting under his figtree lay behind the story of the 'cursing' of the figtree.

imply that their roots were close together.[1] It would be difficult in practice to be under both. Thus the most satisfactory interpretation of Zech 3: 10 would be that in the Age to Come each man will give and receive invitations under his vine or his figtree as the case would be. To do what? Perhaps to join the companions of Joshua? The text leaves it open.

As proof that this is what St John has in mind we turn to Zech 4. Jesus in Jn 1: 51 announces that Nathanael shall see greater wonders. 'Ye shall see the heaven opened and the angels of God ascending and descending upon the Son of Man.' The dream of Jacob will be shared, in a special way. It has already been urged that Jesus is made to refer to the cross, as the means whereby heaven and earth were reconciled.[2] In Zech 4 we have a dream carefully connected with what went before: the stone reappears, but Zerubbabel is introduced. There is the curious vision of a great lampstand, like the Menorah in the Temple, with an olive tree on each side of it. The lampstand is identified with God, and the trees with 'sons of oil' that stand by him (Zech 4: 14). That is not the end of it. Though the text implies that the lampstand is God himself, other interpretations are current, that it is the righteous, or it is Israel.[3] The bowl on the top of it is said to be an allusion to the Redeemer (*gō'alah* for *gullah*).[4] Further, in Zech 6: 11–13 we learn that Joshua the High Priest is to be crowned and is to be told that the Branch (undoubtedly the Messiah) will build the Temple. The rabbis say that there have been two founders of the Temple, Solomon and Zerubbabel, and there will be a third, namely the Messiah.[5] Clearly this passage is shot through with messianic allusions, and although the rabbis identify the men 'worthy of a sign' with Hananiah, Mishael and Azariah,[6] it does not follow that they cannot be visualized as a company assembling to see the Messiah's work begin. It does not seem too fanciful to suggest that if the cross can be Jacob's ladder it can also be Zechariah's candlestick.

There can be no doubt but that Jesus acclaims Nathanael as worthy of a greater sign than the fact that Jesus himself saw him under a figtree,

[1] *Mishnah*, Kilaim (based on Lev 19: 19, Deut 22: 9–11). Ibid., Kil. VI. 4 (Danby, *Mishnah*, p. 35) relates an incident outside the Land of Israel. Kil. VI. 5 speaks of a figtree as always potentially fruitbearing, a point to be watched if one figures in a vineyard (cf. Lk 13: 6).

[2] Cf. *Law in the New Testament*, pp. 415–16.

[3] *Midr. R. Lev.*, XXX. 1–2, Soncino trans., p. 383; *Midr. R. Num.*, XIII. 8, trans., p. 520. The Targum says the Stone itself is the Messiah and the two trees are 'sons of princes' (angels?). The Targum links the two dreams.

[4] *Midr. R. S. of S.*, IV. 7, 1, Sonc. trans., p. 205 (cf. Isai 47: 4); so Midr. R. Lev., XXXII. 8, trans., p. 417.

[5] *Midr. R. Gen.*, Sonc. trans., p. 901.

[6] *Midr. R. Gen.*, LVI. 11, Sonc. trans., p. 503; *Exod.*, IX. 1, trans., p. 121; b. Sanh. 93a, Soncino trans., p. 623.

and, with his 'ye', he extends the qualification to all those that have already assembled. Thus I should be prepared to assert that the figtree was intended to be symbolic of the dawning of the New Age, by no means out of place in the first chapter of St John.[1]

It would not be unreasonable to ask, was Nathanael actually under a figtree? It has been suggested that the question was some sort of test analogous to the test applied to the elders in Susanna.[2] The similarity does not seem close. All that we can draw from the curious passage seems to be that Jesus saw Nathanael being invited under a figtree and connected this with Zech 3: 10, reading it with 3: 8, which certified the 'companions' ' fitness for a sign and their connection with the Messiah. Were we expected to enquire whether it was such a tree? Is not Nathanael's admission and submission (v. 49) the point of the passage? Jesus could recognize potential recruits from the signs of the New Age approaching, and what we should place in such a bald abstract form is placed by St John in poetic and dramatic terms. Not only were these recruits, who, according to St Mark, were impressed by Jesus' apparently supernatural knowledge of fishing (an episode placed by St John or his continuer at the end of that gospel), impressed by his knowledge of them, but he promised them in an appropriately indirect fashion that they would participate in the story of Redemption, as the prophet Zechariah, on this interpretation, indicated that Joshua's companions would. This was the kingship, and such was the kingdom, to which Nathanael's extraordinary submission must be related.

---

[1] The abrupt and unexplained intervention of a figtree would be less bizarre if St John's church were fully informed about the symbolic significance of figtrees in the synoptic gospels; and if my guess about the *sycomore* of Lk 19: 4 (see above p. 256, n. 2) is right they had a perfect precedent.

[2] C. F. D. Moule, in 'A Note on "Under the Fig Tree" in John I. 48, 50', JTS, N.S. V (1954), pp. 210–11, finds the peace-and-plenty motif of Mic 4: 4, Zech 3: 10 not obviously to the point, and both he and C. H. Dodd thought the Joshua references in Zech 3 'far-fetched', but he asks whether 'under which tree?' was a stock question to put to a *witness*, alluding to Susanna and to *Mishnah*, Sanh. V. 2 (b. Sanh. 41a = Sonc. trans., p. 266) where Ben Zakkai enquired of witnesses (who said the victim was killed under a figtree) what kind of figs they were (a hyperbole of judicial scrupulosity). Communicating with Professors Dodd and Daube, Professor Moule was unhappily, by chance, not put into contact with the haggadah to which Mic 4: 4 and Zech 3: 10 make their essential (but partial) contribution. R. Bultmann, before him, missed these possibilities and failed to react even to the sound suggestions present in that 'Note': R. Bultmann, *Das Evangelium des Johannes* (ed. 17, Göttingen, 1962) p. 73 with *Ergänzungsheft* (Göttingen, 1957), p. 19 (referring to p. 73).

APPENDIX

C. Bassus, *Geoponica* X 83 (ed. H. Beckh, Leipzig, 1895, 319).

1. Συζωσάμενος καὶ ἀνακομβωσάμενος, καὶ λαβὼν πέλεκυν ἢ ἀξίνην, μετὰ θυμοῦ πρόσελθε τῷ δένδρῳ, ἐκκόψαι τοῦτο βουλόμενος.   2. προσελθόντος δέ σοί τινος, καὶ παραιτουμένου τὴν τούτου ἀποκοπήν, ὡς ἐγγυητοῦ περὶ τοῦ μέλλοντος καρποῦ γινομένου, δόξον πείθεσθαι καὶ φείδεσθαι τοῦ δένδρου, καὶ εὐφορήσει τοῦ λοιποῦ.   3. καὶ ἄχυρα δὲ κυάμινα παραβαλλόμενα τῷ στελέχει ποιεῖ τὸ δένδρον καρποφορεῖν.

FURTHER ANNOTATION

Tit. H. Giesen, 'Der verdorte Feigenbaum — Eine symbolische Aussage? Zu Mk. 11, 12-14, 20f.,' *BZ* 20 (1976) 95-111. On the calling of Nathanael see J. Jeremias, *Angelos* 3 (1930), 2-5, also S. Pancaro, *N.T.S.* 21 (1975), 398. On this version of the Golden Age see E. L. Dietrich, *Šûv s̆'bût. Die endzeitliche Wiederherstellung bei den Propheten* (B.Z.A.W. 40) (Giessen, 1925).

LAW IN THE NEW TESTAMENT:
THE PALM SUNDAY COLT

The mysterious pericope (ALAND, s. 269) is doubted by some [1]) and rejected by others [2]), on the footing that the influence of Old Testament prophecy is demonstrably so great that little or nothing of the factual background can be recovered. Even those who are not ready to reject it must recognise that it is full of difficulties (especially in the Matthaean version) to which no solution has yet been forthcoming. The latest short and at the same time comprehensive treatment [3]) leaves it an open question whether Jesus really did send for a colt in the manner described; and no commentator finds a criterion whereby to determine whether Jesus deliberately worked out, or mimed, as it were, the prophecy in Zech. ix 9; or whether things fell out, by coincidence, so as to appear, on later reflection, to have fulfilled the prophet's words [4]).

---

[1]) E. KLOSTERMANN, Das Markusevangelium (Tübingen, 1950), 112. E. HAENCHEN (infra). Cf. G. D. KILPATRICK, The Origins of the Gospel according to St. Matthew (Oxford, 1946), 81, 94; C. F. D. MOULE, The Birth of the New Testament (London, 1966), 84-5, 229 n. 3.

[2]) R. BULTMANN, The History of the Synoptic Tradition (Oxford, 1968), 261-2. M. DIBELIUS, From Tradition to Gospel (London, 1934), 121-2. T. KEIM, History of Jesus of Nazara, V (London, 1881), 92-104. W. E. BUNDY, Jesus and the First Three Gospels (Cambridge, Mass., 1955), 417. See particularly E. ERDMANN, Die Vorgeschichte des Lukas- und Matthäus-Evangeliums und Vergils vierte Ekloge (Göttingen, 1932), 61. That Jesus was not influenced by Zech. ix 9 is the view of W. L. KNOX, The Sources of the Synoptic Gospels, I (Cambridge, 1953), 77-8. V. TAYLOR says (The Formation of the Gospel Tradition, London, 1933, 150-1), that no legend would break off with an anti-climax (v. 11): but this is not conclusive in itself.

[3]) E. HAENCHEN, Der Weg Jesu (Berlin, 1966), 372-7. W. TRILLING, 'Der Einzug in Jerusalem. Mt.21.1-17', in J. BLINZLER, O. KUSS, F. MUSSNER.,edd. Neutestamentliche Aufsätze. Festschrift Josef Schmid (Regensburg, 1963), 303-9, V. TAYLOR, Behind the Third Gospel (Oxford, 1926), 236-7, believed that Proto-Luke gave a surer understanding of the event than Mark with his greater detail.

[4]) St. John Chrysostom believed the events fulfilled many prophecies. EDERSHEIM and GORE saw the ass-drivers willingly cooperating with Jesus.

St. John's account seems to support the latter solution, and yet his words 'finding the colt of an ass' do not deny the story as the synoptic gospels outline it, a story he must have had before him.

Lately there has been a recrudescence of an opinion unhappily mooted by EISLER [1]), that what really happened was a deliberate political demonstration with messianic overtones, intended to capture the holy city with the object of ousting the Roman and pontifical governments [2]) It seems, at first sight, not implausible that Jesus might have led his followers in a rash movement, which culminated in a riot. Holy men are known to have led rash uprisings [3]).

Yet it is not beyond our powers to clarify what St.Mark was trying to say. We can even conjecture why St. Matthew and St. Luke differed from their predecessor. The commentaries available to us give no useful details about the underlying motifs in Mark xi 1-7. The skill and precision with which St. Mark tells his story has gone utterly without recognition. Let us reconstruct the scene as the first hearers will have understood it. This is the only way open to us to conjecture what Jesus's mind must have been at that time; bearing in our own minds, as we must, that the episode of the Cleansing of the Temple, which is a companion piece to this pericope, has been identified as a practical application, a kind of midrash in action, of Zech. xiv 21 [4]). In this article our account of the factual background will be supplemented by a reexamination of the

---

M. GOGUEL, *Life of Jesus* (London, 1933), 410: Jesus may have been deliberate. V. TAYLOR, *The Gospel according to St. Mark* (London, 1952), 451ff., summarises the viewpoints. N. H. SNAITH, *Studies in the Second Part of the Book of Isaiah* (Leiden, 1967), 209; F. V. FILSON, *A New Testament History* (London, 1965), 128; and R. V. G. TASKER, *St. Matthew* (London, 1961), 197, illustrate the common field of opinions.

[1]) R. EISLER, ΙΗΣΟΥΣ ΒΑΣΙΛΕΥΣ(Heidelberg, 1929), II, 439ff., 459ff.; *Messiah Jesus* (London, 1931), 471ff., 480ff. W. GRUNDMANN, *Das Evangelium nach Markus* (Berlin, 1959), 226, has no time for EISLER's ideas, but he stresses the allegedly legendary aspect of the story.

[2]) S. G. F. BRANDON, *Fall of Jerusalem* (London, 1957), 1957), 103; *Jesus and the Zealots* (Manchester, 1967), 349-50. W. R. FARMER, *Maccabees, Zealots and Josephus* (New York, 1956), 198-9, asks whether the Holy War was not the context— Jesus showed his trust in the Lord of Hosts by contrast with violent men. H. J. SCHONFIELD, *The Passover Plot* (London, 1965), 112, shows whither the idea that Jesus had a prearranged plan may lead.

[3]) JOSEPHUS, *Bell.* II. 262 (THACKERAY, ii, 425); *Ant.* XX. 169 (FELDMAN, ix, 481.)

[4]) E. TROCMÉ, 'L'expulsion des Marchands du Temple', *N.T.S.* 15 (1968), 1-22, and especially C. ROTH, 'The cleansing of the Temple and Zechariah xiv.21', *N.T.* 4 (1960), 174-181, are particularly to be consulted now.

midrashic background of our pericope, essential for a true appreciation of the treatment by St. Matthew, a treatment which has suffered misunderstanding, and even ridicule.

Angaría

In the ancient world transport on the state's behalf was operated in a somewhat haphazard manner. The ruler might 'impress' (commandeer, requisition) means of transportation to meet needs as they arose. The bible refers to the right of the king to impress asses at 1 Sam. viii 17, and the same passage shows how men could be impressed to bear burdens as if they were animals.[1] The postal system of the Persian empire, which operated under a system of relays, was the envy of the world, from India to Rome[2]. Known under the name ἀγγαρεία[3], a loan-word in Hebrew, אנגריא[4]), the system was universally in use, and was so burdensome to the general public that that word ended in Hebrew and even in Greek by meaning 'compulsory service' in general. A great deal is known about the institution in the ancient world[5]. It is clear that officials used to impress men, asses, and other means of transport, for the state's needs and sometimes, illegally, for their own. The public were protected from time to time from the abuses to which they were subjected on pretext of *angaría*, as contemporary documents

---

[1] Num. xvi 15 may be an example: 'I have not taken (even) one ass from them'.

[2] HERODOTUS, VIII, 98. XENOPHON, *Cyr.* VIII, 6, 9, 17. JOS., *Ant.* XIII, 52 (Marcus, vii, 251) (cf. 1 Macc. x 33). A. M. RAMSAY, *J.R.S.* 10 (1920), 79 ff.; C. FRIES, *Klio* 4 (1904), 119. O. SEECK, 'Cursus publicus', Pauly-Wissowa, *R.E.* IV, 1846 ff., 1850, 1851.

[3] NAPHTALI LEWIS, *Inventory of Compulsory Services* (Am. Stud. Papyr., vol. 3, New Haven-Toronto, 1968), p. (4). F. PREISIGKE-K. KIESSELING, *Wörterbuch der gr. Papyrusurkunden* IV (1944) ἀγγαρεύω; suppl. I (1969) ἀγγαρεία, ἀγγαρεύω.

[4] S. KRAUSS, *Griechische u. Lateinische Lehnwörter im Talmud* (Berlin, 1898), pt. 2, p. 63. See esp. Pes. Rab. 42 (Braude, 1968, ii, 743). For an appropriate instance see Mishnah, *B.M.* VI, 3 (Danby, p. 358). S. KRAUSS, *Talmudische Archäologie* (Leipzig, 1911), II, 327, 374.

[5] M. ROSTOWSEW, 'Angariae', *Klio* 6 (1906), 249-258 is the leading article. F. PREISIGKE, *Klio* 7 (1907), 241 ff. at 275. P. FIEBIG, *Z.N.W.* 18 (1918), 64-72 is excellent, but it never occurred to the author to apply the learning to Mark xi 1-7. A. DEISSMANN, *Bibelstudien* (1895), 81 f. or *Bible Studies* (1901), 86-7, gives splendid references. L. MITTEIS and U. WILCKEN, *Grundzüge und Chrestomathie* I (1912), 372 ff. F. ZUCKER, *S. B. Preuss. Akad. d. Wiss. Berlin, Phil. hist. Kl.*, 1911, 801 ff. at 803-5. M. ROSTOVTZEFF, *Gesellschaft und Wirtschaft im Römischen Kaiserreich* II (Leipzig, 1930), 93-4, 96, 227, 325 nn. 34, 36. F. OERTEL, *Die Liturgie* (1917), 24 ff., 88 ff.

testify ¹); and Libanius gives a pathetic account of abuses continuing
centuries later ²). Villages would dispute with each other about their
duties to provide unpaid transport over stretches of road between
them and adjacent towns ³). In self-protection owners of asses,
camels, etc., in Egypt banded together into guilds or unions ⁴),
perhaps to regularise the incidence of compulsory supply of ass-
transport for the government, providing a pool, from which animals
would be taken, enjoying (no doubt) arrangements of their own
whereby animals abandoned by the impressing soldiery or com-
misariat at the next stage could be returned to their owners.

That soldiers in Jesus's time could exercise their right of *angaría*
with the utmost freedom is shown by the experience of Simon of
Cyrene ⁵); and Jesus himself advises the righteous almost hyper-
bolically to offer to go further than the stage to which the 'impresser'
had required them to go with, one must understand, a man-load ⁶).
Now Jesus himself impressed a colt, and we must examine his
method, and investigate his right to do it.

The right to impress was a royal right. It goes back into Jewish
social history which (as the passage at 1 Sam. viii cited above
shows) illustrates the preference of the group to allow labour and
transport to be requisitioned *ad hoc* to a regular system of public
finance. The ruler and his servants needed transport, and the people
on the spot provided it. Similarly the rabbis, when in need, were
entitled to have their particular type of aristocracy recognised in
the same way. That is why we find impressment exercised on the
part of disciples of rabbis, in their master's interest. There is a
story ⁷), not to be taken quite literally, of a rabbi so devoted to
study that he wandered in pursuit of it though he had great wealth
and servants whom he had never seen. Some of them once impressed
him to carry something for their master whose name they invoked.

---

¹) For example P. Lond. 1171 (c)² (= III, p. 107), of A.D. 42 (a proclamation of the prefect, L. Aemilius Rectus); P. Tebt. I, 5, 178ff., 182, 252 (B.C.
118) (see PREISIGKE at *Klio* 7, 275-6 (note changed reading of the key word)).
Ditt. *Or. Gr.* 665. Ulpian, *Dig.* XLIX, 18. 4, for the later imperial situation.
²) Lib., *Or.* XVIII. 141-5 (FOERSTER, ii, 296-8). P. PETIT, *Libanius et la
vie municipale à Antioche* (Paris, 1955), 158-9.
³) W. H. C. FREND, 'A third-century inscription relating to Angareia in
Phrygia', *J.R.S.* 46 (1956), 46ff.
⁴) *B.G.U.* I, No. 15² (A.D. 118) and ROSTOWSEW, *Klio* 6, p. 253 (ὀνηλάται)
'... jeder κτηνοτρόφος ist wohl zur ὀνηλασία verpflichtet'.
⁵) Matt. xxvii 32, Mark xv 21.
⁶) Matt. v 41.
⁷) b. Yoma 35b = Sonc. trans. 163-4 (tannaïtic).

He protested that he was a scholar, and rabbis and their students were indeed customarily exempt, for it would be absurd for one scholar to be impressed in the service of another [1]). However, this rabbi's servants were unwilling to release him, until, we gather, he revealed his identity and confounded them.

Readers of my *Law in the New Testament* (1970) will already be familiar with the fact that in the Land of Israel two systems of law were in force and effect. The condominium of the Romans and the Jewish hierarchy had its own blend of laws: and the Torah was observed as far as possible by the pious. Nothing done by Herod or Pilate could amend or in any way affect the Torah. The rabbis might differ as to its meaning, but all would have agreed that it could not be amended or abolished. According to the Torah the king of the house of David was the true or ideal ruler, unless a Jewish ruler from another house (e.g. Saul) was appointed by God temporarily [2]). Not that every descendant of David was a king in the eye of the Torah, but one who was also anointed would surely be entitled to be accepted by the pious as the true king, whoever might actually occupy the throne. Respect was owed to the actual *de facto* ruler, but the pious could well believe that another was *de jure* sovereign. The case of David himself was in point (1 Sam. xvi 13; 2 Sam. ii 4). Zealots might claim that only God's anointed of the house of David could be their ruler, and would reject all others, Greek, Roman, or Jewish. Roman soldiers would exercise *angaría* on behalf of the κύριος Καῖσαρ; and the disciples of a rabbi who was thought to be the Son of David would hardly hesitate to try to execute an order by their master to impress an animal for his personal transport when he deemed it necessary.

The public objected to *angaría*, but not more than they would object to any enforced contribution. There was no knowing whether impressed animals would be returned [3]). The soldiers might turn them loose. The peasantry may well have tried to limit the effects of this by voluntarily combination, as in Egypt. By such means they could prevent soldiers from entering courtyards and perhaps pilfering there. A few animals might be kept in the broad road that

---

[1]) b. Ned. 32a = Sonc. 97; b. Soṭ. 10a = Sonc. 46.

[2]) MAIMONIDES, *Mishneh Torah* (The Code of Maimonides), XIV, V, i. Subject to the reservation that claims in favour of a priestly Messiah of the house of Aaron or Levi were aired in apocryphal literature, which must have responded to widely-held notions.

[3]) Mishnah, *B.M.* 98a-b, and gemara thereon, noticed by FIEBIG (supra).

surrounded the honeycomb or warren of narrow lanes and cramped dwellings which made up a Palestinian village. Villagers were aware that the right of *angaría* overrode the private right of owner-ship of pack animals and carts: in the eyes of the pious a true Israelite king had this right also *de jure*, whereas Pilate and the Herods had it only *de facto*. Epictetus explains what people felt in Greece, and it must have been the same everywhere. The ass-driver who objected to his ass's being impressed, even when he was already going along with it loaded with his own goods, was in danger of a beating himself, followed by the total loss of his ass [1]).

A typical royal impressment would take place by sending messengers ahead to arrange for the next stage. Jesus's requirement was for an ass for one short stage. The method in general would simply be to seize the object impressed (to ask permission would seem to waive the right of *angaría*), and to explain the action by such words as 'I, or the army, or the ruler (as the case may be) require(s) this'. In the case of a secular ruler the word would be 'king', 'lord'. In the case of a rabbi, 'our master (*mārān*)'.

But the formula which Jesus instructs the disciples to use is very peculiar. ὁ κύριος αὐτοῦ χρείαν ἔχει means [2]) 'Its lord (i.e. its true owner) is in need'. This is an impressment, since it presupposes want of hindrance to the taking. It asserts that, whoever is the legal owner (whose identity would certainly be known to the by-standers), its lord and master in some other terms is *in need* and therefore they are taking it away. It is a righteous impressment, because the return of the animal is promised shortly. And the fact that the individual claiming to be 'lord' (apparently the rabbi of these men who must have been recognisable as religious students)

---

[1]) ARRIAN, *Epictetus* IV. i. 79-81, esp. ἂν δ' ἀγγαρεία ᾖ καὶ στρατιώτης ἐπιλάβηται, ἄφες, μὴ ἀντίτεινε μηδὲ γόγγυζε. εἰ δὲ μὴ πληγὰς λαβὼν οὐδὲν ἧττον ἀπολεῖς καὶ τὸ ὀνάριον . . .

[2]) The manuscripts do not differ, and in the light of this the dropping of the αὐτοῦ in some versions, though understandable, is not authentic. Professor G. D. KILPATRICK has assured me that in Marcan Greek αὐτοῦ cannot depend on χρείαν. The rarity of ὁ κύριος in reference to Jesus in Mark has been commented upon frequently: an explanation was awaited until now. TAYLOR on Mark, p. 454. K. H. RENGSTORF was more right than he knew when he said (*Das Evangelium nach Lukas*, Göttingen, 1962, 219) that the secret of the whole Entry is bound up with the formula of requiring the animal. The notion that Jesus was in association with the actual owner of the animal (who could quite possibly have been a visitor temporarily lodged in Bethphage for the Feast!) is widespread, but it has no foundation whatever.

was indeed *in need* was vouched for by the evidence of two adult males, the disciples themselves (Deut. xix 15). Naturally pious Jews would admit the right of a rabbi to borrow in case of *need*. But the solemn formula will have warned them that some esoteric matter was afoot, and they will have been all the more reluctant to refuse. Jesus's instructions precluded all further explanation, but on these terms none would have been required!

Indeed within the wall of Bethphage such a request could find, as it were, a homely precedent. David, when he was *in need* (Mark ii 25) obtained bread for himself and his 'pure' young men (1 Sam. xxi 1-6) by virtue of two things, his need and his inherent royal right, which together overrode the ordinary law, under which it was highly questionable whether others than priests should eat that bread (it was their property) [1]). At that moment David was not the *de facto* king, to whom he was in opposition through no fault of his own, but he had a kind of spiritual sovereignty which time alone would reveal. Bethphage was one of the places in which such bread could be obtained, and the people of Bethphage no doubt retained a general interest in that part of the David story. It is no coincidence that the Babylonian Talmud (b. Men. 95 b) relies on 1 Sam. xxi 6 to illustrate the sanctity of the showbread which might be baked (Mishnah, *Men.* XI. 2) in Bethphage. Small wonder that when Jesus set off on the ass which they led firmly to him [2]) the accompanying throng said 'Blessed be the kingdom of our father David which is coming'!

Whether the actual legal owner of the colt was present does not matter: given the right of impressment the concurrence of the owner was superfluous, provided that the impresser had notified before competent witnesses (as, through the disciples, he did) what his intentions were. I have already suggested the extreme likelihood that a rudimentary pool system existed, at least, so that a few bystanders would have custody of the animals of several villagers [3]).

---

[1]) There is a connection between the five loaves of David and the three loaves required by the friend who comes at midnight (Luke xi 5) but I abstain from entering into that topic now. The midrashic material on David is given in its entirety by BILLERBECK, *ad loc.*

[2]) φέρειν is a characteristically Marcan word. C. H. TURNER, *J.T.S.* 26 (1924-5), 12-14. It means 'to bring', keeping a firm hold upon, distinguished from other means of introducing: Mark i 32; vii 32; ix 17, 19; xv 22. I suspect Mark wants to exclude the disciples *riding* it up to Jesus.

[3]) An ass might well have co-owners in the sense that the keeper might feed him until he was old enough to bear burdens and thereafter take the

I have spoken of an ass. In common with others I cannot believe that the colt was in fact the colt of a horse [1]). Horses would not be kept in the open street. They were too valuable. The ordinary villager would not know how to look after them, and their range of utility was far more limited than that of the ass. But the words πῶλον δεδεμένον at Mark xi 2 are delightfully ambiguous. The Jewish reader would be put immediately in mind of Gen. xlix 11. But since πῶλος by itself could naturally mean the colt of a horse, as BAUER insisted, the momentary impression is that here we have an impressment of a horse, such as any real king might desire to ride.

Why does Jesus require one which had not been ridden before? Even an inexpert rider would anticipate difficulties if one chose such a mount for a steep, rough, down-hill journey [2]) amongst shouting people, who could not be guaranteed to avoid making a commotion. The usual explanation is that Jesus regarded the ass as a sacred implement, which, according to taboo, must be new [3]). Whether or not there is truth in this, I suggest that a true king would not choose an animal which had been ridden (or rather *sat on*, whether or not astride) before (and so might conceivably convey ritual uncleanness) both because of the possibility of contamination and because of dignity. No commoner was ever

---

half of the profits as his reward. Mishnah at b. B.M. 68a = Sonc. trans. 397. But it is more than likely that the men referred to in our text were, as it were, the 'duty ass-keepers' of the 'pool'.

[1]) W. BAUER, *J.B.L.* 72 (1953) 220-9 (also *Aufsätze*, Tübingen, 1967, 109-121), followed by ARNDT-GINGRICH (πῶλος). Contradicted by H. W. KUHN, 'Das Reittier Jesu in der Einzugsgeschichte des Mc-Evangeliums', *Z.N.W.* 50 (1959), 82-91 (an excellent article). Since the LXX at Zech. ix 9 itself used πῶλος in the obvious sense of ass, BAUER is contradicted *ipso facto* at the very place where his argument should have been strongest.

[2]) C. KOPP, *The Holy Places of the Gospels* (Freiburg, Edinburgh, 1962), 270ff. My own inspection of the ground confirms KOPP's cautious description. None of the existing paths can be referred back certainly to first-century times, either in contour or gradient or specific route. An additional advantage in imagining two asses would have been that since even a *hirer* had no claim against the lender if the chosen mount was unsatisfactory (b. B.M. 79a) an alternative mount would have been prudently furnished.

[3]) Num. xix 2, Deut. xxi 3, 1 Sam. vi 7, 2 Sam. vi 3, Luke xxiii 53. This is noticed since EDERSHEIM by everyone. But outside the special biblical instances the ass stands for something altogether secular. Later rabbinical and early Christian allegories see the ass of Zech. ix 9 as the wicked (Pes. R. 34, Braude, ii, 667-8, and St. John Chrysostom agree here).GUNDRY (cit. inf.) at p. 198 tries to refute BACON and KUHN to the effect that the unridden mount is derived from πῶλον νέον. But it could well have been Jesus's own midrash upon *ʿayir ben ʾatonot* (the original of π. νεόν).

allowed to ride an animal which a king had once ridden [1]). Here was
a moment for Jesus to show his royal dignity, and the mount must
be unridden by man. The words do not mean 'unbroken', for it will
often have run along with its dam, and will have been familiar with
people, with work, and with an ass's life. We are not to suppose that
it had not carried *non-human* burdens (such as could not defile)—
as the text accurately indicates. The words ἐφ' ὃν οὐδεὶς οὔπω
ἀνθρώπων ἐκάθισεν would not be a bizarre piece of pedantry, after
all! And as far as suspicion of impurity goes, the disciples placed
clothing on the animal's back, so that that aspect was removed. It
is worth remarking in passing that in making his royal progress
down to the Temple—and as a king he could make his way on or
off the paths which already existed (Mark ii 23)—Jesus ran the risk
of passing over something which would have polluted him with the
taint of death. He could not enter the Temple area in that condition.
But seated on an animal he would have been to some extent
protected, for an animal does not afford a passage to impurity which
would otherwise be contracted by overshadowing. Our text does
not justify our pursuing that point beyond its mere mention.

Loans of Animals

So much for Jesus's *angaria* of the ass. But St. Mark's story,
though quite consistent with *angaria*, is also a flawless account of
a borrowing consistent with Jewish law on that subject. St. Mark
is fascinated by the borrowing, which did not interest St. Matthew
or St. Luke equally. To them it is the *angaria* which counts. To
them the irony of the gospel is more important. The real king came,
but the busy city went on with its buying and selling. St. Luke even
dispenses with the direct reference to David. But to St. Mark the
beauty of the episode lay in its being at one and the same time, by
the same steps, the same actions, and the same words, both an
impressment and a borrowing. What a paradox! But it is the paradox
of Zech. ix 9, as we shall see below.

A borrower, as contrasted with a hirer, does not pay for the use
of the thing borrowed. Borrowing is understood by everyone, for
apart from the economic aspect it manifests social solidarity. Now
the Jews had the strictest law of borrowing in legal history [2]). For

---

[1]) Mishnah, *San.* II. 5 (Danby, 385).
[2]) Some schools of Islamic law are equally strict, but not all: cf. *Minhaj
et Talibin*, trans. VAN DEN BERG and HOWARD (London, 1914) (Shafii law)

this there must have been a substantial reason as well as the
technical reason. Socially it was desirable that there should be
ready lenders at all times: and lending is encouraged if the borrower
is bound by an absolute liability to restore the article or its value.
The technical reason is that the bible stated the law in unusually
precise terms. Ex. xxii 14-15 reads:—

> When a man borrows a beast from his neighbour and it is injured or dies
> while its owner is not with it, the borrower shall make full restitution; but
> if the owner is with it, the borrower shall not make restitution. If it was
> hired, only the hire shall be due.

Briefly, what this meant was that the borrower must replace the
animal in *all* eventualities, even those amounting to unavoidable
accident ('*onēṣ*) [1]), unless (a) the animal died in the normal course
of work to do which it had been borrowed, or (b) the owner was
present in such a sense that he could ascertain for himself that the
loss of the animal (or, in appropriate circumstances, its fall in value)
was not due to fraud or negligence or misuse on the part of the
borrower (*sho'ēl*). The rule that the owner-lender (*mash'iyl*) should
be *with it* was a rule of common sense, but a very rough and ready
one, not effective for all situations. There were at least two ways
in which it could be construed. As Philo takes it [2]) the *sho'ēl* is
free from liability to restore the animal (or make good its deprecia-
tion) if the owner is physically associated during the use to which
the animal is put [3]). This could operate adversely to the interests of
owners if both they and their animals were borrowed, and the
enterprise were such that neither the *sho'ēl* nor the *mashe'iyl* could

---

and C. HAMILTON, trans., *The Hedaya*, 2nd. edn. (London, 1870), 478-482
(Hanafi law). For the Roman law, which excluded liability for *vis maior* see
F. SCHULTZ, *Classical Roman Law* (Oxford, 1954), 508, 514-6; M. KASER,
Das Römische Privatrecht I (Munich, 1955), 423-6, 445. B. COHEN, *Jewish and
Roman Law* (1966) does not touch this subject. G. R. DRIVER and J. C. MILES,
Babylonian Laws I (Oxford, 1952), 438-40. For the English law see *Halsbury's
Laws of England*, 3rd edn., II (1953), s. 202.

[1]) Mishnah, *B.M.* VII. 8-10 (Danby, 360); b. B.M. 93 a-b. The whole law
is set out conveniently at MAIMONIDES, *Mishneh Torah* XIII, II, i (trans.
J. J. RABINOWITZ, *Book of Civil Laws*, New Haven, 1949, pp. 52 ff.). I. HERZOG,
Main Institutions of Jewish Law II (London, New York, 1967), 176-185 (at
p. 177 line 3 read '(c) and (d)' for (b) and (c) and line 6 read '(b)'?). D. W.
AMRAM, 'Borrower', *J.E.* III (1902).

[2]) *De Spec. Leg.* IV. 37-8. E. R. GOODENOUGH, *Jewish Courts in Egypt*
(New Haven, 1929), 173-4. B. RITTER, *Philo und die Halacha* (Leipzig, 1879),
64 f. is of little help.

[3]) COLSON (viii, 31) translates συνδιατρίβοντος as 'living on the spot', but
συνδιατρίβειν means to accompany, keep in association with.

save the animal from damage or loss. Therefore the rabbis developed the rule which is now the *halakah* to the effect that the phrase 'if the owner is with it' meant simply that the owner personally authorised the borrowing, and by his personal cooperation waived his right to absolute restoration of the animal (always saving fair wear and tear in the course of the contemplated labour). This was taken to absurd lengths. If the *sho'ēl* could induce the *mashe'iyl* to load the beast for him, or even to saddle it, his liability for unavoidable accident was removed. If he could induce the owner to get him a drink of water prior to his taking the animal out of his possession the *sho'ēl* could claim that he had borrowed the animal *with its owner* [1]).

Liability for the animal began from the moment when the animal was *drawn* [2]) (i.e. led by the rope) and so went out of the owner's possession and power into the quasi-ownership of the *sho'ēl*. To draw the animal by taking its tethering rope was to submit oneself immediately [3]) to responsibility to return the animal or its value in any event, unless it died in the course of the work for which it was borrowed. A young colt, needless to say, was not likely to die in the course of a two-mile journey, however steep or rough, nor on the homeward route (for it would surely have been ridden by Jesus, unless it had become lame, and unless Jesus preferred to walk back). But there was one situation in which drawing would not have this effect. If at the time the rope was taken in the hand of the borrower or his agent the animal was in the lender's *courtyard* the animal did not enter the borrower's possession and quasi-ownership until the animal had left the courtyard: for a courtyard possesses for its owner(s) [4]). Thus if the question were whether the owner was *with it*, and if this question depended upon any conversation between the borrower (or his agent) and the owner (or his), the

---

[1]) Mishnah, *B.M.* VIII. 1; b. B.M. 94a-97a. MAIMONIDES, *ubi cit.*, ch. ii (trans., 55 f.).

[2]) b. B.M. 94b, 99a.

[3]) 'A cow is acquired only by *meshiykah*' (b. B.M. 94b: Sonc. trans. 544). It would be the same for an ass. *Meshiykah* (drawing) is a recognised method of acquisition. See explicitly MAIMONIDES, *ubi cit*, ch. i, s. 5 (trans., 53).

[4]) A well-known proposition of Jewish law. See b. B.M. 94b (also 118a), where the point is made precisely. In our context a close study of Mekilta *Nez.* 16 (LAUTERBACH, iii, 127) is desirable. 'From his neighbour' at Ex. xxii 14 is construed with reference to passage out of the domain of the lender. *Reshūtā'* is (1) control, (2) territory, domain. A. SCHLATTER, *Markus* (Stuttgart, 1935), 208, nearly saw the point.

fact that the animal had been drawn effectively into the possession
of the borrower would be significant, and the fact that the animal
was tethered in the public domain, out in the open street surround-
ing the block of habitations and within the wall or its remains [1]),
would be especially significant.

In effecting a borrowing it is necessary that the purpose should
be indicated and the expected duration, for after the duration has
expired, it becomes a hire, and the borrower becomes liable as a
hirer. Jesus's instructions thus contain many important legal
implications. The disciples, who are his agents, first take the rope
and untie the ass. By so doing they establish Jesus's liability for
the safe return of the animal from that moment, and not from the
moment when the animal reaches Jesus's own personal possession [2]).
It would have been possible for the disciples to hire the animal, or,
if borrowing, to induce the owner to send it by his own servant:
but they were to do neither. They were to borrow it on Jesus's
behalf, and to assume liability immediately. They were to submit
Jesus to liability for the ass's safe return to the village itself (and we
note in passing that in St. Mark's account Jesus completes his
formal entry and immediately returns). Now it fell out that the ass
was, as Jesus had indicated with his words εὐθὺς εἰσπορευόμενοι,
in the public domain (πρὸς θύραν ἔξω ἐπὶ τοῦ ἀμφόδου) and the
disciples, by untying it, assumed the rigorous liability of the
Jewish law. Jesus's instructions precluded either the owner's
participation in any direct contractual arrangement (Luke's
οἱ κύριοι looks like guesswork, but it serves to emphasise the
esoteric character of ὁ κύριος αὐτοῦ), or the owner's participation
in the enterprise itself. The people standing there 'allow them to
go', i.e. they accept that the disciples are entitled to take the ass
on the footing of what had been said. The putting of garments on
an ass does not normally have the effect of violating the contract

---

[1]) For ἄμφοδον see MOULTON-MILLIGAN, *Vocabularly*, s.v. PREISIGKE,
Fachwörter des öffentlichen Verwaltungsdienstes (cit. inf.), s.v. GRENFELL and
HUNT, *Oxyrhynchus Papyri* II, No. 242, p. 189 n. 12 explain the word as
more than a street and its houses and less than a quarter. Oxyrhynchus had
at least fourteen of them. POLYBIUS, *Hist.* XXXIX. 3. 2: ἄμφοδον is the
road as contrasted with a threshold. The suggestion that our ἀμφόδου should
be changed to ἀμπέλου (Couchoud, Lohmeyer, Grundmann) is unnecessary
and unreasonable.

[2]) Mishnah, *B.M.* VIII. 3; b. B.M. 98 b-99 a (Sonc. trans., 565). Maimonides,
ubi cit., ch. iii, ss. 1-3 (trans., pp. 58-60).

of borrowing [1]), and everything, we understand, went according to plan.

Now it is fair to ask, could this have been a deliberate preparation for a political demonstration, possibly involving a riot and stone-throwing? Could Jesus have contemplated that he himself and his disciples might have been arrested and the ass stolen? On the contrary Jesus quite gratuitously took every care to have the use of this ass as a borrower (not as a hirer), and subject to the highest liability known to the law. He had only to ask the owner or his agent to accompany him the two miles or less to the Temple, and that liability would have been obviated. But he took care not to do so. This can be explained partly because the action was also an impressment, partly because Jesus was actually (and in midrashic symbolism) 'poor' (see below), and partly because he was righteous [2]). But I cannot see why a 'poor' man should accept higher responsibility than a clever person who is not poor would care to assume, if he could as easily avoid it. The answer must lie somewhere else. Jesus's ability to combine Old Testament themes in action seems to have come once again into play.

'Despoiling the Egyptians'

It is a curiosity of the Old Testament that the story of the First Redemption includes at a very early stage a quite unnecessary motif of borrowing. Every Israelite had to borrow from his neighbour (Ex. iii 22, xi 2-3, xii 35-6). The effect was that valuable items (Gen. xv 14) were taken from the Egyptians, implements of silver and gold and raiment, and since these were not returned the borrowing seems indistinguishable from theft. In fact the words in xii 36 (*wa-yᵉnatsᵉlū et-Mitsᵉrāyim*) which are conventionally translated 'and they despoiled (or plundered) the Egyptians' coincide with a problem which has pursued the Jews from ancient times: they were little better than thieves. This is corroborated by the Jewish concern to show that the loans were, in a sense,

---

[1]) The pedantic discussion at Mishnah, *B.M.* VI, 5, further at b. B.M. 79b. What applies to a hirer will apply *a fortiori* to a borrower. Jesus's justice is shown not only by the way in which he treats the owner (i.e. consulting his welfare) but also by the use to which the animal is actually put.

[2]) A Jew might obtain a reputation for *piety* by stipulating to be liable as a borrower although in fact he paid for the use of the animal and so was actually a hirer: a theoretical instance is discussed at b. B.M. 94a. Hence it was righteous to be absolutely liable for returning the beast.

recovered later [1]) ; or that it was a means whereby the Jews were, voluntarily, recompensed for their years of slavery, the account was settled, though by a form of settlement which we should call deception [2]). And good feeling was restored through which the Egyptians might profit (see Zech. xiv 18). To this end scholars have pointed out that the conventional translation is almost certainly wrong and that the correct translation would be 'and they saved (in a spiritual sense) the Egyptians' [3]). The garments (compare the betrothal gifts brought by Eliezer for Rebecca) are a point of contact with our story, and it is worthwhile realising that the word for 'implement' (*k^{e}liy*) can mean something upon which one sits (Lev. xv 4, 6, 22). Thus, whatever it may be to which these details point, a grand borrowing took place before the First Redemption, and it would be appropriate that a ceremonial borrowing should take place before the Second, namely that Redemption which Jesus was about to set in motion. In connection with the Exodus story it is notable that in Jewish law loans of such a character are not recallable at will by the *mashe^e'iyl*, so long as no duration is agreed. Then no period was put to the loan, and technically the Egyptians were not robbed at all! In the case of the ass, as we have seen, the duration was indicated with sufficient precision. To revert for a moment to the case of David at Nob, the transfer of the five loaves to David (and his young men) was a gift and not a loan, so that (if one wanted to be midrashically precise) the unfortunate end of the priests, caught up in politics (1 Sam. xxii 18), was in no sense an inauspicious precedent for the ass-drivers of Bethphage.

---

[1]) b. Pes. 87 b = Sonc. 464; ibid. 119 a. See on this Philo, *Vita Mos.* I. 141 f. Jos. *Ant.* II, 14 ('gifts'). PEAKE, 179 G. J. H. HERTZ, *The Pentateuch* (1930) *ad loc.* and references. Midr. R. Exod. III. 11 (Sonc. 69). Mekilta, *ad loc.* At Midr. R. Gen. LXI the incident of 'spoiling the Egyptians' is explained as being a means whereby the children of Israel obtained their accumulated 'back pay' (see footnote 3 infra).

[2]) Hindu law and Jewish law agree that there are cases in which a creditor is entitled to resort to deception, or trickery, in order to recover his rights or reestablish his legal position. For the present it is sufficient to refer to Mishnah, B.M. VI. 1 (DANBY's *Mishnah*, 357) for a passing illustration of this concept.

[3]) From KUHN's *Konkordanz* it may easily be verified that NTSL occurs 212 times in the senses 'snatch, rescue, recover', with the direct object of the thing recovered, whereas only at Ex. iii. 22 and xii. 36 is our alleged meaning 'despoiled' found. The instance at 2 Ch. xx 25 could easily be taken as 'gathered'. The root in the hiphil form, *hitsiyl* is regularly used in the spiritual sense: Prov. xxiii 14, Isa. l 2; lvii 12; Ezek. xiv 20, Amos iv 11.

Old Testament Asses and their Midrashic Background

Most Old Testament asses are real asses, even Balaam's. The ass might be ridden by a nobleman, and to ride an ass was not a sign of humility in itself [1]). No doubt one who rode an animal was 'superior' to one who went on foot [2]), but that was an everyday experience. To connect riding an ass with the Second Redemption we must look for metaphorical asses. There are only two of them, though they figure in three places. The Messiah's ass (*'iyroh*) at Gen. xlix 11 is automatically identified with the ass to be ridden by the Messiah at Zech. ix 9 (*ḥamor*). Yet the ass which is Issachar (Gen. xlix 14-15) is also *ḥamor*. The reader of the esoteric blessings in Gen. xlix will be struck by the fact that two metaphorical asses   * appear so close together. Jewish interpretation eliminates both! In the blessing upon Judah the Messiah is said to usher in an age of unexampled plenty, in which the ass disappears in the metaphor [3]). From the words πῶλον δεδεμένον at Mark xi 2 we know that the evangelist intended to alert us to the awareness of Jesus that the rule of the king Messiah, king by descent from Judah, was about to begin. Thus all of the passage Gen. xlix 10ff. must be understood to be present to Jesus's mind. Passing to Issachar, Jewish interpretation, with fair consistency, insists upon eliminating the ass: unlike the proverbial donkey, Issachar is superlatively wise, able to teach the other tribes their duties [4]), and even exclusively occupied with the Torah [5]). The Sanhedrins were copiously supplied

---

[1]) Jg. v 10, x 4. J. DE FRAINE, *L'Aspect religieux de la Royaulté Israélite* (Rome, 1954), 198 n. 9. DANIEL-ROPS, *Jesus in his Time* (London, 1955), 341-2. On asses as mounts see M. REHM, *Der König Messias* (Kerelaer, 1968), 335 n, 352 (on Zech. ix 9f see *ibid.*, 333-8).

[2]) 1 Sam. xxv 20, 23.

[3]) The Targumim are exhaustively discussed by J. BOWKER, *Targums and Rabbinic Literature* (Cambridge, 1969), where see pp. 278-9, 284-5. See also the small but interesting variations of the celebrated (but in no sense exhaustive) Neofiti MS. edited by A. DIEZ MACHO (1968), 635. Ps. Jon. has, of Issachar, 'he is a strong tribe knowing the determined times', while Neofiti I has 'Issachar is a strong tribe lying between two territories' (cf. RASHI, below). For Judah all versions agree, but Midr. R. Gen. XLVIII, 9 says that the Messiah will teach Torah. See b. Ket. 111b = Sonc. 722.

[4]) 1 Chr. xii 32-3 is constantly referred to. See for variants Midr. R. Gen. LXXV, 6 = Sonc. 697-9; LXXV. 12 (the ass at Gen. xxxii. 6 also means Issachar); b. B.K. 17a = Sonc. 75 (Is. xxxii. 20 refers to Joseph and Issachar).

[5]) Midr. R. Gen. XCVII = Sonc. 908 (see also LXXII, 5 = Sonc. 665); XCVIII, 12 = Sonc. 960. Midr. R. Num. XIII, 15-16 = Sonc. 532-3; XIII, 17 = Sonc. 539.

by this tribe. If he dwells between two bounds, or limits (the word is of unknown meaning) [1]), far, as Rashi says, from a dwelling, out upon the outskirts of inhabited places [2]), he is a bond-slave to the Torah, to which he lends his shoulders, or to his fellow Jews who subject him to the onerous task of prescribing their duties for them [3]).

It is remarkable that, in only apparent defiance of geography, Jesus is shown sending for the animal in a region betwixt and between [4]). St. Matthew sensibly leaves out the reference to Bethany, since midrashically Bethphage is the significant place, whence, we need not doubt, the animal was borrowed—but in so doing the between-ness of Jesus's situation was obscured. Again, the ass is actually found right upon the entrance of the village (St. Mark intends the prediction to be fulfilled, we may be sure), not in a courtyard or in any inhabited place, but in the high street (though only just on the right side of the threshold!), between the relevant 'block' of the village and its bounds or the remains of its wall. It is notable that Issachar is a bond-slave (*maṣ-ʿovēd*: the men of Issachar in ancient times were often carrying loads of crops on their backs, we may be sure), and what we are watching is precisely an impressment. Thus, midrashically, the ass upon which Jesus rode was Issachar! The ritual purity of the animal was doubly requisite!

Judah is said to possess the kingship until he comes to Shiloh (or until Shiloh comes), that unintelligible expression which, from the Dead Sea Scroll rendering onwards [5]) is to be interpreted 'until he comes to whom it (the kingship) belongs' [6]). Until, in fact, the

---

[1]) *hammıshᵉpᵉtāyım* is a puzzle. See p. 255 n. 3 sup. JEROME has *termini*; Midr. R. Gen. XCVIII, 12: rows of disciples, or sheepfolds or plains, so XCIX. 10 = Sonc. 984. The LXX has 'lots', another Greek version 'streams', and another (?) 'neighbourhoods'. RASHI's explanation is 'hearths' = 'boundaries of towns'. Targ. O., see BOWKER (285), 'borders'. Pess. 'paths'.

[2]) RASHI explains (trans. S. Bamberger, Hamburg, 1928, 131-2) that this is because of his bringing in loads and being unable to enter the built-up portions of a town!

[3]) See p. 255 n. 5 sup.

[4]) The comments of W. SCHMAUCK, *Das Evangelium d. Matthäus* (Göttingen, 1956), 294 ff. will typify many such comments, which, however, tend to the reflection that St. Mark knew little of Judaean geography.

[5]) J. M. ALLEGRO, *J.B.L.* 75 (1956), 174 ff. G. VERMES, *Scripture and Tradition in Judaism* (Leiden, 1961), 53 and nn. For the previous position see J. SKINNER, *Genesis* (Edinburgh, 1951), 521 ff.; O. PROCKSCH, *Die Genesis* (Leipzig, 1913), 268-9.

[6]) LXX: τὰ ἀποκείμενα αὐτῷ. Otherwise: ᾧ ἀποκεῖται. V.L.: cui reposita

master (ὁ κύριος αὐτοῦ) comes! When the Messiah comes he will be a king, and whatever he *needs* will be his by regalian right.

Now we may examine the passage from Zech. ix 9, the rabbinical connection of which with the Messiah is notorious to all students of the passage:—

> Rejoice greatly, daughter of Zion, shout aloud, daughter of Jerusalem; for behold your king is coming to you, just (or righteous) and saved (or saving [cf. Mark x 52], or victorious), poor (or humble) and riding on an ass *and* (i.e. *namely*) on a colt, the son of she-asses.

To comply with this picture the rider must be mounted on a young animal, with which an untried mount would correspond; and he must be coming in a kingly style, with which a progress upon an impressed animal would correspond. He must be poor, which implies that he begged the animal, borrowed it as a matter of charity, and did not hire it. Thus the paradox of the king who begs the loan of, not a horse, but an ass, is fulfilled. His 'justice' is shown by his juridical scrupulosity, even as 'king'.

St. Matthew has not incompetently misunderstood the Zechariah passage [1]). Nor does he fail to notice the semitic idiom. He is to be visualised as hinting that though Zech. ix 9 mentions *one* animal twice, there must have been two animals in terms of the symbolism, because if one is Issachar, the other is the colt tied to the vine. If one is a colt, the other is its mother (a she-ass); or if not the story would not have been at the same time a fulfilment of two biblical passages. Whether Jesus rode the mother or the colt, or both alternately, the picture of the colt running with its mother is true to life, and reasonable in view of the possibility that it would make a poor mount on the rough descent. As usual, St. Matthew gives his reader the benefit of a midrash as he goes along.

St. John obviously had a tradition, possibly but not necessarily an independent one, to the effect that Jesus rode on an ass, a young

---

sunt. Targ. Jo. Neofiti: 'whose is the kingship' (cf. Bowker, 284). Thus BRATCHER, *E.T.* 64 (1952), 93, was right, without knowing why.

[1]) As feared by O. MICHEL in his learned study (KITTEL, TWNT V, 283·7); K. PIEPER, *B.Z.* 11 (1913) at p. 401; E. LITTMANN, *Z.N.W.* 34 (1935), 28; F. C. GRANT, *The Gospels* (London, 1957), 148; and many others. A close study of St. Matthew's use of Zech. ix 9 appears at R. H. GUNDRY, *The Use of the Old Testament in St. Matthew's Gospel* (London, 1967), 120, 197-9. It is most balanced, and corrects errors in previous sceptical discussions. F. F. BRUCE's 'The book of Zechariah and the Passion narrative', *B.J.R.L.* 43 (1961), 336ff., 339, 346-7, gives an excellent background to the event.

ass, which he 'found'. This fits impressing, since asses were impressed as they were found on the highway. St. John says nothing about its previous occupation. The synoptic gospels visualise the disciples going off the road down to a village which is 'opposite' to them. St. John visualises the ass being already within view, perhaps on the crowded road. The possibility of a borrowing is even there left quite open.

Not less important information was brought forward by H. J. Schoeps in 1949[1]). The ass of Zech. ix.9 was eventually said by the rabbis to be no other than the ass on which Abraham rode (Gen. xxii.3) when he went to sacrifice Isaac (who was sacrificed on Mt. Moriah, the Temple Mount), the same ass (Exod. iv.20) on which Moses rode[2]). The action of Jesus therefore combines the messianic and prophetic roles along with the kingly, and appropriately leads him on to his great prophetic act, the Cleansing of the Temple[3]), and the announcement that for this Temple, temporarily cleansed, he himself would provide a lasting substitute and successor, his house a house of prayer for all nations.

[1]) *Theologie und Geschichte des Judenchristentums* (Tübingen, 1949), 92.
[2]) Pirqe de R. Eliezer, XXXI; Yalqût § 573; Rashi on Exod. iv.20. Observe how late these traces are—yet the haggadah illuminates Jesus's behaviour.
[3]) Sup., p. vii, n. 1.

FURTHER ANNOTATIONS

Tit. H. Patsch, 'Der Einzug Jesu in Jerusalem,' *ZTK* , 68 (1971), 1-26.

p. [243], n. 5. Epictetus on *angaria* figures curiously at Claudius Salmasius, *Diss. de Foenore Trapezitico* (Lug. Bat., 1640), i, 276-7. G. Webster, *The Roman Imperial Army* (London, 1969), 261-2.

p. [244], n. 1. L. Mitteis - U. Wilcken, *Grundzüge und Chrestomathie der Papyruskunde* I, 2 (1912), 439.

p. [245], l. 31. S. with caution Z. W. Falk, ed., *Dine Israel; an Annual* 1 (1969), a short essay on Jewish quasi-commercial law, including a limited form of insurance which excluded negligence, applicable to ass-drivers and ship-owners.

p. [247], l. 18. The wall of Bet Pagi was as the wall of Jerusalem: b. B.M. 90a = Sonc. 518.

p. [255], l. 12. J. A. Emerton, *J.T.S.* 19 (1968), 245-6; C. M. Carmichael, *JBL*, 88 (1969), 435ff, 437-8. See also J. Coppens, 'La bénédiction de Jacob. Son cadre historique à la lumière des parallèles ougaritiques,' *Volume du Congrès. Strasbourg 1956.* Supp. V.T. IV (Leiden, 1957), 97-115.

p. [257], l. 3. In reply to E. Lipiński, *VT* 20 (1970), 50-3, B. Köhler, 'Sacharja ix.9. Ein neuer Übersetzungsvorschlag,' *VT*, 21 (1971), 370 : 'triumphing and riding on an ass', taking *'atōnôt* as fem. sing. That this would be known to Jesus's contemporaries or their disciples is doubtful.

p. [257], n. Exhaustive but concise : J. H. Hertz, ed., *Pentateuch and Haftorah* (London, 1956), 201-2.

Midrash in the New Testament:
The Origin of Luke XXII 67–68

The overworked word 'midrash' is producing an increased impact on New Testament studies. Difficult passages are submitting to elucidation,[1] and easy passages are finding new contextual values. Here is a case where an Old Testament passage, with its intellectual ambience, not only seems to have provided our gospel passage, but gave to its surroundings their proper point and meaning. Apart from the Last Supper, no part of the gospel has been studied so intensively as the Passion and Resurrection narrative. St. Luke's contribution to the former has been minutely examined, in the pages of this journal as of others, and in specialist treatises. However, xxii. 67–68 have received very little attention (if we except Schneider, *v. inf.*) and they have only a narrow commentatorial cauda, as a glance at a bibliography will confirm. The basic question, as ever, is whether they represent what Jesus answered in fact, what he *might* have said, or what he can fairly be taken to have meant, whether he uttered the words or not. It will emerge from what is said below that my own view (based on the use of scripture in Jesus' *deeds* as well as *words*) supports St. Luke in a particular understanding of Mark, viz. that Jesus consciously played out the scriptural role he understood himself to have assumed: thus the words belonged to him, and were truthfully believed to have belonged to him, whether he actually uttered them or not.

67. λέγοντες,[2] Εἰ σὺ εἶ ὁ Χριστός, εἰπὸν ἡμῖν. εἶπεν δὲ αὐτοῖς, Ἐὰν ὑμῖν εἴπω οὐ μὴ πιστεύσητε· 68. ἐὰν δὲ ἐρωτήσω οὐ μὴ ἀποκριθῆτε.[3]

[1] E. g. Derrett, 'Figtrees in the New Testament', *Hey. J.* 14/3 (1973), 249–65.

[2] The subject is inconveniently placed and one suspects an editorial suture.

[3] The reading ἀποκριθῆτε μοι ἢ ἀπολύσητε, though evidently ancient, seems to be a gloss devised by men already unaware of the allusion to Isaiah (see below) and supposing Jesus to have avoided a direct answer as useless. The alternative view (preferred by Schneider, infra at p. 118: references), that the reading is original and excised to avoid Jesus' appearing to wish to be freed, is theoretically valid, practically implausible. If Jesus' words are Luke's identification of Jesus with the Servant, he is not pleading, but condemning.

'. . . Saying, if you are the Messiah, tell us! He said to them, "If I tell you you will not have faith. And if I ask you you will not answer." '

The uninstructed reader will ask, why should Jesus *ask* anything? That was not in question. But, indeed, it might be, if we retranslate ἐρωτήσω as *eš^e'ālēm* (on which see below). Our bibles show no marginal references. The allusion has remained unknown. The specialised studies of Rese[4] and Schneider[5] have not detected it, though the latter rightly excludes a free composition by Luke (p. 115). Lightfoot, Schöttgen, Wetstein and Billerbeck have nothing to offer. Blinzler's short, but uniquely well-informed study[6] sees nothing behind our passage but Lk. xx.3, 8 and (wrongly) Jer. xxxviii.15. If it was, in fact, St. Luke's invention, he left no recognisable trace. Below I give the answer, and try to sketch in its meaning. It is usually supposed that Jesus' words reflect his consciousness that the assembly was prejudiced, and that it was futile to converse with it.[7] This is not factually implausible, but the point could well be much deeper.

The implications of any successful search may be vital to recovering an understanding of St. Luke's technique, the sources he used, the beliefs he assumed in his hearers, and, of course, his understanding of Mark.

---

[4] M. Rese, *Alttestamentliche Motiven in der Christologie des Lukas* (Gütersloh, 1969); cf. p. 199.

[5] G. Schneider, *Verleugnung, Verspottung und Verhör Jesu nach Lukas 22, 54–71* (Munich, 1969), 105–132, especially 114–118, and p. 35, n. 69. The prophetic style is recognised at p. 169.

[6] J. Blinzler, *Der Prozess Jesu*[3] (Regensburg, 1960), pp. 120–2, esp. 122.

[7] M. Kiddle, 'The Passion narrative in St. Luke's gospel', *J. T. S.* 36 (1935), pp. 267ff, at 272. N. Geldenhuys, *Commentary on the Gospel of Luke* (London/Edinburgh, 1956), p. 587 (cf. Lk.xx.4). A truthful answer would require time to explain and define, and this was being denied him: A. E. Harvey, *Companion to the New Testament* (Oxford, Cambridge, 1970), p. 292. He shows his knowledge and his own authority: A. Vanhoye, 'Structure et théologie des récits de la Passion dans les évangiles synoptiques', *Nou. Rev. Théol.* 89 (1967), pp. 135ff, at p. 146. Jesus' answer is equivocal: J. A. Bailey, cited below (n. 13). Klostermann thinks it evasion (so did A. B. Bruce in *Expositor's Greek Testament* I, 1910, p. 635): Conzelmann (n. 10) denies this at p. 84 n. 3. G. B. Caird too takes it to be a refusal to answer (*Saint Luke,* London, 1963, 245). An indirect reply: Hooker (n. 15), p. 88. Schneider (n. 5), p. 33 says Jesus' words are no answer to the question at all; they are evasive (p. 35). Schmid and Grundmann (below, n. 18) both see Jesus' answer as evasive, the latter commenting that discussion was useless since there was no common ground between the prospective disputants in the scene as shown. J. M. Creed, *The Gospel according to St. Luke* (London, 1950) gives no explanation of the passage. A. R. C. Leaney, commenting on the passage, calls Jesus' words a 'substitute for . . . silence'.

It was suspected that Luke had no separate source of his own for this area.[8] The view that he possessed an independent source with the aid of which he modified and completed Mark, widely held,[9] may be losing ground. That xxii. 66–71 is no less 'editorial' than traditional is regarded in some quarters as obvious. The reason for this, expressed by Conzelmann rather in passing than by strict proof,[10] is that St. Luke wishes to demonstrate to his church that their existing evaluation of Jesus as (1) an (undefined) entity of messianic significance, (2) the 'Son of Man', (3) the Son of God was endorsed by Jesus himself in the face of an assembly of the elders of the Jewish people, both chief priests and scribes, at the crisis of his earthly life. This was understood by them formally as such an act as might be the direct justification for their taking Jesus before Pilate. Luke is concerned to exhort and console his church in their conflict with the Jews, who had, by that time, formally excommunicated

[8] Or if he did he did not use it here: R. Bultmann, *The History of the Synoptic Tradition* (Oxford, 1968), p. 271. For Finegan see n. 12 below. Bultmann (p. 438 *ad* p. 272) praises Finegan for attributing Lk. xxii.66 to Mk. xiv.53b and xv.1. G. Bertram, *Die Leidensgeschichte Jesu und der Christuskult* (Göttingen, 1922), pp. 56–60 (Luke apologises for Jesus' want of clearer speech) took the view that if Luke had a separate source it had no particular historical value. Schneider (above, n. 5) guesses that the passage may originally have belonged outside the crisis in Jerusalem, see Lk. xx.1–8. Grundmann gently doubts Luke's special source.

[9] Schneider, pp. 30–1, 116, 118. A. M. Perry, *The Sources of Luke's Passion-Narrative* (Chicago, 1920), pp. 98–9, 105. V. Taylor, *Jesus and his Sacrifice* (London, 1937), p. 197. J. B. Tyson, 'The Lukan version of the trial of Jesus', *N. T.* 3 (1959), pp. 249–58. G. Schneider, 'Gab es eine vorsynoptische Szene, «Jesus vor dem Synedrium»?', *N. T.* 12 (1970), pp. 22–39 (Lk. xxii.66–71 was based on Luke's special passion source). The belief in a source totally independent of Mark is weakly supported by P. Benoit, *Exégèse et Théologie* (Paris, 1961), pp. 295–6. ⌐. ⌐. Catchpole, 'The problem of the historicity of the Sanhedrin trial', in E. Bammel, ed. *The Trial of Jesus* (London, 1970), p. 65 (semitically coloured, more primitive, it deserves great respect).

[10] H. Conzelmann. *The Theology of St. Luke* (London, 1960), pp. 84–7, 140–1, 170–1, 188 n. 7. See also A. George, 'Jésus Fils de Dieu dans l'évangile selon Saint Luc', *R. B.* 72 (1965), pp. 184ff., 207. At 'La royauté de Jésus selon l'évangile de Luc', *Sciences Ecclésiastiques* (Montréal), 14 (1962), pp. 57–69 (*New Testament Abstracts* 6.793) Fr. George finds that Jesus asserted his royalty throughout *vv.* 67–70. R. H. Lightfoot (n. 13) at p. 181 points to the steady development of the church's belief about the person and office of its Master. Catchpole (cited above) questionably believes that the separate enumeration of the titles proves that the church in a semitic area had *not* yet equated them (Luke had equated them at iv.41 = Mk. i. 34). Grundmann sees Luke's church as having no longer any dialogue with the Jews (below n. 18, at p. 420).

Christians,[11] and had (we do not know how persistently) brought Christians before heathen rulers for punishment (a feature or trait found amongst Jews down to quite modern times). Jesus, the pattern, spoke out and identified himself boldly, though not in any terms which 'the Jews' could propound, or could sympathetically understand. Such an understanding of Luke need not take very seriously the question whether St. Luke did have any traditional source[12] behind *vv.* 67–68, which have no true parallel elsewhere, saving some Johannine passages. Jaubert has seen in the (supposed) awkwardness of *v.* 68 a suture betraying Luke's editorial hand. Now the likeness to the Johannine material has been noticed by many writers besides her.[13] The most obvious explanation is probably the right one.[14] John knew the source of the Lucan passage, if not (as Schneider admits is possible) St. Luke himself; and provided his interpretation of it. We shall turn to St. John presently.

Element (1) is the so-called vague self-revelation. Its origin seems plain to me, provided we take the word πιστεύσητε in the sense not of 'believe me' (which is very natural) but in the sense of 'have faith (*sc.* in the gospel)'. Professor Hooker's *Jesus and the Servant*[15] would reject a direct

[11] Cf. Lk. vi.22 ἐκβάλωσιν with Mt. v.11 διώξωσιν M. Goulder, *Midrash and Lection in Matthew* (London, 1974), p. 281.

[12] See n. 8 above, and next n. (Bailey). It is notable that F. Rehkopf, *Die lukanische Sonderquelle. Ihr Umfang und Sprachgebrauch* (Tübingen, 1959) does not deal with our verses! P. Winter's peculiar view, that *vv.* 66b–71 are a post-Lucan interpolation ('The treatment of his sources by the Third Evangelist: Luke xxi-xxiv', *St. Theol.* 8/2, 1955, pp. 138ff. at 162–3 [66a is based on Mt. xxvii.1, cf. Mt. xxvi. 63–5]; 'Luke xxii.66b–71', *ibid.*, 9, 1955, pp. 112–15) is rejected by Conzelmann at p. 84 n. 3, also J. Blinzler (n. 6) at p. 122. J. Finegan, *Die Überlieferung der Leidens- und Auferstehungsgeschichte Jesu* (Giessen, 1934), pp. 25, 36 (Luke merely explains Jesus' silence and has no separate source). If Luke is merely expanding Mark's report of silence the verses would qualify for treatment in E. P. Sanders, *Tendencies of the Synoptic Tradition* (Cambridge, 1969), ch. 2 or 3, but they do not figure there.

[13] Schneider, pp. 61, 68, 115–16. A. Jaubert, 'Les séances du Sanhédrin et les récits de la passion', *Rév. de l'hist. des Réligions* 166 (1964), pp. 143ff., 165–6 (she believes he did have a source: p. 166). Perry, cited above, links Lk. xxii.67–8 with Jn. xvii.21. See n. 34 below. R. H. Lightfoot, *History and Interpretation in the Gospels* (London, 1935), p. 180. J. Schniewind, *Die Parallel-Perikopen bei Lukas und Johannes* (Darmstadt, 1958), p. 43. D. R. Catchpole (n. 9 above), p. 64. Similarly J. A. Bailey, *The Traditions Common to the Gospels of Luke and John* (Leiden, 1963), pp. 55–63. He links the passage with Jn. x.24b–25a (correctly). Bailey suggests a possibly historical written, un-Markan account of the trial. Similarly, G. Schneider. Winter, *St. Theol.* 9, pp. 112–15. Benoit (cited above, n. 9).

[14] V. Taylor, *Formation of the Gospel Tradition* (London, 1953), p. 53.

[15] London, 1959, reviewed by J. Jeremias, *J. T. S.* 11 (1960), pp. 140ff. See p. 91.

connection between the evangelists' Passion story and Deutero-Isaiah. But, if I am right, this view must be revised. We may start with Is. xlii: 'Behold my servant, whom I uphold; my chosen, in whom my soul delights: I have put my spirit upon him; he shall bring forth judgement to the gentiles.'[16] Spirit suggests utterance, expression; judgement we shall see is a prominent theme in the whole; the gentiles and heathenism likewise pervade the prophecy: the Servant will denounce them. The First Servant Poem does not in fact commence the servant theme. This figures literally even in earlier passages which, historically considered, deal with prophecy of the victories of Cyrus and the discomfiture of heathen cults: a historical view of Is. xli, for example, does not, by any means, exhaust its midrashic potential. The one whom God raises up, at xli.2 and 25, need not be a political ruler, still less a foreign one. Israel is the servant (xli.8, 9), the chosen one (ibid.), or perhaps it is true to say that the Servant is the ideal Israel. 'Be not dismayed, for I am thy God: yea I will help thee; yea, I will uphold thee with the right hand of my righteousness. Behold, all they that are incensed against thee shall be ashamed and confounded: they that strive with thee shall be as nothing, and shall perish (vv. 10–11).' 'Thou shalt seek them, and shalt not find them, even them that contend with thee: they that were against thee shall be as nothing and as a thing of nought. For I the Lord will hold thy right hand, saying unto thee, Fear not; I will help thee (v.12).' Is. xli.15–16, 25 are on the same theme: the Servant will search out, enquire and judge, and, in justice, punish. The brings us to vv. 26–28, the Hebrew of which requires careful scrutiny. The Dead Sea Scroll readings are of interest, but the Masoretic Text remains our fixed point of reference.

xli.26: mî higîd mē ro'š wᵉnēdā'āh   ûmilᵉfānîm wᵉno'mar ṣadîq
         'af 'ên magîd 'af 'ên mašmîa'   'af 'ên šomᵉ'a 'imrêchem.

27: ri'šôn lᵉṣîyôn hinēh hinām   wᵉlîrûšālaim mᵉvaśēr 'etēn.

28: wᵉ'ēre' wᵉ'ên 'îš   ûmē'ēleh wᵉ'ên yô'ēṣ
     wᵉ'ešᵉ'ālēm   wᵉyāšîvû dāvār.

A literal translation:
'Who announced from the beginning and (i.e. so that) we know it? And from beforehand and (i.e. so that) we say "Just"? Indeed there is no announcer, indeed no proclaimer, indeed no one who hears the words you (plur.) speak. First to Sion, "Here they are, here they are". And to Jerusalem I shall give a bearer of good news. I looked but there is no

---

[16] See S. L. Edgar, 'New Testament and rabbinic messianic interpretation', *N. T. S.* 5 (1958/9), p. 50.

man; and among them, and there is no counsellor that shall answer a word when I ask. . .'

This passage is linked with Is. xlviii.5 in relation to God's persistent warnings and the utter nothingness of idols, and is concerned with the importance of the bringer of good tidings who is also a warner; and we have seen that the context is God's servant as judge and an avenger within the history of redemption. The Septuagint translators had some difficulties. But revisers made (it would seem) no improvements on their efforts. The LXX rendered v. 26 literally; v. 27 is handled differently: 'I shall give beginning/dominion to Sion and exhort Jerusalem towards the way', which is a clever paraphrase (r'šwn as if punning on r'š, head, king). It possibly took into account the rabbinical interpretation of that verse, viz. that it refers to the Messiah, who is the *first* referred to, and who will restore exiles to Jerusalem.[17] The LXX takes v. 28 to refer to the gentiles, the idolaters: 'Behold none of the nations, and from their idols there was no messenger (or reporter) (i.e. the idolaters have defaulted at the trial)'; the Hebrew leaves it vague who are those of whom a question is asked. The word yw'ṣ is taken by the LXX to mean a delegate, one who brings advice, rather than counsellor. The question is paraphrased and detached from the reporter/counsellor: 'And if I shall ask them (viz. the idols) "whence are you", they will not reply to me.' That the words καὶ ἐὰν ἐρωτήσω αὐτούς. . .οὐ μὴ ἀποκριθῶσίν μοι have some connection with Lk. xxii.68 was seen by Adolf Schlatter,[18] but he did not know what to make of that similarity of form. The latest researcher, who has given intensive study to our passage, is likewise unimpressed by it.[19] The Targum sticks much closer to the Hebrew text. The Dead Sea Scroll takes away two *waws*: at v. 26 we read the equivalent of 'we know it beforehand': at

---

[17] The name of the Messiah is revealed in Is. xli.27: b.Pes. 5a = Soncino trans., p. 17; the verse is messianic: Midr. Rabb. Gen. LXIII.8 = Sonc. 562; Midr. Rabb. Lev. XXX.16 = Sonc. 395. This has been widely known since A. Edersheim at the latest (*Life and Times of Jesus the Messiah*, London, 1906, ii, p. 726) who referred also to the Pesiqta. For confirmation see *Pesikta Rabbati*, trans. W. G. Braude, ii (New Haven, 1968), 860 (Piska 51.3). The Targum on Is. xli.27 (J. F. Stenning, *Targum of Isaiah*, 1953, p. 138) can indeed be taken to identify the bringer of good news with the Messiah as at xliii.10 it renders 'my servant' as 'my servant the Messiah'.

[18] A. Schlatter, *Lukas* (Stuttgart, 1931), p. 438. See also J. Schmid, *Das Evangelium nach Lukas³* (Regensburg, 1955), p. 340, and W. Grundmann, *Das Evangelium nach Lukas²* (Berlin, 1964), 418–20, both of whom ignore Schlatter's recognition of the parallel.

[19] G. Schneider (n. 5 above) at p. 35, n. 69.

v. 28 'I shall ask and they shall answer nothing'. The latter change, slight in itself, is helpful to us. Further at *v.* 27, by reading *hnwmh* instead of *hinām* the version seems to produce the meaning, 'First to Sion behold (him) who shall speak!' In other words the bringer of good tidings is actually introduced, instead of a sarcastic comment. However, this rendering, though adopted in the NEB, is not finally agreed.[20]

The concept of man's asking God, and God's hearing (and responding) is familiar.[21] God will answer even before he is called upon.[22] Along with this comes the equally familiar idea that God speaks, and is not listened to; God calls, and no one answers.[23] The theme has a relation to judgement. God will call upon the wicked to defend themselves: but they have nothing to say.[24] God's complaint is a variation of that that men are disobedient, like children who, if they hear in a literal sense, do not 'hear' in the sense of obeying. Of the Servant, on the other hand, it is said that he is a good learner and a good teacher (Is. 1.4). The orthodox Jewish pattern is to obey first and to understand the reasons afterwards.[25]

It remains to show how Is. xli.26–28 are related to Lk. xxii.66–68. Luke uses the word πρεσβυτέριον. The council of the nation was assembled; it is from such that counsel is to be expected; they were (after all) the council of Jesus' nation! The word *yo'ēṣ* fits well enough with this. πρεσβυτέριον occurs nowhere else in the New Testament except Acts xxii.5, where it has the same meaning, viz. the social and religious governing body of the Jews.[25a] As the word occurs only once in the LXX (Sus. 50) and then too in a different sense, and as Mk. (xiv.55) and Mt. (xxvi.59) are content with συνέδριον (not in a locative sense as in Luke), which would obscure the 'counselling' character of the assembly in question, note must

---

[20] A. Guillaume, 'Some readings in the Dead Sea Scrolls of Isaiah', *J. B. L.* 1957, pp. 40ff. J. R. Rosenbloom, *The Dead Sea Isaiah Scroll: A Literary Analysis* (Grand Rapids, 1970), pp. 50–1.

[21] Ps. xvii.6, xxvii.7, lxxxvi.7, xci.15; cii.2, cxxxviii.3; Is. lviii.9; Jer. xxxiii.3. Cf. Prov. i.28.

[22] Is. lxv.24. Cf. Job. xiv.15.

[23] Is.1.2, lix.16, lxiii.5, lxv.12, lxi.4; Jer. vii.13, 27, xxxv.17. Jer. xxxviii.15 (LXX xlv.15) is (*pace* Blinzler and Schneider) not relevant in substance, though, if we did not know of Is. xli.27–28, it might seem appropriate in context (which is in any case hardly significant in comparison with Jesus' predicament). Add Jer. xxii. 21 LXX.

[24] Job ix.3, 14, 15, 32, xxv.4, xxxi. 14, xl.4. Ps. cxxx.3, cxliii.2 (cf. Is. 1.8). See also, for the train of ideas, Job xxxiii.32.

[25] Ex. xxiv.7. Ps. cxi.10. b.Shab. 88. I. Grunfeld, Introd. to S. R. Hirsch, *Horeb* (London, 1962), I, lxxii–lxxiii.

[25a] See A. E. Harvey, *J. T. S.* 25/2, 1974, 323.

surely be taken of it.[26] It is not, further, the work of the High Priest, as in Mk. and Mt., to question Jesus, and to elicit the 'blasphemy' which (it is generally agreed) caused his transmission to Pilate and so to death. It is the anonymous body which puts the leading question. Luke himself omits the comment that the answer was blasphemous. Naturally, if I am right. The sequence of ideas is firmly hooked onto a prophecy from Isaiah and is therefore authentic. The commencement to the self-revelation is an assertion that Jesus is the Suffering Servant. That Luke so believed is known for certain from the quotation of Is. liii.12 at xxii.37.[27] Mark, of course, led him in this, for Mk. xiv.65 (= Lk. xxii.63–64) is based on Is. 1. 6.[28] This does not mean that Luke believed, any more than did Mark,[29] that Jesus, as the Servant, personified the New Israel. But the context of Is. xli certainly suggests polemic against the then elders of Israel as if they were idolaters.

The bringer of good tidings (cf. Is. xl.9) was identified with the Messiah by the rabbis, as we have seen, at least at Is. xli.27. The Servant would find that though he was the first to come and announce the good news he would look (for *w're'* can as easily be read 'and I shall look' as 'I looked') and find no one, viz. to believe him, to take him seriously. Incredulity is a characteristic of reception of the Servant: Is. liii.1 says 'Who has believed our report. . .?' and that this is to be taken in this sense in Christian midrash is evident from Pauline and Johannine use (see below). And Luke uses the verb πιστεύειν mostly in this manner (only vi.11 is an exception): Zechariah was punished for want of faith (i.20); the mother-to-be is praised for her faith (i.45); the persistent believers in the word are saved (viii.12–13); their belief saves others (viii.50); men such as our assembly did not believe in John the Baptist (xx.5: by common consent a relevant passage for comparison with ours); the disciples lacked faith in the (Christian interpretation of the) prophets (xiv.25: another highly relevant passage). Want of faith on earth is exactly what Christ feared (xviii.8). When he says what he is, he must be believed, or the fate of the Jews is the fate of the unbelieving!

[26] See A. F. J. Klijn, 'Scribes, Pharisees, Highpriests and Elders in the New Testament', *N. T.* 3 (1959), pp. 259–67.

[27] Lk. iv.18–19, xxii.27, 37, xxiii.35 (alluding to Is. xlii.1) are discussed by A. George at *R. B.* 72 (1965), 207.

[28] *Pace* Hooker, pp. 90–91. She is against the evangelists' having contrived to adapt the story to Isaiah. See C. Maurer, 'Knecht Gottes und Sohn Gottes im Passionsbericht des Markusevangeliums', *Z.Th.K.* 50 (1953), 1–38.

[29] P. Richardson, 'The Israel-idea in the Passion narratives', in E. Bammel, ed., *Trial of Jesus* (London, 1970), pp. 1ff., at p. 28.

Thus the Servant, when he came in the form of the Messiah, which is exactly what v. 67b seems to mean in response to 67a, will according to prophecy, find incredulity when he brings the good news. Luke is concerned to show, here as elsewhere, that the story of Salvation was foreordained.[30] Furthermore, when he puts questions to them to test their faithfulness (in both senses), he will find them without an answer. Not out of perversity, obstinacy, hostility, perhaps, but out of consciousness of guilt (as at 1 K. xviii.21), an absence of a defence. Not merely out of ignorance, but out of foreordained incompetence: no counsellor (σύμβουλος) can 'teach' the 'spirit of the Lord' (Is. xl.13–14)! The Hebrew 'eše'ālēm can well imply a semi-judicial enquiry. At all periods the root šā'al covers inquiries (into law as well as fact) besides the meaning 'beg, borrow'.[31] We have already noticed the highly curious episode of the fire by which Peter warmed himself:[32] Jesus was the true High Priest (so Mark suggests) and his triers were really the defendants in a trial conducted in effect by him. At that very time, says Luke (and not merely 'shortly'), the Messiah operates as judge.[33] Thus though they appear to be enquiring into Jesus, in reality his situation is an inquiry or challenge for them. They are silent because, if he questioned them, they would have no (adequate) answer to give, and it is amusing to note that St. Luke does indeed represent the 'council' as making no sort of answer to Jesus, irrespective of his amazing claims.

Thus, if I am right, Jesus asserts, in answer to the question whether he is the Christ, that he is the Servant come to judge, the Son of Man, and, letting the ambivalent terminology remain apparently on their lips (not his), the Son of God. What further need had they, or the church, of witness? His own testimony had declared all that needed to be known.

---

[30] H. Conzelmann, cited above. Schneider, cited above, at pp. 174–81. S. Schulz, 'Gottes Vorsehung bei Lukas', Z. N. W. 54 (1963), pp. 104–16. One notes especially Lk. xxiv.46; Acts iii.18, xxvi.23.

[31] M. Jastrow, Dictionary II, pp. 1506–7. ἐρωτάω itself has the sense of cross-question in dialectic: Liddell-Scott-Jones, Lexicon, s. v. II. 2. The note of M. Polus, Synopsis Criticorum IV (London, 1669), col. 1114 is worth reproducing in part: 'sed interrogandi munus proprium est judicis ac proinde nec Christus eas partes sibi sumerit, nec id negari sibi quereretur. (quid ergo dicendum? 1. Sensus est) Si qua argumenta proponam quibus me Christum probem. Argumenta enim Hebraei, non minus quam Graeci, solebant interrogando. Saepe ita utitur Sextus philosophus, et hinc apud Aristotelem fallacia plurium interrogationum. . . 2. Verbum hoc ex Haebraeorum usu sumendum: quibus τὸ sh'l est agere cum aliquo. . .'

[32] Derrett, Law in the New Testament (London, 1970), pp. 410–11.

[33] This meaning may be read into the verb 'sitting': Liddell-Scott-Jones Lexicon, καθίζω II.3. Ps. ix.4. See also Sim. Enoch for the son of Man and Judgment.

St. John certainly believed that Jesus was the Servant: Is. liii.1 is quoted at Jn. xii.38 and is the *reason* why Jesus' signs were not believed. Isaiah had foretold the incredulity (Jn. xii.37–41). That this was common Christian tradition is evident from the same appearing at Rom. x.16. It is significant that Paul refers to Is. liii.1 immediately after he uses Is. lii.7, a verse that refers back to Is. xl.9 and xli.27. Jn. xviii.19–23 looks at first sight like a rather lame development of Lk. xxii.67–68,[34] but the 'Lucan' passage in fact appears at Jn. x.24 (the Jews) – 39. The connection of the incredulity theme with shepherds and flocks could well be traced to Is. xl.11, where the one who brings good news is indeed Sion's shepherd.

Appended Note : The above was written in ignorance of the midrash on Is. 1.2 to be found at Midr. R. Cant. I.12, §. 2. The text is there represented as a complaint on God's part that when he assembled the Children of Israel to receive the Law at Mt. Sinai, after giving them ample warning of what would take place, he discovered that they were asleep. This is why trumpets were needed to bring them to their senses. The divine complaint of the heedlessness of Israel even after she has been warned, and at the moment when a new covenant is about to be given to her seems by no means out of place in the mouth of Christ at the climax of his 'confrontation' with his 'enemies'.

---

[34] As if Jesus' testimony would be of no ´avail (as might well be the case). So Perry. It is understandable that Jn. xviii is not considered by P. Borgen at *N. T. S.* 5 (1958–9), pp. 246–9 or I. Buse at *N. T. S.* 7 (1960–1), pp. 65–76 (both on Jn. and the Passion narratives in the synoptics).

CURSING JESUS (I COR. XII. 3): THE JEWS AS RELIGIOUS 'PERSECUTORS'

The many recent studies[1] of the inauspicious and mysterious phrase ΑΝΑΘΕΜΑ ΙΗΣΟΥΣ leave its implications uncertain. Cullmann believed[2] it reflected persecution (by, he surmised, pagans); others that it referred to the behaviour of Christians under spirit-possession,[3] shouts in a Jewish synagogue,[4] a gratuitous proposition of Paul's own to make a contrast with the confession of faith,[5] or an esoteric test by gnostics keen that the earthly Jesus should be denied.[6] Powerfully propounded,[7] this last suggestion is now more or less abandoned.[8] As so often, ingenuity revels where cultural information is scanty. In my view Paul refers *primarily* to an ἀρχισυνάγωγος reported to have tutored a Jewish Christian to say these words in order to save his (the latter's) membership of the community. The last and critical step required by disciplinarians of the synagogue, this procedure would be called διωγμός, which can be translated as well by 'prosecution' as by 'persecution', seeing that religious and social laws were bound to overlap in that context. In

---

[1] K. Maly, 'I Kor. 12. 1–3, eine Regel zur Unterscheidung der Geister', *B.Z.* x (1966), 82–95. J. C. Hurd, *The Origins of 1 Corinthians* (London, 1965), pp. 186–95, places the problem in its scholarly context. C. K. Barrett, *A Commentary on the First Epistle to the Corinthians* (London, 1968), pp. 279–80; also his *Holy Spirit and the Gospel Tradition* (London, 1947), p. 106. T. Holtz, 'Das Kennzeichen des Geistes (1 Kor. xii. 1–3)', *N.T.S.* xviii (1971–2), 365–76. W. C. van Unnik, 'Jesus: Anathema or Kyrios', in B. Lindars and S. S. Smalley, edd., *Christ and the Spirit in the New Testament. Moule Festschrift* (Cambridge, 1973), pp. 113–26, is most ingenious. E. E. Ellis's attempt to link the spirits with angels requires reconsideration: *N.T.S.* xx, 2 (1974), 128 ff., at 132–4.

[2] O. Cullmann, *Les premières confessions de foi chrétiennes*, 2nd ed. (Paris, 1948), pp. 22, 23. He guessed that renegades would claim the Spirit taught them to do this. See Merkel at p. 551 n. 9 below and Lampe (1973) for the guess (after Freudenberger, p. 549 n. 6 below, p. 150) that I Cor. xii. 3 may refer to Jewish persecution. That Jews were the first persecutors was the view of J. Jocz, *The Jewish People and Jesus Christ* (London, 1954), p. 43. Hare's sustained criticism (see below, p. 545 n. 1) of Harnack does not succeed in removing the main accusation. It is curious that he does not mention I Cor. xii. 3!

[3] Lietzmann, *Z.N.T.W.* (1923), 262. A. Deissmann, *Paul* (London, 1926), p. 79. Barrett (1968). See R. Scroggs (n. 8 below) (freedom in the spirit; no devaluation of the earthly Jesus (!!)). W. Bousset, *Kyrios Christos*, 5th ed. (Göttingen, 1965), 87 (perhaps ecstatic).

[4] For references see Hurd, n. 1 above.

[5] G. de Broglie, 'Le texte fondamental de Saint Paul contre la foi naturelle (I Cor. xii. 3)', *R.S.R.* xxxix (1951–2), 253–66. He approves the interpretation of Moffatt and Holtzmann. H. D. Wendland, *Das Neue Testament Deutsch* 7. *Die Briefe an die Korinther* (Göttingen, 1962), 92–3; Barrett (1968), ubi cit. n. 1 supra; H. Conzelmann, *Der erste Brief an die Korinther* (Göttingen, 1969), 241. The sophisticated notion that Jesus *ought* to be called accursed, since he was 'a curse', hardly convinces, though its ingenuity is attractive: W. Grundmann in J. Murphy-O'Connor, ed. *Paul and Qumran* (London, 1968), 101; van Unnik adds that though Jesus *was* anathema he is now much more. Alas, the idea that Jesus ever *was* anathema is fine-spun theologizing by Paul, and here, if ever there was one, is a case where the reading of theology into a text is dangerous. Knox, p. 549, n. 3 infra.

[6] See next note.

[7] W. Schmithals, *Die Gnosis in Korinth*, 2nd ed. (Göttingen, 1965), 117–22 (English trans., Nashville, 1971, 124–30). U. Wilckens, *Weisheit und Torheit* (Tübingen, 1959), 121 n. 1. N. Brox, '"ΑΝΑΘΕΜΑ ΙΗΣΟΥΣ" (1. Kor. 12. 3)', *B.Z.* xii (1968), 103–11 (a Gnostic *confessio*).

[8] R. Scroggs, 'The exaltation of the spirit by some early Christians', *J.B.L.* lxxxiv (1965), 359–73 (the church exalted its possession of the spirit). K. Maly (cit. sup.). B. A. Pearson, 'Did the Gnostics curse Jesus?', *J.B.L.* lxxxvi (1967), 301–5. Conzelmann (cit. sup.).

my view the Old Testament framework within which Paul's discussion is to be read is Deut. xviii. 17–22 (cf. I John iv. 1), and he is in the course of replying to a general question how one may know whether a Christian has the gift of the Spirit, given that piety and prophetic power are claimed to survive *sub modo* in elders authoritatively expounding scripture. Paul's reply is neat and sarcastic, and has not been explained so far.

Studies, ignoring Juster and Tcherikover, proceed upon the questions of persecution and church discipline,[1] and Professor Lampe has investigated Peter's denial.[2] Persecution figures *passim* in the New Testament, and many think it was exaggerated there in the interests of ancient theology. Could it have been a juridical phenomenon before Nero? Were Paul's activities against the church[3] not exaggerated after all? Can we exempt from essential editorial activity those passages in the gospels which allude to[4] prophesy,[5] and relate[6] persecution,[7] however much the vocabulary and location of the passages may owe to that procedure? From what will appear below it will not at all surprise us that *prophets* figure amongst those marked out for persecution,[8] and whether this goes back to the time of Jesus must remain an open question!

The studies of Lampe, Hare and van Unnik leave small gaps, filled (it is hoped) now with an extended footnote to all of them. A translation-paraphrase of I Cor. xii. 1–3 is left until near the end. We must briefly re-create the situation in which the churches of the diaspora found themselves.

Jerusalem maintained contact, by letters and their bearers, with synagogues of different complexions, all of which sent their Temple-dues to the centre. Whatever the composition of ethnic Jews, proselytes and Godfearers

---

[1] G. W. H. Lampe, 'Church discipline and the interpretation of the Epistles to the Corinthians (1 Cor. 5. 1–6)', in W. R. Farmer and others, edd., *Christian History and Interpretation: Studies Presented to John Knox* (Cambridge, 1967), pp. 337–61. D. R. A. Hare, *The Theme of Jewish Persecution of Christians in the Gospel according to St Matthew* (Cambridge, 1967) strictly disciplines unauthentic claims about Jewish persecution.

[2] G. W. H. Lampe, 'St Peter's denial', *B.J.R.L.* LV, 2 (1973), 346–8.

[3] διώκω: Gal. i. 13, 23; Phil. iii. 6 (διώκων); Acts ix. 1–5 (διώκεις), 13, xxii. 7–8, xxvi. 11 (πολλάκις τιμωρῶν αὐτοὺς ἠνάγκαζον βλασφημεῖν, περισσῶς τε ἐμμαινόμενος αὐτοῖς ἐδίωκον ἕως καὶ εἰς τὰς ἔξω πόλεις), 14–15. Oepke, *T.W.N.T.* II, 229–30. L.S.J., *Lex.*, s.v. IV, shows that διώκω also means to prosecute as a plaintiff. Hare would write the word down as (merely) 'harass', which is whitewashing.

[4] διωγμός (see also below, n. 6): Mark iv. 17/Matt. xiii. 21 (note Luke's *comment*: it is a trial, in both senses πειρασμός); διωγμοί: Mark x. 30; Rom. viii. 35; II Cor. xii. 10; II Thess. i. 4; II Tim. iii. 11. Rom. xii. 14 is interesting as it brings persecution and cursing into juxtaposition.

[5] δεδιωγμένοι Matt. v. 10; διώξωσιν...ἕνεκεν ἐμοῦ (11); v. 44 (διωκόντων), x. 23. Mark iii 9; (ἕνεκεν ἐμοῦ)/Luke xxi. 12 (διώξουσιν...ἕνεκεν τοῦ ὀνόματός μου); Matt. xxiii. 34/Luke xi. 49. John xv. 20, xvi. 2. The best corroboration comes from parallel ideas *without* the technical vocabulary: persecution begins in the home: Mark xiii. 12–13/Matt. x. 21–2/Luke xxi. 16–17.

[6] διωγμός: Acts viii. 1. The position is correctly stated at John ix. 22, xii. 42 (see below). In Acts xiii. 50 the word has both spiritual and secular connotations. So John v. 16?

[7] As supplied by critical scholars referred to by Hare, *op. cit.* pp. 19, 85 ff.

[8] ἐδίωξαν τοὺς προφήτας τοὺς πρὸ ὑμῶν(!): Matt. v. 12. προφήταις: Luke vi. 23. Matt. xxiii. 34/Luke xi. 49 (on which see G. Klein, 'Die Verfolgung der Apostel, Luk. 11. 49', *Neues Testament und Geschichte ...Oscar Cullmann zum 70. Geburtstag* (Zürich/Tübingen, 1973), pp. 113–24). I Thess. ii. 15–16 is important and difficult: see O. Michel in W. Eckert and others, edd., *Antijudaismus im Neuen Testament?* (Munich, 1967), pp. 50–9; E. Bammel, 'Judenverfolgung und Naherwartung', *Z.T.K.* LVI (1959), 294–315 (it may not relate to specific past acts, but chiefly dwell on the signs of the End).

(Jos. *Bell.* vii. 3. 3), the theoretical unity of the whole was unquestioned. In all parts of the Empire the race[1] was entitled to privileges of cultural, political and economic value;[2] the Romans allowed these to proselytes also.[3] The stability of the Jewish residential communities[4] depended on their not forfeiting those privileges. Sources of tension were pervasive: quite apart from purely religious problems, the solidarity and continuity of the Jews with the *ethnos* having its headquarters in Jerusalem[5] was an ideal of which no synagogue elders could ever lose sight. Hare's realistic comments on the effects of religious schism are entirely in point. My own experience of a caste society in which inbreeding is practised and a distinctive speech, clothing, diet, and the worship of a common and peculiar deity in a common fashion are essential prerequisites of reserved occupations and livelihoods, and my professional interest in the phenomenon of 'excommunication' (a living issue in Indian politics and sociology) have made it easy for me to visualize the Jews' dilemma.

The first Christians thought they were purifying Judaism from within.[6] Did they anticipate that overseas Jews would be faced with schism as a consequence? Could the problem have presented itself, if at all, realistically? The privileges rested upon the *race*, though they could be renounced. But since they related specifically to the practice of the Jewish religion-and-law (often called simply *nomoi*) no one who ceased to profess the religion by actively professing one evidently inconsistent with it could claim its privileges. John ix. 22 is thus realistic not merely for Judaea but for the diaspora also: ἤδη γὰρ συνετέθεντο οἱ 'Ιουδαῖοι ἵνα ἐάν τις αὐτὸν (sc. 'Ιησοῦν) ὁμολογήσῃ Χριστόν, ἀποσυνάγωγος γένηται, i.e. he would be excommunicated. Self-governing communities, in which the synagogue played the role of townhall as well as church, must insist upon a decent minimum requirement of orthodoxy, conformity. Otherwise all might lose the rights which their religion had purchased for them, not only to practise their religion but to live within their whole cultural tradition. Relations with their pagan neighbours were

---

[1] J. Juster, *Les Juifs dans l'Empire Romain. Leurs Conditions juridique, économique et sociale* i (Paris, 1914), 232–3. V. Tcherikover, *Hellenistic Civilization and the Jews* (Philadelphia/Jerusalem, 1959) is of great value (see pt. ii, ch. 2).

[2] Juster, i, 354 ff. Tcherikover, pp. 306–8, 325, 332.

[3] Juster, i, 233 n. 1. Referring to Josephus, *Ant.* xiv. 10. 13–16 Juster explains the need for, and point in, excommunicating Christians. See the behaviour of Samaritans as explained by Josephus, *Ant.* xi. 8 (341). That the practice of excommunicating 'idolaters' existed long before Christ is proved by CD xix. 34–xx. 13 (Lohse, *Die Qumran Texte*, 102–5). All the 'Saints of the Most High' have *cursed* (er⁽ᵉ⁾rûhû) them.

[4] It is not known how many Jews in the diaspora lived in non-Jewish environments, but the orthodox will always have tended to congregate together. Tcherikover, pp. 304–5, 308.

[5] Juster, i, 414–15, 418, 422–4. Josephus's particulars at *Ant.* xiv. 115–17 regarding the judicial powers of Jewish communities have been overlooked since Juster. The correct analogy is with the Millet system known in the Ottoman Empire. See Juster, ii, 110–12. Gallio (Acts xviii. 15) understood the Jews to have exclusive domestic competence, or so Luke understood this would be believed without doubt.

[6] P. Richardson, *Israel in the Apostolic Church* (Cambridge, 1969). Gal. vi. 16; Rom. ix. 6; Jas. i. 1; 1 Pet. i. 1, ii. 9; Heb. xiii. 22–4.

delicate; proselytism was a part of Judaism[1] (as it is of Christianity)[2] but the Jews undertook not to insult non-Jewish religions.[3] It was not impossible that, in course of time, Rome might extend the ethnic concept 'the Jews' to include a new sect which welcomed proselytes of all races on terms which waived observance of the Sabbath, the dietary laws and circumcision, and which, on the contrary, required the worship of a dead Messiah whom it related in some poorly defined way to the Deity. But the former recipients of rich proselytes would take note of the competition. The difficulties, however, might be ignored by a group professing to be disinterested in worldly matters. Further, the church, taking Jesus to be Messiah, called him *kyrios*, which was a royal title regularly appropriated to the emperor.[4] The possibility of misunderstanding arose very early. Whether Jesus himself encouraged the belief that he was the Messiah (I believe he did) is beside our present point.

The new sect must sooner or later drive trustees of synagogues into some attempt (not necessarily efficient or apt) to make them conform. John ix. 34–5 (ἐξέβαλον αὐτὸν ἔξω) expresses to my mind a historical fact, viz. politically and socially motivated conformism – the passage must be read along with John xi. 48 which (though it is St John's own reconstruction) seems verbally accurate: ἐὰν ἀφῶμεν αὐτὸν οὕτως, πάντες πιστεύσουσιν εἰς αὐτόν, καὶ ἐλεύσονται οἱ Ῥωμαῖοι καὶ ἀροῦσιν ἡμῶν καὶ τὸν τόπον καὶ τὸ ἔθνος. The excruciating irony in both protasis and apodosis is beside our present point.

This must be understood from the inside. Judaism was familiar with sects of severe purity, e.g. the Pharisees and the Qumran sect. Hare is right: they posed no such strident threat as did the Christians. Yet tensions certainly existed (Acts xxiii. 6–10) between groups all of whom acknowledged portions of the Hebrew scriptures. 'Conformity' therefore did not mean anything approaching comprehensive agreement. The governing bodies of the *ethnos* comprised men of various persuasions or none. But a group which flouted universal practices, denounced individual rulers, spiritual and temporal, and tendered as its own leader a human being (i.e. not a synod or company), came obviously within the scope of the Law's provisions against 'rebellious elders'.[5] The position was worse if that leader had led an apocalyptic, messianic movement, and deserved his death penalty by a flagrant breach of

[1] W. G. Braude, *Jewish Proselyting in the First Five Centuries of the Common Era* (Providence, 1940). B. J. Bamberger, *Proselytism in the Talmudic Period* (Cincinnati, 1939).

[2] A recent decision of the Orissa High Court (India) holds, after lengthy examination of the Bible and 'Vatican II' that Christians have the right, under Art. 25 of the Constitution, to propagate their religion, provided they did not interfere with public order, morality or health, and a local statute, passed in order to prosecute/persecute Christians, was struck down as *ultra vires*. The modern Gallio is obliged to accept jurisdiction in the 'secular state'.

[3] Juster, I, 233. Jos. *Ant.* XIX. 5. 2, 3 (190); *Con. Ap.* II. 237. On the delicacy of Jewish–pagan relations see W. C. van Unnik, 'Die Anklagen gegen die Apostel in Philippi', *Mullus. Fests. Th. Klauser* (Jahrb. Ant. Christ., Ergänzungsbd. 1) (Münster/W., 1964), pp. 366–73. W. H. C. Frend, *Martyrdom and Persecution in the Early Church* (Oxford, 1965), ch. 3.

[4] Juster, I, 343. Philo, *Leg.* 45. Cullmann, ubi cit., 21.   [5] See e.g. Deut. xvii. 11–13, xviii. 20.

generally accepted religious rules. The traditional elders would be under a conscientious as well as political duty to retrieve the scattered flock from its dangerous antisocial path. Those that led the people astray had been denounced from the time of the book of Deuteronomy at the latest. Moreover, inordinate affection for a human being is idolatry and its consequences could only be evil.[1]

All religious groups living within a more or less tolerant and would-be neutral state possessed and possess the power of excommunication, cutting off (cf. διχοτομεῖν at Matt. xxiv. 51 = Luke xii. 46!) the offender (if he did not conform) from the privileges vested in the group. It is usually insufficient. The existence of the power in Jesus's day cannot be doubted:[2] the technical vocabulary is present;[3] what is less clear is what procedure(s) might be employed. Some of our texts may have been overdrawn and to that extent confuse the issue, but the 'editors' certainly alluded to known practices. Before applying excommunication, which is always the ultimate weapon in the armoury, other measures were (we can assume) tried, e.g. a 'disciplinary flogging',[4] such as is constantly referred to in Maimonides's *Code*. Paul, it seems, underwent this. It is clear why. He first preached in synagogues as a Pharisee, and then, unless prevented by those who knew his methods, went on to preach Jesus not only as the Messiah but as the crucified into the bargain.[5]

Hare makes much of the lack of evidence that non-missionary Christians were flogged or excommunicated (the passages in John being left out of account). It is enough for us that the Christian *prophet* was in danger and forced to abjure. In the time of Bar Kochba closely similar methods seem to have been used with ordinary Christians,[6] and Justin[7] speaks of a more systematic kind of 'persecution'. The threat posed by the presence of a Christian prophet *inside* a traditional synagogue must have entailed a warning, a flogging, and, ultimately, excommunication if he did not abjure

---

[1] Correctly Rom. i. 23, 25; Col. iii. 5; cf. Gal. v. 20; I Cor. v. 11, vi. 9. W. D. Davies, *Paul and Rabbinic Judaism* (London, 1948), pp. 29–30. 'Idol' means 'false god': I John v. 21.

[2] Paul applied anathema himself: I Cor. v. 2, 4–5, 13. For CD xix. 34–xx. 13 see p. 546 n. 3 above. Simeon b. Sheṭaḥ (1st cent. B.C.) threatened Ḥoni with *niddwy* (Mishnah, Taanit, iii. 8).

[3] ἀφορίσωσιν (Mark vi. 22), ἐκβάλωσιν (ibid.), John xii. 42 (οὐχ ὡμολόγουν), xvi. 2. All instances of ἐκβάλλειν may be scrutinized to see whether they covertly allude to excommunication: Matt. viii. 12, xxi. 39, xxii. 13, xxv. 30? Hare would interpret the word as 'social ostracism', but could this be effected without an institutional act, seeing that to separate oneself from a 'brother' was socially and religiously objectionable?

[4] *makkat mardût*. Matt. x. 17, xx. 19, xxiii. 34; Acts v. 40–1; II Cor. xi. 24. Hare's scepticism of this penalty is traceable to his reluctance to admit exclusive competence in the synagogue with reference to moral offences. The NT sources are here corroborated by later, but culturally continuous information. Epiphanius, *Haer.* xxx. 11 (PG 41. 423). Maimonides (p. 551 n. 9 inf.), vii. 1 (stripes are usually more appropriate than excommunication). Juster, ii, 161. Z. H. Chajes, *Student's Guide* (London, 1952), p. 35.

[5] I Cor. i. 23, ii. 2. To preach Jesus as Lord was attributed to apostles in Palestine also: Acts ii. 36, x. 36.

[6] Justin, I. *Apol.* 31. 6. Hare makes political aspects more significant than religious aspects here: true, but *we* are interested in the formula at I Cor. xii. 3.   [7] *Dial.* 117 (see next note).

by cursing Jesus – that being the method established in the periods just referred to.

The stumbling-block for the 'orthodox' synagogue was not so much the novelty of the method by which pious, revivalist concepts were propounded, but the very fact (emissaries would insist)[1] that Jesus was himself rejected by the Jewish authorities, not indeed by any formal ban, but by sentence to be handed over to the power possessing the *ius gladii*, as a sequel to manifest blasphemy.[2] He was crucified and thus exemplified the scriptural notion that he who is impaled is accursed.[3] Furthermore he failed to confirm the words of the Law, as Deut. xxvii. 26 puts it. On two counts at least Jesus was accursed. Ἀνάθεμα, a word about which there is no doubt, means 'under a ban', 'accursed'.[4] To associate with such a person is a sin in itself.

It would be wrong to think of the trustees as glad to expel a schismatic. Unless a 'prophetically' gifted Christian (as at Acts xviii. 26) went out, or were silenced, schism was inevitable. The post-Mishnaic Hebrew word for apostatizing is semantically interesting: *šamad* means both 'to cut off' (cf. διχοτομεῖν above) and 'to destroy';[5] to leave one's religious community was social and political destruction (the same is the case in South Asia today, with results only now beginning to be regarded as anachronistic). No word approximately equivalent to our (voluntarily) 'apostatizing' seems to have existed earlier, and it is not clear that even later it was possible to avoid the overtones of compulsion. Now new synagogues founded by and for proselytes who favoured this new persuasion might feel no inconvenience with these 'prophets', perhaps the contrary; but if they were allowed to continue the normal intercommunion with the orthodox, traditional synagogues the whole *ethnos* would be compromised, and pogroms might ultimately be threatened.

Pliny's well-known letter to Trajan[6] strongly suggests that Romans learnt

---

[1] *Dial.* 17. 1, 108. 2. These may be taken as typical. There is no need to hesitate to date the practice back to Paul's time since Paul himself was sent as an envoy καὶ τοῖς ἔξω!

[2] Derrett, *Law in the New Testament* (London, 1970), pp. 424–5, 453–5. Hare avoids considering the effects of Jesus's own utterance before the meeting. J. C. O'Neill, 'The charge of blasphemy at Jesus's trial before the Sanhedrin', in E. Bammel, ed., *The Trial of Jesus* (London, 1970), pp. 72–7 ignores Jesus's provocative words. What I Tim. i. 19–20 means is not clear, but their 'blasphemy' of something or someone (Paul himself?) made him curse or excommunicate them.

[3] Gal. iii. 13. I should unhesitatingly link Deut. xxi. 23 with Lev. xxiv. 16 since Josephus does so: *Ant.* iv. 202. See 4QpNah. 7 f. (G. Jeremias, *Der Lehrer der Gerechtigkeit*, Göttingen, 1963, pp. 134–5). The notion that the curse undergone by Jesus terminated the curse at Deut. xxvii. 26 and enabled believers to revert to the promise made to Abraham is explained by W. L. Knox, *St Paul and the Church of Jerusalem* (Cambridge, 1925), p. 230 n. 19.

[4] For ἀναθεματίζω see C.I.Att., App. (I.G. III. 2), pp. xiii f., R. Wünsch, *Antike Fluchtafeln*, Kl.T. xx (1912), no. 1 (p. 5 nn.). G. A. Deissmann, *Light from the Ancient East* (London, 1927), p. 95. Juster, II, 159–60. Ch. Michel, 'Anathème', D.A.C. I, 1926–1940. Behm, *T.W.N.T.* I, 354–5. On its figuring (as in the Birkat-ha-Minim) as a liturgical factor (G. Bornkamm, *Early Christian Experience*, London, 1969, pp. 169–70) I feel bound to reserve doubts.

[5] Jastrow, *Dict.*, 1591–2.

[6] Pliny, *Epp.* 10. 96 (maledicerent Christo, Christo maledixerunt). D. Ayerst and A. S. T. Fisher, edd., *Records of Christianity*, I (Oxford, 1971), 14–16. A. N. Sherwin-White, *The Letters of Pliny* (Oxford, 1966), pp. 691–710, esp. 700–1. The same, 'Early persecutions and Roman law again',

from 'orthodox' Jews that refusal to curse Jesus would detect a Christian who, by that period, could no longer take advantage of the Jews' privileges to ignore the state cults. The formula[1] seems to have been put by the 'inquisitor' to the accused, and to save his life (as in our period his status) he must repeat it verbatim, denying his saviour.[2] At our period the ἀρχισυνά-γωγος might well explain how and in what sense Jesus was 'accursed'. The suspect might be bold enough to reply that Antiochus Epiphanes had provided the Jews with martyrs, who were currently honoured like the children in the fiery furnace before Nebuchadnezzar. If he thrice refused solemnly to say 'Cursed is Jesus' he could be thrown out. Since 'persecution' was thought by Christians to be a sign of the End the process might get out of hand. Especially with young members, it might be more politic to flog them at intervals until they came to a sounder frame of mind. At what stage Paul's contemporaries would go to the Roman authorities for help to supplement their internal sanctions we do not know.

Christians, whether Jewish or non-Jewish (Acts x. 45; Gal. iii. 1–6) claimed to be 'Israel' and therefore still technically 'Ιουδαῖοι. This is the burden (as B. S. Easton showed in 1955) of the story in Acts xiii–xxviii: their religion was the *religio licita*. Could individuals curse Jesus formally in order to conserve their financial position and still remain, and even prophesy (!) in the church? Could they appropriate to themselves I Chron. xvi. 21–2: '...touch not mine anointed ones and do my prophets no harm'?! To honour elders is a religious duty; not to separate from one's community is also an ancient spiritual and social obligation.[3] Would what seemed a mini-mum compliance be fatal to the new status of Christian? If not, why not? The church believed[4] that it had the revived gift of the Spirit.[5] Gospel texts then circulating (in an unknown form) may have contained something like the information they now give us on the subject. Ordinary people 'prophesied'. It is difficult to grasp the effect on a community understanding, by 'edu-

---

J.T.S. III, 2 (1952), 199 ff. Mr Sherwin-White informs me (16 July 1973) that there was no *Roman* persecution of Christians anywhere (so far as we know) during the period when I Corinthians must have been written. G. E. M. de Ste-Croix, 'Why were the Early Christians persecuted?', *Past & Present* 26 (1963), 6. P. Freudenberger, *Das Verhalten der römischen Behörden gegen die Christen* (Munich, 1967).

[1] Does ἀποστοματίζω at Luke xi. 53 recall the process of putting to a suspect a formula which he must accept or reject? The verb normally means to teach to repeat by word of mouth: Plato, *Ethyd.* 276c, 277a, and therefore to correct mistakes in repetition, tutoring. ἀποστομίζω means 'know by heart', 'be word-perfect': Or., *sel. in Jes.* (6. 26) (PG 12. 824B).

[2] Lampe (1967), 355.   [3] Mishnah, Avot II. 5(4).

[4] And therefore valued (Acts viii. 20). There need be no doubt but that they believed that the Spirit was conferred in baptism (Matt. iii. 16, cf. Acts viii. 16–17): A. Wikenhauser, *Pauline Mysticism* (Freiburg/Edinburgh, 1956), p. 119, refers to I Cor. vi. 11, xii. 13.

[5] See references at G. Vermes, *Jesus the Jew* (London, 1973), p. 91 n. 30. Hence the widespread concern about false prophets: citations at Lampe (1967), p. 361, also G. W. H. Lampe, 'Grievous wolves', *Christ and the Spirit* (above, p. 544 n. 1), pp. 253–68. On the significance of the coming of the Spirit as anticipation of the End see G. B. Caird, *The Apostolic Age* (London, 1955/1966), p. 58. On blasphemy of the Spirit as suggesting 'false prophet'/'deceiver'/μάγος see the rich material at K. Berger, 'Die königlichen Messias-Traditionen des N.T.', *N.T.S.* xx, 1 (1973), at p. 10 n. 38. I set store by Acts iii. 25: ὑμεῖς ἐστε οἱ υἱοὶ τῶν προφητῶν.

cation', only rote-learning, the sudden appearance of untutored, spontaneous religious utterance. When one of these gifted ones was publicly accused the texts seem to have said that he *must* trust to the Spirit for his defence.[1] Ironically this was not to save him from a penalty, but as a witness for the faith.[2] The common Jewish principle that the Name must be glorified[3] was understood by the church[4] as requiring that their risen Lord must be *confessed* and *testified to* on all such solemn occasions![5] Jesus himself, so it was said, made this confession[6] at the climax of his testimony, and so supplied the pattern.

It could hardly be argued that those who cursed Jesus under pressure were possessors of the Spirit any more than those that tutored them with the obnoxious formula. Above all those *were* possessors who said 'Jesus is Lord!' (Rom. x. 9). The Spirit gave many gifts, but it was not present in one who actually cursed Jesus: not a naïve, or gross judgement, as has been suggested, for the Spirit is a matter of *utterance* (not calculated thought) after all! We do not know how Paul would have treated one who 'failed' the test: perhaps he would have readmitted him subject to penance. We know that Paul would excommunicate offenders whose presence in the church he felt noxious.[7]

One might, indeed, suspect that hope of early reintegration was held out to the 'failures' by the story of St Peter. After Lampe's description,[8] Peter's denial strikes one as having been constructed as an independent story, a pattern of the ironic futility of the threefold solemn abjuration of the Lord – he actually cursed Jesus.[9] Could this legitimately comfort renegades? No! Momentary enthusiasms apart, the builder of the story assures us, the Old Israel, when it came to the pinch, denied (as she still denies) that Jesus is Lord. But the New Israel, the true Israel, is permanently hinged to the Old in the person of Peter, the great witness to the Resurrection.

[1] Mark xiii. 11–12/Matt. x. 17–20/Luke xii. 11–12, xxi. 14–15. S. Schulz, *Q* (Zurich, 1972), pp. 442–4. See John xiv. 26. The procedure is actually illustrated at I Cor. ii. 3–5!

[2] Lampe (cited p. 545 n. 5 above), p. 355.

[3] Lev. x. 3; Ezek. xxviii. 22; Hag. i. 8; Isa. xlix. 3 ('Thou art my servant, Israel, in whom I will be glorified').

[4] Matt. v. 16, xv. 31; Luke xxiii. 47; John xii. 28, xiv. 13, xv. 8, xvii. 1, 4; Rom. xv. 9; Gal. i. 24; II Thess. i. 12; I Pet. iv. 11.

[5] Lampe (1967), p. 355. The technical words are ὁμολογέω, μαρτυρέω or, on the contrary, ἀρνεῖσθαι. See II Macc. vi. 6.

[6] I Tim. vi. 13. The 'confession' = 'not denying' image is to be found *passim* in our texts, e.g. John i. 20; Rom. x. 9. The Jews *denied* Christ before Pilate: Acts iii. 13 (Cullmann, ubi cit., pp. 20–1). On the theme see K. Berger, cit. sup., p. 550 n. 5, at pp. 18–20. See Rev. iii. 8–9 (trial at v. 10!).

[7] I Cor. xvi. 22; Gal. i. 8; Rom. ix. 3; I Cor. v. 11.

[8] G. W. H. Lampe, 'St Peter's denial' (cit. sup.).

[9] Presumably saying '*ārūr*: CD xx. 8; b. Shev. 36a (Judg. v. 23). Maimonides, *Mishneh Torah* I, *Study of Torah*, 6, 4 (b. M. Q. 17a, Soncino trans. p. 106; j. M. Q. III. 81a, b). The synagogue formula will have been 'J. *meḥaram*' (he has been accursed/excommunicated). M. Arm, *Histoire de l'excommunication Juive* (Nîmes, 1882). Jesus is alleged to have been put under a ban (b. Sanh. 107b), but this is irrelevant even if it reflects post-A.D. 135 practice. A. Schlatter, *Paulus*, 3rd ed. (Stuttgart, 1962), p. 333. Lampe (1967), p. 357. H. Merkel, 'Peter's curse', in E. Bammel, ed., *The Trial of Jesus* (cit. sup.), pp. 66–71 (rightly connecting οὐκ οἶδα τὸν ἄνθρωπον [cf. Matt. xxv. 12; Luke xiii. 25, 27!?] with ostracism, see b. M. Q. 16a).

Jesus must have known that his novel movement, with its peculiar rituals and millenarian programme, would produce conflict with any social organization then known, for totally 'neutral' states did not exist. 'Blasphemy' of, i.e. denigrating (including cursing) Jesus was, as he is represented as saying more precisely in Luke (xii. 10) than in Mark (iii. 28, cf. ix. 39), not a desperately serious matter and could be forgiven;[1] but to deny the Spirit upon which the church was founded (as Ananias did in contrast with 'the apostles': Acts v. 3, cf. 32) was to disqualify oneself for the Messiah's banquet. In one place (II Cor. iii. 17) Paul equates Jesus, the Lord, with the Spirit, and indeed denial of Jesus is in one place said to be fatal. Matt. x. 33 (ὅστις δ' ἂν ἀρνήσηταί με ἔμπροσθεν τῶν ἀνθρώπων, ἀρνήσομαι κἀγὼ αὐτὸν ἔμπροσθεν τοῦ πατρός μου ἐν τοῖς οὐρανοῖς) is more harsh than Matt. xii. 31, which can be taken as an extended (as well as casuistical?) commentary upon it. The gospel passages we now possess would authorize Paul to receive a penitent apostate provided he had gone no further than cursing Jesus. But they do *not* touch the question whether one who had gone so far, whether or not he claimed to be a Christian, could be taken to possess the Spirit. They might authorize absolution – they did not leave untouched the baptismal acquisition of the Spirit. Moreover all Jews held the *kohens* in respect, and it was popularly believed that they had the power of prophecy by the Holy Spirit (b. Yoma 73 b). Here is a further context in which priestly status, Christian aspirations, and worldly prudence might come into conflict. The gospel passages, if they provided then the portfolio of authorities we have still, left room for much question and answer. But to deny that Jesus himself historically foresaw something at least of the difficulties into which his disciples would be thrust is virtually to argue that the church later manufactured (as well as welcomed) its own 'persecution'. For this no one at that time remembered any precedent in any religion.

We turn, at last, to Paul's comment at I Cor. xii. 1–3. He is utilizing a passage from Habakkuk, and alludes to the biblical theme of God's *leading or sending* the errant people into the range or scope of idolatry (Deut. xxviii. 36–7; Ps. lxxxi. 12; Ezek. xx. 39; Acts vii. 42, xiv. 16; Rom. i. 24–32). The latter notion authorizes the expectation that Jews will be, as they were, led to imitate idolaters. Idolaters were known to drag Jews before their idols and compel them to blaspheme: Ass. Mos. viii. 5; and Jews can be made to swear by demonized pagans (Mark v. 7). Pagans are worshippers of 'dumb idols'. Jews liked to ridicule idols as 'dumb' (Ps. cxv. 5, cxxxv. 16–17; Is. xlvi. 7; Jer. x. 14; III Macc. iv. 16). Would one expect them to be otherwise? The

---

[1] Matt. xii. 31–2 conflates two versions of this promise. Lampe, *B.J.R.L.* LV (1973), 357. The passage is not dealt with in detail by Hare. R. Schippers proposes to reconstruct an Aramaic original (a single sentence) rendered differently by Ur-Markus's source and by Q; he approves the Q version, but finds the contrast between the Son of Man and the Holy Spirit intelligible only after Easter: 'De Zoon des Mensen in Mt. 12, 32–Lk. 12, 10, vergeleken met Mk. 3, 38' in *Ex Auditu Verbi, Berkouwer Festschrift* (Kampen, 1965), pp. 233–57, summarized at 'The Son of Man in Matt. xii. 32 = Lk. xii. 10...', in F. L. Cross, ed., *Studia Evangelica* IV (Berlin, 1968), 231–5.

point was that Yahweh speaks (λαλεῖν) through his prophets, and the idols lack πνεῦμα. Hence prophets are contrasted with idols. Those that have the gift of spirit-speech are the heirs of the prophets of Old Israel, whom the representatives of the latter honour only in their tombs (Matt. xxiii. 29). Israel was formerly dragged, as if to trial,[1] before the idols of Babylon and elsewhere. Daniel shows how the heroes responded. The Habakkuk malediction[2] completes the picture:

What profit is an idol when its maker has shaped it, a metal image, a *teacher of lies* (*môreh šāqer*)? For the workman trusts in his own creation when he makes dumb (κωφά, Σ. ἄλαλα) idols! Woe to him who says to a wooden thing, Awake; to a silent stone, Arise! This one shall teach! Behold he is caught up by (or 'sheathed in') gold and silver, and there is no spirit (πνεῦμα) in his inward parts! But the Lord (κύριος) is in his holy temple; let all the earth keep silence before him.

Paul takes for granted persecution (hence 'leading' with overtones of an ordeal), and the rather illogical combination of attributing this experience to God's will[3] on the one hand, and invective on the other, against the orthodox (under whom he had suffered repeatedly) as little better than idols. The Qumran commentary on Hab.[4] shows that this text denounces destruction against not merely the idolatrous people of this world but also the wicked.[5] The Lord speaks in the temple, which is the church,[6] and all the rest ought to be silence. In the Babylonian Talmud Hab. ii. 19 is applied to an incompetent (silent) Jewish teacher.[7] So we paraphrase our passage:

As for men gifted with spirit, brothers, I am keen to inform you. You recollect that when you were merely nations[8] [as opposed to the true Israel in which Jews and gentiles are one] you were (often) borne off before the speechless[9] idols, however it was that you were impelled thither. On that basis I insist that no one who gives tongue[10] by means of the Spirit of God says 'Jesus is accursed' and no one is

---

[1] See L.S.J., *Lex.*, ἀπάγω iv. 2: 'to bring before a magistrate and accuse'. Dem. 22. 27. Matt. xxvi. 57; Luke xxi. 12; Acts xxiii. 17, xxiv. 7 (TR); Dan. iv. 22 (LXX).

[2] ii. 18–20. For a most important close discussion of the Qumran text in comparison with the MT see Brownlee (below).

[3] Hence the passive in ἤγεσθε. Would John vi. 44 be relevant?

[4] W. H. Brownlee, *The Text of Habakkuk in the Ancient Commentary from Qumran* (Philadelphia, Soc. Bibl. Lit., 1959), pp. 81–7 proves how little substantial deviation from the MT need be feared when reconstructing a midrash of Paul's type.

[5] For a translation see A. Dupont-Sommer, *The Essene Writings from Qumran* (Oxford, 1961), pp. 267–8.

[6] I Cor. iii. 16–17, vi. 19; cf. II Cor. vi. 16 (. . .nothing to do with idols).

[7] b. Sanh. 7b, Soncino trans. 29.

[8] The Jews themselves were a mere *ethnos* before Yahweh chose them, and they are an *ethnos* still in terms of the Roman privileges and their own self-image. The Corinthians included Jewish Christians (I Cor. vii. 18).

[9] ἄφωνος means (if capable of uttering *non-meaningful* sounds, as at Sapph. 118; II Pet. ii. 16; Isa. liii. 7 LXX; Philo, *Vita Mos.* I. 83) incapable of communicating (I Cor. xiv. 10). Thus the word is very appropriate in a discussion which will cover spirit-possession and glossolalia.

[10] λαλεῖν is the technical word for prophetic speech! H. Jaschke, 'λαλεῖν bei Lukas', *B.Z.* xv, 1 (1971), 109–14.

capable of saying the (confession)[1] 'Jesus is Lord' unless it is the Spirit that speaks through him.

In other words, it is evidence of the absence of spirit that one may either tutor accused persons, or repeat the formula in question. Those that demand and those that utter the denial are the accursed ones (cf. John xvi. 8–10; I John iv. 3!). Whatever else may be said about their past or present performance, they are not possessors of the Spirit and we can ignore them when we discuss the relative merits and prestige of individuals who manifest other attributes of the Spirit. The extreme example proves that no one is indeed elevated, socially or otherwise, by spirit-possession unless it would (according to Deut. xviii. 18, Matt. x. 20, and Acts xxii. 10) determine, absolutely, his behaviour in the context of interrogation in the synagogue.

[1] 'Confession' primarily, and only secondarily 'invocation' (F. Hahn, *Christologische Hoheitstitel*, Göttingen, 1963, p. 119) or 'acclamation' (W. Kramer, *Christos Kyrios Gottessohn*, Zurich, 1963, pp. 61, 165). On the importance of κύριος Ἰησοῦς see also C. F. D. Moule at *J.T.S.* x (1959), 261–2, and E. Schweizer, *Ev. Theol.* xvii (1957), 12. R. N. Longenecker, *The Christology of Early Jewish Christianity* (London, 1970), pp. 125, 127.

MIDRASH IN MATTHEW[1]

The overworked word 'midrash' is useful and should not be discarded. Jewish traditional interpretation of scripture is now widely recognized as a technique operating in the composition of, e.g., the infancy narratives. Many are willing to believe, further, that it provides a clue to other obscure New Testament passages, including the framework and many details of parables. To find the inward meanings, discovering the biblical allusions in obscure texts, and therefore, also, possibly in texts never thought difficult, one must tolerate traditional Jewish techniques, and even delight in them. This contrasts with the (mockingly called) 'Anglo-Saxon' method of reading the New Testament ('the text says what it means and means what it says') so that the older generation cannot stomach the idea, and the challenge is evaded.

The recent work of M. D. Goulder, awaited with enthusiasm by those who heard his lectures at Oxford, is a landmark in what we may call the 'midrashic' approach to the New Testament. As a sign of its originality it effectively offers Chronicles as a remote but none the less real parallel to Matthew's midrashic activity. To exemplify the latter is indeed à la mode.[2] Unique as a contribution to synoptic studies, it is the product of a gifted and massively persistent mind, written with verve and a pervasive sense of humour, necessary for a reader whom much detail, assembled with vigour, might otherwise put off: thus the 'poem' on p. 232 lightens what could seem a dense lump. It must be said straight-away that Goulder attempts too much,[3] proving more than even an enthusiast could wish: but in so doing he throws a brilliant light on Matthew, especially on his poetry (minutely analysed),[4] imagery and language, which the 'blind and the lame' (p. 250), viz. the majority, will need in order to maintain their position (that Matthew was an editor: p. 136), and improve upon it.

[1] *Midrash and Lection in Matthew. The Speaker's Lectures in Biblical Studies 1969–71.* By M. D. GOULDER. Pp. 528, London, SPCK, 1974, £8·50. A valuable contrast is E. P. Sanders, *The Tendencies of the Synoptic Tradition* (Cambridge, 1969).

[2] An excellent example of critical evaluation of midrash in Matthew is in E. Nellessen, *Das Kind und seine Mutter. Struktur und Verkündigung des 2. Kapitels im Matthäusevangelium* (Stuttgart, 1969), pp. 61–8.

[3] 'The Beatitudes . . . if these are Matthew's creation, his midrash on Mark 10 from Exodus and Isaiah and the Psalms, then comes the wild surmise, why not the whole Sermon? Why not the whole Gospel? Why, indeed' (p. 279).

[4] Goulder has not thought of breaking the material into its cantillation/recitation-units (presyllabic poetry), an easy operation which would have confirmed almost all he has discovered from the text printed (as usual) as prose. Amongst the 'lines' so identified some stand out because they are syllabically anomalous: those, I suspect, are the dominical bits Matthew inherited and incorporated in his composition.

Farrer and Kilpatrick are appreciated, but Jülicher, Dodd, Jeremias, Black, Cullmann, Strecker, Stendahl, Lindars, Gundry, and others are shown to have misdirected themselves.

Goulder's case, briefly, is that Matthew was a single person[1] with a definite style, identifiable by its transcriptions, omissions, abbreviations, inconsistencies, fatigue (here one may be sceptical: p. 298), doublets, modifications, changes of meaning, antitheses, expansions, blending of materials, hyperbole, and the style of the parables in greater detail (one wonders if the distinction, on p. 50, between indicative and imperative parables is not unreal).[2] The frank acceptance of Matthew's *allegorical* style (pp. 56ff.) is most welcome, as is the notion that allegory does *not* increase with time (p. 418). Matthew, it seems, was inspired by Paul's letters[3] and Ephesians,[4] and by the rabbinical background[5] in which he, as a Christian 'scribe', with an Aramaic mind,[6] was brought up. He had only our Mark in front of him, and his Hebrew bible as well as the LXX (p. 363), and he invented all that we now attribute to Q and M. His main motive was creatively to provide his church (in Antioch?) with a lectionary, since Mark had provided one for only half the year.[7] In Goulder's view Mark (whom this reviewer sees as very much a midrashic editor himself) represents a dominical tradition (conjectured on pp. 140ff.). What is not copied, adapted, or expanded from Mark (four parables were made up out of the Markan Doorkeeper: p. 65!), was built out of other bits of Mark, in the light of a generation's piety, Pauline theology, and the mentality of one who, unlike Luke, and still less like John, believed contact with the synagogue to be fruitful: to him the reconciliation and even conversion of Pharisee-dominated Palestinian Judaism was a real hope. Nothing which is Matthaean is a substantial contribution to the Christian gospel.

The result is unwelcome. Jesus gave no sermon on that mount (the idea was developed out of the Rich Man), there was no transfiguration, no temptations, no centurion's boy, no questions from John, no violation of the Kingdom, no woes on Galilaean cities, no thanks to the Father, no yeast in the dough (but see

---

[1] See p. 31. No doubt he profited from a decade's experience and inspiration: p. 248.

[2] On the Workers in the Vineyard (here pp. 54–5) see Derrett in *Journal of Jewish Studies* XXV (1974), pp. 64–9 (see above SNT I. 48ff.).

[3] P. 152. 'The evidence for a direct link from Paul to Matthew may be described as massive' (p. 170). See also p. 361.

[4] See p. 389.

[5] See pp. 62, 63 (hell—see also p. 168—and angelology). As for hell as a characteristically Matthaean interest what of Mk 9: 43–7 (contra p. 368)?

[6] '. . . it is impossible but that [the parable's] author is Matthew, the Christian scribe.' See pp. 117, 121 (he spoke Greek), 134–6, 357; also 10–17. Jesus did not abrogate the Sabbath in the Cornfield episode (see Derrett in *Journal of the Royal Asiatic Society* above SNT I)nor did he abolish the dietary laws (Goulder sees the episode clearly at p. 19, but read καθαρίζον). 'As a synagogue official, Matthew might be expected to turn his mind to the Rites of Passage'(!) (p. 108). '. . . the theory of a common source in Jesus behind the non-Marcan parts of Matthew is invalid' (p. 115). Matthew was fighting simultaneously Antinomians and Pharisees (p. 284).

[7] See p. 201.

Gen 18: 6 and think of Proselytes, the miraculous fermentation of the Kingdom and 1 Cor 5: 6; Gal 5: 9!), no treasure in the field, no pearl, no blessing of Simon bar Jonah, no lost sheep, no unmerciful servant, no two sons, no virgins, no talents, and, saddest of all, no labourers in the vineyard! Goulder is aware of the reluctance with which these will be bade farewell. His attempt to show that Jesus never taught the Lord's Prayer is famous,[1] and is repeated in substance here (the sources were Mk 11: 25, 14: 36—but could Mark not have taken features of Gethsemane from the Prayer?): the technique is being worked out to the bitter end, while the world laughs. This reviewer is favourable to the notion that Matthew wrote a commentary on Mark in all the evidently Markan passages, and is eager to see the midrashic matrices of apparently invented material, e.g. the infancy narratives. But Goulder does not really occupy himself with midrashic *content*. He is not tracing the Jewish traditional stimuli behind the Matthaean passages exhaustively, for he economically proves his case, and neglects what might distract the mind from it, however interesting and enlightening in itself.[2] Conventional in another respect, he mostly ignores the factual background of parables, concerned overwhelmingly with their literary characteristics (exceptions are at pp. 62 and 229 n. 11). The handling of the Magi at p. 238 n. 37 seems under-imaginative for a midrashist (the Alexander legend seems to be the clue to such material).

However numerous the instances where reminiscence/tradition is wanting behind the Matthaean invention, Goulder is keen (in an Anglo-Saxon way) to assume that there is one answer and that a simple one. But there are multiple possibilities. Probability is not enough before we scrap history behind so many pericopes. That one man ultimately composed the gospel need not be doubted seriously, but no one acquainted with ancient authorship can imagine that one man produced it in all its stages and provided the *imprimatur*, as it were, as well. Hence the conventional tests of vocabulary are futile,[3] however impressive to the western mind. Worse, the possibility is neglected that Jesus himself was 'acquainted with' Pauline theology (i.e. was its ultimate source!), and that Jesus himself (who knew something of rabbis) was the ultimate author of the 'rabbinical' bits of Matthew (a view which Goulder's foes, the form-critics, e.g. Braun, would of course abhor). That we cannot trace the route by which the elements reached the latter does not settle the question in favour of Matthew's inventive genius. That the church itself was lacking in rabbis (p. 28) is an assumption, however. Moreover the apparently telling query why Matthew threw away a hypothetical non-Markan *narrative* source, retaining 300 verses of dominical teaching (p. 143) takes no account of the fact that *Pirqe Abot* has

---

[1] JTS, N.S. XIV (1963), pp. 32ff. Here pp. 296ff. Did not Mark summarize and paraphrase the Prayer as teaching (cf. pp. 297-8)?

[2] For example a connexion between the Magi and Gen 37: 25 would be 'midrashically' fertile.

[3] Always suspicious of these, I find the concept 'semi-Matthaean' or 'semi-Lukan' useless.

not a scrap of narration; teaching catenae may well have pre-existed Mark, let alone Matthew. Paul's *allusive* method (cf. p. 148) is not to be interpreted as evidence of his and his churches' ignorance (as on pp. 144ff.).[1]

Let us notice occasions where Goulder's case impresses, and those where it does not. Amongst the first come the connexion of 2: 17–18 with Gen 28: 9–31 as well as Jer 31: 15 (p. 239); 7: 1 with Mk 4: 24 (p. 304) (but if 7: 3–4 is rabbinical why could Jesus not be its author?); the pairing of blind men (p. 315); Isai 59: 19 (at p. 321) is relevant (but why not in Jesus's mouth?); the Queen of the South and Noah (p. 334); Mt 10 and the Twelve (pp. 339, 342); material on *works* (11: 19c) (p. 358); 11: 28–30 and Sir 51 (p. 362); 13: 44 and Mk 10: 21 (p. 372); the handling of 15: 29–31; Jonah at 16: 17 (p. 387); Zech 3–4: 7 (p. 394); the *didrachm* (pp. 395ff.); the Woes contrasting with the Beatitudes (p. 421); various Zechariahs (p. 429); and too many happy touches to list.

Inadequate, to this mind (and more worthy to be treated seriously), are the attempts to handle the following: 18: 17, 20 with 1 Cor 5: 3–4 (name/gathered)—(p. 154); 5: 34–6 with 2 Cor 1: 17 (p. 159); 12: 5 with 1 Cor 9: 13 (pp. 161–2); 5: 13 with Mk 9: 50 (can the latter really be the origin of the former?) (pp. 255, 282); 5: 38–42 (do Ex 21: 24 and Isai 50: 6f [LXX] with the Passion story cover *enough?*) and is ἱμάτιον really covered by Ex 22: 26f? (p. 293–4); 5: 47 as based on Mk 12: 38 (p. 295); ἐλθάτω 6: 10 and Mk 1: 14, 1 Cor 16: 23 (p. 300); 6: 25 and Ps 147 (p. 302: somewhat thin); 7: 9 with 4: 3 (p. 306); 7: 13–14 with Mk 10: 17; 7: 24–27 and Noah's Flood (p. 309); 8: 8 with Mk 2: 14 (p. 319: weak); 8: 19–22 and Mk 4: 38 (p. 322: weak and farfetched); there is no explanation why the harvest metaphor of 9: 37–8 follows the sheep metaphor (see 1 Sam 12: 17; Jer 50: 16–17 = LXX 27: 6–7)—(p. 327); a very slender point of departure at Mk 9: 25 for 12: 43–4; there is no source for 10: 24 (p. 348: *b. Ber.* 58b is on sufferings); nor for the striking saying at 10: 34 (p. 351); 11: 11 ἐγήγερται is rather absurdly derived from ἐγήγερται at Mk 6: 14 (p. 356); Mk 4: 26–9 is a very thin source for Mt 13: 24–30 (pp. 367–8); 13: 47–50 and Mk 1: 17 (p. 373); the suggested source of 14: 22–36 is entirely conjectural; Mk 11: 25 and Eph 4: 32 are too thin to provide 18: 21–end (p. 402). Far fetched are the relation of the prophet's reward, the salt and the light to the blessedness of persecution (p. 256); and it is quaint to link the Sixth Beatitude with 5: 28 (p. 259); there is no satisfactory source (p. 301) for σής and βρῶσις (it could well be Isai 51: 8!); and the singular at 6: 21 is possibly due to the fact that only an individual can have a καρδία (p. 302). Moreover, Mark's *brass* (6: 8) need not indicate that his church was poor: for while brass will include gold *a fortiori* in such a context, a commentator might well do as Matthew has done, namely spell out the forms of coinage (cf. pp. 9, 110). *Our* Mark is not *always* prior.

---

[1] On the Corinthians' possession of bits of our gospels see Derrett in 'Disposal of Virgins', *Man* IX (1974), 23–30. Goulder, p. 154, is capable of the opposite conjecture (John's words on sheepfolds—see *Studia Theologica* XXVII [1973], 25-50—are not from Paul, are they?). Does δωρεὰν ἐλάβετε, δωρεὰν δότε come from 2 Cor 11: 7 (see p. 345)?

Several of the passages cited above suggest that we are right to posit a nucleus *outside* Mark, Paul, rabbinism and the church's piety which cannot be attributed to 'Mat the faker'. Citations common to Matthew and Paul (pp. 168–9: the works theory and the stone of stumbling) can easily be explained by a common tradition anterior to all gospels. And is there no history whatever behind 26: 24, 3: 13ff.? Paul's and Matthew's (see pp. 284–5!) very different evaluations of the Law (pp. 158, 170) take some explaining! The 'slip' between 'transcending' and 'fulfilling' (p. 262 et al.) is not convincingly worked out: too much is left to an assumed want of clarity in a professed genius. Goulder is not aware, it seems, that there was a pre-Mishnaic *halakah*, and this vitiates his argument at pp. 22, 425. From the list at p. 47 a significant omission is Hag 2: 11–14. On διχοτομεῖν either amputation[1] or excommunication[2] or both (!) may be contemplated. On Matthew's 'grand scale' and trees (Matthew and Luke) (p. 61) one must not neglect the messianic *haggadot*.[3] Wages are misunderstood at pp. 145–6. The Syro-Phoenician woman is called a Canaanite, perhaps, because of Jdg 1: 4–7.[4] It is not at all clear that Jesus would *exclude* the Jewish authorities from the Kingdom (as at p. 157).[5]

These comments do not hinder the compilation of an impressive list of gains due to Goulder's method. Note will be taken apropos of Deut 13: 1–3 (p. 126); Zech 11: 13 (pp. 127, 130); Mt 2: 23 (pp. 129, 240); 18: 20 (pp. 148, 154 *tantum quantum*); 23 with 1 Thess 2: 15f. (p. 165: but are not these Jesus's words?); 24: 59 and Noah (p. 192); on the genealogy (pp. 228ff.); 4: 5 and Dan 9: 25–7 (p. 246); the meaning of εἰρηνοποιοί (p. 256); an interesting interpretation of 7: 6 (pp. 265, 278: rather betrayal in secular contexts?); an identification of the behaviour called 'mourning' (p. 267); 'seek'=scavenge (p. 268); ἐκβάλωσιν (Lk 6:22)/διώξωσιν (5: 11) were contrasted (p. 281); λόγος (*dābār*) at 5: 31–2 (p. 291: an old crux surprisingly illuminated); 6: 6 with Isai 26: 20, 2 Kgs 4: 23 (p. 296: a word of Jesus?); ἐπιούσιος and manna (p. 300); the printing of 7: 14–15 (p. 307); 12: 32e as rabbinic (p. 333); and the correct translation of 28: 17 (p. 344).

The second part of the case, that Matthew catered for the Jewish festal year,[6] filling blank periods with more or less appropriate arrangements, with self-conscious forward or backward borrowings from his Mark, is very well sustained. This had been suspected of Luke, and can now be taken as *prima facie* true of Matthew. Professor Guilding's attempts with John, sadly traduced by impatient

[1] See Derrett in *Revue Internationale des Droits de l'Antiquité* XX (1973), pp. 11–36.
[2] See a forthcoming issue of NTS (on religious persecution).
[3] Cf. HJ XIV (1973), pp. 249–65.
[4] Cf. NovT XV (1973), pp. 1–26.
[5] Cf. JJS XXV (1974), pp. 88–90.
[6] Chs. 9 and 10. The Sermon on the Mount is far longer than a normal lection because it was the church's (eight-day) Pentecostal lection (pp. 186, 188). 17: 24–end is placed to coincide with Dedication because the church must still show willing to subscribe to the Temple (p. 190). Purim is associated with the Marriage-feast (correctly: see Derrett, *Law in the New Testament* [London, 1970], p. 129) (pp. 190–1).

critics unable to see the jewel in the pinchbeck setting, are brought to mind; eventually, one may hope, a Guilding rediviva will rehabilitate, while reforming, a Johannine lectionary hypothesis.

The minor study of the poetically less gifted (p. 85) Luke ('not in the Jewish tradition': see p. 50) towards the end[1] must be reviewed separately in its own right, though admittedly experimental. That Luke knew Matthew, but no Q or L seems unnecessary as well as embarrassing—but Luke too was a commentator (see Lk 12: 33, p. 74).

The book is beautifully produced. Three misprints, each insignificant, highlight the quality of the work. At p. 169 *vaqûm* should read *yāqûm;* and πενθεῖν might have been listed at p. 483, though it does not meet basic criteria, as an evidently Matthaean word (and there must be more such which would slip through too mechanical a net). The summaries, the diagrammatic schemes, and the list of parables at pp. 66ff. enhance a workmanlike thesis, as modest in tone as it was bold in conception.

---

[1] Ch. 21. See also **pp. 7** and 8, n. 11.

CORRIGENDA AND ADDENDA TO VOL. I

CORRIGENDA

p. 46 ad p. [189], l. 4 : wax tablet.

p. 52, l. 26 : affect.

p. 94 n. 53 : for 'ed. 1769', 'ed. Finkelstein'.

p. 126 ad p. [5], l. 22 : women.

p. 142, l. 7 : theme.

ADDENDA

p. 31 ad p. [34]. On breeding worms : Hdt. 4.205, Diog. L.4.4, cf. Exod. xvi.20.

pp. 42, 44. On *ekdikos* s. Adinolfi, *Bibb. Or.* 19/1 (1977), 10-12. On 'blackened' s. 3 Bar. xiii.1.

p. 68. On multiplication of covenants see R. Banks, *Jesus and the Law in the Synoptic Tradition* (Cambridge, 1975), 31-2.

p. 99, last para. A study of the Cornfield episode in an attempt to improve on Daube's hypothesis appears from M. Cohen (Lille), 'La controverse de Jésus et des Pharisiens à propos de la cueillette des épis, selon l'évangile de Saint Matthieu,' *Mél. Sc. Rel. 34 (1977), 3-12.*

p. 107, n. 1. E. Gutwenger, '*Auferstehung und Auferstehungsleib Jesu,*' *ZKT* 91 (1969), 32ff.

p. 110. On Jewish practice : Test. Job. liii.6-7! On Scheintod, M. Nemiroff, *Scientific American* (*Observer*, London, Aug. 21, 1977).

p. 167, n. 1. Psychiatry has advanced in this direction. A Auerbach, ed., *Schizophrenia* (New York, 1959), D. D. Jackson, ed., *Schizophrenia* (New York, 1960); D. D. Jackson, 'Conjoint family therapy ...,' *Psychiatry*, Supple. 24 (1961), 30ff; J. E. McKeown, 'The behaviour of parents of schizophrenic, neurotic and normal children,' *Am. J. Sociology* 56 (1950), 172ff; S. S. Nathawat at *Indian Family in the Change and Challenge of the Seventies* (Indian Social Institute, New Delhi, New Delhi, Sterling, 1972), 34ff; B. B. Wolman, 'Schizophrenia' in Wolman, ed., *Handbook of Clinical Psychology* (New York, 1965).

p. 174, ad p. [102], l. 2. We do not know precisely what was the vow that even Paul himself took, but it involved head-shaving : Acts xviii.18! See also H. Salmanowitch, *Das Naziräat in Bibel und Talmud* (Wilna, 1931).

p. 183. J. Neusner, *The Idea of Purity in Ancient Judaism* (Leiden, 1973), 61. The question whether unclean food is bad for one's soul (a perennial Asian notion) is dealt with positively at 4 Macc. 5.2ff, viii.1, 12 (c.A.D. 50); the interpretation of Ezek. iv.14 at b. Ḥull. 37b. A view much nearer to Jesus's but quite otherwise phrased appears at Test. Benj. viii.3 : the pure mind when caught in the defilement of the earth rather seeks edification, and is not itself defiled.

p. 184. On the community at Corinth an intriguing attempt is A. Schreiber, *Die Gemeinde in Korinth. Versuch einer gruppendynamischer Betrachtung der Entwicklung der Gemeinde von Korinth ...* (Münster, 1977).

p. 195. 'At the feet of' implies custody (see Acts vii.58).

p. 201, ad. p. [227], l. 22. D. L. Mealand, 'Community of goods and Utopian allusions in Acts ii-iv,' *J.T.S.* 28/1 (1977), 96.

p. 201, ad p. [227], l. 36. For a release of a *ketubah*, *R.B.* 61 (1954), 184 (A.D. 134).

p. 201, ad p. 228. E. F. de Ward, *JJS* 23 (1972), 1-27, 24 (1973), 145-66.

INDEX OF SCRIPTURAL REFERENCES (II)

(in the order of the Jerusalem Bible)

[For the index to Vol. I see that volume.]

I. OLD TESTAMENT

Genesis		ii.13-15	99, 100, 101	xii.2	37(9)
ii.7	52	iii.22	177, 178	xv.4, 6	178
iii.16	35	iv.20	182	xv.22	178
iii.17	150	iv.22	96	xix.9-15	117
iii.18	51, 53	iv.24-26	17, 42	xix.14	64, 117
iii.38	53	ix.29	119	xix.16	73, 126
iv.10, 11	71	xi.2-3	177	xix.28	70
ix.6	72	xii.23	40	xxi.20	130
xiii.8	100	xii.35-36	177, 178	xxii.4	70
xiii.11-13	101	xiii.2	35	xxiv.16	199
xv.14	177	xiii.12-13, 15	35	xxv.1-7	111
xxi.2	35	xvi.16-18	2	xxv.18-22	111
xxii.3	182	xvi.20	211	xxv.20-22	111, 116
xxv.27	93	xvi.22-27	111	xxv.21	112
xxvi.12	152	xviii.21	1	xxv.23	119
xxvi.27-28	153	xviii.25	1	xxvi.4-6	151
xxvi.29	108	xix.5	119	xxvi.10	116
xxvii.27	41	xix.22, 24	134, 135	xxvi.13	152
xxviii.15	112	xx.5	71		
xxviii.22	108	xxi.1	129	Numbers	
xxix.8	147	xxi.37	125	v.2	70
xxxv	36, 41	xxii.1(2)	124-5, 129, 137	ix.6, 7	70
xxxvii.25	26, 207	xxii.2	126, 145	ix.10	70
xxxviii.29	134	xxii.8-12	127-8	xi.5	2
xli.25-31	112	xxii.14-15	174	xi.6	3
xli.35-36	111	xxii.24	117	xi.20	3
xli.41-56	112	xxiii.2-3	117	xi.32	111
xli.48-49	111	xxiii.6, 7	117	xiv.13	119
xli.56	111	xxiii.10-11	111	xiv.18	71, 96
xliv.22	71	xxiv.7	190	xvi.13	101
xlvii.14	111	xxv.30	112	xvi.15	167
xlviii.5	41	xxx.12f.	9	xix	47
xlviii.15	119	xxx.23	26	xix.2	172
xlix.8ff.	41	xxxiv.7	71, 96	xix.13	70
xlix.10	95	xl.13-14	112	xx.1-2	3
xlix.11	172, 179			xx.8	151
		Leviticus		xxii.18	119
Exodus		ii.2	26	xxiv.15-20	25
i.15-21	51	ii.16	26	xxvii	124
i.19	35	x.3	201	xxvii.1-7	101
ii.2	35	xi.1	105	xxvii.15-20	132, 141

II. FURTHER INTERTESTAMENTAL AND APOCRYPHAL LITERATURE

III. NEW TESTAMENT

INDEX OF NAMES AND TOPICS (II)

(including references to Midrash Rabbah, Mishnah, and 'Test. XII Patr.', but not to the Talmuds)

[For the Index to Vol. I see that volume.]

Morris, L.   129n
Moses   17, 23, 36, 42, 100n, 101, 134, 139, 141 & n, 151
Moule, C.F.D.   60n, 92n, 109n, 163n, 165n, 204n
Mount, Sermon on the   vii, 85ff.
Münderlein, G.   151n, 153n
Murray, R.   148n
myrrh   26

Name, glorifying the   201
Nathan, Fathers according to R.   51n
Nathanael   149, 155n, 160f.
Nazareth   15
necessities   106
negligence   64
Nellessen, E.   4n, 18n, 19 & n, 20n, 23n, 25n, 30n
nepheš   70 & n, 113n
Nero   19, 23n
Nestle, E.   4n, 8, 10, 23n
Neusner, J.   109n, 211
Nimrod   23n
Nock, A.D.   21n, 30n, 130n
Noll. P.   82

Oaths   6-7, 13, 128, 140
obedience   190
Odeberg, H.   121n, 122n, 139n
Oedipus   23n
Oesterley, W.O.E.   103n
Ogg, G.   5n
Olschki, L.   26n
O'Neill, J.C.   199
onēs   139
Orlinsky, H.M.   73n, 125n
orthodox liturgy   10n

Pancaro, S.   147, 164
Pannenburg, W.   49n
papyri   1n, 11n, 13nn, 14nn, 22n, 24n, 28n, 110n, 111n, 168n
parables, various   1, 60, 92, 99, 123, 136n, 155, 158-9
paradox   103
parapet   61, 64
Parthian   19, 25
partition   101-3
Passover   1, 61n
Patsch, H.   183
Paul, St.   202-4, 211
peace, making   100
Pearson, B.A.   194n

pedigrees   14
pentecontarchos   1n, 3
Perez   135
Perez Fernández, M.   158n
perisseuein   103
Perrot, C.   23n, 37
Perry, A.M.   186n
persecution   194ff.
Pesiqta Rabbati   109n, 135n, 156, 172n, 189n
Peter, St.   201
Pfleiderer   2n
Pharisees   106
phatné   17, 18, 55-57
Philo   17n, 21n, 35, 37, 58n, 100n, 102n, 109n, 110n, 112n, 114n, 116n, 125n, 137n, 144n, 174, 178n, 197n, 203n
piety, Jewish   viii, 105-6, 177n
pious, *see ḥasîdîm*
Plato   17n, 30n, 58n, 200n
Pliny   22n, 26, 199n
Plumpe, J.C.   36n
Plutarch   23n, 24, 26n
Polus, M.   103n, 107n, 192n
Polybius   26n
Potterie, I. de la   140n
Préaux, C.   11n & ff.
pregnancy, divine   8
Preisigke, F.   1n, 15n, 167nn, 176n
Priene, inscription at   29n
priests, Jewish   202
privileges   11, 13, 16, 196
prodigality   109
prophets   68ff., 200
proselytes   140
Protevangelium Jacobi   34
pruning   159
puns   8, 64n, 67, 70, 73, 75, 114, 120, 131
purity, ritual   17

quails   2, 3
Quasten, J.   121n
Quirinius   5ff.
Qumran   vii, 30; *see also* Dead Sea Sect

rabbinical law   16, 45n, 61n, 68n, 73, 99 & n, 107n, 116-17, 125, 139, 159, 173-6, 198
rabbinics, adventures into   vii
Rabin, C.   1
Rachel   36
Rahab   9
Red Heifer   46
referees, duty of   117